SACRED SONG IN AMERICA

PUBLIC EXPRESSIONS OF RELIGION IN AMERICA
Conrad Cherry, Series Editor

A list of books in the series appears at the end of this book.

Published in cooperation with the Center for the Study
of Religion and American Culture
Indiana University–Purdue University at Indianapolis

Sacred Song in America

Religion, Music, and Public Culture

STEPHEN A. MARINI

UNIVERSITY OF ILLINOIS PRESS

URBANA AND CHICAGO

Library of Congress Cataloging-in-Publication Data
Marini, Stephen A., 1946–
Sacred song in America : religion, music, and public culture /
Stephen A. Marini.
p.   cm. — (Public expressions of religion in America)
Includes bibliographical references (p.   ) and index.
ISBN 0-252-02800-7 (alk. paper)
1. Sacred songs—United States—History and criticism.
2. Church music—United States.
3. Music—Religious aspects.
I. Title. II. Series.
ML2911.M37   2003
782.25'0973—dc21   2002008741

*To the members of Norumbega Harmony,
with gratitude for twenty-five years
of making sacred song together*

CONTENTS

Preface and Acknowledgments   *ix*

Introduction: What Is Sacred Song?   *1*

PART 1: GREAT TRADITIONS OF AMERICAN SACRED SONG

1. Songway: Sacred-Song Traditions of Native America   *17*

2. Pilgrimage and Penitence: Sacred-Song Traditions of the Hispanic Southwest   *39*

3. Sacred Harp Singing: Continuity and Change in the American Singing-School Tradition   *68*

4. "Is It Going to Save Someone?": The Black Church at Song   *100*

5. Klezmorim and Sephardim: The Jewish Music Revival   *130*

PART 2: SACRED SONG AND CONTEMPORARY AMERICAN RELIGION

6. New Music of the Spheres: From the New Age to Neo-Paganism   *163*

7. Contested Praise: A Tale of Two Hymnals   *184*

8. Mormons and Music: Maintaining and Mainstreaming Sectarian Identity   *213*

9. Troubadour for the Lord: Catholic Charismatics and Sacred Song   *239*

10. The Conservatory Tradition: Interviews with Daniel Pinkham and Neely Bruce   *264*

11. Gospel Music: Sacred Song and the Marketplace   *296*

Conclusion: American Sacred Song and the Meaning of
Religious Culture   *321*

Appendix: Music Examples   *331*

Index of Titles and First Lines   *377*

Index of Names and Subjects   *383*

PREFACE AND ACKNOWLEDGMENTS

This book began with a 1991 commission from the Center for the Study of Religion and American Culture at Indiana University–Purdue University at Indianapolis, Indiana. Conrad Cherry, director of the Center, invited me to contribute a volume on "the public expression of religion and music in contemporary America, with particular attention to diversity" for its book series, Public Expressions of Religion in America. The series was part of a larger program that also included research consultations and public conferences conducted by the Center from 1991 to 1996 under the auspices of a grant from the Lilly Endowment, Incorporated.

The Center's invitation was exciting for me as a historian of American religions and a lifelong performer of sacred music. It was a daunting one as well. To do any justice to the Center's agenda, I would have to master new research methods, explore entirely new fields of scholarship, and learn how to write about a notoriously difficult subject that lay far outside my familiar historical territory of early American Protestantism. Yet it was also a challenging intellectual opportunity that held out the prospect of exploring a vital but still obscure place in human religiousness where ritual action, sacred text, and music join together to articulate the deepest meanings of self, community, and cosmos.

The proposed topic was immense and impossible to address even in one large volume. After long deliberation I decided to concentrate on sacred song, the genre of American religious music that would provide the greatest formal diversity and theoretical range. That focus required me to gain access to a wide range of contemporary sacred-song traditions. Accordingly, from 1991 to 1997 I traveled across America to witness sacred-song performances and record song texts in a dozen different religious traditions, and to interview singers in order to learn how they understood the meanings of their sacred songs. The burden of this book is to place those performances, song texts, and interviews into a set of interpretive frames that provide insight into their specific religious meanings and to address the larger question of the place of sacred song in religious culture. In the course of this work, I have found that the medium of song expresses sacred meaning in many different ways, and that those differences have much to teach us about human religiousness.

I am indebted to many people who made this book possible. Conrad Cherry, Tony Sherrill, and Jan Shipps at the Center for the Study of American Religion and Culture took the risk of entrusting me with this project. Anita Gillette, Clay Harper, Jeanne MacRae, Tom Rossi, and Jack Welch helped me find sacred singers to interview. All of the sacred-song performers and religious leaders I have met were extraordinarily giving of their time and their experience. They spoke from the heart as well as from the head. This book is grounded in their insight and candor.

I am grateful to Howard Bad Hand, Neely Bruce, Polly Lewis Cropsey, James Crawford, Kay Gardner, Ben Isaacs, Michael Moody, Hankus Netsky, Daniel Pinkham, Mary Frances Reza, Don Ripplinger, Jeff Sheppard, Shelbie Sheppard, John Michael Talbot, Judith Wachs, Stuart Wilson, and Terry York for their permission to include portions of their interviews with me in this book.

This work has also benefited from the helpful criticism of many scholars. The Center gathered a superb group of consultants to meet regularly with the book series authors. Those meetings were the highlight of my intellectual experience at the Center. The consultants' thoughtful discussion of my book proposal decisively shaped the inquiry. David D. Hall, William R. Hutchison, and the graduate students of the Harvard Divinity School Colloquium on American Religious History read an early draft of the introduction and suggested the narrative literary strategy I have used for integrating the interview material with interpretation. Peter W. Williams and the Department of Religion at Miami University of Ohio provided an opportunity to present a later version of the introduction as the 1995 Edward A. Puff Memorial Lecture.

Carlos Vega, professor of Spanish at Wellesley College, generously provided new translations of the sacred-song texts for chapter 2. Tova Leigh Choate, Sharon Elkins, Barbara Geller, Edward Hobbs, and Lee M. Smith read various chapters while Harvey Cox, Richard Crawford, Conrad Cherry, and Stephen J. Nelson read the entire manuscript. All of these readers provided sensitive and careful commentaries for which I am deeply grateful. Special thanks go to my editors at the University of Illinois Press, Elizabeth Dulany and Therese Boyd. Their thoughtful and meticulous work improved the manuscript in countless ways.

I also wish to thank the librarians and staff of the Jewett Music Library, the Jewett Art Library, and the Margaret Clapp Library at Wellesley College, the Andover-Harvard Theological Library and the Harry Elkins Widener Library at Harvard University, the Franklin Trask Memorial Library at Andover Newton Theological School, and the Episcopal Divinity School–Weston Jesuit School of Theology Library in Cambridge, Massachusetts, for their expertise and cooperation in providing me with bibliographic resources for this study.

A book about sacred song should provide music scores for the reader to consider, and this one does. I am grateful to the following copyright holders for their permission to print these musical works: Oregon Catholic Press/New Dawn Music for "Grita Profeta," © 1980 Emilio Vincente Matéu and Ediciones Musical Pax, all rights reserved, sole U.S. agent OCP Publications, 5536 NE Hassalo, Portland, OR 97213, used with permission, and "De Los Cuatro Vientos," © 1988 OCP Publications, all rights reserved, used with permission, and "One Bread, One Body," © 1978 John B. Foley, S.J., and New Dawn Music, all rights reserved, used with permission; the Sacred Harp Publishing Company for "All Is Well" by J. T. White, "Holy Manna" by George Atkin and William Moore, "Love Divine" by Charles Wesley and Thomas Waller, "Parting Hand" by J. Blain and William Walker, "Stratfield" by Isaac Watts and Ezra Goff, and portions of "The Gamut"; Largo Music and Hal Leonard Publ. for "What a Friend We Have in Jesus," arranged by Carol Cymbala and Hubert Powell; Transcontinental Music Publishers for "Six Settings of Lecha Dodi"; Canyon Records Productions for "Zuni Song"; Caduseus Publications for "Chart of Color, Sound, and Energy Correspondence" and "Design for Lunamuse"; Janice Knapp Perry for "I Walk by Faith"; Birdwing Music/BMG Songs for "I Corinthians 13" and "Psalm 95"; New Jerusalem Music for "Our God Reigns," © 1974, 1978 by L. E. Smith Jr., New Jerusalem Music, Box 225, Clarksboro, NJ 08020, all rights reserved, used by permission; and Albert E. Brumley and Sons for "I'll Fly Away" by Albert E. Brumley, © 1932 in "Wonderful Message" by Hartford Music Co., renewed 1960 by Albert E. Brumley and Sons/SESAC (admin. by ICG), all rights reserved, used by permission.

Finally, I wish to acknowledge the people whose personal support made it possible to write this book. Louise Marlow and Daniel Lewinstein bore with grace and good humor the daily burdens and sometimes spectacular disruptions that this project brought into our home. To Conrad Cherry I owe special thanks, not only for his initial confidence and splendid editorial skills, but most of all for his extraordinary patience and good judgment, without which this book would not have been completed. Above all, I want to thank the more than one hundred past and present members of Norumbega Harmony to whom this book is dedicated. Their joyful embrace of the American singing school tradition over the past twenty-five years has inspired me to sing sacred songs and to write about them.

SACRED SONG IN AMERICA

INTRODUCTION:

WHAT IS SACRED SONG?

The United States is one of the most religiously committed and religiously diverse nations in the world. According to polling data, virtually all Americans believe in a supreme being, more than half of them hold membership in a religious community, 40 percent attend religious services regularly, and more than one-third claim to have had a personal experience of the sacred. These levels of religious commitment are exponentially higher than in any other developed nation.

The array of religious traditions in our public culture is also remarkable, embracing at least five hundred denominational varieties of Protestantism, another five hundred Native American tribal religions, most forms of Judaism and Eastern Orthodoxy, significant enclaves of Muslims, Sikhs, Hindus, and Buddhists, one of the world's largest and most heterogeneous Catholic communities, and an ever-growing number of New World faiths from Mormons to Scientology to Santería to New Age goddesses.[1] While nations like India, Russia, and Brazil also harbor hundreds of religious groups, the sheer range of America's global religious diversity is unparalleled.

Each of America's religious communities has its own unique tradition of sacred song. Racial, ethnic, class, and regional styles further subdivide those musical traditions. The result is a national sacred-music culture that ranges from Native American drum songs to Bach cantatas, from black Pentecostal shout to the Mormon Tabernacle Choir, from Sacred Harp singing to New Age toning, from bluegrass gospel to hard-rock gospel, from Catholic pilgrimage songs and charismatic concerts to Jewish varieties of Sephardic song and Hasidic klezmer music. The list goes on and on to functional infinity.

It is impossible to address the problem of religion and music in contemporary America through individualized attention to this plethora of traditions and styles. Yet without some effort at comprehensive examination, it is hazardous to venture any overarching interpretation of music's place in religious culture. How then to proceed? For me, the inquiry has come down to three central tasks: to define sacred song, the most widely shared form of American religious music, as the object of study; then to explore the meanings and functions of sacred song across a representative range of American religious communities; and, finally, to consider how those findings might contribute to a larger understanding of religious culture. The first of these tasks is the subject of this introduction.

What Can Music Express?

What kind of music is religious? The question has defied a precise and convincing reply for centuries. I do not expect to provide one here, but a few steps toward that end can be taken. The burden of modern opinion tends to deny that music per se can be religious or anything else other than music. The twentieth century dismissed the Romantic idea of "absolute music" that contains universal spiritual or moral meaning, though contemporary music theorists still generally grant the capacity of music to promote powerful emotions. How this happens, however, remains a subject of intense debate.

One school of thought insists on music's capacity directly to express or communicate emotional meaning. British musicologist Deryck Cooke made the most ambitious argument of this sort in his 1959 book *The Language of Music.* Cooke compiled a "musical vocabulary" based on the notions that a rise in pitch creates "outgoing emotion" while downward pitch sequences produce "incoming emotion" and that major key expresses joy while minor key renders sorrow. Another variant of this approach came from American musicologist Leonard Meyer, who argued in *Emotion and Meaning in Music* (1956) that musical patterns of tonal and rhythmic tension and relaxation trigger patterns of psychological frustration and release that the listener experiences as the emotive and aesthetic meaning of the music.[2]

Other theorists have resisted such a direct connection between music and its attendant emotional responses. Philosopher Suzanne Langer, for example, argued in *Philosophy in a New Key* (1942) that the relationship between music and emotion is an inherently symbolic one in which musical forms present an open-ended range of feelings to the listener. For Langer, music is a necessarily incomplete or "unconsummated" symbol that conveys the "morphology" of emotions but not the emotions themselves. Pioneer ethnomusicologist Kurt Sachs asserted a rather different perspective in *The Wellsprings of Music* (1962), claiming that music's origin lies in two dimensions of human experience, the cry of joy or pain and the capacity for verbal communication. The primal emotive cry or "tumbling strain," he claimed, is musically transformed into intervallic jumps in melody, especially the ascending and descending octave, and in sharply accented rhythmic forms. The verbalization of cognitive meaning, on the other hand, takes the form of sustained rhythm and "one-step melodies" built around a tightly circumscribed tonal center.[3]

During the 1950s and 1960s the work of Cooke, Meyer, Langer, and Sachs sparked a rich theoretical discourse on the problem of music and emotional meaning. The most recent generation of theorists, however, has tended to oppose all claims for direct or symbolic relationships between music and emotion. Preeminent among these thinkers are the postmodern deconstructionists Peter Kivy and Malcolm Budd. The title of one of Kivy's books, *Music Alone* (1990), neatly summarizes their position. The only thing music can express, they insist, is musicality itself, through the syntactic and formal structures of tone and rhythm. In their view, all theoretical efforts to make music a medium for or symbol of emotional expression have failed. Kivy and Budd insist that the non-musical associations we bring to music—say, a response of religious emotion to a hymn-like passage in a Brahms or Mahler symphony—while certainly understandable, have nothing to do with the music itself.[4]

Recently, psychologists John A. Sloboda and Anthony Storr have answered the deconstructionists by using a psycholinguistic model of the mind to argue that music expresses our inward states in much the same way as a religious belief system, by providing an ideal order through which to perceive the world and thereby ourselves. Storr adds that both music and religious belief can accomplish this task because they closely resemble and therefore can analogically or symbolically express the linguistic structure of the unconscious mind.[5]

A more powerful physiological counter to the deconstructionists, however, has been offered by Robert Jourdain in his 1997 book *Music, the Brain, and Ecstasy.* Working from Oliver Sacks's extraordinary findings on music's capacity to alleviate the symptoms of Parkinson's disease and the discovery of the "Mozart Effect," the experimental demonstration of improved memory after listening to compositions by the eighteenth-century master, Jourdain argued that our brains respond directly to music by producing pleasurable emotional states, the highest of which is ecstasy.[6] While the auditory cortex is not as large or developed as the visual cortex, its complex linkages to the frontal cortex and the limbic system make sound a more emotive stimulus than light. Our response to tone, Jourdain suggested, is physiologically structured to generate great pleasure, even ecstasy, from the perfection of musical form. "By providing the brain with an artificial environment, and forcing it through that environment in controlled ways," he wrote,

> music imparts the means of experiencing relations far deeper than we encounter in our everyday lives. In this perfect world, our brains are able to piece together larger understandings than they can in the workaday external world, perceiving all-encompassing relations that go much deeper than those we find in ordinary experience. . . . It's for this reason that music can be transcendent. For a few minutes it makes us larger than we really are, and the world more orderly than it really is. We respond not just to the beauty of the sustained deep relations that are revealed, but also to the fact of our perceiving them. As our brains are thrown into overdrive, we feel our very existence expand and real-

ize that we can be more than we normally are, and that the world is more than it seems. That is cause enough for ecstasy.[7]

The argument between Kivy and Budd's deconstruction and Storr's psycholinguistics or Jourdain's physiology is the latest but surely not the last word in a perennial debate as inconclusive as it is important. My own judgment is that some substantive linkage between music and emotion cannot be denied, whether it be formal, symbolic, or physiological in nature. Despite the vogue of deconstructivist theory, emotivist or symbolic views of music remain attractive to Americans when applied to sacred music because of the importance we have traditionally attached to the emotions in interpreting the nature of religion itself. Our classical theorists of religion, Jonathan Edwards, Ralph Waldo Emerson, and William James, all located the principal seat of human religiousness in the emotions, describing it alternatively as affection, intuition, and psychological experience.[8] Twentieth-century popular religion has retained this strongly emotional cast, with conversionistic and charismatic styles predominating. Americans have a cultural tendency to identify both religion and music with heightened emotional states, and therefore to grant the idea that music itself can convey religiousness.

Sacred Lyric and Ritual Performance: Toward a Definition of Sacred Song

In the case of sacred music, however, music's apparent ability to express emotion proves too much. For many listeners, Beethoven's Fifth Symphony induces feelings of inspiration that they associate with authentic spirituality. I would argue, however, that such feelings are not in themselves sufficient to constitute religious expression properly defined. Music that does not move us emotionally is not likely to be effective religiously, but there is more to sacred music than emotionality.

If music is not religious per se, something else is required to make it so. Religious belief, or mythic content, as historians of religion would say, is the principal element that sacralizes music. Beliefs expressed through mythic language add an explicitly sacred conceptual dimension to music's protean emotional power. By naming the sacred powers, articulating the sacred cosmos, and disclosing how sacrality interacts with humanity, verbalized beliefs specify sacred content in a way that music alone cannot. Mythic language supplies a criterion by which musical emotion qualifies to be a carrier of sacred meaning. The harnessing of musical expression to mythic content defines sacred song.

What do sacred lyrics express? How do they accomplish their task in sacred song? And how do they relate to the musical forms to which they are "set"? Critical opinion about the religious capacities of lyric varies as much as it does about the religious qualities of music. Some interpreters insist on the independence of sacred poetry, understanding the role of music in sacred song as merely the contouring and highlighting of mythic meaning poetically expressed by the lyrics. Other interpreters emphasize the musical qualities of lyric poetry itself, claiming an inherent musicality, and therefore sacred meaning, for the words apart from their explicitly mythic content.

Two critics, Mark Booth and Andrew Welsh, may stand as exemplars of the range of contemporary literary criticism addressing the problem of sacred song. In his 1981 book *The Experience of Songs,* Booth argued that song lyrics constitute a distinctive genre of literary expression: "Certain qualities of the individual words and of the patterns into which they fall, are appropriate for song while others are not." In making his case, Booth cited the argument of W. H. Auden, who asserted that those words best suited for song are "those which require the least reflection to comprehend [the] most dynamic and immediate interjections [and] imperatives; verbs of physical action or physical concomitants of emotion."[9]

Booth concluded that sacred-song lyrics possess a "low density of information," that is, qualities of redundancy and simplicity rather than those of originality and complexity. "A poet on paper has much greater freedom to test the patience and ingenuity of the reader and to stretch his comprehension," Booth wrote. "He can aspire to enlarge the reader's world and experience and ideas. But a song, hedged by the demands of unity and clarity, must say things that are simplifications, and generally familiar simplifications. The experience of a new song must be the imagining anew of some simplification of life that is more or less in our possession already."[10]

This conservative function of song lyric pointed Booth to the song theory of philosopher Victor Zuckerkandl, who argued that the experience of the singer is a twofold process of transcendence. Singing, Zuckerkandl claimed, first joins the individual singer to a community of other singers, then the singers together seek identity with those things that are sung about. For Zuckerkandl, musical tones and harmonies function to "remove the barrier between person and thing, and clear the way for what might be called the singer's inner participation in that of which he sings."[11] This suspension of the self leads singers to enter, through lyrics, the realm of a shared mythic identity. "People sing," Zuckerkandl wrote, "in order to make sure, through direct experience, of their existence, where distinction and separation give way to authentic togetherness."[12]

Booth, following Zuckerkandl, said that singers participate in mythic experience and expression, and that songs exist principally as "iterative" phenomena, words and music that pronounce essentially "static" formulae of shared mythic beliefs. "Songs give us, for matter, something we can recognize," Booth wrote. "They present it in language sparing of surprises, consisting for the most part of well-chosen phrases rather than well-chosen words. The experience of song lies distinctly aside from [the] process [of] experience. The experience [of song] accumulates rather than develops. The patterns [that] songs show are common as opposed to unique, standing patterns as opposed to linear sequences of growth, evolution, discovery, catharsis."[13]

Andrew Welsh took a quite different approach to the problem of music and lyrical meaning in his 1978 book *Roots of Lyric: Primitive Poetry and Modern Poetics*. Examining a vast range of lyrical texts from ancient, medieval, and tribal societies as well as poems from the twentieth century, Welsh asked Wordsworth's question: what is the poet's language? He answered that it is lyric's powers of image and music, or as Aristotle called them in *Poetics, opsis* and *melos*. Lyrical *opsis* is the use of visual imagery to heighten meaning. Welsh cited Northrop Frye's definition of *opsis* as "a fusion of sensation and reflection, the use of an object of sense experience to stimulate a mental activity in connection with it." A classic example of *opsis* in Christian sacred poetry is Milton's employment of extraordinary visual and other sensory images in *Paradise Lost* to amplify and nuance the Genesis narrative.[14]

The more important lyrical element for sacred song in Welsh's analysis is *melos*, lyric's inherently musical qualities. Welsh observed with Paul Valéry in *The Art of Poetry* that "for centuries poetry was used for purposes of enchantment. Those who took part in these strange operations had to believe in the power of the word, and far more in the efficacy of its sound than in its significance." The power of *melos*, Welsh agreed, lies in "coincidences of sound-pattern. If full end-rhyme is rare [in lyric poetry], the internal soundings of consonance, assonance, alliteration, and word-repetition are common."[15] The words of a sacred song, then, can of themselves possess powers of incantation quite apart from their musical setting.

How do these words gain such power? Welsh's exploration of this question took him to the nature and use of chant. In his view chants are "words that act" as myth on the social and communal level, aided by the driving force of music. "Chant is poetry organized by both the internal rhythms of language and the external rhythms of music," Welsh wrote. The primal narrative of chant is communal myth and its social action is communal dance. "A chant, particularly a mythological chant, *needs* to be expressed in a regular rhythm, in a public rather than a private and secretive rhythm. The goal of the chant is an ambitious one: through the dance, through the social action of the ritual, through the shared knowledge of communal origins, it attempts to create and maintain a rhythm uniting individuals into a community."[16] For Welsh, chant conveys mythological meanings to the believing community through the regularity of its rhythm, whereby it is "fused with the sacred" and thereby rendered publicly efficacious.[17]

Whether one agrees with Booth that sacred lyric is a simplified poetic vehicle for mythic content or with Welsh that sacred lyric as a language form possesses potencies of rhythm and myth that directly manifest sacrality, language is an essential element of sacred song. Mythic language therefore gives a first answer to our question about how music can be sacred: music can be sacred song when it conveys specifiable mythic meaning through sacred lyric. This formulation, however, must be taken in the most flexible way possible. Specifiable mythic meaning can be conveyed musically by the most delicate of verbal gestures, even by syllabic vocalizations that have little apparent conceptual meaning.

Sacred song must at least combine music with mythic content. Under what conditions, however, does such a song become religious? The answer to this final defining question lies in sacred-song performance and the complex realm of sacred ritual. The most characteristic form of sacred song is the hymn. Commencing with the *Vedas* of the ancient Indus Valley, the hymn is at once the oldest literary form and the earliest musical form known to cultural history. In defining sacred song as religious expression, I find instructive the ancient standard of St. Augustine, Christianity's premier authority on matters of praise, who defined the hymn as "a song of praise to God."[18] To make a hymn Augustine required in addition to music both a fixed text—either biblical or original—and a specific intention and occasion to praise divinity. In my view, Augustine's elements of the hymn translate quite well into the modern anthropological concepts of belief content and ritual process. For a song to be sacred, it must possess not only belief content but also ritual intention and form. Ritual is the defining performance condition for sacred song, as mythic content is its defining cognitive condition.

In order for song to be religious expression it must be presented with sacred intentionality as part of effective ritual action. By "sacred intentionality" I mean simply that the song is presented as a sacred activity, like a prayer or a scripture reading, in a social and physical context consciously prepared to facilitate such a religious event. By "ritual action" I mean symbolic behavior that moves participants out of everyday awareness into a state of shared mythic consciousness and creative community. Sacred song is an extraordinary vehicle for conducting believers into the ritual dimension. It may indeed be the single most powerful medium of the ritual process.[19]

This ritual process, however, does not occur only in traditional religious environments like churches, synagogues, or mosques. In those sacred spaces, the ritual intention and context of sacred song are made categorically explicit. Everything that happens there has sacred meaning by definition and the problems of belief content and ritual action are thereby largely mooted. But there are other sacred-song contexts in which mythic content is less explicit and ritual itself becomes the principal vehicle of religious meaning.

At American ethnic and tribal celebrations, for example, the mythic universe often recedes into tacit or shorthand references that nonetheless still inform the sacred identity of the community. In such situations songs can articulate sacred meaning more through their ritualized performance modalities, like dances, than their articulated mythic content. This same kind of ritualized sacrality, as distinguished from the mythicized sacrality of more familiar texted varieties of sacred song, also appears in religious celebrations of the life cycle, especially marriage and death. At Italian and Jewish weddings and Irish wakes in America's northeastern cities, traditional songs and dances without any words at all can convey powerful sacred meanings through ritual performances that evoke the sacred cosmos of otherwise long-lost times and places.

These reflections suggest a cautious approach to defining sacred song. It is a protean medium that effortlessly moves across received categories of musical, literary, and religious analysis. Perhaps it is enough to say that sacred song is music that expresses religious meanings through the interaction of mythic content and ritual performance. Musical setting is, of course, a given, but both myth and ritual also seem necessary conditions for sacred song. The synergy of these elements creates a spectrum of expressive possibilities from mythicized, textually driven songs to ritualized, nontexted forms. Any definition of sacred song, in America or anywhere else, must be adequate to the range of practice on the ground. This interactive model of sacred song as music, myth, and ritual is offered, therefore, as a provisional definition. Whether this definition accomplishes its task will depend, ultimately, on the explorations of specific American sacred-song traditions that make up the body of this book.

The Public Realm

To a significant degree, sacred-song performance in contemporary America has moved out from explicitly sacred space into secular concert halls, theaters, auditoriums, stadiums, museums, and gymnasiums. Likewise, the audiences assembled in such places are no longer defined by a specific religious identity, but rather by a generic one as listener or fan. Performances like these introduce yet another dimension of our inquiry, the problem of sacred song as public expression.

The term *public* has enjoyed a lively recent history. In 1972 German philosopher Jürgen Habermas touched off a decades-long debate with his claim that a "public sphere," an open cultural dimension in which all political alternatives were tolerated and disputed, was a necessary precondition for civil society.[20] Subsequent argument has questioned whether such a public sphere has ever existed and whether it is a hopelessly limited Western political idea, but as a result of that discourse, scholars across the social sciences have explored the theoretical potential and historical reality of the public realm.

Sacred song can be performed in both the private and public domains, but it almost always requires a social rather than individual context. One can read or meditate alone upon a sacred song, or play it on a solo instrument, but it is extraordinarily difficult and uncommon to sing a sacred song alone. The form itself discourages such closeted performance, and if ritual context is a requisite for genuine sacred song, then it is by definition a social rather than individual medium.

On the other hand, the reality of sacred-song performance puts different glosses on the notion of publicity. To the extent that the word *public* means a representative sample of the American citizenry, polling data has long established that any public audience for sacred song is made up of theists, most of whom identify with religious institutions in some sense. One can also assume, however, that the more genuinely "public" and not religiously preselected an audience is—the more religiously plural it is—the less likely it is to provide a ritual context for sacred song.

The word *public* also has a very different meaning as it is used in the phrase *public worship*. Since one in every two American church members belongs to a religion other than their family's tradition, and since many among the one-third of all Americans who move their domicile each decade also seek out a new religious affiliation, we know that public access to worship services is in fact frequently exercised. It is also clear, however, that in practice "public worship" is primarily a private matter for closely drawn communities. Anyone who has done participant-observation research in a small religious congregation knows the disruptive effect that even one outsider can have on the flow of ritual process. From such evidence, it is not unreasonable to conclude that the more circumscribed the public access to worship is, the more likely that efficacious ritual process will accompany the performance of sacred song.

Both kinds of audience, the general public and the worshipping public, share a common characteristic that adds yet another dimension to the problem of sacred song in American public culture. These audiences are all in some sense consumers of sacred song as a product. The public dimension of sacred song today extends far beyond church and concert hall to the realm of commodity and commercialization. One of the most common things Americans do in public is shop, and they buy a lot of sacred-song recordings, more than a half-billion dollars worth each year in gospel music alone, and half again as much if traditional and classical sacred music is included. Live gate, performance fees, and production costs generate tens of millions more per annum. Add to this amount the church music budgets of every congregation and religious community in the land, and sacred song becomes big business indeed. Television and the Internet have created vast new audiences for sacred-song recordings and videos exponentially larger than ever before possible. Much of the "public" audience for sacred song in America today never needs to leave home to consume the product: they can just queue it up on their cable TV or electronically order it for their video screen or sound system.

What difference does this commercial transformation of the public realm make for sacred song in America? In one sense the new media act as a conservative force, establishing canonical styles and standards for sacred-song performance that preserve many traditional elements. The remarkable success of white gospel singer Sandi Patti, "the new Kate Smith," in the 1980s and 1990s illustrates this tendency, as does the generally unexceptional performances of sacred-song classics on local and regional religious broadcasts.

In another sense, however, the media have become the new arbiters of taste for much of American sacred song. Nationally syndicated religious broadcasts, like those of evangelist Pat Robertson, have had major impact on the selection and styling of white Evangelical Protestant sacred song over the past twenty years. Similarly the opportunity to "cross over" from gospel to pop has shaped the development of many Black Church singers, most notably Aretha Franklin. The power of the media in the twenty-first century to shape the style and content of sacred song is unprecedented, and it raises the question whether the future of sacred song will be determined by the religious communities from which it has traditionally sprung or by commercial artists and production specialists skilled in creating new markets for sacred song products. The answer to that question is fateful, for if sacred song becomes simply a commercial commodity, can it truly still be sacred?

Sacred Song and American Religious Culture: The Plan of the Book

There is a great deal more to the problem of sacred song than these matters of definition and public practice. Sacred song performs complex and diverse functions in the larger domain of religious culture. Among many definitions of religion employed by scholars today, the formulation of anthropologist Clifford Geertz is especially suitable for assessing the many roles of sacred song. In his 1973 essay "Religion as a Cultural System," Geertz offered a now-classic definition of religion as a dynamic system of symbolic expressions and behaviors: "a religion is 1) a system of symbols which acts to 2) establish powerful, pervasive, and long-lasting moods and motivations . . . by 3) formulating conceptions of a general order of existence and 4) clothing these conceptions with such an aura of factuality that 5) the moods and motivations seem uniquely realistic."[21]

Geertz's definition may be roughly translated into four major components—systematic beliefs, institutional structures, ritual behaviors, and spiritual or moral practices—that combine to produce a religious culture. As sacred song interacts with and articulates these different elements of religious culture, it takes on a multitude of roles and significations that reach far beyond matters of musical setting, sacred words, and ritual performance. Within any single religious culture or tradition, sacred song may act in many ways. It can provide identity, move to action, cause dissent, promote growth, alter belief, deepen faith, galvanize or anesthetize worship. To understand the deeper significance of sacred song, it is necessary to ask about these roles and functions.

The meanings of sacred song in America can best be addressed through a detailed examination of representative examples. This book presents a series of cases drawn from the immense diversity of contemporary American religion in order to outline the principal ways in which sacred song works in religious cultures. I do not pretend that the cases are exhaustive, nor do I claim to address all of sacred song's significance in each tradition. I do mean, however, to suggest a framework for understanding what sacred song means by testing the definition of it as a synergistic form of music, myth, and ritual against salient examples of its most important functions in major American religious traditions.

Five of those traditions—Native American, Chicano Catholic, Sacred Harp, Black Church, and Jewish—represent the historic deep structure of American sacred song. Each of these song traditions extends back at least to the seventeenth century in the New World, the Native American far beyond that, and all of them have been maintained continuously since then. It is not surprising, therefore, that they perform fundamental functions in their religious cultures. Exactly which aspects of religious culture they preserve and articulate, however, varies in each case, as does the form and manner in which sacred song accomplishes those functions. The exploration of these five constituting sacred song traditions occupies part 1 of this book.

Beyond traditional sacred song lies the realm of contemporary religious groups and their musics that perform additional functions in religious culture. Two examples, the New Age movement and the recent hymnals of the Southern Baptist Convention and the United Church of Christ, suggest alternative ways in which sacred song shapes religious beliefs. The Church of Jesus Christ of Latter-day Saints, by contrast, provides a textbook case of a rather different function for sacred song in America: its ability to legitimate sectarian religious movements. The career of John Michael Talbot, founder of the Brothers and Sisters of Charity and America's most popular Catholic sacred-music artist, offers a complementary and contrasting example of how sacred music and musical leaders can influence the institutional dimension of American religious communities. Finally, the worlds of the concert hall and gospel music address how sacred song functions at the interface of contemporary religious culture and commercialization. Examination of these contemporary movements and musics makes up part 2 of the study.

This book is an inquiry into the question: what do we learn if we place sacred song at the center of our attention as a public expression of contemporary American religious culture? To answer that question I have used a variety of methods, applying them to each sacred-song tradition and movement under examination. Description is the first task. Sacred song must be observed in performance in order adequately to describe it. I have therefore included in each chapter my personal observations of live sacred-song performances (with the exception of chapter 10, which contains interviews with two conservatory-trained composers). These entail what Geertz called "thick description" of detail, especially setting and sequence.[22]

Next, it is essential to establish the religious meaning of sacred song for those who sing it. The researcher of sacred song is obligated to let singers articulate the sacrality of their own songs. To that end, I have interviewed at length the performers of the songs described at the beginning of each chapter, relying on their eloquence, as well as supplemental written sources, to articulate how and why they consider their songs sacred. These descriptions and interviews are the principal primary sources to be interpreted in this study.

I have used three major disciplines to interpret this evidence: history, musicology, and religion theory. As a historian of American religion, I believe it is impossible to understand a phenomenon like sacred song without placing it in historical context. Some of these songs are very old, others quite new, but all require an explanation of the historical processes that created them. It is especially important to know something about the beliefs, institutions, and rituals that inform the text and music of sacred song. To that end each chapter also contains a brief historical treatment of its respective religious tradition.

The need for at least some musical and musicological commentary in a study like this one is obvious. I am not a trained musicologist, but I have performed, directed, and taught about American Protestant sacred song for more than forty years. The purpose of this book is not to provide expert comparative analyses of sacred-music texts, but rather to explore sacred song as an integral element of religious culture. For that more modest purpose, and to assist the non-musician reader, basic description of musical examples and commentary on music history and performance practice have been provided.

Finally, in order to uncover the complex role of sacred song in religious cultures, it is necessary to apply a wide range of conceptual tools from the theory of religion. These ideas help define religion and explain how it works. I have drawn primarily upon sociology, anthropology, and history of religion theories, the major social scientific approaches used in the study of religion today. Every sacred-song tradition we will examine could be interpreted by any or all of these theories, but I have found that each tradition especially illuminates a different theoretical category or concept. I have therefore used religion theory to explain different aspects of each sacred-song tradition, rather than to conduct a theoretical exercise about the nature of religion for which sacred song simply provides the data.

Descriptions and interviews provide the frame of evidence for the chapters that follow. History, musicology, and religion theory supply their interpretive fuel. The problem of commercialization appears in every chapter, but it is focused principally in the first and last chapters. This book is also a vehicle for a larger journey, however, an exploration of that little understood region where religion and music meet. Our itinerary will take us to many places to hear different kinds of sacred song and consider different understandings of what it means and how it works. If we travel far enough, we might also learn something new about religion itself and how to understand it in twenty-first-century America.

Notes

1. Diana Eck and the Pluralism Project at Harvard University, *On Common Ground: World Religions in America* (New York: Columbia University Press, 1997). See also Diana Eck, *A New Religious America: How a "Christian Country" Has Now Become the Most Religiously Diverse Nation* (San Francisco: Harper San Francisco, 2001).

2. Deryck Cooke, *The Language of Music* (New York: Oxford University Press, 1959), 113–67; Leonard Meyer, *Emotion and Meaning in Music* (Chicago: University of Chicago Press, 1956).

3. Suzanne K. Langer, *Philosophy in a New Key* (Cambridge, Mass.: Harvard University Press, 1942); Kurt Sachs, *The Wellsprings of Music* (New York: Da Capo Press, 1962).

4. Peter Kivy, *Music Alone: Philosophical Reflections on the Purely Musical Experience* (Ithaca, N.Y.: Cornell University Press, 1990), 146–72; Malcolm Budd, *Music and the Emotions: The Philosophical Theories* (New York: Routledge and Kegan Paul, 1985), 121–77. See also Peter Kivy, *Sound and Semblance: Reflections on Musical Representation* (Princeton, N.J.: Princeton University Press, 1984), *Sound Sentiment: An Essay on the Musical Emotions, Including the Complete Text of The Corded Shell* (Philadelphia: Temple University Press, 1989), *New Essays on Musical Understanding* (Oxford: Clarendon, 2001), and *Introduction to a Philosophy of Music* (New York: Oxford University Press, 2002); Malcolm Budd, *Values of Art: Pictures, Poetry, and Music* (New York: Penguin, 1995).

5. Anthony Storr, *Music and the Mind* (New York: Free Press, 1992); John A. Sloboda, *The Musical Mind: The Cognitive Psychology of Music* (Oxford: Clarendon Press, 1985).

6. Robert Jourdain, *Music, the Brain, and Ecstasy: How Music Captures Our Imagination* (New York: Morrow, 1997); Oliver Sacks, *Awakenings* (New York: HarperCollins, 1975).

7. Jourdain, *Music, the Brain, and Ecstasy*, 331.

8. Jonathan Edwards, *A Treatise on Religious Affections*, ed. John E. Smith, vol. 2 of *The Works of Jonathan Edwards* (New Haven: Yale University Press, 1957–); Ralph Waldo Emerson, *Nature*, ed. Robert E. Spiller, vol. 1 of *The Collected Works of Ralph Waldo Emerson* (Cambridge, Mass.: Harvard University Press, 1971–); William James, *The Varieties of Religious Experience*, ed. Bruce Kuklick, vol. 1 of *The Works of William James* (New York: Library Classics, 1987–).

9. Mark W. Booth, *The Experience of Songs* (New Haven: Yale University Press, 1981), 7.

10. Ibid., 14.

11. Victor Zuckerkandl, *Man the Musician*, trans. Norbert Guterman, Bollingen Series 44, no. 2 (Princeton, N.J.: Princeton University Press, 1973), 29.

12. Cited in Booth, *Experience of Songs*, 20.

13. Ibid., 25.

14. Andrew Welsh, *Roots of Lyric: Primitive Poetry and Modern Poetics* (Princeton, N.J.: Princeton University Press, 1978); Northrop Frye, *Anatomy of Criticism* (Princeton, N.J.: Princeton University Press, 1957), 280; Stephen Halliwell, *The Poetics of Aristotle: Translation and Commentary* (Chapel Hill: University of North Carolina Press, 1967); John Milton, *Paradise Lost: An Authoritative Text, Backgrounds and Sources, Criticism*, ed. Scott Elledge, 2d ed. (New York: Norton, 1998).

15. Paul Valery, *The Art of Poetry*, trans. Denise Folliot, vol. 7 of *The Collected Works of Paul Valery* (New York: Pantheon, 1958), 74; Welsh, *Roots of Lyric*, 139.

16. Welsh, *Roots of Lyric*, 166, 175.

17. Ibid.

18. See *St. Augustine on Music: Books I–VI*, trans. R. C. Taliaferro (Annapolis, Md.: St. John's Bookstore, 1939).

19. Victor Turner, *The Ritual Process: Structure and Anti-Structure* (Ithaca, N.Y.: Cornell University Press, 1969), 94–130.

20. Jürgen Habermas, *Knowledge and Human Interests* (Boston: Beacon Press, 1972), 301–17.

21. Clifford Geertz, "Religion as a Cultural System," in Geertz, *The Interpretation of Cultures* (New York: Basic Books, 1973), 90.

22. Clifford Geertz, "Thick Description: Toward an Interpretive Theory of Culture," in Geertz, *Interpretation of Cultures*, 3–32.

PART 1

Great Traditions of American Sacred Song

Songway: Sacred-Song Traditions of Native America

The story of sacred song in America begins with the original peoples of the continent. Centuries before the arrival of European colonists, Native American tribal societies developed extraordinarily rich and diverse traditions of sacred song. These songs, and the dances and ceremonial rituals associated with them, stood at the center of Native American religion. Transmitted orally and elaborated over countless generations, sacred songs addressed virtually every aspect of tribal life. Native American song gathered together the cycles of the year and the seasons, life and death, birth and health, human purpose and natural process into a circle of shared meaning joined to the powers of the sacred cosmos.

Pre-Columbian Americans created an immense variety of sacred-song cultures, from the calendric spectacles of the Maya, Aztec, and Inca to the ancient celebrations of the Pueblo peoples of the Southwest, from the clan rituals of the Woodland, Plains, and Western Coastal nations to the shamanistic practices of sub-Arctic societies. Despite five centuries of systematic attack by European colonialists and the U.S. government, much of this diversity still survives. Five hundred remaining Native American nations maintain a unique and powerful legacy of sacred meaning expressed through song.

Native American peoples divide sacred song into two types, ceremonials and socials. Ceremonials, sung in the high sacred rituals of tribal religion, are employed to make spiritual beings present and to purify participants. Ceremonies of initiation, planting, hunting, healing, harvest, and war proceed through songs sung by spiritual men and women entrusted with their performance and the exercise of their powers.[1] While some ceremonials, notably the Plains Sweat Lodge, have recently been performed for non-Indians, they are usually reserved for tribal members and scrupulously fenced. Even public rituals like Pueblo Feast Day ceremonies in the Southwest may be witnessed by non-Indians only with tribal permission, and the outside observer will not obtain any significant interpretation from participants.

Sacred song also expresses traditional spirituality on social occasions. At these socials—games, holiday celebrations, and dance competitions—song may lack the cultic meanings of high ceremonial, but it maintains its potency as a sacred medium. The most important form of socials is the powwow, a public ritual gathering of one or more clans or tribes dedicated to skill competitions, feasting, and dancing. Given the very private nature of ceremonials, powwow provides the best way to explore the significance of publicly expressed sacred song for Native American peoples. To experience firsthand the power of this kind of sacred song, I traveled to Colorado in the early spring of 1994 for the twentieth annual Denver March Powwow, one of the oldest and largest intertribal powwows in the United States.

Denver March Powwow

The Denver Coliseum is a two-story 1950s-vintage concrete arena that seats about five thousand people. Built originally for stock shows and rodeos, the facility stands in an old stockyard area on the north side of the city. On the second night of the Denver March Powwow, an unseasonably warm early spring Friday evening, the Coliseum lobby was jammed. Men, women, and children pressed close, seeking a way into the arena as the time for the evening's Grand Entry approached. Vendors lined both sides of the hallway, narrowing the streams of people negotiating passage.

Every imaginable kind of Indian paraphernalia seemed to be on sale at more than 275 booths packed into the circular hallway. On the low end of the scale were "dreamcatchers," handwoven grass circles with intricate webbing and a small feather attached, said to capture bad dreams and prevent them from coming true. More expensive items included pottery, sand paintings, carvings, lamp stands, posters, prints, flutes, recordings, and Indian jewelry. At a few stalls materials for powwow dancers' outfits were on sale: chicken, turkey, and macaw feathers; beads and necklaces; small tin cones and packs of Copenhagen chewing tobacco lids known as "jingles." More predictable merchants hawked commemorative tee-shirts, caps, and jackets. At this hour the most popular concessions sold frybread and Indian tacos to patrons and dancers alike.

The powwow had begun Thursday afternoon with the consecration of the dancing ground by spiritual leader Byron Brady. The first Grand Entry had stepped off at noon Friday, followed by a three-hour round of contest dancing, the coronation of the Powwow Princess, and two special women's competitions. At six o'clock on Friday evening, however, dinner break had left the arena quite empty so that the ritual space could be easily seen. An announcer's table domi-

nated the west end, about a dozen rows above the floor. The powwow organizing committee had set aside seats below the announcer's table, with a long
judges' table on the floor directly in front of them.

Large numbered signs on metal poles ringed the blue-carpeted arena floor.
At each of these stations, a circle of six to ten folding chairs had been arranged
for the singers. In the center of each circle stood a large drum, handmade and
well used, each one at least three feet across. Some of the drumheads bore
painted images of eagles; others displayed mountain peaks. A few of the drums
were set up vertically, like bass drums in a marching band, but most were placed
horizontally, like tympani, so that each person in the circle could comfortably
strike a mallet on the drumhead. During this powwow recess, tufted drumsticks
had been carefully arranged on top of the drumheads, in some cases surmounted
by a small group of eagle feathers.

Shortly after 6:30 Dale Old Horn, veteran powwow master of ceremonies and
chairman of the Department of Crow Studies and Social Sciences at Little Big
Horn College, called the assembly to order with a short speech that located the
powwow in a specifically religious context. "For those of you who may be new
to Native American culture," Old Horn said, "we are probably one of the most
religious groups of people on the face of the earth, as we acknowledge the power
of our maker at all times. We believe that this power comes to us in many different ways. And one of these ways is the dance way, and one of them is the song
way. The Native American experience is known through motion and song. By
this we appeal to our Maker. For we know that all things are His creation, and
that we are only a small part. Through this way we pray."

Old Horn introduced Walter Pennekeep, a respected elder from Mandan, North
Dakota, "to pray for us in this way tonight." Pennekeep began in traditional Plains
fashion with a brief speech expressing the circumstances of the occasion: "It's
always a big honor for me to do something like this among so many people who
are from different tribes. A lot of times we get up and say a prayer in our own
tongue, but there are so many among us today who have lost that understanding
and the true meaning of their tongue. Today I want to say a prayer in a universal
language that we all can understand and know what this man is praying about,
even from the smallest among us up to the elders and the oldest ones."

Pennekeep delivered a bilingual prayer in Lakota and English, consisting of
invocations to Tunkashila, the Sioux grandfather of all spirits. His prayer eloquently stated the fundamental spiritual purpose of powwow—to bring "joy and
understanding" to all through the celebration of song and traditional dance:

> We ask that you help everyone here tonight, Tunkashila,
> Help us during the day and during the night, Tunkashila,
> And especially give your help to the singers, Tunkashila,
> Help them so that they may bring joy to each and every one,
> And help every one to understand one another, Tunkashila,

And especially for those on the arranging committee,
Those that have put this event on, Tunkashila,
Have pity on them and watch over them in their daily lives.
And each one that is here tonight, Tunkashila,
Help them to return to their homes in safety.

After this prayer, Dale Old Horn began the drum roll call. "Drum" refers not only to the instrument itself, but also to the singing group that plays it and sings to its rhythms. The number of drums indicates the significance of a powwow: the more the better. At Denver forty-eight drums, a very large number, had assembled from every point on the Plains from Alberta to Oklahoma. Drum names also represent powers of the spiritual entities specially invoked by each group. The drum-beings at Denver included Medicine Warrior, Good Wood Creek, White Shield, Cherry Creek, Red Rose Crossing, White Ridge, Redstone, Spotted Eagle, Little Wind, Morning Star, Bad Medicine, Heartbeat, Ironwood, Rising Hail, Black Stone, Whirl Wind Eagle, Little Otter, White Ghost, Spotted White Wolf, and Wind River. When Old Horn called each drum name, one of its singers responded with a single stroke on the drumhead. Roll call, however, entailed more than merely taking attendance. As the varied, resonant voices of the drums rolled through the hushed hall, they announced the presence of the spirit-beings without whom powwow could not properly occur.

As Grand Entry time approached, dancers in brilliant outfits crowded into the east end of the arena. Some of them practiced their steps, while out on the floor singers occasionally broke into song. Finally the Grand Entry commenced with the singing of "A Living Hoop," the Denver March Powwow Song, by its composer Howard Bad Hand of Taos, New Mexico, and his Heartbeat Singers. The singers moved toward the center of the floor beating their large drum and singing in Lakota:

> He Ska Oyate ki!
> Oskate kile luhapi ki
> Cangleska ca niun welo
> Sitomniya, Tunkasila nan
> Unci Maka ko
> Oniciyapi nan
> Wiyuskinya waci au welo

> White Mountain People!
> This Celebration that
> You have is a living hoop!
> From all over the universe,
> Even Grandfather Creator and
> Grandmother Earth help you, and
> All joyfully come to dance.

The song addressed the "White Mountain people," Native Americans of Colorado's Mount Evans Range who host this annual event, and honored the Denver Powwow as "a living hoop," Sioux symbol of community life. To animate that hoop of celebration, the song invoked all ancestors and cosmic powers, including the spirits of the Creator and of the Earth, to join in the dance.

After the first rendition of "A Living Hoop," a procession of more than 1,000 dancers, led by an eagle-feather staff bearer, flag bearers, and honored guests, entered the arena dancing to repeated iterations of the song. The lead party moved past the Heartbeat Singers' drum to face the reviewing stand. Next came the "royalty," young women chosen by each tribal community to represent it in competitions of dancing, outfit, and speaking. The newly crowned princess marked out a clockwise spiral path that all dancers followed around the arena. Competition groups processed in strict traditional order, classified by their status, outfit, and dance form: Senior Men's, Men's Northern Traditional, Southern Straight, Men's Fancy, Men's Grass, Women's Fancy Shawl, Women's Jingle, Senior Women's, Women's Northern Traditional, Women's Southern Buckskin, Women's Southern Cloth, Teen Boys' Traditional, Teen Boys' Fancy, Teen Boys' Grass, Teen Girls' Traditional, Teen Girls' Fancy, Teen Girls' Jingle, Little Boys, Little Girls, and Tiny Tots.

The spectacle slowly wound its way into a great serpentine procession of dancers performing traditional steps and joining in the spirit of the powwow song. Grand Entry was the only event of the powwow in which every dancer participated. As such it was the defining act of "joy and understanding," transcending the competitions soon to begin. Brief formalities followed the Grand Entry. A patriotic flag song and an honor song were sung, and the Powwow Princess delivered a message of greeting. Then Dale Old Horn called for several "intertribals," a special variety of song in which all are encouraged to dance. Blackstone Singers, a popular group of Cree, Choctaw-Chickasaw, and Ute singers from Alberta, Canada, were the "special guest" drum group at the Denver March Powwow that year and accordingly they led the intertribals. Such songs are textually very simple in order to encourage maximum comprehension and participation by the dancers. Blackstone Singers sang intertribal songs that said, "Dancers! Come and enjoy yourselves!" and "The dancer knows how to enjoy himself in the Indian way."

Two important ritual observances govern the flow of singing and dancing at powwow: the feather and the whistle. During one of the first intertribals, a sacred eagle feather became dislodged from a dancer's outfit and fell to the floor. The floor manager informed the master of ceremonies, who immediately called out, "we have a feather!" and all singing and dancing ceased. The eagle is the prime Plains symbol of the Great Spirit. For its feather to touch the ground during dance is a profanation of the sacred powers, the assembly, and the dancer responsible for it. Before dancing can resume, restoration must be made.

A group of select elders carefully recovered the fallen feather while they sang and danced a "Brave Man" song that restored its sacred powers. The elder chosen to recover the feather offered a speech about bravery that rekindled the spirit of the powwow. An advocate for the dancer spoke for his honor and sincerity in the ways of the powwow, removing the onus of weakness and impurity. The dancer's family made a "giveaway" of gifts to the elders and offered a special prize for one of the competitions, thereby reuniting with the community and healing the profane rupture. Only then did the intertribal resume.[2]

The ritual opposite of the fallen eagle feather is the blowing of the eagle whistle, which occurred later in the evening during another intertribal. Carved from the wing bone of the sacred eagle, the whistle is worn by noted dancers as a sign of skill and accomplishment. When one of those dancers feels the sacred power of a song especially keenly, he blows the whistle, making the cry of the sacred eagle to honor the offering of song. When the whistle sounded at Denver, the master of ceremonies cried, "we have a whistle," and the singers gave it honor by repeating the song at a quicker tempo. The whistle-blower danced over to the drum and repeated the whistle-blowing ritual, redoubling the energy and enthusiasm of singers and dancers. On Friday night alone five whistles amplified the intertribals. The Grand Entry and the intertribals together consumed a full hour and a half of intense, virtually nonstop singing and group dancing by every powwow participant.

After a fifteen-minute pause, competition dancing began, conducted in groups of twelve to twenty dancers and judged by three or four expert masters of the style. Every dance required songs, which were assigned by numerical order to the forty-eight assembled drums. The judging of each competition included not only the dancing itself, but also the dancer's outfit and overall presentation of traditional style. On Friday evening, competition dancing began around 9:00 and continued until 11:30 with only brief breaks for competition groups to enter and leave the floor. Competition songs are textually similar to intertribals. Blackstone Singers, for example, sang a contest song by one of its Cree members, Randall Paskemin, that said, "Let's enjoy this powwow as we sit around the circle."

Powwow requires a fundamental commitment by participants. It is very demanding of time, money, energy, and skill for people who are neither wealthy nor specially trained. Most of them do not participate for the prize money that large powwows now offer for dance and drum competitions. The 1994 Rocky Boy's Powwow sponsored by the Chippewa Cree Nation, for example, offered $50,000 in regular competition prizes and $12,000 for special competitions. Such prizes support a small class of professional dancers, and drum groups attract a significant market for their recordings, but even for these elite powwow performers the costs are high, the rewards slim, the risks great.

The massive number of singers, dancers, and audience at Denver comprised only a mere fraction of Native American participants on the contemporary powwow circuit. The 1993 edition of Eagle/Walking Turtle's *Indian America: A Traveler's Companion* listed 573 powwows in virtually every state and reservation in the United States.[3] More than one million people, most of them Native Americans, attended those powwows. Singers traveled endless miles to offer up their songs. Dancers spent large sums of money on handmade outfits furnished with precious hereditary artifacts, costly feathers, expensive animal hides, ornamental shoes, bells and jingles, and spectacular sewn beadwork and sequins decoration. Audiences devoted substantial time and treasure to witness what appears to be a singing and dancing contest. Why? Something more than prize money and competition must account for the powwow movement. That force is a profound dedication to the traditional spiritual ways of Indian peoples combined with a growing sense of intertribal solidarity and cultural identity.

The Powwow Movement

The origins of powwow lie deep in the traditions of Native American peoples. "The Algonquin word 'pauau' or 'pauwau' has been Anglicized into the word powwow," according to Henrietta Mann Morton, a Southern Cheyenne, "which also has become a pan-Indian term. . . . A powwow is an outgrowth of the religious and social dances of the Plains tribes, it is a celebration of culture with dancing as its primary focus." Cliff Roberts, a lifelong student of powwow, provides more context: "Historically, tribes in North America held certain ceremonies celebrating successful hunts, food gathering, or warfare. These ceremonies allowed the people to give thanks, to mourn their deceased relatives, or deal with special honors such as name-giving ceremonies, adoptions, and coming of age rites. Many times they were held to renew allegiances and maintain friendships with members of visiting tribes. The ceremonies often involved dancing and feasting."[4]

The modern powwow movement may be traced to the late-nineteenth-century war dances of the Hethuska Societies of the Pinca tribe in Oklahoma and the grass dances of the Omaha and Pawnee peoples in Nebraska. "Oklahoma tribes were the center of the powwow emergence," Roberts reported.

> The Pinca's Fair and Powwow originated in 1877. The dances lasted four days and attracted people from over 100 miles away. They travelled by foot, horseback, and wagon. 1916 saw the beginnings of the Anadarko Fair [in Nebraska]. In 1925, the Haskell Institute in Lawrence, Kansas, held a dance contest to determine the world's championship. The old Omaha grass dance became fancied up with colorful feathered bustles, and fancy dancing was born. Indian people have always borrowed from each other and the new style of costuming and dancing quickly spread to other Plains tribes. (22)

By the mid-twentieth century the powwow had developed into a fragile vehicle for intertribal celebration, creating understanding even among former enemies. Boye Ladd, a prominent Winnebago Fancy Dancer, remembers that transition: "Back in the fifties there was still a lot of animosity between tribes. You wouldn't see Crows and Cheyennes or Crows and Sioux sitting at the same drum, let alone being at the same powwow. Today intertribalism is very much alive. The modern-day powwow has brought a lot of tribes together, it's brought unity. We are saying 'we' now as opposed to saying only 'Sioux,' 'Cheyenne,' or 'Crow'" (33).

During the 1950s and 1960s the powwow movement diversified. Ladd explained its growing geographical configuration: "Powwows take place in geographic circuits which are roughly a half-day's drive in diameter."[5] Roberts wrote, "These circuits overlap. I've been able to identify about sixteen in the US and Canada. The two primary circuits are the northern and the southern. The more formal southern Plains influence is centered in Oklahoma and the looser northern style is centered in the Dakotas, Montana, and the Canadian Provinces of Alberta and Saskatchewan" (33).

Powwows also differentiated according to their intention. "There are five kinds of powwows," Roberts wrote, "some of which overlap: holiday, honoring, memorial, benefit, and large annual commercial powwows. The southern powwow circuit, centered in Oklahoma, hosts many of the honoring and benefit powwows. The northern circuit seems to favor holiday and large commercial events" (29–31).

As the powwow circuit developed, however, it fought a difficult battle against the overall decline of Native American cultural traditions in postwar America. During the 1960s, reservation populations decreased, urban Indians acclimated to Anglo lifestyle, and a new generation seemed focused on nontraditional pursuits. After the deadly 1974 confrontation between Native American rights activists and federal government officials at Wounded Knee, South Dakota, Indian leaders took a new cultural strategy designed to promote, restore, and—where necessary—reconstruct their traditions.

Today's powwow movement emerged as part of that strategy. Powwows promote intertribal social dancing in which many different peoples come together, rejoice in the power of their numbers and their unity, and share their song and dance traditions with each other. If enough different tribes participated in dance and drum competitions, leaders believed, a pan-Indian cultural synthesis could develop through nonconfrontational expression of difference. While some traditional tribal leaders still consider any public sharing of their social dances a secularizing profanation, the powwow movement's intertribal agenda has enjoyed success over the past two decades beyond even the highest hopes of its founders.

Tony Brown, a prominent Oneida/Sioux/Flathead Fancy Dancer, has given eloquent voice to the qualities that draw so many to powwows today. "There is no single word that describes the powwow," Brown said. "Powwow is Indian. [It] is a place of healing, praying, dancing, and singing. A place to join others in pride and respect. A place to feel good. Powwow means the gathering of relations, of people. A place people come to get well, feel good about themselves, about their people. It is a place of good spirits. When you're feeling sad, come to a powwow and you'll be happy again. There will be a feeling you didn't have when you first came there" (29).

Precisely because powwow is a nonexclusive form of spiritual and ritual sharing among Native Americans, however, it can also accept the presence of non-Indians. Because singers and dancers may be hearing new songs for the first time, it is acceptable for non-Indians in the arena also to be doing so. And because the intertribal powwow is explicitly designed to open Native Americans to new awareness of their own collective identity, it can open the souls of non-Indians as well without violating its own integrity. Powwow is unquestionably the most important public expression of Native American sacred song. Song is the medium that makes powwow possible by supplying musical form to facilitate communal dance. The spiritual power released through song and dance animates powwow and reveals the sacred way of being Indian.

The Song

At Denver March Powwow, as at the Blackfoot Nation's North American Indian Days at Blanding, Montana, and the Kootenai Nation's Standing Arrow Powwow on the shores of Flathead Lake, Montana, it seemed to me that the driving force behind the songs was the drum. I had surmised that singers predicated their performance on the throbbing percussive figures of their particular drums. I had made that assumption because of what I had long been taught about the primal power of rhythm in Western music. Many interpreters of Western sacred music ascribe fundamental potency to rhythm as the musical link between the body and the holy, and the form of Native American sacred song seemed only to enhance that importance.

Howard Bad Hand, creator of the Denver March Powwow Song, saw the drum quite differently, however, as structurally subordinate both to the song and to the singer's own performance. "The drum helps me and it's a friend and if it's a good friend you give it a name and treat it as a person," said Bad Hand, a fourth-generation Lakota singer and healer from the Rosebud Sioux reservation in South Dakota, "but it's a person and it doesn't have any more mystical power than any object that is useful." He acknowledged other approaches to the relationship between singer and drum, but found that the greatest power lies elsewhere in sacred song. "You do get some folks who get so into the mystical aspect of it," he said, "that the drum takes on a persona, a personification. And the New Age movement gets into drumming to promote religious feeling. But in my way of singing it is only helping me. The real movement is in the music, not the drum. I tend to sing even if I don't have the drum."[6]

Words, too, are important in powwow and ceremonial singing, but they also do not carry the same cognitive burden associated with them in Western religious traditions. In fact, powwow and ceremonial songs come in both worded and syllabic or "vocable" forms. I asked Howard Bad Hand whether he experienced worded and nonworded songs differently. To my surprise he answered, "It's just the same."

There are quite complex reasons, however, behind this simple answer. William Powers, a prominent scholar of the Lakota tradition, has studied them. Powers argues that over the course of long generations of use, original Lakota song texts were gradually blurred into "incomprehensible terms" that heightened rather than diminished their sacrality. Powers grounds this claim in a theoretical principle from the French anthropologist Lucien Levy-Bruhl. "That which finally proves the mystic worth and power of words as words," Levy-Bruhl wrote in 1928, "is the widespread custom, in magic ceremonies and even in ritual and religious ceremonies, of using songs and formulas which are unintelligible to those who hear them, and sometimes even to those who utter them."[7] Rudolf Otto said much the same thing about words and the expression of sacrality in his groundbreaking 1912 book *The Idea of the Holy*. The "uncomprehended" quality of the sacred, Otto wrote,

> finds its most unqualified expression in the spell exercised by the only half intelligible or wholly unintelligible language of devotion, and in the unquestionable real enhancement of the awe of the worshiper which this produces. Instances of this [include] the ancient traditional expressions, still retained despite their obscurity, in the Bible and hymnals; the special emotional virtue attaching to words like "Hallelujah" [and] "Selah," just because they are "wholly other" and convey no clear meaning.[8]

Nonintelligibility, in other words, can enhance the sacrality of a song text, especially if it has been transmitted by venerated traditional means. In the Native American case, this element has been developed so far as to permit songs with texts consisting simply of syllables like "ehe" or "ye hi" to convey tremendous spiritual power and sacred significance. In sharp contrast to Western practice, indigenous song traditions like the Lakota do not create a musical setting for a text that already bears independent sacred authority. Rather text and tune are married in a single expression through which the intention of the song is made real to the singer and through him or her to the people. The spiritual reality that the song manifests is far greater than the meanings of its words.

The drum, then, is "friend," but not indispensable agent, to the singer. The text and the tune have no special metaphysical status. What then makes these songs sacred? I asked Howard Bad Hand about how he created his Denver March Powwow Song. I learned first that powwow songs are not "composed," they are "made," while ceremonial songs are "taught," and that their makings are always close to nature, the fundamental spiritual reference point for being Indian.

In his influential book *God Is Red: A Native View of Religion* Sioux lawyer and philosopher Vine Deloria Jr. describes the essence of Native American religions

as a series of spiritual relationships between the individual, the community, the
natural world, and the sacred cosmos:

> The Indian is confronted with a bountiful earth in which all things and expe-
> riences have a role to play. The role of the tribal religion . . . is to determine
> the proper relationship that the people of the tribe must have with other liv-
> ing things and to develop the self-discipline within the tribal community so
> that man acts harmoniously with other creatures. . . . The world that he ex-
> periences is dominated by the presence of power, the manifestation of life
> energies, the whole life-flow of creation. Recognition that the human beings
> hold an important place in such a creation is tempered by the thought that
> they are dependent on everything in creation for their existence.[9]

Howard Bad Hand's story illustrates this intimacy between nature, community, cosmos, singer, and song, all understood as parts of the larger whole of
spiritual being. The Powwow Committee had waited an entire year for Bad Hand
to make the song, yet as he drove from his home in Taos, New Mexico, to Denver for the first Powwow in March 1974, he had not yet made it. On the way,
inspiration came to him while gazing on the sacred mountains of the Evans
Range in Colorado. "Driving into Denver," he recalled,

> I was looking westward to Mount Evans, so I used the skyline of the moun-
> tain to make the song, the silhouette of the mountain. If you listen to the
> melody, you will hear how it's structured high, then comes down low, then
> bounces around a little bit. If you look at the horizon west of Denver that's
> what it is. The Indian people who settled in Denver are called in our language
> the White Mountain People. Those are the White Mountains, the central lo-
> cation where the spirit people we work with are located. So tying that togeth-
> er, because it was a committee of those people who had asked me to make this
> song, I tried to formulate an idea that would capture the essence of that lo-
> cale. And the silhouette of the mountains provided it.

In Bad Hand's songmaking, visual perception of nature, sense of sacred site, the
patron's spirit, and melodic creativity all blended into the balanced expression
of the song.

Technically, Native American melody is quite complex. In her 1918 collection of 240 Lakota songs, Frances Densmore found Sioux melodies to be built
on five different scales comprised of the tones G, A, C, D, and E. Each scale used
the same tones, but began on a different tonic note, similar to the seven modes
of classical Greek music. In modern Western terms, Densmore's songs were
equally divided between major and minor keys. The songs covered a wide tonal
range, usually an octave or an octave and a half, and sometimes extending to
as much as seventeen steps, more than two octaves. Other distinctive musical
qualities of Native American song include the first note of the song lying an
octave or more above the keynote, an initial downward phrase, predominant

2/4 or 3/4 rhythm, serial rhythm, polyrhythm between singer and drum, and a characteristic lag of the drum behind the singer.[10]

According to William Powers, the basic form of Lakota songs is A1–A–B–C–B–C: "A corresponds with the introductory phrase by an individual or the entire chorus (known in English as the 'second'). B corresponds with the theme of the song; and C with the cadential formula. In actual performance, the Oglala Sioux do not distinguish B and C; they are both regarded as the song proper (*olowan*)."[11] In other words, the song consists of a repeated introductory phrase sung first by the leader and then by the entire group, followed by the main melody and a strongly rhythmic ending. This structure is illustrated by "Song of the Grass Dance," a powwow song collected by Frances Densmore in 1913 (example 1 on page 332).

In Lakota the first introductory or A phrase is called *yawankicu*, "to take the voice upward," and the second is termed *pawankiye*, "to push the voice upwards," from which they have come to be known colloquially as "push ups." They are also called "the head" of the song; B and C are called *sinte*, "the tail." In performance, the head of the song is sung in an extremely high range and with a cultivated wide vibrato. Powers reports that in Lakota the proper way to sing the first iteration of the introductory phrase is called *pan*, "to whine, cry," and the second is to be sung *akis'a*, "yelping." Both sections may also be sung *yus'a*, which Powers translates as "the squeaking sound produced by rubbing one's finger around the rim of good crystal." As the song nears its end, the group leader signals a repetition by striking heavy drumstrokes at the tail's cadence. These beats inform the lead singer to begin another "push up" and thus repeat the song. In powwow performance, songs are repeated many times, sometimes more than twenty times, lending them a chant-like quality of ceaseless repetition.[12]

These observations provide a brief technical description of Lakota and most Plains Indian powwow songs, but the power of Native American sacred song depends ultimately not so much on its musical structure as on its intrinsic sacrality as delivered in performance. Powwow song expresses a uniquely Native American sacred synergy between melody, rhythm, word, dance, ritual, and belief that challenges Western assumptions. Through brief yet highly complex melodies sung in unison to the incessant beat of the drum, the song reaches the borders of language as it draws both singers and dancers into interaction and union with their sacred cosmos. For Native Americans, this song tradition is a sacred way essential to their identity. It is preserved by rigorously disciplined traditional dancers and by dedicated singers who submit their lives and skills to the spirit world in order to make its songs.

Dancers and Singers

Powwow song acts in different ways for different participants. For dancers, song is the sound to which they move and through which they experience a profound sense of spiritual and physical transformation. For singers, song makes them instruments through which spirit itself becomes manifest. In the largest sense, song serves both dancer and singer as a unique spiritual link between past and present, earth and spirit world, self and community.

For the dancer, powwow is far more than an exhibition of skill, though it is also certainly that. In the performance of traditional dance movements to the beat and melody of sacred song, dancers experience spiritual and emotional union not only with one another but with the sacred source of being itself. In his pioneering 1957 book *Sacred and Profane Beauty: The Holy in Art* Gerardus van der Leeuw, a Dutch scholar of religion, described dance as the most direct expression of the sacred. His words captured a sense of how movement and the rhythmic power of song join the Native American dancer to the sacred cosmos. "Movement reaches out and overpowers all things, until the stars, the clouds, and the flowers join the dance and become a roundelay which includes the entire world. . . . Rhythm literally sweeps everything along, and transfers itself to everything that comes under its influence. . . . The dance overpowers whatever it finds in its path. Thus movement finally becomes universal. Everything spins and circles; everything leaps to the rhythm of the universe."[13]

George Horse Pasture, director of the Buffalo Bill Historical and Cultural Center in Cody, Wyoming, gave a moving account of Native American dance experience in his 1989 book *Powwow* that echoed van der Leeuw's description of the power of rhythm and movement, primal elements of sacred song.

> As I adjust the space between the people in front and in back of me, I am part of a widening circle of dancers, each a living part of the tradition that is Indian. As the perspiration begins, I dance my best, continuing to enter clockwise in ever-tightening circles. . . . Soon, the chemistry, the ambience, and the magic are just right. While vigorously dancing, an irrefutable awareness arises that I am close to the center, the essence of life. As the world dissolves in color and music around me, a warm spiritual feeling spreads throughout the heart and body, and the song and dance carry me away from the heat and earth. Another zone of awareness, a detachment is entered: my feet, body, and arms move automatically to the rhythm of life. My fellow dancers are a part of me and I a part of them. I realize that life could not get much better than this moment and it is a gift from the creator. As the countless eagle feathers flutter before my eyes, I realize that this is Indian—this is powwow.[14]

This eloquent passage describes in detail an experience of altered awareness and behavior, but in what sense is it sacred or holy or religious? Several current theories of religion could be applied to Horse Pasture's description of powwow dancing. It could be regarded as an example of spirit possession or of sacred time and space, religious phenomena often associated with sacred song. Horse Pasture's dancing experience, however, can best be described as a ritual experience, one of the most fundamental elements of religion.

While no Western theory can fully comprehend the experience of powwow dancers and singers, anthropologist Victor Turner's analysis of ritual provides a helpful way to approach powwow as public religion. In his 1969 book *The Ritual Process: Structure and Anti-Structure,* Turner described ritual as a symbolic action in which individuals and groups divest themselves of the cultural norms of everyday life and temporarily experience spiritual and social realities far more fluid and flexible than normal. Turner applied the term *structure* to traditional standards and institutions and *anti-structure* to the short-lived but intense manifestations of ritual transformation. Drawing on a wide range of multicultural data, Turner proposed a four-stage model of the ritual process.

In the first stage, participants prepare themselves by consciously leaving the structural arena and removing to the ritual space where they begin to change their identity through special behaviors like wearing costumes, consuming special foods, or performing purifications. Next, participants engage in prescribed ritual actions, often involving song, dance, or some other kind of symbolic movement. Through these ritual actions, Turner claimed, participants cross a psychophysical barrier that he termed the *limen*—Latin for "threshold"—and enter the realm of anti-structure. In the third stage of the ritual process, participants, now called "liminars," move from "liminality" into the full experience of anti-structure, which Turner called *communitas* because of its often intensely egalitarian and communal qualities. When communitas has been completed, liminars gradually return to the structural realm of everyday experience and behavior through ritual actions of closure that he termed *reaggregation.* Turner made many finer-tuned distinctions within this general theory, but his model of structure, preparation, liminality, anti-structural communitas, and reaggregation has found wide acceptance among interpreters of sacred ritual.[15]

George Horse Pasture's account strongly suggests that something like Turner's notion of the ritual process occurs among powwow dancers.[16] The stages of preparation, liminality, and communitas are most important for understanding Native American sacred song and dance, for it is in those dimensions that the transformative power of ritual action is most manifest. Horse Pasture began his account with the apparently mundane matter of positioning himself properly in the Grand Entry procession line. Yet this simple act located him squarely in the preparatory preliminary phase. Horse Pasture had already traveled physically from the structure of his home and work to the anti-structural location of the dancing ground. The elaborate and careful preparation of his handmade outfit and those of the other dancers bespoke an enduring commitment to traditional Native American ways, while the outfits themselves bristled with natural objects—feathers, horns, skins, stones—that identified the spirit beings of the anti-structural realm. Under these conditions, to find his proper place and spacing in line symbolized Horse Pasture's break from everyday structural existence and his embrace of the social and sacred order of Native American life to be manifested in the dancing to come.

As he joined the dance of the serpentine circle, Horse Pasture crossed the threshold into liminality. The inspiration of the event moved him to ever greater physical exertion in his own dance—sweating, stepping, hyperventilating—which triggered "the chemistry, the ambience, the magic" of ritual consciousness. As he sweated and stepped in ritual dance, Horse Pasture encountered "an irrefutable awareness that I am close to the center, the essence of life." Suddenly Horse Pasture found himself inside the traditional Lakota picture of the world as a circle oriented around the principal directions and rooted at its sacred center. No longer focused on the details of preparation, Horse Pasture through the experience of song, rhythm, and dance had become a liminar for whom the symbols of the sacred world had taken on an "irrefutable" reality of their own.

Another wave of ritual effects dissolved the sacred world into its constituent elements of color and sound. Heat, the sacred symbol of life, poured from Horse Pasture's chest and carried him into yet another "zone of awareness" where his body became detached and moved on its own "to the rhythms of life" while his spirit merged with those of the other dancers. "My fellow dancers became a part of me and I a part of them." Horse Pasture's words describe a profound experience of communitas in which his own personal identity was subsumed into a larger sacred modality of common being. Horse Pasture's culminating experience of communitas moved beyond the union of dancers to union with the Creator. He realized that dance was the Creator's gift, and as the sacred eagle feathers "floated before" him in ritual space, he attained his final transforming ritual insight: to be Indian is to dance to the songs of powwow, and to dance is to participate in the divine.

For the singer, powwow also entails a ritual process, but one with a different configuration. In Native American traditions proper sacred singing requires even more preparation than dancing, and its liminality and communitas are more radically transformative. The Native American singer's world is one of constant spiritual preparation. The singer does far more than simply preserve oral and ritual tradition. The task also includes creation of a spiritual force to be shared through the song by the entire community. To accomplish this vital function the singer, unlike the dancer, must live permanently in the sacred dimension, employing daily the moral and musical standards necessary for true spiritual singing.

"[Singers] are really responsible for the traditions of the culture," Howard Bad Hand explained, "because everything that we do culturally and religiously is related to song." This sacred vocation requires of the singer a disciplined and prayerful way of life. "If you're really following the spiritual path," he said, "you use your capabilities and talents and song to make effects among people. When you are both a great singer and consciously able to move the spiritual, you have a greater responsibility to keep those things in your mind as a way of living and virtue." Bad Hand explained that the singer's "highest values and the highest ideals have to be sacrificed to the divine. The truly divine doesn't manifest itself apart from that. The supreme revelation of God appears in the prophets,

holy men, and musicians. So to venerate that form, that reality, is the true veneration of God. You're expressing that in your song." In Turner's terms, Bad
Hand describes a life of "permanent liminality" in which the singer sacrifices
personal goals to the higher values and moral disciplines of the tradition in order
to remain constantly distanced from the structure of the profane world and
thereby prepared to sing in a genuinely sacred way.[17]

If the singer's liminal preparation is more constant than the dancer's, the
communitas experienced in sacred singing is also more complete. In singing,
as in dancing, physiological effects on the body facilitate altered spiritual states.
Repeated reach for very high notes produces hyperventilation, high blood oxygen, skeletal vibration, ultrasonic overtones, and brain endorphins, all of which
help induce transnormal consciousness.[18] Dancing produces many of the same
phenomena, but for the singer the physical dimension of the ritual process is
not the external movement of limbs and body, it is rather the internal exercise
of lungs and larynx whereby the body vibrates to produce vocal sound. Extended
singing alters awareness quite as efficiently as dancing, but the alteration is of a
different kind. In both cases everyday consciousness is swallowed up in sacrality,
but the Native American singer unites directly with the sacred to become its
voice, its instrument, a living manifestation of its reality, and thereby transmit
its power to the powwow community.

For Howard Bad Hand the experience of singing involves direct participation in the divine. "When I sing, it's showing the reverence for divinity, and that
brings the past into place," Howard Bad Hand said. "And when you hit that
high—those overtones—you are becoming in a sense the personification of that
divinity at that moment. You are bringing heaven and earth together in mystical contact." "Hitting that high" is not a matter of preparation or practice. According to Bad Hand it is entirely unplanned, a spontaneous instance of
communitas that joins the singer not to other singers or dancers, but to the
divine. "I do not prepare [vocally]," he said; "the experience comes from the
performance itself. Those who prepare lack certainty and self-knowledge."

The sacred song that issues from such a performance also possesses its own
qualities of communitas according to Bad Hand. "In our own language, we
say that song is the Creator's language," Bad Hand said, "because it's the one
force of life that cuts through all obstructions and tensions." Song "has power
to ease tension within the heart and to loose the grip of obscure emotions in
people, so the enthusiasm of the heart only can express itself when it invol-
untarily responds to song. The dance and rhythm and movement of the body
results from that."

The communitas of song also involves sacred consciousness of the ancestors,
whose ways and myths are embodied in singing and dancing. Bad Hand said,
"When you look upon music as something serious and holy, designed to purify the feelings of people, it falls to music to glorify the virtues of heroes, and
what you're really doing is constructing a bridge to the world of the unseen. . . .

Because it is uniting the past with divinity, [singing] is a great solemn moment. It does create a religious inspiration that establishes the bond between what we believe is the Creator [and] the human."

But how do singers transmit their experience of sacred song to the dancers and the rest of the community? The answer involves the social dimensions of liminality and communitas. While the singer's personal discipline is necessary for effective performance, it is not sufficient because powwow also requires spiritual sharing among all the people. This social agenda is not as simple as it might seem. Since each nation bears its own sacred-song tradition, powwows are spiritually dissonant at their outset. "When you come into a large meeting like [Denver]," Bad Hand said, "you are looking at a prolonged state of tension. As a musician you go in with at least the intention to resolve that tension. And when you resolve it, you experience joy and relief." That "tension," in Turnerian terms, is the deadening effect of structure, the social separation maintained by disparate tribal identities. Singing alone can relieve it. To overcome it is to enter into liminality. To transform it is to enjoy the anti-structural fruits of communitas.

Once released, the powers of song unite the people together in sacred consciousness and join the visible world to the invisible one in communitas. Bad Hand said, "To me, it's the inspiring effect of the invisible sound that moves all hearts, that draws them together, so it has a mystical aspect to it. Our belief as singers is that all that is visible must grow beyond itself and extend into the realm of the invisible where it receives its true consecration. [Through singing] it takes firm root in the cosmic order."

While Bad Hand acknowledged that traditional ceremonials provide more explicit sacred action and mythic language, he valued the powwow as a greater opportunity to extend the powers of sacred song precisely because of the openness of its social environment. The reason for this, he said, is the unique sharing of songs and hence of spiritual and cultural values among many different peoples. Powwow is in principle less constrained or restricted than particular tribal rites. This sharing in turn amplifies each community's understanding of what it means to be Indian, thereby creating greater unity among all.

When powwow ends and the people "reaggregate" into the structure of their everyday lives, they return with a renewal of their traditional culture and sense of identity as Indian. "To me the powwow is the function of many different tribes to share their songs," Bad Hand said. "So in a sense it is addressing the cultural superstructure of our society. The powwow introduces the new songs to them, and they take those and integrate them into their structure of their ritual and ceremony. It's the way we nourish the spirit. These people take that experience back into their own community and individual selves. This is where the culture and civilization itself reaches its religious culmination. They make it spiritual."

Native American sacred song is more than simply a medium or vehicle of religious expression. It is a complex, synergistic manifestation of sacrality, a holy being whose blessing endows singers, dancers, and all the people with their spiritual essence. In powwows, song stimulates the intense physical energies of the dance. Emotionally, song cuts through negativity and division and invites healing and union. On the metaphysical level, song binds the visible world to the spirit world and historical time to sacred timelessness. For the dancer, song is the way out of daily consciousness into ritual communitas. The singer, as the bearer of this sacred synergy, becomes transformed through the "sacrifice of song" into the very personification of divinity. And the people, whether actively participating in the dancing and singing or witnessing powwow with respectful attention, join with the ancestors and spirit-beings in the renewal of their most fundamental sense of being Indian.

The Politics of Powwow

In recent years Native American sacred song has attracted the interest of ever-increasing numbers of non-Indians. Since 1990 non-Indians have flocked to Native American reservations, historic sites, cultural performances, and powwows in unprecedented numbers. Industry sources predict that Native American sites will become the most popular domestic tourist destination in the beginning of the twenty-first century. This new celebrity has also helped to promote powwow singing "supergroups" who now enjoy star status and booming sales of tapes and compact discs.

This new public interest presents Native Americans with difficult choices. The prospect of millions of non-Indians visiting reservations, seeking admission to powwows and traditional ceremonies, and purchasing recordings and memorabilia has raised fundamental questions of privacy, cultural preservation, and religious authenticity for Native American tribal and business leaders. Their dilemma raises an unusual perspective on the problem of the public expression of religion. Is it possible for public expression to be too public? Put differently, under what conditions does public performance of sacred song become profane?

The question is especially torturous for Native American leaders and entrepreneurs, who have responded with a wide and impassioned range of answers. The facts demonstrate that Native Americans have created a flourishing tourist industry by providing performances of sacred songs and ceremonials for non-Indians. From Taos to Tulsa, even the most casual tourist can readily find song, dance, and ritual performances at upscale motels, resorts, and trading posts. These performances are unauthorized, and the performers are usually ostracized by traditional tribal leaders, but they reap significant financial rewards in an impoverished reservation economy, even among such powerful communities as the Pine Ridge Sioux and the Navajo. To the extent that they succeed, they undermine traditional cultural and religious authority. Public expression in this sense is at best a mixed blessing, bringing economic gain while violating the very tradition it wishes to display.

Responsible Native American leaders decry the presentation of ceremonial and social rituals outside of their traditional context, but they also acknowledge the economic and cultural opportunity that the new non-Native interest represents. The problem of how to deal with such a this-worldly opportunity without compromising the sacred ways is one of the most controversial issues in Native America. Perhaps the most important single forum for addressing it has been a series of conferences titled "Indian Country Tourism 2000," first convened in 1994 at Denver during the three days before March Powwow by Ben Sherman, a Lakota businessman and president of the Western American Indian Chamber. Sherman's organization provides entrepreneurial resources, technical assistance, and governmental interface for a nationwide "network of Native American tourism interests" dedicated to "the protection of tribal property rights and tribal member privacy."[19]

I attended the first Indian Country Tourism 2000 conference along with nearly three hundred men and women into whose hands the future of public access to Native American ritual expression, including sacred song, has been entrusted.[20] On the first morning of the conference, Ted Wright, general manager of the Sitka Tribe of Alaska, rose to ask advice for promoting his community's only cultural asset, its nationally recognized company of traditional dancers. Wright said. "We are one of those isolated, landlocked tribes with no resources and no gaming. We are proud of our dancers and want to promote them, but we don't want to perpetuate the stereotype that [the dances show only] how it was. We also want to share something of what our culture is like today, and not give the image that our culture is dead or died one, or two, or five hundred years ago. It's still alive and growing. How do we do that?"

Wright's question opened the fundamental question of whether Native American sacred song and dance can and ought to be presented to the non-Indian public as a living reality. Two Sioux leaders answered him most directly. Randy Ross of the Oglala Tribe cautioned against presenting "our private [ceremonial] dances" to non-Indians. "We must be very careful" in this regard, he warned. On the other hand, appropriate social songs and dances, including powwow, should be presented authentically in their full power. Ross said, "In performing those dances, let's make sure that we do it right, that they are the dances we do, and not only for show, and that it's acceptable especially to the older people on the reservation. We're going to do this and to display it as really our way of life, and not just for the fifteen minutes that we do it."

Alex White Plume of the Pine Ridge Sioux Reservation agreed with Ross, but argued further that non-Indians should not be allowed to participate in social dancing unless they properly understand the traditional meaning of the songs and the dances. "They've got to learn about that song [to which they will be dancing]," he said, "there's got to be a certain amount of interpretation about those types of dances." White Plume spoke for many other tribal leaders when he called for maintaining strict community control of all performances and distribution of profits. "On Pine Ridge," he said, "we have social dancing and every one enjoys it, and [non-Indian] people come back year after year. [But] these things have to be written and defined and agreed within the tribe, or one of the elders is going to accuse you of exploiting the culture."

Most conferees at Indian Country Tourism 2000 agreed with Ross and White Plume that the most appropriate way to handle the potentially polluting cultural effects of tourism is to strike a careful standard of what is to be shared and then to present it as authentically as possible, offering a clear, tribally authorized interpretation. Other Native American leaders, however, are adamantly opposed to cultural tourism, especially New Age and Men's Movement appropriations of Plains traditions like the Sun Dance, the Sweat Lodge, and the Vision Quest.

One of the most outspoken opponents has been Ward Churchill, a Creek/Cherokee Metis and codirector of the American Indian Movement of Colorado. Churchill's recent book, *Indians Are Us?: Culture and Genocide in Native North America*, blasted the embrace of Native American ritual by non-Indians. "Spiritual traditions cannot be used as some sort of Whitman's Sampler of ceremonial form, mixed and matched," Churchill wrote. "To play at ritual potluck is to debase all spiritual traditions, voiding their internal coherence and leaving nothing usably sacrosanct as a cultural anchor for the peoples who conceived and developed them, and who have consequently organized their societies around them." Churchill claimed that the expropriation of living Native American cultures, including sacred song, has already reached critical proportions. "Native American societies," he wrote, "*can* and *do* suffer the socioculturally debilitating effects of spiritual trivialization and appropriation at the hands of the massively larger Euro-immigrant population which has come to dominate literally every other aspect of our existence." The only way to stop this process, Churchill concluded, is to declare war against it.[21]

Churchill helped to persuade the principal Sioux nations—the Dakota (Santee), Lakota (Teton), and Nakota (Yankton)—to do just that. A "Declaration of War Against Exploiters of Lakota Spirituality" was ratified in June 1993 by the three nations. It denounced "the unspeakable indignity of having our most precious Lakota ceremonies and spiritual practices desecrated, mocked, and abused by non-Indian 'wannabes,' hucksters, cultists, commercial profiteers, and self-styled 'New Age Shamans' and their followers." The "Declaration" declared "war against all persons who persist in exploiting, abusing, and misrepresenting the sacred traditions and spiritual practices of our people" and called upon "all Lakota, Dakota, and Nakota brothers and sisters . . . to actively and vocally oppose this alarming take-over and systematic destruction" by "whatever specific tactics are necessary and sufficient.[22]

While most Native Americans might stop short of declaring war on non-Indians for cultural expropriation, there can be no doubting their categorical opposition to it and their growing reticence to share their sacred ways with outsiders.

This growing seclusion of Native American sacred-song traditions at a time of fast-rising popular interest in them places increased pressure on the powwow as the most available and explicitly public expression of Native American sacred song.

Powwows occupy a unique position among the sacred-song traditions of contemporary America. Powwow has survived near extinction to re-emerge as a powerful public expression of sacred song's qualities and functions to both Native Americans and a non-Indian society that has lost much of its own sense of sacrality. The religious functions of Native American sacred song have been preserved because the nations have been able to maintain their oral traditions. That ability in turn has been made possible principally by the geographical and cultural isolation of Native American peoples in the United States.

Today, however, the integrity of oral tradition is threatened by the very popularity it is beginning to enjoy. The commercialization of powwow is already well advanced: large cash prizes encourage the emergence of a professional dancer elite, something utterly new in Native American tradition and certainly at odds with powwow's spiritual and communal purposes. The recording business burgeons, creating an even larger class of professional singing groups who now produce songs to be heard by an audience rather than shared by a dancing community. And crowds fill with non-Indians, leading to the possibility that this fragile lifeline of sacred celebration and traditional community might become encased in an uncomprehending layer of entertainment and secular promotion. One clear sign of growing commercialization was the creation in 2001 of the first Grammy Award for Native American Music.

The irony of this situation is extreme: after struggling for centuries against white dispossession of their land and their economy, Native Americans have begun to create a more powerful pan-Indian culture through the public intertribal powwow. Yet only a few years after the powwow movement's emergence into American public culture, it has become commercialized to the point that some of the movement's founders express serious concern. As the crowds grow, prizes increase, and recording sales skyrocket, will the powwow be able to sustain its own traditional form and intention? Or will it succumb to market forces and become just another entertainment commodity?

Powwow illustrates with particular poignancy the larger cultural situation that all sacred song faces as public expression in America today. On the one hand powwow songs play essential and complex roles in Native American religious cultures, roles that are absolutely necessary for the maintenance of the sacred cosmos and the people's access to it. On the other hand, because they can be performed and commodified outside of traditional religious contexts, powwow songs are available for promotion and consumption in the secular world, where their sacred meaning is inevitably altered, if not destroyed altogether. In twenty-first-century America, no form of sacred song is immune to these upper and nether millstones of cultural production, but Native American sacred song in particular inhabits a profoundly paradoxical relationship to the very forces that help it flourish in public culture.

Notes

1. See Leland C. Wyman, *Blessingway* (Tucson: University of Arizona Press, 1970), 3–9; Ake Hultkrantz, *The Religions of the American Indians* (Berkeley: University of California Press, 1979), 103–15; Ruth Murray Underhill, *Singing for Power: The Song Magic of the Papago Indians of Southern Arizona* (Berkeley: University of California Press, 1938; reprint, Tucson: University of Arizona Press, 1993), 1–19.

2. Chris Roberts, *Powwow Country* (Helena, Mont.: American and World Geographic Publishing, 1992), 55.

3. Eagle/Walking Turtle, *Indian America: A Traveler's Companion,* 3d ed. (Santa Fe, N.M.: John Muir Publications), 386–451.

4. Roberts, *Powwow Country,* 14, 20. Subsequent page references appear in the text.

5. Quoted in ibid., 33.

6. Howard Bad Hand, telephone interview by author, April 17, 1994. All subsequent quotations are taken from this interview.

7. William K. Powers, *Sacred Language: The Nature of Supernatural Discourse in Lakota* (Norman: University of Oklahoma Press, 1986), 11–41; Lucien Levy-Bruhl, *The Soul of the Primitive* (Chicago: Henry Regnery, 1928), 156.

8. Rudolf Otto, *The Idea of the Holy,* trans. John W. Harvey (London: Oxford University Press, 1923), 64–65.

9. Vine Deloria Jr., *God Is Red: A Native View of Religion,* 2d ed. (Golden, Colo.: North American Press, 1992), 880.

10. Frances Densmore, *Teton Sioux Music* (Washington, D.C.: Smithsonian Institution, 1918), 9–39.

11. Powers, *Sacred Language,* 55.

12. Ibid., 56.

13. Gerardus van der Leeuw, *Sacred and Profane Beauty: The Holy in Art,* trans. David E. Green (New York: Holt, Rinehart, and Winston, 1963), 28.

14. George P. Horse Pasture, *Powwow* (Cody, Wyo.: Buffalo Bill Historical Center, 1989), 38.

15. Victor Turner, *The Ritual Process: Structure and Anti-Structure* (Ithaca, N.Y.: Cornell University Press, 1969), 94–165.

16. Horse Pasture, *Powwow,* 38.

17. Turner, *The Ritual Process,* 147–49.

18. Andrew Storr, *Music and the Mind* (New York: Free Press, 1992), 24–48.

19. "Indian Country Tourism USA Objectives," Western American Indian Chamber Web site <http://indiancountry.org>.

20. This account is based on presentations recorded and interviews conducted at the Western Indian Chamber's Indian Country Tourism 2000 conference, Denver, Colo., March 17–19, 1994.

21. Ward Churchill, *Indians Are Us?: Culture and Genocide in Native North America* (Monroe, Maine: Common Courage Press, 1994), 213.

22. Ibid., 273–77.

CHAPTER 2

Pilgrimage and Penitence:
Sacred-Song Traditions of the
Hispanic Southwest

Mexican and Chicano Catholic sacred song is the oldest Euro-American sacred music tradition in the New World. Since the 1521 arrival in Mexico of the first company of Spanish Franciscan missionaries—known as the Twelve—the Catholic music of Iberia has mingled with the indigenous sacred song of Mesoamerican and South American peoples.[1] Over nearly half a millennium, this musical crossfertilization has produced a rich heritage of Hispanic American Catholic sacred song. Many of its variants flourish in the United States today, including important popular Afro-Caribbean forms, like Santería, brought to the East Coast in the late twentieth century from Puerto Rico, Cuba, and the Dominican Republic. In historical and numerical terms, however, the most important Hispanic American sacred-song tradition in the United States is unquestionably that of Mexican Americans and of Chicanos, the indigenous Mexicans of the Southwest.[2]

Today twenty million Chicanos and Mexican Americans comprise more than 60 percent of Hispanic citizens in the United States, the vast majority of them Catholic. They represent by far the largest single ethnic constituency in American Catholicism, numbering nearly one-third of the church's 64 million members. The most important forms of their sacred song are pilgrimage songs associated with journeys to sacred sites and traditional spiritual ballads called *alabados,* songs of praise and penitence. These songs comprise the heart of the distinctive sacred-song tradition and characteristic Christian spirituality of Chicanos and Mexican Americans.

To understand these Chicano sites and sounds, they must first be placed in the context that formed them: the complex mixture of Mesoamerican and Catholic cultures that followed the Spanish Conquest of 1519–21. Chicano sacred songs and rituals follow religious archetypes for pilgrimage and penitence rooted deep in the pre-Columbian past. These in turn began to fuse with Spanish Catholicism almost immediately after Hernán Cortés subdued the Aztec capital of Tenochtitlán, today's Mexico City. The most important product of that encounter was the emergence of the Virgin of Guadalupe, a uniquely Mesoamerican Christian symbol whose songs and pilgrimages define the spirituality of Mexican and Chicano Catholicism to the present day.

La Virgen de Guadalupe

According to the *legenda* of Guadalupe, the official account authorized by the church in 1754, the Virgin Mary appeared to an Aztec Catholic convert named Juan Diego on five different occasions between December 9 and December 12, 1531, at Tepeyac, a hill on the northern perimeter of Mexico City.[3] Mary's first appearance, formally termed an "apparition," occurred at dawn when, framed in the eastern light and saluted by songs of heavenly birds, she uttered to Juan Diego the words that forever joined Catholicism to the native peoples of Mesoamerica:

> I am truly the eternal Virgin, holy Mother of the True God, through Whose favor we live, the Creator, Lord of Heaven, and the Lord of Earth. I very much desire that they build me a church here, so that in it I may show and make known and give all my love, my mercy and my help and my protection—I am in truth your merciful mother—to you and to all the other people dear to me who call upon me, who search for me, who confide in me; here I will hear their sorrow, their words, so that I may make perfect and cure their illnesses, their labors, and their calamities.[4]

After Juan Diego failed on several occasions to convince Franciscan Juan de Zumárraga, first bishop of Mexico, that the apparition was true, the Virgin instructed him to pick some of the roses of Castile that had miraculously sprung up in her presence, wrap them in his *tilma*—his cloak—and show them to the bishop as a sign. When Juan Diego dropped the flowers before Zumárraga, however, his cloak bore an image of the Virgin depicted as a beautiful Aztec woman arrayed in the symbolism of the Immaculate Conception, robed in a blue-green mantle studded with the planets and stars, surrounded by a rainbow aura, and standing on a crescent moon supported by an angel. The bishop knelt before the image and vowed to build the Virgin's church at Tepeyac.

She immediately became known as "La Virgen de Guadalupe," the Virgin of Guadalupe. Why this name? Zumárraga and the Spanish Franciscan missionaries apparently associated this new Marian apparition with one that had occurred in 1326 in Spain's west-central province of Extremadura. There the Virgin had revealed to a simple shepherd the location of an ancient, precious, and long-lost statue of herself buried in a local cave. Recovered and installed at the nearby Jeronimite monastery of Guadalupe, this image of the Virgin was credited with crucial military victories during the *Reconquista,* the Christian crusade that in 1492 finally expelled Moroccan Islamic forces from Spain after seven hundred years of invasion and occupation. Inspired by Spain's extraordinary success at home and in the New World, and imbued with powerful expectations that Christ's millennial kingdom was about to dawn in New Spain, Franciscan missionaries in Mexico found in Juan Diego's story an ideal opportunity to convert the Aztecs. They called the new apparition Our Lady of Guadalupe.[5]

The new Mexican Guadalupe, however, was also emphatically Mesoamerican. Juan Diego's Aztec name, Cuauhtlatohuac, meant "Singing Eagle" and his hometown of Cuauhtitlán was an Aztec center for the noble order of the Eagle. Juan Diego clearly was a messenger of the eagle, ancient Mesoamerican symbol for its high god, the sun. The Virgin appeared at the hill of Tepeyac, site of the main temple to the Aztec goddess Tonantzin, mother of the gods. The Aztec capital of Tenochtitlán was ringed at the principal compass points by temples to female deities, including Tonantzin. Great calendric pilgrimages venerated these female sacred beings long before the Spanish knew Mexico existed. The Virgin's legend and miraculous image incorporated Aztec sacred symbols including music—the language of the gods—birds, flowers, stars, the eastern light of dawn, and the blue-green color of Ometeotl, the Aztec god of cosmic being. Above all, Nuestra Señora gathered into her sacred persona the powers of life and death, suffering and destiny wielded by the goddesses of the Aztec pantheon, and especially by Tonantzin, whose role best matched Mary's Catholic theological status as Mother of God.[6]

The few Aztec converts whom the Franciscan missionaries had made during their first decade in Mexico embraced the apparitions, but a miraculous healing by the Virgin's image shortly after the new church opened brought native peoples flocking to Catholicism for the first time. By 1539 an estimated eight million Aztecs had converted. Guadalupe's legend became a fundamental element of Mexican folklore and popular belief. In 1639 the Virgin was credited with ending the worst flood in colonial Mexican history. Twenty-five years later, Mexican church and political leaders first petitioned Rome for official approval of the apparition. Meanwhile, popular devotion to La Virgen continued to grow. The Old Basilica of Our Lady of Guadalupe, built by Pedro de Arrieta between 1695 and 1709, soon became the most popular pilgrimage site in Latin America. The healing cult of Guadalupe spread still further after 1737, when the city's worst recorded plague subsided after the capital was placed under the Virgin's protection. In acknowledgment of her apparition and miraculous blessings, Benedict XIV in 1754 bestowed upon Guadalupe the title "Patroness and Protectress of New Spain" and authorized a feast day Office and Mass to her on December 12 in the liturgical calendar; a revised Office and Mass was promulgated by Leo XIII in 1894.[7]

During the twentieth century, devotion to the Virgin of Guadalupe has eclipsed that of every other saint, perhaps even of Jesus himself, in Mexico and much of Latin America. In 1910 Pius X proclaimed Guadalupe "Patroness of

Latin America," and sixty years later Paul VI added "Queen of Mexico" and "Empress of All the Americas" to her titles. To accommodate the ever-increasing volume of pilgrims, the New Basilica, an enormous concrete bowl mounted under a self-supporting roof, was designed by Pedro Ramirez Vasquez and consecrated in 1976. The New Basilica's interior offers unobstructed views of Juan Diego's tilma to forty-thousand pilgrims. The framed image stands above and behind the central altar; two moving stairways run through an opening behind the altar to afford pilgrims a closer look at it. Devotion to Guadalupe reached a new peak with the canonization of Juan Diego by Pope John Paul II in 2002.[8]

Despite the immense popular embrace of Juan Diego's vision, however, Mexico's cultural politics has been divided since 1539 by two Guadalupes, the Spanish Virgin of Extremadura who sustains the Spanish identity of the *criollo* elite and the Virgin of Tepeyac who suffers with and empowers the *mestizos* and the *indios*. The cult of the former legitimized the Iberian origins and ethnic purity of "the Forty Families," descendants of the conquistadors who dominated colonial Mexico. Over against criollo oppression, Juan Diego's Virgin of Tepeyac developed into the focal symbol of political justice and national aspiration for the mestizo and Indian majority. In 1810 the priest Miguel Hidalgo y Costilla declared the Insurgencia—Mexico's revolt against Spain—in her name and under her banner his mestizo army swept to the gates of Mexico City. Eleven years later Agustín de Iturbide, first ruler of independent Mexico, named Guadalupe the patroness of the new nation and committed its destiny to her will. During the nineteenth century, however, the colonial cultural dynamic returned with frequent European and American interventions supporting the traditional elite. In 1910 the troops of Emiliano Zapata and Francesco Maderno again wore Guadalupe's image as they successfully fought the dictatorship of Profirio Díaz in the modern Mexican Revolution.[9]

In the twentieth century the Virgin of Guadalupe has been appropriated by both parties, inspiring both reactionary and radical cultural movements to compete for her symbolic authority. Long enshrined by the dominant Institutional Democratic Party (PDI) as the symbol of nationalist order and submission of the poor, Guadalupe since the 1960s has served yet again as the banner of radical political movements from Cesar Chavez's La Causa among Mexican American farm workers in California to the Zapatista revolutionary movement in Mexico's Chiapas province.

In religious thought, Chicano liberation theology has reconstructed Guadalupe as "Mother of Creation" and patroness of political and economic justice over against her traditional theological role as guardian of doctrinal orthodoxy and moral conservatism. In yet another new dimension of cultural conflict, during the 1980s and 1990s Guadalupe has become a contested symbol of traditional gender relations. Recent *mujerista* critiques of traditional *machismo* have invoked Guadalupe both as a legitimator of women's oppression by men in the Mexican household and as a source of liberation from traditional gender roles.[10]

With this enormous array of meanings, Guadalupe today has become the master symbol of Mexican and Chicano religious and cultural identity. Her image is everywhere in Mexico and the Chicano Southwest—mounted in cars, buses, and taxicabs, painted on murals, printed on decals in shops, venerated in churches and cathedrals, and displayed in countless domestic altars with their ever-present offering of flowers. She is the supreme public expression of Mexican Catholic piety, and the defining form of that piety is pilgrimage. From every corner of Mexico and Mesoamerica, companies of the faithful take the arduous journey to the New Basilica to make their offerings and bring their prayers to Nuestra Señora. Even on the quietest days the immense Plaza de Guadalupe outside the New Basilica is alive with pilgrim groups dressed in traditional costumes, bearing flowers and banners, presenting pre-Columbian dances and rituals in the Virgin's honor. It is a great ongoing Mexican fiesta, complete with mariachi bands, fireworks, and special foods. During Advent season the number of pilgrims increases daily until, on December 12, the Feast of Our Lady of Guadalupe, more than a million pilgrims pack the plaza.

What accounts for the intensity of Mexican pilgrimage and its immense devotion to Guadalupe? Poet and essayist Octavio Paz, Mexico's Nobel Prize laureate in 1990, offered an answer in his 1961 prose masterpiece *The Labyrinth of Solitude*. Paz understood the Mexican as trapped in a desperate postcolonial separation from his own being, hidden behind masks of formalism and unable to reunite the cosmos either by going back to the Aztec past or by going forward into an authentic revolutionary future. For Paz, Mexico was a world of suffering, pain, excess, and penitence. "In the Valley of Mexico man feels himself suspended between heaven and earth," Paz wrote, "and he oscillates between contrary powers and forces. [The Mexican] has forgotten the word that ties him to all those forces through which life manifests itself. Therefore he shouts or keeps silent, stabs or prays, or falls asleep for a hundred years."[11]

In Paz's view, the very violence of Mexican solitude, its legacy of colonial oppression and postcolonial poverty, generates the need to submerge itself in communal festivity, most potently released in the fiesta of Our Lady of Guadalupe: "During the days before and after the twelfth of December, time comes to a full stop, and instead of pushing us toward a deceptive tomorrow that is always beyond our reach, offers us a complete and perfect today of dancing and revelry, of communion with the most ancient and secret Mexico. Time is no longer succession, and becomes what it originally was and is: the present, in which past and future are reconciled."[12]

For Mexican and Chicano Catholics, the Virgin reconciles the desperate condition of solitude by offering genuine conviviality and real hope for the future. As the only human being immaculately conceived, completely obedient to God's will, vessel of God's incarnation, mother of God, apostolic founder of the church, and *la Morenita*—"the little brown girl" who appeared to Juan Diego—the Virgin has become the unique sacred persona to whom the solitude and suffering of the Mexican people can be brought. In the words of Chicano theologian Virgil Elizondo, Guadalupe has become not only "the protector and liberator of the poor, the downtrodden, and the disenfranchised," but what is more, "the beginning of a new creation, the mother of a new humanity, and the manifestation of the femininity of God." While her fiesta releases all of the symbolic excess and social leveling that Paz explained, for believers it also reaches a spiritual completion that cures the Mexican curse of solitude he so eloquently described. If the soul of Mexico is beset with solitude, then Guadalupe calls it to a new pilgrimage of healing and hope.[13]

Over nearly five hundred years the Guadalupe pilgrimage has acquired a rich repertory of songs, the most universally sung of which is "Mañanitas a La Virgen de Guadalupe" [Morning song to the Virgin of Guadalupe], the traditional greeting song to the Virgin based on the legend of her apparition to Juan Diego. It is quite a song: part greeting, part love-song, part prayer, part song of the people, part Spanish devotion to the Immaculate Conception, part indigenous Mesoamerican cosmology, part penitence, part petition. In "Mañanitas a La Virgen de Guadalupe" (example 2 on page 333), the many strands of the Virgin's meaning and significance for Mexican pilgrims blend into one expression in a way only sacred song can create:

1   Oh Virgen, la más hermosa del Valle del Anahuac,
     tus hijos muy de mañana te vienen a saludar.

     Chorus:
     Despierta, Madre, despierta;
     mira que ya amaneció,
     mira este ramo de flores que para ti traigo yo.

2   Cuando miro tu carita llena de tanto candor,
     quisiera darte mil besos para mostrarte mi amor.

3   Madre de los Mexicanos dijiste venías a ser;
     pues ya lo ves, Morenita, sí te sabemos querer.

4   Recibe, Madre querida, nuestra felicitación
     hoy por ser el día tan grande de tu tierna aparición.

5   Aquella alegre mañana en que apareciste a Juan
     mientras Dios me dé la vida nunca se me olvidará.

6   Mira que soy Mexicano y por eso tuyo soy;
     busca en vano en el mundo quien te quiera más que yo.

7   Recibe, Madre querida, nuestra felicitación;
     míranos acquí postrados y danos tu benedición.

8 Envidia no tengo a nadie sino al ángel que a tus pies
  hace cuatrocientos años que te sirve de escabel.

9 Salve, Virgen sin mancilla, de belleza sin igual,
  de Guadalupe es tu nombre y tu trono el Tepeyac.

10 Tú brillaste, Virgen Santa, como estrella matinal,
   anunciando la alborada que iba pronto a comenzar.

11 Hoy a tus pies acudimos, dígnate, Madre, mirar
   a tus hijos que llorando venimos ante tu altar.

1 O Virgin, the prettiest in the Valley of the Anahuac,
  Your children early in the morning come to greet you.

  Chorus:
  Awake, Mother, awake;
  Look and see that dawn has broken.
  See this bouquet of flowers that I bring for you.

2 When I see your pretty face full of so much candor,
  I would like to kiss you a thousand times to show you my love.

3 Mother of the Mexican people you said you came to be;
  Now you see, Morenita, how much we love you.

4 Accept, dear Mother, our congratulations
  for being today the great day of your dear apparition.

5 That happy morning when you appeared to Juan
  as long as I have life, I shall never forget.

6 See that I am a Mexican, and for that reason I am yours;
  Seek in vain through the world for anyone who serves you more than I.

7 Accept, dear Mother, our congratulations.
  See us at your feet; grant us your benediction.

8 I am envious of no one, but the angel at your feet;
  it has been four hundred years that he serves as your footstool.

9 Hail, Immaculate Virgin, most beautiful of all
  of Guadalupe is your name and Tepeyac is your throne.

10 You shined, Holy Virgin, as a morning star,
   announcing the dawn that soon was to begin.

11 Today we come to your feet; deign, Mother, to look
   at your children who, crying, come to your altar.[14]

This great pilgrim song achieves a complex layering of mythic images, from indigenous Aztec religion and medieval Spanish Catholicism, what ethnomusicologist Philip Bohlman has called the "remixing of scaffolded meanings." Many symbols of "Mañanitas"—the eastern light of dawn, the morning star, the flowers, the figure of the Holy Mother—are sacred symbols shared by both Aztec and Spanish religious cultures that the cult of Guadalupe has blended into uniquely Mexican form. Most fundamentally, the song affirms the Virgin's identity as powerful and caring mother of the people and the people's identity as her faithful and suffering children whose pilgrimage commemorates and renews the great events of 1531. Through "Mañanitas" the complex mixing of belief, action, and history at work in the Guadalupe pilgrimage is compressed into song.[15]

What happened at Guadalupe permanently determined the style and substance of Mexican Catholicism. Colonists from Mexico brought Guadalupe's syncretistic sensibility with them in 1598 as they explored the headwaters of the Rio Grande and established the province of New Mexico. They would apply that same sensibility to their own spiritual experience at a place called Chimayó and create there Chicano America's premier tradition of pilgrimage, penitence, and sacred song.

El Santuario de Chimayó

If there is one time and place in the United States at which Chicano sacred song is publicly expressed in its most definitive form, it is during Holy Week at Chimayó, New Mexico. The small agricultural community of Chimayó, population 2789 in 1990, nestles along the Old Taos High Road in the Sangre de Christo Mountains about thirty miles north of Santa Fe. Chimayó is home to three important Chicano Catholic institutions: the flourishing Franciscan mission parish of Sagra Familia (Holy Family), a large "pious fraternity" popularly known as Penitentes, and El Santuario de Chimayó, the most visited Catholic pilgrimage site in the United States. These three institutions embody the interaction of Franciscan piety with indigenous beliefs and practices that has informed Chicano religion since the Spanish colonization of New Mexico. Through those long centuries the sacred song of the people has endured, carrying with it a quest for spiritual and moral meaning in a harsh and oppressive world. To encounter the Chicano tradition of sacred song at its source, I traveled to Chimayó for the beginning of the Holy Week pilgrimage.

I awoke early on Palm Sunday morning, 1994, in my motel room at Los Lunas, a small town on the Rio Grande twenty miles south of Albuquerque. I hoped to reach Chimayó, one hundred miles to the north, in time for the noon Eucharist that would begin the Holy Week pilgrimage. Between Albuquerque and Santa Fe, however, the cool desert spring morning turned into a late-winter mountain snowstorm. As the road ascended into the Sangre de Cristo Mountains, snow transformed their dry forested slopes into great white pyramids studded with the deep green of junipers. I took a turnoff to Chimayó that sent me the back way into town, past isolated farms and ranches. Along the winding road I passed solitary figures on foot, pilgrims walking the last miles to the sacred site despite the inclement weather. By Good Friday, less than a week away, these few will have been joined by nearly one hundred thousand other pilgrims, many of them also walking the highways and byways around Chimayó in penitential pilgrimage to El Santuario's holy objects: the miraculous crucifix of Our Lord of Esquipulas, the effigy of the Holy Child of Atocha, and the healing earth of El Santuario.

El Santuario is an unassuming sacred site, especially given the fame of the place. Only a gift shop and the Potrero trading post flank the church to the right and the left of the plaza. Opposite the church a few houses rise on a low hillside. The plaza is unpaved, and on this sloppy day it had become a muddy parking lot packed with cars, pickup trucks, and four-wheel drive vehicles. A Chimayó police officer directed me to park in the steep driveway of one of the houses opposite the church. Snow was still falling as I hurried through three inches of mud to the church.

El Santuario itself, built in 1815, is a classic of New Mexico church architecture. Entering from the plaza through thick adobe walls, the visitor encounters an atrium filled by a formal garden of flowers, shrubs, and trees. It is a space that remains sheltered and green all year round, a symbol of sacred fecundity in a land of harsh climatic extremes. The atrium also serves as a cemetery to five generations of the Abeyta family, original builders of El Santuario, whose tombs are marked by marble slabs. Two adobe belltowers rise above the front entrance, surmounted by wooden belfries and connected by a wooden porch. A narrow narthex leads to a stone stairway that descends through a massive carved wooden door to the church.

The interior is a simple block of space sixty by twenty-four feet defined by three-foot-thick windowless adobe walls and differentiated only by a central aisle. Twenty-four painted wooden beams support a flat timbered ceiling. The nave's twenty-four rows of pews will seat perhaps 450 people. A brightly painted balustrade separates the nave from the altar placed just in front of the east wall. A low door to the left of the altar leads to two narrow rooms built against the church's north wall. The smaller of the rooms, adjacent to the altar, has no wooden floor. An otherwise unmarked hole about two feet wide and two feet deep called *el posito,* "the well," has been dug in the bare earth at the center of the room. The larger room serves as the sacristy where votive images hang, sacred articles are stored, and priests vest for worship services.[16]

The decoration of El Santuario follows the style of colonial New Mexican church architecture, including a rich display of painted iconographic images in the traditional *santero* style of Chicano folk art by three masters, José Rafael Aragón (fl. 1826–55), Miguel Aragón (fl. 1830–50), and Antonio Molleno (1804–45?).[17] In the niches of three wooden screens, or *reredos,* along the apsidal wall behind the altar and on the north and south sidewalls of the church appear painted *santos* (saints) and other sacred symbols rendered in brilliant reds, oranges, blues, and greens. Not surprisingly, the Virgin Mary, especially in her image of Guadalupe, appears frequently among the santos of El Santuario. Each reredos also contains a large carved statue, called a *bulto,* of a principal saint. Among the bultos are statues of San José, Santiago, San Rafael, and most prominently Jesus Nazareno, a large image of Christ crowned with thorns and robed in purple, bearing his cross to Calvary. Mounted in the central niche of Molleno's principal reredos behind the altar is the Crucifix of Our Lord of Esquipulas, the sacred object to which the church is dedicated. On the altar below the crucifix stand several commercial ceramic statues of the Holy Child of Atocha, whose votive cult has also been incorporated into El Santuario.[18]

On this Palm Sunday midday the church was packed with worshipers. Most of them seemed to be local Chicano families. Pilgrims and Anglo visitors from Santa Fe filled out the congregation. The only place I could find to stand was on the narthex steps just inside the front doors, where I received a palm frond. Franciscan Father Miguel Mateos had just begun the Mass by proceeding down the central aisle, blessing the worshipers with holy water that he splashed over us using a juniper branch as his thurifer.

I had expected an entirely Spanish service, but instead Father Mateos conducted the Palm Sunday liturgy of the Word—scripture readings, creed, litany, and homily—in English, including a lengthy reading of the Passion narrative from the Gospel of Luke. Mateos's homily depicted Christ's Passion as unique and transcendent, a sacrifice that not only cannot be approached by our human suffering, but in fact was caused by the evils we create and for which we deserve divine punishment. The songs, however, were multilingual. A Spanish processional hymn, "Alabado de Dios" [Give praise to God], accompanied the blessing of the palms. Later in the service, the congregation sang the African American spiritual "Were You There?" For the second part of the service, the liturgy of the Eucharist, Father Mateos reverted to Spanish. He recited the most sacred of all Catholic Christian words, by which offerings of bread and wine become transformed into the true body and blood of the risen Christ, in the vernacular language of the people, calling them into encounter with sacrality through their Chicano identity.

While the bread and wine were being distributed at the brilliantly painted altar rail, the congregation sang in unison the traditional Chicano eucharistic hymn "Alabado Sea El Santísimo," [Blessed be the Holy Host] (example 3 on page 334). Its musical form, a simple two-line verse and chorus in two-part harmony, suggested great antiquity. Its intense piety and emotional imagery expressed the depth of the people's devotion to the Blessed Sacrament.

> *Chorus:*
> Alabado sea el santísimo sacramento del altar.
> En los cielos y en la tierra, aquí y en todo lugar,
> En los cielos y en la tierra, aquí y en todo lugar.

1   Angeles y serafines ayudadme a bendecir
    a Jesús sacramentado que ya voy a recibir,
    a Jesús sacramentado que ya voy a recibir.

2   Sea en el cielo y en la tierra alabado sin cesar
    el mansísimo cordero que hasta mi quiere llegar,
    el mansísimo cordero que hasta mi quiere llegar.

3   Vuestro cuerpo sacrosanto, benignísimo Señor,
    es de fuertes alimentos y de débiles vigor,
    es de fuertes alimentos y de débiles vigor.

4   Vuestro cuerpo sacrosanto es mi vida, paz, y unción.
    Es salud y dulce calma que mitiga mi dolor,
    Es salud y dulce calma que mitiga mi dolor.

5   Vuestro cuerpo sacrosanto es suavísima mansión
    donde el alma aprisionada goza libre a su amador,
    donde el alma aprisionada goza libre a su amador.

Chorus:
Blessed be the most holy sacrament of the altar.
In heaven and on earth, here and everywhere,
In heaven and on earth, here and everywhere.

1   Angels and seraphs, help me to bless
    Jesus in the sacrament which I just received,
    Jesus in the sacrament which I just received.

2   Be blessed in heaven and earth constantly
    The gentle lamb who wishes to come to me,
    The gentle lamb who wishes to come to me.

3   O benign Lord, your sacred body
    Is food for the strong and vigor for the weak,
    Is food for the strong and vigor for the weak.

4   Your sacred body is my life, peace, and unction.
    It is health and sweet calm that lessens my pain,
    It is health and sweet calm that lessens my pain.

5   Your holy blessed body is a most sweet mansion
    Where the imprisoned soul enjoys, freely, its lover,
    Where the imprisoned soul enjoys, freely, its lover.[19]

Just before Mass ended, Father Mateos announced a penance service that evening at Sagra Familia parish, the Franciscan mission church in Chimayó. Catholic sacramental theology requires the faithful to make full confession of and penance for their sins during Holy Week in order to be ritually pure for the

Easter Eucharist. Mateos said that the *hermanos,* the Penitente brotherhood, would attend the service to sing alabados, their traditional songs of Christ's Passion. The penance service "is the most beautiful way to present ourselves [to God] for this Holy Week," he said, urging everyone to attend the singing, which he called "a beautiful part of our religious tradition."

At dismissal the congregation sang the traditional Chicano Lenten hymn, "Perdona a Tu Pueblo" [Forgive your people]. The text reflected the atonement theme of Father Mateos's sermon: Christ's sacrificial death for our sins and the presence of the Virgin to help the faithful. Again the singing was unison, this time to a haunting minor melody, proceeding by the same verse-and-refrain form as "Alabado Sea El Santísimo," with simple words that conveyed their sacred message not by art but by depth of heartfelt petition to Christ for pardon.

After dismissal, many worshipers remained in their pews to pray. Others rushed forward to receive Father Mateos's blessing. Parents carried babies or sick children; old people handled medals or votive images. His blessings finished, Father Mateos hurried out of El Santuario bound for Sagra Familia, but the church emptied slowly. Many worshipers crowded toward the small side room to obtain some holy earth. Surprisingly, this act did not require any official ritual. No priest was present, no liturgy performed, no prayers said, yet the event carried utmost sacred importance for its participants. The pilgrims simply waited in line until a spot opened in the circle around el posito, into which the sacred soil had been dumped. They stooped to fill whatever containers they had brought with the holy earth. The containers themselves made a commentary on the homely yet intimate character of the sacred in this place. The pilgrims did not bring ornamental vessels emblazoned with holy images, as one might expect, but rather humble coffee cans, plastic pitchers, and Tupperware to bear away soil that supposedly carries curative and providential powers.

I learned from Father Mateos that sacred soil from El Santuario is used like the famed chili powder on sale at Potrero Trading Post across the plaza: liberally in a host of different applications. It is mixed in fruit juice to make a healing drink for the sick, sprinkled in feed for farm animals to ward off disease, and sewn into infant garments for protection against evil spirits. The holy earth is also burned with incense for special petitions before home altars to Our Lady of Guadalupe and scattered wholesale on the floors of homes during ritual cleansings to ward off disease and evil from the family hearth. Tiny amounts are sprinkled into food for the sick to promote divine healing, and it is poured over farm vehicles to insure their good repair.

Everything that happens at Chimayó, from the Holy Week pilgrimages to El Santuario and its sacred soil to the songs of the people before the Miraculous Cross of Esquipulas and the Holy Child of Atocha and the alabados of the Penitentes, typifies the Chicano way of holiness. As at Guadalupe, that pilgrim way is a fusion of many different indigenous and Hispanic religious traditions. To understand how Chimayó works, it is necessary to examine the religious history of El Santuario more closely and to explore more deeply the ritual process of pilgrimage. Only when the complex strata of sacred traditions and processes at this place have been exposed can the genius of its sacred song be fully comprehended.

From Tsimayo-Pokwi to Chimayó

From time immemorial, the unusually fine muddy earth pitted in the glassy stone banks of the Santa Cruz River headwaters has been regarded as sacred. The Tewa Indians, who occupied the site from 1100 to 1400 C.E., called the place *tsimayo-pokwi*, "obsidian rock-water pool," and celebrated its soil as *nam po'uare*, "blessed earth." The Tewa revered tsimayo-pokwi in their sacred beliefs and frequented the place for healing rites that included eating the "blessed earth." Sometime after 1400, the Tano people occupied tsimayo-pokwi and embraced its sacred powers. They transmitted the Tewa myth of healing earth to Mexican colonists who in 1695 established a settlement on the site that they called Chimayó.

Among Chimayó's original settlers was Diego de Veitia. His family prospered along with the young settlement. A century later Diego's descendant Bernardo Abeyta (c. 1770–1856) married Rita Valerio and bought land near her home at a place called El Potrero, "the pasture," a few miles up the Santa Cruz River from Chimayó center on the banks of tsimayo-pokwi. As the legenda of Chimayó tells it, Bernardo Abeyta, now a member of the Penitente brotherhood, was performing his spiritual duties in the hills around El Potrero during Holy Week, 1810, when he saw a bright light shining from a hole in the ground near the Santa Cruz River. Rushing to the spot, he dug out the hole with his bare hands and found a crucifix of Our Lord of Esquipulas, a copy of a sixteenth-century Guatemalan ritual object whose vaunted healing power was well known throughout colonial Hispanic America. Abeyta called the people of the village together to witness his remarkable discovery, then organized a procession to bring the crucifix to Father Sebastian Alvarez, the priest at nearby Santa Cruz, the main town of the region, who placed it on the altar of the church there.

Next morning, however, the crucifix was gone, having returned by its own powers to its hole at El Potrero. Abeyta recovered it and led a second procession to Santa Cruz, but overnight the crucifix again returned to its hole, *el posito*. After a third procession and overnight return, Abeyta and the people understood that the crucifix wished to remain at El Potrero. Soon the soil of el posito was found to contain miraculous powers and pilgrims flocked to the site to pray before the crucifix and to consume the holy earth. Abeyta built a small chapel or *hermita* on the site. Three years later he wrote a series of letters to the bishop of Durango requesting permission to build a church at Chimayó "to honor and venerate, with worthy worship, our Lord and Redeemer of Esquipulas." The bishop approved his request in 1815, whereupon Abeyta at his own expense constructed the building now known as El Santuario.

This legenda is promulgated at El Santuario and accepted by its pilgrims. The story resonates with several different mythic archetypes from Native American and Spanish Catholic beliefs. The location of the crucifix in a hole from which light pours, for example, recapitulates an element that appears in Aztec, Mayan, and Pueblo Indian creation myths. In those stories, human beings first appeared on earth through an opening from the underworld after the surface had been made safe by the triumph of the Ancient Ones over the powers of the under-world. For the indigenous peoples of the Santa Cruz valley, such a story had always existed to explain the powers of the healing earth of Chimayó. With Abeyta's discovery of a miraculous Christian image in an illuminated hole, the soil of which could heal, the legend of Chimayó superimposed Christian myth over indigenous belief.[20]

For colonial Spanish settlers, the Chimayó story also bore powerful structural similarities to Old World Catholic sacred narratives of the shepherds' cycle, *el ciclo de los pastores*.[21] During the Christian Reconquista of Spain from Islamic Moors, many miraculous images were discovered or recovered at remote sites, it was said, by shepherds or other simple lay people. Our Lady of Guadalupe in Extremadura, a "black Virgin" of darkened wood, was one of the most celebrated of such images. Stories of their recovery invariably contained providential guidance of the discoverer by divine light and natural anomalies, "refusal" of the images to be moved, and instruction to build a church on the sacred discovery site. The legend of Our Lady of Guadalupe in Mexico itself has been interpreted as a variant of the shepherd's cycle. The story of Bernardo Abeyta and the miraculous crucifix of Esquipulas held even more closely to that archetype, supplying the Chicano settlers of New Mexico with their own version of this traditional Spanish sacred narrative, thereby conferring credibility and legitimacy on El Santuario.[22]

The holy image that Don Bernardo discovered had its own New World legenda that was also superimposed onto the meaning of Chimayó. It was a life-sized crucified Christ carved from balsam wood and fixed to a green painted cross decorated with sculptured vines and painted golden leaves. This crucifix was a replica of the original created in 1594 at Esquipulas in southeastern Guatemala by the great colonial sculptor Quirio Catano and known throughout Latin America as Our Lord of Esquipulas. The city of Esquipulas was founded by Spanish conquistadors in the mid-sixteenth century. Catano was commissioned to create a crucifix to honor the peaceful conversion of the indigenous Chorti Maya people there by Dominican missionaries. Catano's work became a masterpiece of the Antigua style of colonial Central American sculpture and decorative arts. The dark hue of Christ's balsam body, blackened further by the constant burning of candles and incense, earned the crucifix the title *el Cristo Negro*, the Black Christ. Placed in a chapel near the hot springs of Esquipulas, the crucifix gained a reputation for miraculous cures. In 1737, the same year that the image of Guadalupe saved Mexico City from typhus, Archbishop Pedro

Pardo de Figueroa of Guatemala was cured of a life-threatening fever at the hot springs. Honoring the crucifix for his healing, Figueroa built a vast basilica on the site. Consecrated in 1758, the new church and its precious crucifix became a major pilgrimage destination for Hispanic America. In addition to veneration of the miraculous crucifix, the cult of Esquipulas also included the eating of clay. Pilgrims purchased little tablets of fine white local clay called *benditos* or *tierra del Santo,* stamped with images of the miraculous crucifix or the Virgin of Guadalupe. Blessed by the priests at the basilica, benditos were eaten or dissolved in water and drunk to cure a variety of physical ailments.

In 1810 Bernardo Abeyta of Chimayó, living on the far northern frontier of colonial Hispanic America, knew the cult of Esquipulas and its clay-eating ritual, as well as the Tewa myth of sacred earth at Chimayó. It cannot be determined whether the Guatemalan clay-eating practice provided a conscious point of identification for Abeyta between the Esquipulas cult and the tsimayo-pokwi myths, but geophagy was certainly an important ritual element common to them both. By whatever the mode of transmission, Mesoamerican myth, Hispanic American Christianity, sacred earth, and miraculous healing all came together at El Santuario.[23]

Mythic elaboration of the Chimayó site continued during the nineteenth century when a second cult, that of the Santo Niño de Atocha, became associated with El Santuario. The legenda of the Santo Niño tells of a miraculous appearance by the Christ child who answered the prayers of the pious women of Atocha, near Madrid, during the last years of the Moorish occupation of Spain. Dressed in the costume of a pilgrim, the Holy Child gave food, water, and blessings to local Christian men imprisoned there by Moorish authorities. In early modern Spain and late colonial Mexico the Santo Niño developed into the patron of the helpless, especially children, captives, and travelers.[24] The cult of the Holy Child of Atocha reached Chimayó after New Mexico was ceded to the United States in 1848. Shortly after Don Bernardo Abeyta's death in 1856 the Medinas family, local rivals of the Abeytas, built a private chapel to the Santo Niño just off the plaza of El Potrero. By 1890 the Santo Niño had replaced Our Lord of Esquipulas as the most powerful votary at El Santuario and became the acknowledged source for the healing power of the blessed earth.

At Chimayó, the Holy Child legend included nocturnal travels by the Santo Niño during which he bestowed blessings on children of the faithful and combated nocturnal evils perpetrated by *brujas* or witches. Because his shoes would wear out during these visitations, baby shoes became a popular votive image for pilgrims to the shrine after 1900. So popular did the Santo Niño de Atocha become that in the early twentieth century the Chaves family, then owners of El Santuario, rededicated the church to the Holy Child and three of his helpers, San José, San Rafael, and Santiago, all of whom also travel at night doing the Santo Niño's bidding. To further their devotion, the Chaveses added bultos of the three saints and several ceramic statues of the Santo Niño to the iconography of El

Santuario. In the twentieth century, the cults of el posito's holy earth, the miraculous crucifix of Esquipulas, and the Santo Niño de Atocha have combined to make El Santuario the supreme pilgrimage site of the Chicano Southwest.

Los Peregrinos de Chimayó

Mary Frances Reza, noted composer of Chicano sacred songs, director of the Office for Liturgy of the Archdiocese of Albuquerque for eight years, and an editor of *Flor y Canto,* the most popular Hispanic Catholic hymnal in America, explained to me the significance of pilgrimage for Chicanos. "Pilgrimage," she said, "is an action that joins together *iglésia,* the church, with *misión y testimonio,* mission and witness. We are a pilgrim church, always moving toward God in our lives. And this is our mission to travel together to God, and this is our testimony. By participating in pilgrimage we express all of these things."[25]

Reza's theological description of Chicano pilgrimage confirms the anthropological understanding of it as a ritual process described by Victor and Edith Turner. As we saw in our examination of Native American sacred song, Victor Turner explained ritual as rite of passage that moves the participant out of the "structure" of everyday individual consciousness and social order across a "liminal" threshold into an "anti-structure" of free spiritual experience and a "communitas" of new collective consciousness, thence returning through "reaggregation" to the normal structures of society.[26] In their later work *Image and Pilgrimage in Christian Culture,* Victor Turner and Edith Turner classified pilgrimage as a "liminoid" form of the ritual process, not quite a rite of passage, but rather a voluntary activity in which the pilgrim individually chooses to join a transformative experience mediated by physical travel and the experience of song. Yet pilgrimage is a fundamentally anti-structural activity. "Pilgrimage has some of the attributes of liminality in passage rites," the Turners wrote,

> release from mundane structure; homogenization of status; simplicity of dress and behavior; communitas; ordeal; reflection on the meaning of basic religious and cultural values; ritualized enactment of correspondences between religious paradigms and shared human experiences; emergence of the integral person from multiple personae; movement from a mundane center to a sacred periphery which suddenly, transiently, becomes central for the individual; movement itself, a symbol of communitas, which changes with time, as against stasis, which represents structure; individuality posed against the institutionalized milieu; and so forth.[27]

All of these elements are present in the Chicano pilgrimage to El Santuario. Some are more salient than others; they tend to be the ones that the pilgrims sing about.

Chicano pilgrimage begins with a vow, a *promesa,* by individual pilgrims to bring their "intentions," their prayer requests, into the sacred presence at the pilgrimage site. Such vows are typically made to holy beings like the Lord of

Esquipulas or the Holy Child of Atocha at life-and-death moments. In traditional Catholic societies like that in New Mexico, when the faithful face the possibility of death by accident or the loss of a loved one by illness, their instinctive response is to pray to Jesus, Mary, or the saints for aid and to promise a pilgrimage in humble acknowledgment of blessings received.

Mary Frances Reza talked about how pilgrims prepare for the journey. "Pilgrimage is both spiritual and physical. It is not easy to walk a hundred miles in our country!" she said. "The preparation takes months, and they will pray on retreat for a week or more before the pilgrimage to be spiritually ready for it." As diverse individuals gather at their local parishes they take on new individual spiritual identities as pilgrims to Chimayó, each one bearing his or her promesa to the Lord of Esquipulas or the Holy Child of Atocha. Along the way the pilgrim functions as a "spiritual athlete," in the language of St. Paul, praying and singing continually while walking the arduous miles to El Santuario. "Many of the peregrinos have composed their own songs which have become popular among those who participate in pilgrimages," Reza said. "These are sung on the journey."

A recent Chimayó pilgrim song, "Grita, Profeta" [Cry out, prophet] (example 4 on page 335), by Emilio Vicente Matéu, voices this dimension of proclamation and witness so essential to pilgrimage's anti-structure. As a pilgrim, the believer makes a visible, public expression of commitment to the faith while suspending his or her everyday life patterns to pursue a new vision of God's future. This song gathers that risky religious self-presentation into a powerful expression of pilgrimage as a prophetic calling:

1   Has recibido un destino de otra palabra más fuerte,
es tu misión ser profeta: Palabra de Dios viviente.
Tu irás llevando la luz en una entrega perenne,
que tu voz es voz de Dios,
y la voz de Dios no duerme.

Chorus:
Ve por el mundo, grita a la gente,
que el amor de Dios no acaba,
ni la voz de Dios se pierde.

2   Sigue tu rumbo, profeta, sobre la arena caliente.
Sigue sembrando en el mundo, que el fruto se hará presente.
No temas si nuestra fe ante tu voz se detiene,
porque huimos del dolor y la voz de Dios nos duele.

3   Sigue cantando, profeta, cantos de vida o de muerte
sigue anunciando a los hombres, que el Reino de Dios ya viene.
No callarán esa voz, y a nadie puedes temerle,
que tu voz viene de Dios, y la voz de Dios no muere.

1   You have received your call from another, stronger word;
    your mission to be prophet: the living word of God.
    You shall carry the light of a perennial delivery,
    because your voice is God's own voice,
    and the voice of God never sleeps.

    Chorus:
    Go through the world, shout to the people,
    that the love of God never ends,
    neither the voice of God is ever lost.

2   Follow your own road, prophet, on the ardent sands,
    keep sowing seeds in the world, because the fruit will come.
    Don't be afraid even if our faith wavers before your voice;
    we flee from suffering and the voice of God hurts us.

3   Keep on singing, prophet, songs of life or death;
    Go on announcing to men that God's kingdom is at hand.
    They will not silence your voice, you can't fear anyone
    because your voice comes from God
    and the voice of God never dies.[28]

Large pilgrimages often organize local parish networks and groups to pray for special intentions. At Chimayó the Catholic church sponsors special Holy Week pilgrimages for "vocations," God's calling of men and women to serve as priests and religious. Young men volunteer to take these special pilgrimages, walking one hundred miles to El Santuario from each of the four cardinal directions, north, east, south, and west. Companies of women, called *Guadalupanas* for their devotion to Our Lady of Guadalupe, also join the pilgrimage for vocations. Often a young man intent on finding his true spiritual calling leads a group of vocation pilgrims bearing a full-sized wooden cross on his shoulders for the entire distance. As many as five hundred people will thus descend upon Chimayó from the four corners of the compass in Holy Week.

Often pilgrim songs have been spontaneously composed as the pilgrims walked the long miles to El Santuario. One such Chimayó song is "De Los Cuatro Vientos" [From the four winds] (example 5 on page 337), by Arsenio Córdova. As an expression of Chicano religious syncretism, the song's chorus references the ancient Native American understanding of the sacred center of the world, in this case Chimayó, bounded by the four principal directions and their winds. Yet in its simplicity and directness, the song also expresses the characteristic Chicano pilgrimage intention "to bring our sufferings to Christ," along with the powerful bond of spiritual and social union that the experience of pilgrimage creates.

Chorus:
Somos peregrinos, de los cuatro vientos;
somos caminantes de Cristo el Señor;

1   Venimos del oriente, norte, sur y oeste,
     y te presentamos todo nuestro amor.

2   Hermanos peregrinos, de lejos venimos
     a traerle la gloria a nuestro Señor.

3   Todo el sufrimiento, que traemos, mi Cristo,
     hoy, lo ofrecemos en signo de amor.

4   Te damos las gracias porque nos uniste
     con nuestros hermanos de todo lugar.

Chorus:
We are pilgrims from the four winds;
We are pilgrims of Christ, the Lord.

1   We come from the east, north, south, and west
     and we offer you all our love.

2   Brother pilgrims, we come from afar
     to bring glory to our Lord.

3   All the suffering that we bring, my Christ,
     today we offer in sign of love.

4   We render thanks because you have united us
     with our brethren from everywhere.[29]

Whether undertaken for a personal *promesa* or an ecclesiastical petition like vocations, pilgrimages begin with individual decisions to make the journey. They end, however, in a new experience of sacred *communitas*. Pilgrimages by their very nature seem to create a powerful, if transient, sense of community among the company of seekers. The process was so well known in medieval Europe that Chaucer could premise his *Canterbury Tales* on it. The Turners have recovered it in modern social-science theory, and their analysis points to why sacred song is such a powerful element in pilgrimage. The pilgrim's individual liminal identity gradually melds into a new *communitas*, an anti-structural community marked by wearing symbolic colors or images of the holy site, and above all by singing sacred songs like "De los Quatro Vientos" and "Grita, Profeta."

These sacred songs function as a potent medium of contemplation to keep pilgrims focused on their holy purpose as they move through the wild New Mexico landscape. Step by step they keep rhythm to songs of their holy aspiration. That same rhythm assists meditation upon the pilgrim vows they have made and the sacred powers that await them at El Santuario. Such singing is in one dimension the most private of religious expressions, yet in another it is the most public of sacred utterances, sung as the pilgrim band passes through towns on open roadways, heard by any and all who might encounter their liminal personae as they pursue healing and hope.

As they approach Chimayó, the pilgrims have through sacred song created a new communitas, a sense of sacrality quite specific to their arduous physical achievement and spiritual discipline, yet indissolubly linked to the cosmic powers to whom they have brought their petitions. When Holy Week pilgrims finally arrive at El Santuario, they find the plaza decorated for fiesta and filled with vendors of food and souvenirs. Once arrived, they melt into the immense congregation of the faithful, joining its larger communitas in celebration and praise, singing together once more the sacred songs that have brought them all safely to the fulfillment of their promesas.

For Chicano and Mexican American Catholics the world is a harsh and dangerous place where evil and oppression rule and human beings fail to obey the royal examples of Christ and the Virgin. Yet at the same time they know that through their faith they will be forgiven, restored to the family of Jesus and his mother, and ultimately rejoice in the final victory of justice. Pilgrimage is the most powerful expression of this movement from sinful disobedience to redemptive reunion with God, an act that expresses the faith simultaneously through physical movement, spiritual transformation, and above all through songs that embody in melody and words the hopeful humility and prophetic proclamation of the people of God. "It is our mission to travel together to God," Mary Frances Reza told me. At Chimayó, pilgrims raise their offering of prayer, penitence, and praise to the Lord of Esquipulas and the Holy Child of Atocha, two images of Christ's ministry that assure them that their purity of heart and their human suffering are known, honored, healed, and redeemed by God.

Hermanos y Alabados

Interwoven with the pilgrimage songs of El Santuario is another corpus of closely related songs also sung during Holy Week. These are the alabados of the Penitente brotherhood. At the Palm Sunday noon mass Father Mateos had announced that the brotherhood would be singing the penance service at Sagra Familia parish later in the day. By the time I arrived at the church shortly before 5 P.M., a steady stream of pickup trucks and four-wheel drive vehicles were pulling into the muddy unpaved parking lot delivering families for the service. At the edge of the lot a long double line of perhaps fifty men had formed. They appeared to be typical farmers and working men of the region, dressed in jeans and colorful shirts with boots and cowboy hats. As I walked by, I overheard the men greeting one another warmly. At the head of the line, processional banners were unfurled and snippets of song filled the air. These men were the hermanos of the Fraternidad Piedosa de Nostro Señor Jesus Nazareno, the brothers of the Pious Fraternity of Our Lord Jesus the Nazarene or, as they are popularly known, the Penitentes of Chimayó, preparing to sing their songs of penitence and praise.

The modern sanctuary of Sagra Familia seats more than five hundred people. It is built in three-quarters round with a beamed ceiling supported by wooden pillars. Indirect natural lighting flows from narrow horizontal second-story windows characteristic of traditional northern New Mexico churches. Confessionals and function rooms punctuate the sidewalls of the building. The central altar rises three steps above the sanctuary floor, backed by a massive wall of natural cedar wood. A crucifix modeled on the Lord of Esquipulas surmounts the wall above the altar. A large wooden cross stands to the right of the altar. The only other images in the church were the Twelve Stations of the Cross painted in santero style from the old church. At the time of my visit, large purple banners, the noble vestment color for Holy Week, flanked the crucifix reading "Return to Me with All Your Heart," a motto that exhorts all to complete their spiritual and physical pilgrimage to Christ. Shortly after 5 o'clock, five priests, including Father Miguel Mateos, entered stage right of the altar to begin the service. From the back of the church came the sound of the hermanos singing a processional song as they walked through the atrium outside the church. The doors opened and the brothers entered the sanctuary. Three men led the procession. The first bore a small wooden crucifix with a white skirt around Christ's waist, mounted inside a painted white diamond-shaped candelabrum and covered with a white veil. Behind the crucifix bearer, the first pair of men carried the standards of the fraternity. The brothers proceeded down the central aisle of the church by pairs, singing, then sat as a group in pews stage right of the altar. There were men of every age among them, elderly and middle-aged, young fathers and youthful novices.

After a short service of penance, Father Mateos announced that the priests would hear individual confessions while the hermanos sang their alabados. The singing began with a pair of lead singers striking up the first verse of a song. The entire group of brothers repeated the same verse antiphonally. The song continued in this way through ten verses. After a very brief pause a second pair of singing leaders called out another song, which was performed in the same manner. And so the singing went for more than an hour without a break.

The brothers knew some of the songs much better than others, and the novices seemed to know neither the songs nor the proper bearing for the occasion. But the singing of the leaders was spellbindingly intense and powerful. They rendered the slow undulating lines of the alabados with full voice, frequent melodic ornament, and a characteristically open tone quality that clearly aroused their spirit. After an hour of nonstop singing, some voices had tired. The brothers began to make their own confessions in small groups so that the body of singers was never significantly diminished. When about two-thirds of the brothers and the congregation had confessed, the leaders finally called for the Ave Maria to be recited several times to give the singers a rest.

After this brief hiatus the singing immediately resumed and continued until the rest of the confessions had been heard. In the end, the brothers sang about ten songs, most of them with many verses, requiring altogether an hour and a half to complete. In the fading March light the church gradually darkened and emptied, leaving the hermanos alone in full cry. After the last song, they left the sanctuary singing their processional song once again. They receded in traditional fashion, walking backwards up the central aisle in the same order they entered so that the last man backed out of the church bearing the Penitente crucifix. In the empty church I asked Father Mateos what they had been singing. "They were singing the scenes of the Passion," he answered. During the next week and especially during the *triduum*—the three days of Christ's Passion between Maundy Thursday and Holy Saturday—the brothers would literally re-enact those scenes in their controversial and bloody initiation and purification rites.

Who are these men, what is their history, and what role do they play in Chicano sacred-song culture? The origin of the Penitentes, like their history and practice, is much disputed. Their dramatic Holy Week observances suggest several possible origins: the Flagellants of thirteenth-century Europe, the passion plays of colonial Mexico, or the penitential *cofradias* or confraternities of sixteenth- and seventeenth-century Spain. But the most likely source of the Penitentes is eighteenth-century settlers who joined the Third Order Franciscans in New Mexico. The Franciscan Rule of 1223 included a provision for a "third order," in addition to the first and second orders of fully professed men and women, respectively. Members of the Third Order, called Tertiaries, live in the world rather than in religious communities and maintain secular vocations and family obligations. Third Order Franciscans do, however, form lay communities committed to the strict observance of piety, chastity, penance, and charity. Christopher Columbus and Queen Isabella of Spain were both Franciscan Tertiaries.[30]

The Franciscans came to newly settled New Mexico in 1616 as the Spanish crown's official missionaries and spiritual custodians. Their principal tasks were to Christianize the Native American population, which they accomplished with limited effectiveness, and to supply priests for the colonial towns of Spanish New Mexico. The Pueblo Indian Revolt of 1680–92 temporarily drove the Franciscans and most of the Spanish settlers out of New Mexico. After 1700, however, resettled missions and towns began to support Third Order communities for the Chicano laity. Yet the New Mexico mission remained small throughout the eighteenth century and declined sharply after 1800. In 1821 the Mexican revolutionary government rescinded the authority of the Franciscan Order over the missions and placed them under the control of the bishop of Durango. The missions continued to languish so that by 1831 Antonio Barriero, legal advisor to the Mexican authorities in Santa Fe, reported that "spiritual administration in New

Mexico is in a truly doleful condition. A great many unfortunate people spend most of their Sundays of the year without hearing mass."[31]

Into this vacuum stepped the Third Order brotherhoods, who took up much of the religious teaching, counseling, moral discipline, and charitable work previously reserved for the missions. The Tertiaries convened worship and song services for the people in the absence of priests to say mass. They built meetinghouses, called *moradas,* for their brotherhoods and gained notoriety for their public displays of extreme penance, including flagellation and scourging, and even reenacted crucifixions during Holy Week. In a few years the brotherhoods had sparked a revitalization of popular Catholicism that began to displace the formal institutions and hierarchical authority of the church.

Church reaction to this laicization came quickly, when in 1833 the bishop of Durango, José Zubiría y Escalante, condemned the Penitentes in general and those at Chimayó in particular. They "practiced immoderate corporeal penances, sometimes publicly," he wrote, "using crosses and other unspecified instruments of mortification. These were kept in rooms—the moradas—which may also have been used for the meetings which the bishop deplores and prohibits." Three months later, Zubiría banned the *grandes maderos,* the "large crosses," and other "instruments of mortification," and demanded that "abuses of this sort" be stopped by local church authorities.[32]

Zubiría's orders proved ineffectual as the downward spiral of priestly vocations continued. Instead, the Penitentes became a secret society ruled by a group of powerful leaders including Don Bernardo Abeyta, founder of El Santuario, who was named in source documents as the "Hermano Mayor Principal of all the Brotherhoods." The church was not able to reassert ecclesiastical authority over New Mexico's religious culture before the Mexican War and the cession of New Mexico to the United States in 1848. It was not until 1856–57 that Jean Baptiste Lamy, first bishop of Santa Fe, could deal effectively with the Penitentes by laying down rules for admission and discipline of the societies.[33]

Over the past century, relations between the Penitentes and the church hierarchy have improved significantly. In 1892 Bishop Juan Battista Salpointe eliminated the secret oath while confirming the hermanos as a Catholic sodality. Formal constitutions for local chapters were approved in 1931. Under the leadership of Penitente Mayor Don Miguel Archibeque and Santa Fe Bishop Edwin Burne, official detente was achieved in 1962. Burne approved the brotherhood as "an association of Catholic men united together in love for the passion and death of our Blessed Lord and Savior" whose purpose was to perform "corporal and spiritual penance" and whose privacy was not to be compromised. In 1974 Santa Fe Bishop Robert Fortune Sanchez restored the brotherhood to full participation in parochial worship, as in the Palm Sunday penance service at Sagra Familia.[34]

In their role as creators and preservers of popular religion, the hermanos have played a vital part in the sacred-song culture of the Chicano people. The

Penitentes have maintained and developed the alabados style, which seems to be the oldest continuous Christian song tradition in North America. These sacred songs are short unison melodies that set two lines of a twelve- or sixteen-line sacred text. Sometimes the two lines are repeated antiphonally, sometimes the second line is repeated, and sometimes a two-line refrain is sung after each verse. Mary Frances Reza has defined *alabado*, "praised" in Spanish, as "a religious hymn related to a Spanish form of poetry of the same name. In the New World the term transferred to a form of hymnody developed and spread under the early Franciscan missionaries. . . . Retaining the free rhythm of plainsong, alabados are sung today at [night vigils], processions, and the way of the cross."[35]

The roots of alabados reach back to the medieval Spanish ballad first popularized by the Carolingians before the Moorish Conquest. Some interpreters claim to hear an element of ecclesiastical chant in the sinuous melodic lines of alabados; others identify liturgical references in its antiphonal structure. Whatever the merit of such assessments, it is clear that alabados became the predominant element in the earliest sacred song of New Spain.[36] Sixteenth-century conquistadors brought the *romance*, an immensely popular form of sacred and secular alabados, with them to Mexico. As early as 1524, Pedro de Gante established a music school at Mexico City to teach the Aztecs music notation, singing technique, instrument building, and ensemble playing. De Gante's repertory included both sacred and secular romances along with settings of the liturgy and the monastic hours.[37]

During the colonial centuries, however, other Spanish song and poetry types were transmitted to Mexico, including the *décima*, a ten-line verse supported by a four-line refrain; the *corrido*, an extended ballad form; and the *canción*, a later variety of sentimental love song. But while those forms became extraordinarily popular among the small criollo elite, the old alabados tradition penetrated ever deeper into the mestizo and indigenous population of colonial Mexico. Several reasons help account for the ongoing appeal of these older ballad styles. One of them was the vital role of song in traditional Aztec religion, which was saturated with song, dance, and costume designed to recite and re-present the myths of its pantheon. This power of indigenous sacred song was not lost on the missionary effort to Christianize New Spain. The earliest and most famous of many successful nonviolent evangelistic efforts using song as a principal medium was the 1530 mission of Dominican Friar Bartolomé de Las Casas at Vera Paz, where he used indigenous melodies to set translations of the Bible and famous Christian hymns.[38]

Musical reasons also contributed to the preservation of the old sacred ballad. According to Mary Frances Reza, new popular song styles were developed to suit new poetic forms, "so ballad musical themes from the early centuries didn't always fit the new words." As elite music culture moved toward new songs of love, war, and worldly achievement, the people continued to tell the stories of the Lord of Esquipulas and the Virgin of Guadalupe in the old ballad style. In that role alabados "encountered indigenous influence as a plaintive note of the people," Reza said, lending the tunes a modal tonality and a highly emotional style of performance still powerfully present in the singing of the Penitentes.

As it emerged in sixteenth-century Mexico, the alabados tradition became the ideal musical tool for evangelization of the Indians and maintenance of the faith among colonial settlers. The Franciscans brought alabados to New Mexico in the early seventeenth century. When the province's missions and parishes were secularized and abandoned after 1800, the hermanos preserved this sacred-song tradition. Even as their Holy Week reenactments and sacred plays became the chief religious events on the New Mexican calendar, so the Penitentes' singing at their moradas and in public became the primary source of sacred song for the people. "Religious song was always called alabados in New Mexico," said Reza, whose grandfather was an active member of Los Hermanos de Jesucristo in Rancho de Taos, "and the hermanos always taught them to the people. People remember the power of song. Catharsis takes place. Through song the prayer is embedded in the soul. In the past it became their form of prayer, a way to express their own religion."

The Penitentes faced the task of preserving their sacred-song culture without printed hymnals. Each Penitente brotherhood has maintained its own tradition of alabados for two centuries or more by constructing its own handmade songbooks containing words only, called "Hymnos Sagrados dedicados a Nuestro Padre Jesus de Nazareno" [Sacred hymns dedicated to our Father Jesus the Nazarene]. These songbooks come in various shapes and sizes, some pocket-sized, some standard book dimension, and a few folios. The binders are mostly leather, the binding hand-sewn or glued. These books are collections of printed alabados texts cut from hymnals that the brothers have encountered over the years. Three sources appear most among Chimayó's Penitente songbooks today: *Cantos Sagrados Populares,* a nineteenth-century Spanish imprint; Juan de Ralliere's *Cánticos Espirituales,* printed at Las Vegas, New Mexico, in 1907; and *Cánticos Mexicanos,* published around 1920 by the Oblate Order at San Antonio, Texas.

"These are delightful hymnals," said Reza, "containing some of the old alabados from Spain and Mexico. [They sing these words to] short, simple, repetitive melodies with many verses to each alabado." These humble books contain the essence of Chicano spirituality as it is lived by the hermanos and modeled by them for the larger community. "They live the liturgical year," Reza said, "and because of their gift of maintaining the faith and song, the theology of their hymns is incredible. The brothers are rehearsing what they know about God."

One of the oldest New Mexico alabados is "Bendito, Bendito" [Blessed, blessed] (example 6 on page 338), said to be brought by the Franciscan missionaries in the seventeenth century. It is a classic illustration of the genre, a twelve-line poem broken into six verses of two lines, the second line repeated.

1   Bendito, bendito, bendito sea Dios,
     los ángeles cantan y alaban a Dios,
     los ángeles cantan y alaban a Dios.

2   Jesús de mi alma, te doy mi corazón;
     y en cambio te pido me des tu bendición,
     y en cambio te pido me des tu bendición.

3   Adoro en la hostia el cuerpo de Jesús,
     su sangre preciosa que dio por mí en la cruz,
     su sangre preciosa que dio por mí en la cruz.

4   A tus plantas llego confuso de dolor,
     de todas mis culpas imploro tu perdón,
     de todas mis culpas imploro tu perdón.

5   Yo creo, Dios mío, que estás en el altar,
     oculto en la hostia te vengo a adorar,
     oculto en la hostia te vengo a adorar.

6   Oh cielo y tierra, decid a una voz,
     bendito por siempre, bendito sea Dios,
     bendito por siempre, bendito sea Dios.

1   Blessed, blessed, blessed be God,
     the angels sing and praise God,
     the angels sing and praise God.

2   Jesus of my soul, I give you my heart;
     and in exchange I ask you to give me your blessing,
     and in exchange I ask you to give me your blessing.

3   I worship in the host the body of Jesus,
     his precious blood given for me in the cross,
     his precious blood given for me in the cross.

4   I come to your feet overwhelmed with sorrow,
     and I ask the pardon of all my sins,
     and I ask the pardon of all my sins.

5   I believe, my God, that you are at the altar,
     and I come to worship you hiding in the Host,
     and I come to worship you hiding in the Host.

6   Heaven and earth! Cry out with one voice,
     blessed for ever, blessed be God,
     blessed for ever, blessed be God.[39]

The lack of a refrain bespeaks the antiquity of this song: it is simply an A–B–B melody rendering two lines of text with each repetition. A quintessential spiritual ballad, "Bendito" tells a story that reveals the very heart of Chicano Catholic identity. Framed by initial and final verses that invoke the *Sanctus* of the Mass, the poem is an intensely personal meditation on the Eucharist in which the singer first rehearses the act of faith in Christ to obtain blessing, moves to adore the host and the divine sacrifice it contains, sorrowfully confesses the many sins brought for pardon, and triumphantly reiterates adoration for the God hidden in the sacrament. Theologically the song expresses the rich paradoxes of a cosmic Christ known to all creation yet hidden in the host, and of a soul faithful to Jesus yet desperately sinful, sorrowful, and needful of pardon. The articulation of these powerful religious ideas and emotions through the simplest possible language and melody is the essence of alabados, and of Chicano piety.

The sacred song of the Chicano Southwest is a complex public expression of music, text, and movement woven around the themes of pilgrimage and penitence, of suffering and hope. In a harsh but beautiful landscape, remote from ecclesiastical authority, Franciscan missionaries and Mexican settlers faithfully preserved their colonial heritage of sacred music and developed it into a true song of the people. That song grew not in the cathedral cultures of New Spain but in the people's ceaseless spiritual and physical movement toward God. Whether on the pilgrimage road to Chimayó or in the arduous Penitente pursuit of holiness by ordeal, Chicano sacred song brings together the most direct sense of the world's sinfulness and suffering with an extraordinary faith in the transcendent power and mercy of Christ.

The great ritual moment of Chicano piety is Holy Week, when the entire community purifies itself and brings its petitions to the dying and rising Lord, singing all the way the alabados of its sacred history. The roots of this practice reach deep into the Mexican experience to the fusion of Aztec and Spanish religions in the figure of Our Lady of Guadalupe. In New Mexico, however, the traditions of penitence and pilgrimage of Old Mexico have been transformed into a unique fiesta of *sagra semana,* of Holy Week, at El Santuario de Chimayó, where the Chicano soul confronts with movement and proclaims through song the great Christian mystery that out of suffering comes salvation, out of death comes life.

Notes

1. Robert Ricard, *The Spiritual Conquest of Mexico* (Berkeley: University of California Press, 1966), 21–22.

2. See Joseph M. Murphy, *Santería: African Spirits in America* (Boston: Beacon Press, 1993); George Eaton Simpson, *Black Religions in the New World* (New York: Columbia University Press, 1978). For a helpful introduction to Chicano and Mexican American worship practice, see Virgilio

P. Elizondo and Timothy M. Matovina, *Mestizo Worship: A Pastoral Approach to Liturgical Ministry* (Collegeville, Minn.: Liturgical Press, 1998).

3. Donald Demarest and Coley Taylor, eds., *The Dark Virgin: The Book of Our Lady of Guadalupe* (New York: Coley Taylor, 1956), is the best sourcebook on the Guadalupe tradition in Mexico.

4. Ibid., 42–43.

5. William A. Christian, *Apparitions in Late Medieval and Renaissance Spain* (Princeton, N.J.: Princeton University Press, 1981), 57–93.

6. Victor Turner and Edith Turner, *Image and Pilgrimage in Christian Culture* (New York: Columbia University Press, 1978), 80–81; Virgil Elizondo, *Guadalupe, Mother of the New Creation* (New York: Orbis, 1997), 49–50.

7. *A Handbook on Guadalupe* (New Bedford, Mass.: Academy of the Immaculate, 1997), 217–21.

8. Patricia Harrington, "Mother of Life and Death: The Mexican Virgin of Guadalupe," *Journal of the American Academy of Religion* 56, no. 1 (1988): 25–50.

9. See John Tutino, *From Insurrection to Revolution in Mexico: Social Roots of Agrarian Violence, 1750–1810* (Princeton, N.J.: Princeton University Press, 1986); John Womack, *Zapata and the Mexican Revolution* (New York: Knopf, 1969), and *Rebellion in Chiapas: An Historical Reader* (New York: New Press, 1999).

10. Elizondo, *Guadalupe*, 81–91; Rudolfo Anaya, "'I am King': The Macho Image," in *Muy Macho: Latin Men Confront Their Manhood*, ed. Ray Gonzalez (New York: Doubleday, 1996), 59–73; Ada Maria Isasi-Diaz, *Mujerista Theology: A Theology for the Twenty-First Century* (Maryknoll, N.Y.: Orbis, 1996), 59–85.

11. Octavio Paz, *The Labyrinth of Solitude and Other Essays* (New York: Grove Press, 1985), 20, 32.

12. Ibid., 47.

13. Elizondo, *Guadalupe*, x–xi.

14. Owen Alstott, ed., *Flor y Canto* (Portland, Ore.: OCP Publications, 1989), 209.

15. Elizondo, *Guadalupe*, 60–80.

16. Marie Romero Cash, *Built of Earth and Song: Churches of Northern New Mexico* (Santa Fe, N.M.: Red Crane Books, 1993), 62–64.

17. Ibid., xix–xxviii.

18. Thomas J. Steele, *Santos and Saints: The Religious Folk Art of Hispanic New Mexico*, 2d ed. (Santa Fe, N.M.: Ancient City Press, 1982), 1–28.

19. Alstott, ed., *Flor y Canto*, 291.

20. See Dennis Tedlock, *Popul Vuh: The Definitive Edition of The Mayan Book of the Dawn of Life and the Glories of Gods and Kings* (New York: Simon and Schuster, 1985).

21. Turner and Turner, *Image and Pilgrimage*, 41.

22. For the persistence of these phenomena in Spain, see William A. Christian, *Moving Crucifixes in Modern Spain* (Princeton, N.J.: Princeton University Press, 1992).

23. Stephen F. deBorhegyi, *The Miraculous Shrines of Our Lord of Esquipulas in Guatemala in Chimayó, New Mexico* (Santa Fe, N.M.: Ancient City Press, 1956), 4–6.

24. Steele, *Santos and Saints*, 109–10.

25. Mary Frances Reza, telephone interview with author, June 19, 1994. All subsequent quotations are taken from this interview, unless otherwise indicated in the text.

26. Victor Turner, *The Ritual Process: Structure and Anti-Structure* (Ithaca, N.Y.: Cornell University Press, 1969), 94–130.

27. Turner and Turner, *Image and Pilgrimage*, 34.

28. Alstott, ed., *Flor y Canto*, 351.

29. Ibid., 358.

30. Kajetan Esser, *Origins of the Franciscan Order* (Chicago: Franciscan Herald Press, 1970), 201–17.

31. Marta Weigle, *Brothers of Light, Brothers of Blood: The Penitentes of the Southwest* (Santa Fe, N.M.: Ancient City Press, 1976).

32. Ibid., 19–25, 195–97.

33. Ibid., 49–56, 201–7.

34. Ibid., 57–65, 110–18, 208–16, 225–27.

35. Mary Frances Reza, "Alabado," in *Worship Music: A Concise Dictionary,* ed. Edward Foley (Collegeville, Minn.: Liturgical Press, 2000), 7.

36. Juan Rael, *The New Mexican "Alabados"* (Santa Fe, N.M.: Ancient City Press, 1964), 1–17.

37. Gilbert Chase, *The Music of Spain* (New York: Norton, 1941), 257–59, 264–66, 271–75; Gerard Behague, *Music in Latin America: An Introduction* (Englewood Cliffs, N.J.: Prentice-Hall, 1979), 2–56.

38. Bartolomé de las Casas, *Historia de las Indias,* ed. Agustin Millares Carlo and Lewis Hanke, 3 vols. (Mexico City: Fondo de Cultura Economica, 1951), 3:330–32.

39. Alstott, ed., *Flor y Canto,* 424.

CHAPTER 3

Sacred Harp Singing:
Continuity and Change in the
American Singing-School Tradition

The most widespread sacred-song tradition in America is Protestant Christian hymnody. At worship every Sunday and at countless hymn sings, prayer meetings, and revivals, tens of millions of American Protestants sing hymns that reflect five centuries of development and embody the extraordinary liturgical diversity of more than five hundred different denominations. The oldest surviving form of white American Protestant sacred song is the singing-school tradition of unaccompanied hymn singing that has been practiced continuously since the 1720s.

This tradition is known by several names. It is often called shape-note singing from the distinctive form of music notation used in its tune books. It is also known as fa-so-la singing from the syllables that are associated with the shape-notes. Shape-note singing has survived the twentieth century, however, because a small band of singers has remained loyal to the tradition's greatest tune book, *The Sacred Harp* (1844), and kept alive the practices of the American singing school.[1] To those singers, people of the rural South, this kind of sacred-song making is known simply as Sacred Harp singing.

Though not a southerner, I too am a Sacred Harp singer and have participated in singings since 1975. My account of this sacred-song tradition is informed not only by the observed performances, interviews with music makers, and historical and musical commentaries that comprise other chapters of this book, but also by my own experience of the people and the singings that have sustained Sacred Harp in the late twentieth century.

Little Vine

Along State Route 5 in Blount County, Alabama, there are more signs for churches than for any other human activity. Leaving the interstate about thirty miles above Birmingham, Route 5's two winding lanes traverse the piedmont below Sand Mountain, southernmost ridge of the Appalachians. Running through dense forests of red oak, poplar, butternut, long-leaf pine, mimosa, sumac, and kudzu, the road occasionally discloses small farmhouses and trailers set in clearings, and little country churches with names like Enterprise Church of God and Harmony Baptist Church.

About seven miles down Route 5 lies Creeltown, a tiny settlement whose only public building is Little Vine Primitive Baptist Church.[2] Little Vine is a one-story, white-painted cinder-block structure measuring about twenty-five by fifty feet. A pediment over front double doors, supported by two wrought-iron pillars, is its only external architectural feature. Inside, a poured concrete slab serves as the floor. Light-blue paint adorns the walls, pierced by two windows on each side. Beautiful tongue-and-groove oak paneling covers the low ten-foot ceiling. Two ranks of twelve pews occupy the floor, separated by a central aisle. The raised sanctuary consists of a simple pulpit flanked by two lecterns; all three structures are hand-made of wood and painted dark gray. There is no internal decoration whatsoever.

Normally the congregation numbers fewer than twenty members, but on a sultry Sunday morning in mid-June 1993, nearly one hundred men, women, and children crowded into the church for Little Vine's annual singing of *The Sacred Harp*. On this day the two front pews had been reversed to face the congregation. Three more pews had been drawn up perpendicularly on each side of the front pews. This arrangement cleared a hollow square roughly ten by ten feet. Three large fans produced a semblance of cross-ventilation in the steamy building, and a large cooler of ice water stood on a table at the rear of the church.

By midmorning enough singers had arrived to begin. Those singing the melody or "lead" part sat facing the pulpit. Most of the lead singers were men, joined by women who sang the melody an octave above. Opposite the leads sat the altos or "counters," all women. Basses gathered to the left of the leads, with sopranos or "trebles," a mixed group of women and men in roughly inverse proportion to the leads, assembled to their right. At the beginning of the singing there were perhaps twelve lead singers and six on each of the other parts. By mid-afternoon the number had doubled.

Shortly after ten o'clock Harrison Creel, a distinguished elder of the church, moved to the center of the hollow square and called the community to order by announcing the first hymn. "Let's begin with page 30, top," he said. While thirty pairs of hands opened their red oblong tune books to the correct tune, Thomas Waller's "Love Divine" (1869), Creel pitched the tonic note of the tune without the aid of a pitch pipe. The singers quickly sounded the first note of their respective parts. Harrison immediately dropped the downbeat, his right hand flat and fully extended, beating time with a simple up-and-down movement.

Instead of words, however, the singers first sang their parts in syllables aligned with the music. Instead of standard round notes, *The Sacred Harp* was printed on oblong pages in a system of music notation called "shape-notes." The notes appeared in their normal place on the staff, but they came in four shapes: triangles, ovals, squares, and diamonds. Each shape was coded to a syllable and sung accordingly: triangles were "fa," ovals were "sol," squares were "la," and diamonds were "mi." When all four parts sang their different lines in these shape-notes, syllabic cacophony ensued. Yet out of the syllabic babble emerged a soaring melody from the leads and primal harmonies from the trebles, counters, and basses.

After the tune had been completely sounded out in shape-note syllables, the singers plunged into the words of the text, a version of Charles Wesley's great 1747 Methodist hymn, "Love Divine, All Loves Excelling," sung to Thomas Waller's 1869 setting, a "plain tune" in which all parts sing the same syllable of text on the same beat (example 7 on page 339):

> Love divine, all love excelling,
> Joy of heav'n to earth come down;
> Fix in us Thy humble dwelling,
> All Thy faithful mercies crown!
> Jesus, Thou art all compassion,
> Pure, unbounded love Thou art;
> Visit us with Thy salvation;
> Enter ev'ry trembling heart.

At the conclusion of "Love Divine," Harrison Creel greeted the singers and asked Mark Davis, a valued younger singer visiting from Oxford, Mississippi, to open the singing with morning prayer. Mark asked God to bless our gathering, to honor the worship we were about to bring, and to keep us on the way of salvation through Jesus Christ. As the singers settled back into their pews, Henry Guthery, vice-chairman of the day's singing, moved to the center of the square and called page 59, "Holy Manna," an 1819 revival hymn by George Atkin set to an 1825 camp-meeting tune by William Moore (example 8 on page 340). Sung first in shape-notes, then with words, the hymn served as a kind of musical invocation for the rest of the day:

> Brethren, we have met to worship,
> And adore the Lord our God;
> Will you pray with all your power,
> While we try to preach the word?
> All is vain unless the Spirit

Of the Holy One comes down;
Brethren, pray and holy manna
Will be showered all around.

Sisters, will you join and help us?
Moses' sisters aided him;
Will you help the trembling mourners,
Who are struggling hard with sin?
Tell them all about the Saviour,
Tell them that He will be found;
Sisters, pray, and holy manna
Will be showered all around.

After "Holy Manna," Creel informed us that the arrangements for the day's singing would be handled by his sister, Edith Creel Tate, like him one of the famed Creel family of Sacred Harp singers, four generations of whom were present on this occasion. It was Edith's task to obtain a list of leaders to conduct a "lesson" of one or two hymns from the tune book, and to call their names in appropriate order. The chairman also noted that Kathleen Robbins would serve as secretary, compiling an accurate list of leaders and their lessons.

"Our first leader will be Kathleen Robbins," Edith announced, "followed by Gertrude Woods." Kathleen rose from her seat calling out "thirty-seven bottom," made her way to the center of the square, faced the lead section, and obtained the pitch from the chairman seated on the innermost lead pew. After the singers found their notes, she launched into "Liverpool," another plain tune arranged in 1835 by M. C. H. Davis to words from *Hall's New Collection* (1804). For her second tune Kathleen chose page 142, "Stratfield," 1719 text by Isaac Watts and 1786 tune by Ezra Goff (example 9 on page 341). One of the oldest American tunes in *The Sacred Harp*, "Stratfield" offered a prayer of praise to the creator through a lively and complex musical setting:

Through ev'ry age, eternal God,
Thou art our rest, our safe abode;
High was Thy throne ere heav'n was made,
Or earth Thy humble footstool laid.

Unlike the previous plain tunes, "Stratfield" had a different structure, called a "fuging tune," featuring a setting of the third and fourth lines of each verse in which different parts entered at different points of the musical figure, combining in a powerful final cadence.

The singing had now fairly begun, and for the next hour and a half leaders were called and tunes sung without a break. By noontime nearly thirty tunes had been sung, an average of one tune every three minutes, always including the shape-notes and several verses. There was little time for rest under such a regimen of extended singing and increasing heat. Yet the voices seemed to gather strength and volume as the morning progressed.

Shortly before noon Harrison Creel adjourned the singing for an hour, asking Davis to bless the traditional "dinner on the grounds" about to commence. And what a feast it was! Six picnic tables were set up end to end in front of the church and laden with homemade dishes. Platters of fried chicken, baked ham, smoked turkey, and barbecued ribs vied for space on the crowded tables with bowls of fried okra, sweet potato pie, black-eyed peas, baked beans, and collard greens. One end of the groaning board was reserved for desserts: peach and cherry cobbler, chess pie, lemon meringue pie, coconut custard pie, chocolate pie. Two ten-gallon urns of iced tea shared space with the desserts.

Singers gathered in small groups, cups and plates in hand, renewing old acquaintances and swapping stories as they ate. Laughter and the relaxed hum of familiar conversation bathed the churchyard. Some singers walked up the hill to the cemetery to reflect on this memorial singing day. Meanwhile more new singers arrived, some from local church services, others visiting from northern cities. At one o'clock everyone returned to the church for the afternoon singing. Edith Creel Tate resumed the calling of leaders. At first the singing was a bit indifferent; the singers' bodies were still digesting glorious southern country cooking into musical energy. After ten tunes or so that energy began to kick in, along with hand fans that sprouted everywhere in the hollow square as the humid room approached 90 degrees. With seventy or so singers, nearly twice as many as in the morning, the singing sharply mounted in volume and spiritual intensity.

Annual Sacred Harp singings typically include a morning "memorial lesson," during which those who have died are named and remembered by a brief eulogy and specially selected hymns. Little Vine, however, was a memorial singing per se: every leader was free to lead a lesson in commemoration of one who has passed on. In the early afternoon, several leaders made such remarks about the tunes they called, exhorting us to "live the words" that we were about to sing. Around two o'clock one of the visiting leaders called page 192, "Schenectady," text by Isaac Watts (1719) and fuging tune by Nehemiah Shumway (1805). He struck a lively tempo and the singers suddenly ran with it, galvanizing their spiritual and vocal intensity into a blazing rendition of this venerable tune. The musical vitality of the singing jumped exponentially, as successive leaders called especially vigorous lessons. The Little Vine singing had reached its zenith of spiritual power and musical energy.

It is difficult to describe what a Sacred Harp singing in a rural southern church sounds like at full cry. The first impression is that of being engulfed by a massive outburst of choral sound. Harrison Creel said that singing at Little Vine "sounds like the inside of a banjo," noting how the building's low wooden roof and dry concrete surfaces create a powerfully resonant sound environment for the singing. The music focuses quadrophonically at the center of the hollow square, delivered by a large closely packed group of singers singing their parts with extraordinary volume, range, and precision. It is hard to believe that these otherwise ordinary-looking people can sing so loud and so high for even a few songs, let alone for two hours straight or all day with only a few breaks. As they do, other characteristics of this relentless succession of powerfully sung tunes become clear.

These people do not produce the round tone and vibrato typical of white church choirs. They produce a flat, piercing vocal tone without vibrato. As in other sacred choral traditions, the Russian Orthodox for example, each part has a specific tone quality and tuning. The basses rumble low and resonant, then stretch out for high phrases reaching beyond middle C. The lead melody line routinely rises to F, G, and even A above middle C, all brought with a full-throated force that sometimes shades over into pure shout. Trebles, on the other hand, tend to float lightly on their harmony part, its range even higher than the leads. Altos, taxed with the least melodically interesting part, make a virtue of necessity by creating subtle tunings for those few notes. Often they will sing their harmonies slightly flat or sharp, lending an archaic modal sound to the ensemble. And they deliver all of this with a laser-like chest tone quality that could shatter glass.

There are other distinctive qualities of Sacred Harp singing beyond volume, range, and tone. Each part has its own melodic interest, and the harmonic relations of the whole, called "dispersed harmony," often produce unusual and powerful effects. This unique synergy of parts seems to embody Walt Whitman's "barbaric yawp" of democratic song. The singers at Little Vine pronounced words according to their Deep South dialect and they did not necessarily sing all the notes on the page. They routinely transformed minor key into Dorian mode by raising the sixth degree of the scale. Complex folk ornaments and inflections—scoops, slides, snaps, even an occasional yodel—embellished virtually every tune. The more lively tunes achieved a driving accent or shake that is impossible to express in musical notation. And in certain tunes the singers defied the most basic rule of choral phrasing, refusing to breathe at the punctuation marks or phrase breaks, pausing instead at points dictated by oral tradition.

As the afternoon wore on at Little Vine, singers sustained an extraordinary level of musical and spiritual energy for more than an hour and a half without a break, until Harrison Creel finally called the singing to a close around 3:30. Kathleen Robbins reported that sixty-one songs had been led by fifty-three leaders. A half-dozen singers announced forthcoming singings later in the year. Edith Creel Tate then called "Parting Hand," the traditional closing plain tune arranged by William Walker in 1835 with 1818 words by John Blain, testifying that it was "the last song my mother ever led" and urging us all to heed its message (example 10 on page 342). Everyone stood, and as the song rang out, the officers of the singing moved slowly around the hollow square shaking hands and bidding farewell to each singer.

My Christian friends, in bonds of love,
Whose hearts in sweetest union join,
Your friendship's like a drawing band,
Yet we must take the parting hand.

Your comp'ny's sweet, your union dear,
Your words delightful to my ear,
Yet when I see that we must part,
You draw like cords around my heart.

Mark Davis offered a closing prayer to ask God's blessing and protection on the singers. Within a half hour the church had been cleaned and secured, the cemetery deserted, and the singers scattered to every point of the compass. The 1993 Little Vine Memorial Singing receded into the murky summer afternoon, ageless as the Alabama woods that gave it birth.

The American Singing School

Sacred Harp singers are not trained in the conservatory sense. They offer their unvarnished praise to God without concern for the sound of their individual voices. Yet their singing is not simply ad hoc vocal expression. It, too, is a learned style, and a unique one at that, for Sacred Harp singing preserves the techniques of the singing school, the oldest American form of music education, even as it maintains one of the last remaining examples of authentic oral tradition in white American Protestant music.[3]

The American singing school began as a reaction to the common practice of unison psalm singing in colonial New England. Following the teachings of Protestant reformer John Calvin, the New England Puritans believed that the only fit texts for Christian worship had been provided in the Scriptures. Those most important were in the Psalms. In the mid-sixteenth century at Geneva, Switzerland, Calvin had prescribed vernacular translations of the Psalms rendered in simple poetic meters and set to tunes for unison singing. The complete *Genevan Psalter*, with texts by Clement Marot and Theodore Beza and tunes by Louis Bourgeois and Guillaume Franc, appeared in 1562. Geneva set the standard for Reformed psalters.[4] In Britain, for example, both Thomas Sternhold and Thomas Hopkins's *Whole Booke of Psalmes* (1562), the first authorized psalter of the Church of England, and John Knox's Presbyterian *Scottish Psalter* (1564), were modeled on Genevan precedent. The Puritans who settled the Massachusetts Bay colony followed the same pattern, issuing their own translation in *The Bay Psalm Book* (1640), the first book printed in British North America. In the 1698 edition, they added thirteen psalm tunes from John Playford's *Brief Introduction to the Skill of Music* (1672) for singing.[5]

By 1720, however, the clumsy texts and limited musical resources of *The Bay*

Psalm Book had created a liturgical crisis in New England's churches. For Thomas Walter of Roxbury and John Tufts of Newbury, the problem lay squarely with the musical decline of what they called the "customary" or "usual" manner of singing the psalms. A major source of this musical declension was the practice of "lining out," in which church deacons or designated "precentors" led psalm singing by reading each line of the text before the congregation sang it. While lining out guaranteed that the people understood the words they were singing, it also ensured that their singing would lose much of its musicality. Walter reported that "the tunes [of *The Bay Psalm Book*] are now miserably tortured and twisted and quavered in some churches into a horrid medley of confused and disorderly noises." In his opinion, the already fragile repertory of psalm tunes had fallen victim to so many evils, including tone-deaf deacons, slow tempos, lower pitches, inaccurate intervals, improvised part singing, "falling-in" from one tune to another, and vocal ornaments of such "quaverings, turnings, and flourishes" that psalm singing sounded like "five hundred different tunes roared out at the same time."[6]

To remedy this crisis of praise, Walter and Tufts prescribed "regular singing," or singing "by rule," *regula* in Latin. By this term they meant that New England Congregationalists should appropriate the rules of music literacy and basic choral technique. The improvement of sacred song, they argued, required that every worshiper know how to read a musical score and how to sing accurately. To that end in 1721 both of them published singing manuals keyed to the small tune repertory of *The Bay Psalm Book:* Walter's *Grounds and Rules of Musick* and Tufts's *Introduction to the Singing of Psalm Tunes.* Walter and Tufts also called for the creation of singing schools, in which qualified singing masters would teach the rudiments of musical notation and vocal production to New England parishes. Walter himself led the first singing school, the Society for Promoting Regular Singing in the Worship of God, from 1720 to 1723 in Boston.[7]

New resources for the singing school lay close at hand. Sudden changes in both poetic style and parish music had transformed English Congregationalist worship at the turn of the eighteenth century. The new texts and tunes easily crossed the Atlantic to assist the fledgling singing-school movement in New England. The crucial moment in the emergence of the new poetics of worship was the "system of praise" proposed and carried out by Isaac Watts (1674–1748), English Congregationalist minister, theologian, and educator. In 1706 Watts published *Horae Lyricae: Poems chiefly of the Lyrical kind,* followed the next year by *Hymns and Spiritual Songs in Three Books* and, in 1719, *The Psalms of David Imitated in the Language of the New Testament and Applied to the Christian State and Worship.* These collections permanently changed both the theory and literary style of the English hymn.[8]

Watts challenged Reformed tradition, claiming that the Psalms were too constraining a standard for Christian worshipers, whose spiritual experience had moved beyond the light of ancient Israel into the blazing noonday of the gospel. Hence, he argued, original songs of Christian experience were warranted, indeed necessary, for authentic worship. He insisted further that the Psalms themselves required modification for Christian worship. While he granted that David was unquestionably a chosen instrument of God, Watts claimed that his religious understanding could not have fully apprehended the truths later revealed through Jesus Christ. The Psalms should therefore be "renovated" as if David had been a Christian, or as Watts put it in the title of his 1719 metrical psalter, they should be "imitated in the language of the New Testament."[9]

To this doctrinal "renovation" Watts brought a new poetic style of subjectivity and emotion. In hymns like "When I Survey the Wondrous Cross," Watts's voice broke down the distance between poet and singer and invested the text with personal spirituality. Yet Watts also achieved what Donald Davie has called an "axiomatic" quality in his verse that presented Christian doctrinal content with the explicit confidence that befits affirmations of faith, as in "Joy to the World" and "From All That Dwell Below the Skies," his setting of Psalm 117.[10] This blend of emotional subjectivity and doctrinal objectivity enabled Watts's poems, as he put it, to "[copy] the most frequent tempers and changes of our spirit, and conditions of our life, . . . our passions, our love, our fear, our hope, our desire, our sorrow, our wonder, and our joy, as they are refin'd into devotion, and act under the influence and conduct of the blessed Spirit."[11]

Watts cast his hymns in a rhetoric deliberately designed to gain widest possible acceptance. His first concern was to promote Protestant consensus by focusing on the most essential beliefs of Reformed theology and the promotion of a deeply emotional piety while "avoid[ing] the more obscure and controverted points of Christianity." To present that agenda in the clearest possible terms, Watts adopted a poetics of extreme simplicity. He employed poetic figures gauged to reach the lowest common denominator of popular understanding. "The metaphors are generally sunk to the level of vulgar capacities," he wrote, "and endeavour'd to make the Sense plain and obvious." Watts also "aimed at ease of numbers and smoothness of sound" by limiting the meters of his poems generally to only four syllabic patterns: Long Meter (8–8–8–8), Common Meter (8–6–8–6), Short Meter (6–6–8–6), and Half Meter (6–6–8–8).[12]

Watts's theology and rhetoric of sacred song gradually gained acceptance on both sides of the Atlantic. In colonial America, Watts became the most published poet of the eighteenth century. Forty-seven American editions of *Hymns and Spiritual Songs* and ninety-nine of *The Psalms of David Imitated* poured from American presses before 1800. Watts's example fostered generations of Evangelical poets including British hymn writers Charles Wesley, Edward Perronet, Anne Steele, Samuel Stennett, Augustus Toplady, John Newton, William Cowper, and Reginald Heber, along with American hymnographers such as Samuel Davies, Timothy Dwight, John Leland, and Peter Cartwright, all of whose lyrics joined Watts's in making up the lyrical content of *The Sacred Harp*.[13]

A new style of English sacred song also informed the rise of the American singing school. Called English country parish music, the new style provided small rural congregations with sacred compositions that were musically accomplished, yet could be well performed by a limited number of singers. It was the sort of music John and Charles Wesley heard and sang growing up in their father's Anglican parish at rural Epworth in Lincolnshire.[14] Composers for the English country parish like William Knapp, Joseph Stephenson, William Tans'ur, and Aaron Williams wrote in three principal musical forms: the plain tune, the fuging tune, and the anthem. The plain tune was simply a harmonized psalm-tune inspired by the chorales of Bach and the other German Baroque masters. The melody appeared in the tenor or lead part and was surrounded by freestanding harmonic lines in the bass, counter (alto), and treble (soprano) parts. Very little ornamentation occurred in any of the parts, and the whole composition was arranged homophonically. The plain tune created a core of worship music that was easy to sing, yet musically and spiritually satisfying.

At the other end of the compositional spectrum, the English country composers created anthems that incorporated more difficult choral elements of the baroque style. The anthem usually set an extended free text rather than a metrical psalm or hymn, typically a biblical passage such as the Song of Solomon, the Lamentations of Jeremiah, or Mary's Magnificat in the Gospel of St. Luke. The absence of metrical constraints provided the composer with a more extensive textual structure as well as more freedom to develop choral effects and tone painting. Melody could move more easily from part to part than in plain tunes, key and rhythm changed suddenly, ornament and harmony amplified the emotional and theological impact of the text. In greatly simplified form the English country parish anthem recalled the complex choral compositions of Bach and the German baroque masters, particularly in its use of extended melismatic melody, complex counterpoint, harmonic suspension, and, above all, the art of the fugue.

The third major form of English country parish music, the "fuging tune," combined features of the plain tune with those of the anthem. The first section or "head" of the tune corresponded exactly to the plain tune, setting the first two lines of a metrical psalm or hymn quatrain in four-part homophony. A fugal section set the third and fourth lines of text, with each part entering separately on a similar musical figure. The most characteristic form of the fuging section commenced with a bass entry, followed in turn by the lead or melody part, trebles, and finally altos. After the entry of all four parts, the composition proceeded by free melody and counterpoint to a final cadence. For emphasis, the fuging section was usually repeated.

It took another generation for these new poetical and musical styles to penetrate the American colonies. The ground was prepared between 1726 and 1755 by the Great Awakening, America's first great religious revival, which created a vast new constituency for the emotionally charged and doctrinally laden lyrics of Watts and his followers. The Awakening was sparked by an intercolonial network of itinerant evangelists led by George Whitefield, Jonathan Edwards, and

Gilbert Tennent. Along with their fiery preaching, the itinerants disseminated Wattsian hymnody to Congregationalists, Presbyterians, and Baptists everywhere in the British colonies.

The classic example of this kind of transmission occurred in 1741, when Whitefield preached at the Northampton, Massachusetts, parish of Jonathan Edwards on his evangelistic tour at the height of the Awakening. During his visit Whitefield gave Edwards a copy of Watts's *Hymns and Spiritual Songs* and *The Psalms of David Imitated* to use in his worship services. Less than a year later, Edwards reported that his congregation had embraced Watts's hymns so ardently that they "sang nothing else, and neglected the Psalms wholly." Their singing was probably worth hearing as well, because the Northampton parish had begun regular harmonized singing of *The Bay Psalm Book* tunes as early as 1722. During a 1736 revival Edwards reported that "our congregation excelled all that I ever knew in [public praise] before, generally carrying regularly and well, *three parts of music,* and the women a part by themselves."[15]

American collections of the new English country parish music began to appear shortly after the Awakening. In 1761 Princeton graduate, Philadelphia singing master, and evangelical Presbyterian minister James Lyon published *Urania; or a Choice Collection of Psalm-Tunes, Anthems, and Hymns,* the first major compilation of sacred music edited and published in America. *Urania* included a large group of four-part English plain tunes along with the first printed music by Americans, including Francis Hopkinson, William Tuckey, and Lyon himself. Meanwhile in New England, Paul Revere engraved 116 English plain tunes and two anthems for Josiah Flagg's *Collection of the Best Psalm Tunes,* published at Newburyport, Massachusetts, in 1764.[16] Comprehensive editions of English collections and manuals of composition, most notably William Tans'ur's *Royal Harmony Compleat* were also reprinted in New England, making the technical details of the new style readily available to aspiring American composers.[17]

By 1770, British Reformed churches in America, especially the Evangelical or New Light Congregationalist parishes of New England, had become seedbeds for a new American synthesis of sacred song.[18] That synthesis was wrought almost single-handedly by William Billings of Boston, tanner, patriot, moderate Congregationalist, and self-taught singing master and composer. In 1770 Billings published *The New-England Psalm-Singer,* the first printed collection of sacred music wholly composed by an American. *The New-England Psalm-Singer* contained 126 compositions in the style of Tans'ur, the great majority of them plain tunes, along with a sprinkling of anthems and fuging tunes. Virtually all of Billings's metrical texts were written by Watts. And Billings acknowledged his debt to Whitefield by printing the great evangelist's own hymn, "Ah! Lovely Appearance of Death," at the end of the book. Whitefield had died at Newburyport, Massachusetts, the same week that Billings completed and signed his preface to the tune collection.

Billings sounded a characteristically American note of cultural independence in his introduction to *The New-England Psalm-Singer*. Rules of composition have their legitimate use, he wrote, but "nature is the best dictator" of musical genius. "I don't think myself confin'd to any Rules for Composition laid down by any that went before me," he continued, "neither should I think (were I to pretend to lay down Rules) that any who came after me were any ways obligated to adhere to them, any further than they should think proper." Over the next thirty years Billings published five more volumes of music, each of them exhibiting greater originality than the one before, and conducted singing schools throughout eastern Massachusetts.[19]

Billings's example of musical originality, prolific composition, and itinerant singing-school mastership created a vocational model for other tunesmiths. Immediately after the Revolution, a cadre of young singing masters fanned out across New England, carrying Billings's music and composing their own. By 1810 they had published more than five hundred sacred music imprints, most of them texted by Watts and the British Evangelical poets. Two centuries later, the most popular of their compositions still make up the musical core of *The Sacred Harp*.[20]

The New England singing school spread rapidly through the early republic, funded primarily by private subscriptions paid to the singing master for two to six weeks of daily instruction. Masters were also permitted to sell their music collections to the students as textbooks. Few singing masters, however, were able to support themselves and their families by musical activities alone until after 1800, when the development of shape-note music notation propelled the singing school from a regional New England institution into the principal vehicle for music education in the new republic.

Shape-notes were based on syllabic systems of scale-singing dating back to medieval times. Guido of Arezzo (c. 995–1035) is credited with the invention of the first Western syllabic system of scale-singing, which evolved into the familiar Italian "do-re-mi" style. In 1597 English composer and organist Thomas Morley published a four-syllable system for singing the scale "fa-so-la-fa-so-la-mi" in his *Plain and Easie Introduction to Practicall Musicke*. Morley's scale scheme was adopted in Anglo-America and transmitted into popular music culture. *The Bay Psalm Book*'s first musical scores, for example, published in 1698, contained not only the pitches on the staff but also letters below the staff indicating their solfa syllables according to Morley's scheme. John Tufts experimented with using these solfa letters on the staff instead of note heads, a form of notation that persisted in New England music imprints as late as 1760.[21]

An experiment by singing masters William Little and William Smith transformed syllabic scale-singing into an effective device for music education. Little and Smith printed their 1801 tune book *The Easy Instructor* in a four-shape notation system that followed Morley's traditional syllables, yet was printed on ledger lines. What made their "shape-notes" so important was their utility as a teaching tool for music literacy. By giving a specific shape to each of Morley's syllables (fa = triangle, so = oval, la = square, mi = diamond) and placing them on the standard music staff, called the "gamut," Little and Smith created a form of notation that could be read by trained musicians and also ciphered out by traditional singers who sang the fa-so-la scale (example 11 on page 343). The latter already knew that the first three notes—fa-so-la—repeated twice in the scale. The new shape-note system allowed traditional singers to visualize these already familiar tonal relationships on the standard five-line musical ledger and thereby enabled them easily to read more than 85 percent of the notes.[22]

Armed with shape notation, a phalanx of singing masters, and a growing repertory of texts and tunes, the singing school spread rapidly everywhere in the new republic after 1800, fueled by another vast upsurge of popular evangelical religion known as the Second Great Awakening (1799–1844). As the singing school took root in the Middle States, the Ohio Valley, and the South, its tune books acquired new musical forms and hymn texts. The most prominent ritual feature of the Second Awakening was the camp meeting, a multiday outdoor assembly featuring round-the-clock preaching and spectacular episodes of charismatic experience. The camp meeting's spontaneity and crowded conditions demanded a simpler form of sacred singing. That form quickly emerged as the camp-meeting song, a plain tune with a repeated refrain often improvised in the heat of revival fervor. The camp-meeting song invited singing masters to incorporate folksongs, popular melodies, fiddle tunes, drinking choruses, and work songs into revival singing. Outside the camp meeting, they adapted traditional folk melodies to create evocative spiritual ballads of evangelical religious experience.

The greatest denominational beneficiaries of the Second Great Awakening were the Methodists. As the singing school spread south and west, composers and editors added the great corpus of Methodist hymnody to their tune books, supplementing the established evangelical Calvinist literary canon of Watts and his successors with the poetry of Charles Wesley and other British Methodists. By 1820 Methodist lyrics like Wesley's "Jesus, Lover of My Soul" and "Love Divine, All Loves Excelling" had gained national popularity equal to any of Watts's lyrics.

A series of accomplished southern and western tune books appeared during the Second Awakening, including John Wyeth's *Repository of Sacred Music* (1813), A. D. Carden's *Missouri Harmony* (1820), and William Walker's *Southern Harmony and Musical Companion* (1835). Georgia Baptist singing masters Benjamin Franklin White and E. J. King added to that list by publishing *The Sacred Harp* (1844), which found an extraordinarily large and loyal following among southern evangelicals. *The Sacred Harp* contained not only the latest camp-meeting songs and spiritual ballads from the South, but also a comprehensive collection of earlier tunes and anthems from New England, the Middle States, and the Ohio Valley.[23]

The Sacred Harp represented the musical zenith of the singing-school tradition, but by 1844 that tradition was already being undermined by the introduction of European sacred music into American churches. Foremost champion of this "better music" for worship was Lowell Mason (1792–1872), Congregationalist composer, church musician, and music educator from Boston. In 1822 Mason published *The Boston Handel and Haydn Society Collection of Church Music,* a collection of sacred music featuring harmonized hymn settings of tunes drawn from noted European composers including Mozart, Haydn, and even Beethoven, that eventually ran to nineteen editions through 1839. Mason's 1826 *Oration on Church Music* presented a blistering attack on singing schools and his own theory of hymnody as oratory and prayer. Mason's work swiftly changed musical taste in wealthy urban congregations on the East Coast and powerfully encouraged the rise of professional church choirs, directors, and organists. Gradually Mason's reforms reached the rising cities of the West. While the singing school and its music still maintained a firm grip on rural and frontier America, by the Civil War the works of Mason and his colleagues had replaced them in America's cities with sacred music determined more by art than by religious tradition.[24]

After the Civil War shape-note singing gradually disappeared from New England, the Middle States, and the Old Northwest, but it retained a hold on popular religious culture in the South. Southern singers organized hundreds of annual singings of *The Sacred Harp* and other tune books at local churches and courthouses. During the early decades of the twentieth century, however, the enormous popularity of gospel hymns drew off much of the shape-note constituency. Gospel hymns were sentimental spiritual lyrics of the mid- and late nineteenth century set to various styles of Victorian popular music. They were first popularized in America during the 1870s by the revival team of Dwight L. Moody and Ira D. Sankey. Southern Baptists and Methodists in particular embraced gospel hymns and sponsored regional singing "conventions" that successfully challenged the singing-school tradition. Between the world wars the advent of modern music education, the automobile, and mass media further circumscribed the cultural niche of the singing school. At mid-century, folklorists and musicologists began to study Sacred Harp singings as part of their effort to record fragile early American cultural forms, and by the 1970s the survival of the tradition itself was in serious doubt.

In the 1992–93 edition of the *Directory and Minutes of Sacred Harp Singings,* compiler Nora Parker listed only 207 annual singings still active and remarked poignantly that "we had only five singings called off this year; this is a big improvement over last year. But in the past nine years we have had seventy one singings discontinued."[25] Annual convention singings of other tune books including *The Southern Harmony, The Social Harp, The Christian Harmony,* and *The New Harp of Columbia* also still existed in the South, but in severely attenuated form. More than two centuries after William Billings and *The New-England Psalm-Singer,* the great American tradition of singing schools and shape-note singing faced a new and uncertain future.

The New North

The Little Vine singing and two hundred like it scattered throughout the rural South faithfully preserve the historic practices of the early American singing school. But Sacred Harp has encountered challenges over the past quarter-century that have created a complex new pattern of religious meanings attached to American Protestantism's oldest sacred-song tradition. If Little Vine represents Sacred Harp singing in a pristine historical form, the national convention at Birmingham exhibits its changing complexion since the mid-1970s.

Organized by Hugh McGraw and Rosa Hughes, the National Sacred Harp Singing Convention first assembled at Birmingham's Samford University on June 11, 1981. The three-day singing drew more than 750 singers, the great majority of them from the Deep South. McGraw and Hughes planned the convention to promote nationwide bonds of musical, social, and spiritual community by revitalizing the singing school and southern Sacred Harp traditions. The national convention, however, did not fare especially well at first. Within five years, attendance at Birmingham had halved, and it sustained at that level for nearly a decade. In recent years, however, attendance has begun to increase, with 451 registrants reported for the 1998 convention.

Many reasons account for Birmingham's career: long distances, the mid-June date, in-house disputes, and the shifting demography of the singers, especially the passing of the oldest generation of traditional southern singers. In 1993, for example, the memorial lesson at Birmingham included names of fifty-seven singers who had died during the previous year. By contrast, nearly one-quarter of the singers at that convention were visitors from the North, Midwest, and Pacific coast. This new infusion of singers began in earnest during the early 1980s and continued to grow steadily through the 1990s. Ironically enough, the national convention seems more likely to fulfill its promise of becoming the central institution of Sacred Harp singing because of its increasing geographical diversity rather than its original mission of promoting the tradition's southern base.

Since 1976 Sacred Harp singing groups have sprung up in northern urban and university centers across the nation, many of them established by scholars and musicians eager to preserve the tradition. Today the tide of Sacred Harp singing runs powerfully toward these new northern singers. The absolute decline in numbers of Sacred Harp singers ended around 1990, but as older southern singers have passed on, their place has been taken by new northern singers rather than by their grandchildren. *Sacred Harp Singings, 1998 and 1999* lists a core constituency of two thousand singers by name and address. More than eight hundred of them live in the North and more are being recruited every week. Editor Shelbie Sheppard reported 264 annual singings for 1998, a vigorous increase of fifty-six since 1992. Part of this apparent growth derives from Sheppard's exhaustive research, but fully fifty of the 264 listed annual singings were northern. And most new singings continue to be organized in the North. Of 128 recently established local singings also listed in *Sacred Harp Singings, 1998 and 1999,* seventy-one are northern.[26]

The revival of northern interest in Sacred Harp began principally in academic circles. During the 1940s and 1950s, Sacred Harp singing was made available to northern scholars and musicians through the writings of Vanderbilt University scholar George Pullen Jackson and the field recordings of Alan Lomax, curator of folk music for the Smithsonian Institution.[27] In the late 1960s and early 1970s this academic treatment of shape-note traditions converged with an upsurge of popular interest in American folk-music traditions, including Sacred Harp singing. At places like Old Joe Clark's in Cambridge, Massachusetts, and the Old Town School of Music in Chicago, and at folk festivals throughout the land, musicians gathered to share an occasional Sacred Harp tune along with the more common fare of folk ballads and fiddle tunes. Awareness of the southern tradition grew slowly, but by the early 1970s copies of *The Sacred Harp* had begun to find their way into northern urban hands, often accompanied by interest in preserving an authentic but threatened American musical tradition.

Meanwhile, music historians took a different approach, seeking to include singing-school compositions in the national music canon. In 1964 Irving Lowens published *Music and Musicians in Early America,* a landmark collection of essays that established the historical importance of Billings and his generation of composers. At the same time H. Wiley Hitchcock began to publish facsimile editions of early tune books in his Earlier American Music Series, which made some of the singing-school repertory available to northern choral conductors and church musicians for the first time in a century. During the 1970s several major music faculties, most notably at the University of Illinois and the University of Michigan, launched extensive research into the lives, careers, and music of the early singing masters and composers. Meanwhile conservatory-trained artists like the Gregg Smith Singers and the Western Wind Ensemble began to perform arrangements of early American compositions.[28]

New England, historic home of Billings and the singing school, was the first region outside the South to convene an annual Sacred Harp singing convention. Organized by Neely Bruce, Larry Gordon, Poppy Gregory, and Juanita Kyle, the first New England convention met at Wesleyan University in Middletown, Connecticut, on October 2, 1976, bolstered by a busload of traditional singers led by Hugh McGraw. Since then the New England convention has drawn two to three hundred singers annually, rotating on a three-year cycle from Wesleyan to churches and grange halls around Montpelier, Vermont, to Wellesley College and Andover Newton Theological School near Boston.

New England at first developed a regional pattern of Sacred Harp singing based not in local communities but rather in performance groups specializing in *The Sacred Harp* and early New England hymnody. Three groups have dominated the New England Sacred Harp revival: Larry Gordon's Word of Mouth Chorus at Montpelier, Vermont, succeeded by his Bayley-Hazen Singers and

Village Harmony; Neely Bruce's American Music Theater Group at Wesleyan University; and my own Norumbega Harmony, founded at Wellesley College.

Over the past two decades these ensembles have presented performances and workshops in New England churches, theaters, libraries, schools, and museums designed to expose audiences to Sacred Harp tradition and to recruit new singers. More recently, members of these groups have helped to establish a network of monthly singings throughout the region, so that by 1998 it was possible to spend virtually every Sunday of the year at a local New England Sacred Harp singing. Just as New England singers sparked the Sacred Harp revival in 1976 by organizing the first annual convention in the North, twenty-five years later they are pioneering the next phase of that revival by creating the first viable regional network of local singings outside the South.

Since 1980 nearly twenty new regional annual conventions have also been organized, more than half of them at northern sites, including Chicago; Central Illinois; Washington, D.C.; St. Louis; Madison, Wisconsin; San Francisco; Ithaca, New York; Boulder, Colorado; Minneapolis; Portland, Oregon; Columbus, Ohio; and Montclair, New Jersey. This list confirms the ongoing connection of the Sacred Harp revival with university communities and urban professionals. Chicago, for example, boasts perhaps the largest regular singing in the nation, held biweekly at Ida Noyes Hall on the campus of the University of Chicago. At each of these locations, new leaders have emerged with their own appropriations of the Sacred Harp tradition. In most cases they have enthusiastically submitted to the traditional standards of southern singing, but each new northern leader in principle represents another strand of Sacred Harp tradition thriving outside the southern ambit.

New northern singers have begun to reshape the public presentation and perception of Sacred Harp singing through mass media, especially recordings, radio, and the press. In 1979 Larry Gordon's nineteen-voice Word of Mouth Chorus recorded *Rivers of Delight,* a collection of tunes from *The Sacred Harp. Rivers of Delight* was the first recording of its kind. Neither southern field recording nor professional studio work, it presented a distinctive style of precision singing by a talented amateur chorus performing traditional tunes in nontraditional choral arrangements and vocal groupings. Gordon, a self-trained Oregon musician who came east to Vermont in the 1960s, and his recording signaled the emergence of new northern Sacred Harp singers with decidedly nontraditional ideas about performance.[29]

An explosion of recordings by other New England groups followed *Rivers of Delight.* Several northern conventions, notably the Midwest at Chicago and the Central Illinois at Springfield, also produced excellent live recordings. The new northern variety of Sacred Harp singing also appeared on radio and in the national press. During the 1990s the Chicago singing was covered by National Public Radio and Norumbega Harmony by Monitor Radio, while Gordon's Bayley-Hazen Singers performed four times on Garrison Keillor's popular *Prairie Home Companion* show on National Public Radio.[30]

This new northern element has in no way replaced public interpretation of Sacred Harp singing by traditional southern singers. The Sacred Harp Publishing Company has produced recordings since 1965, including *Sacred Harp Bicentennial* in 1976 and *Favorite Songs* and *Amazing Grace* during the 1980s. Fine recordings by singing families like the Creels of Little Vine and the Woottens of Ider, Alabama, have also appeared. In 1999 the Smithsonian Institution released two digitally remastered compact disc recordings of the 1959 Alabama State Convention from the Alan Lomax Collection. The most important media presentation of Sacred Harp singing to date, however, has been Hugh McGraw's appearance with traditional singers from Holly Springs, Georgia, in the highly successful 1990 PBS production, *Amazing Grace with Bill Moyers*. Yet while southern traditional singers continue to attract national attention, theirs is no longer the only public expression and interpretation of Sacred Harp singing. National media have begun to discover northern singing groups and to interpret them as a new phenomenon linked to, yet independent of, the southern tradition.[31]

Perhaps most important of all northern activities has been the rebirth of tune writing and tune-book publishing. In 1980 Vermonters Tony Barrand and Carole Moody produced the first edition of *Northern Harmony: A Collection of Tunes by Early New England Composers*, a small paperbound collection funded by Marlboro College. Four years later Barrand and Moody, joined by Larry Gordon, issued the second edition of *Northern Harmony*, a hardcover book containing fifty-five traditional tunes not from *The Sacred Harp*, along with contemporary northern compositions by Gordon, Neely Bruce, Glen Wright, David Gay, and Andrew Christiansen. The second edition of *Northern Harmony* was the first significant new collection of shape-note tunes to appear in more than a century. Successive editions have added new tunes by established northern composers and by Gordon's young Village Harmony singers.[32]

Other New England collections soon followed, most notably Glen Wright and Susan Mampre's *The Sacred Harper's Companion*, thirty-six new tunes by northern and southern contemporary composers. Gordon's *Emerald Streams*, a collection of tunes by Village Harmony's young composers, Timothy Eriksen's *The New Northampton Collection of Sacred and Secular Harmony*, a grouping of twenty-five new and traditional tunes from the Connecticut Valley, and *The Norumbega Harmony*, a collection of 125 traditional and contemporary tunes culled from that group's twenty-five years of singing together, have also been published over the past decade in New England or are now in press. New collections of traditional tunes have also appeared elsewhere, including the Chicago singers' *The Midwest Supplement to the Sacred Harp*, Karen Willard's *An American Christmas Harp*, and *The Eclectic Harmony*.[33] Few if any of these collections will survive a century and a half as has *The Sacred Harp*, but their mere existence demonstrates that new northern singers have engaged the Sacred Harp tradition at its most significant musical level by producing new collections of old tunes and a large and rapidly growing body of competent and sometimes superlative new ones.

Is Sacred Harp Singing Sacred?

Sacred Harp singing presents an example of public sacred song that is difficult to assess. It is not "public" in the usual sense because there is no audience at singings. Everyone sings. It is also not public worship in the sense that churches perform every week, yet the rituals of the hollow square, the content of the words, and the spiritual attitude of traditional singers clearly mark Sacred Harp as a deeply religious activity. What kind of religiousness, then, does it express for traditional singers? The religious status of Sacred Harp is even more complicated for new northern singers. Whereas the great majority of southern singers come to Sacred Harp through religious, familial, and community networks, most northerners discover it through academic or musical associations. Northern singers do not share the evangelical faith of their southern colleagues, yet they are every bit as committed to Sacred Harp and indisputably find deep personal meaning in it. How can that meaning be described and how does it relate to the explicit religiousness of traditional singers?

To interpret such a complex pattern of religious meaning we need a different set of intellectual tools than those we have been using thus far, a set that will interpret how rapid cultural change has transformed religion in contemporary society. A helpful model comes from the sociology of knowledge, specifically the work of Peter Berger and Thomas Luckmann. In his 1967 book *The Sacred Canopy,* Berger argued that religion's most important function was its ability to construct and maintain a symbolic world that integrates the sum of human activity into a meaningful whole. In traditional societies, religious worldviews confer sacred definition and legitimacy on social, economic, and political systems, making them coherent and effective in everyday life. But modernity, Berger warned, has compromised religion's ability to bind together the meanings of societal and individual existence in a single sacred cosmos.[34]

Luckmann's 1967 book *The Invisible Religion* explained how the modern transformation of economic and political systems into autonomous cultural entities governed by their own secular ideologies has defied the authority of religion to contain them. The sheer size and diversity of modern society has rendered religion just one of many cultural forms competing to invest the newly individualized lives of moderns with larger meaning and significance. What Luckmann called "primary" religious institutions—churches, synagogues, mosques—could no longer supply the full range of sacred meanings necessary to construct and maintain a coherent worldview. Modernity condemned individuals either to construct worldviews for themselves or, at best, to appropriate primary religious institutions selectively. In either case, moderns began to use "secondary" means to encounter and express sacred meanings beyond the reach of traditional religious worldviews and institutions.[35]

The religious meaning of Sacred Harp today, I think, reflects the displacement of the sacred from primary religious institutions to secondary expressions that

Luckmann analyzed. It is actually a double displacement in which the realloca-
tion of sacrality has happened for southern and northern singers in two quite
different ways. That difference may be considered the two opposite ends of the
modernization process Luckmann described. Southern singers grew up before
the modernization of the rural South, and in response to its devastating effects
they have shifted their sacred worldview on to Sacred Harp, the last institutional
vestige of the life they have experienced together. Northern singers, by contrast,
have grown up after modernization disenchanted the worldview of primary religious institutions. They are secular urban individuals who have found in Sacred Harp a secondary expression of sacrality that fits well into their disparate
and often eclectic worldviews. That these two processes of displacement should
meet in the unlikely setting of the hollow square underlines the protean dynamism of religion in America and offers a unique opportunity to explore further the role of sacred song in contemporary religiousness.

To better comprehend the experience of southern singers, I consulted Jeff and
Shelbie Sheppard of Glencoe, Alabama, two of the most widely recognized traditional Sacred Harp singers. Jeff is a universally respected leader of annual
singings and conventions; Shelbie is editor of *Sacred Harp Singings,* the official
minutes of stated annual singings and directory of singers. Between the world
wars, Jeff and Shelbie learned Sacred Harp singing in its purest southern form;
today they travel across the nation introducing new singers to the tradition while
maintaining their familiar place most weekends in the front row of local singings
throughout the Deep South. The Sheppards' experience of twentieth-century
Sacred Harp singing provides an invaluable resource for understanding what
is happening to the tradition today. I have known them for years. For this project,
I interviewed them at length during the 1993 National Convention at Birmingham and have followed up on several occasions since.

Like most traditional southern singers, the Sheppards learned Sacred Harp
singing through religious, familial, and community networks. Jeff's grandfather
was a Primitive Baptist preacher who led congregational singing from Benjamin
Lloyd's *Primitive Hymns, Spiritual Songs, and Sacred Poems* (1841), the denomination's words-only hymnal, using tunes from *The Sacred Harp* sung by
memory.[36] Jeff's father was a well-known singing master who squired his growing family around the Sacred Harp community. "Daddy brought us all [to singing school] beginning in 1924," Jeff remembered. "Our family would always sing
at local singing schools and at the Chattahoochee [Georgia] Convention."
Shelbie Sheppard told a rather different story. "I cannot ever remember not singing Sacred Harp," she said, but she learned the tradition in a community context, rather than in church. "In Cleburne County, [Alabama]" she remembered,
"there was a singing somewhere every weekend, and multitudes came. You didn't
have to go out of your county to have huge singings." Yet Shelbie "never went
to a singing school until Jeff and I got married," and she did not regard herself
as a Sacred Harp singer until she received that training.[37]

For traditional singers like the Sheppards, however, the singing school's meaning reached far beyond matters of music education. Singings supplied an intergenerational community meeting place, an arena for courtship, an entertainment and performance center, and a site for the rehearsal of cultural values and practices. Sacred Harp singing joined the family, the school, the church, and the town in defining a seamless community bound together by sacred ties of common beliefs and institutions. As Shelbie Sheppard put it, "in rural communities you knew everyone. If someone was sick, you brought food; if there was a tragedy, you grouped together. If you had a singing school at this church or that one, everybody went."

The relationship of Sacred Harp to primary religious institutions is especially complex for traditional singers. Over the years I have asked dozens of them what the most important aspect of the singings is, and nearly every one has answered the same way: "it's the words." Behind this deceptively simple response stands the complex religious history of the rural South and Sacred Harp's unique role in distilling and expressing its traditional evangelical worldview. It is no exaggeration to say that the culture of the rural South was shaped primarily by its churches. Generations of revivalism and doctrinal conflict created dozens of small regional denominations divided from each other by only a few contested beliefs and practices. Primitive Baptists, for example, agreed in most things with their Anti-Mission Baptist neighbors, except for the use of printed music in worship. The Primitives rejected it as a barrier to the free flow of the spirit, while the Anti-Mission communion employed it as an aid to unity in praise. Yet both of them long preserved the Sacred Harp corpus of texts and tunes.

This legion of denominations also shared the central tenets of Evangelical Protestantism: the necessity of the new birth, the indwelling of the Holy Spirit as a personal moral and spiritual guide, "gathered" congregations of believers only, and the imperative of testimony and witness to the faith. The genius of the singing school was its ability to provide an informal ecumenical setting for sharing these essentials of evangelical faith in song. The classic hymns of Watts and Wesley had been consciously designed to articulate precisely those theological commonalities. A core of their texts and accompanying tunes, shared interdenominationally, enabled the singing school to become the public expression of what we might call the generic religion of the rural South, its consensus doctrines cast in compelling hymnic form. Evangelicals of the rural South expressed their religious difference through their disparate denominations. They celebrated their overarching spiritual and cultural unity through the singing school.

For this reason, Sacred Harp singing is worship for traditional singers, and many of them prefer it to denominational services. Shelbie Sheppard, for example, drew a sharp distinction between the mandated service order of the Southern Baptists, with whom she and Jeff have worshiped often, and the spontaneously shared, free praise of God unleashed in Sacred Harp singing. "In a

[Southern Baptist] church you are regulated by too much structure that tells you when to sing and when to sit down, when to stand up, and when the choir should sing," she told me. "Sacred Harp music is the complete opposite in worshipping the Lord. I get more from going and singing starting at nine in the morning, then seeing people that mean a lot to me, and singing for five or six hours, than going to a regimented service."

Sacred Harp, then, is worship, but it is not church. Jeff Sheppard put his own gloss on the distinction between church and Sacred Harp singing. "[Sacred Harp singing] is not their church," he said of traditional singers, "it is their experience of Christianity, [and] it is better than any particular church. [But] you have to be [at singings] for the right reasons. You have to be receptive. If you're there to play, that's another thing, but if you're there because you were taught to go there just like you were to church, [then] it's a worship service."

If it is something broader and deeper than church, and it is worship, might Sacred Harp be the religion of traditional singers? I asked Jeff Sheppard that question a few years ago. "It's not their religion," he unhesitatingly replied, "it's their fellowship." Religion is a matter of personal faith and denominational identity. Fellowship is a lifetime of relationships with "people you love" and a shared "experience of Christianity" that transcends any particular communion. One must go to Sacred Harp singings "for the right reasons," above all "because you were taught to go there like you were taught to go to church," for praise and prayer and fellowship.

For traditional singers, Sacred Harp is an intact part of rural southern religion and culture. It continues to express their generic evangelical worldview through the specialized musicality and institutional arrangements of the singing school. Sacred Harp has always performed these functions, but in recent decades it has taken on additional meanings of displaced sacrality that have made it transcendently important in the lives of traditional singers. We might call this process a negative displacement of sacrality onto a secondary religious institution because Sacred Harp has taken on a set of larger meanings transferred to it from the cultural world of the rural South that has been otherwise lost.

Jeff Sheppard offered the clue to those meanings when he said to me that Sacred Harp carried "connotations and associations" of life in the rural South before World War II. This eloquent phrase revealed that the singings have arrogated to themselves the cultural memory of a lost world. After 1950 the Sacred Harp fellowship experienced the disintegration of its culture and the attenuation of its evangelical sects. Economic development, urbanization, and the interstate highway system doomed the local farm and with it the traditional social networks that sustained tiny sectarian congregations. Rural whites flocked to rising urban centers like Birmingham and Atlanta, where many of them joined mainstream southern denominations, especially the Southern Baptist Convention, which has enjoyed explosive growth since 1950. Back home, small sectarian congregations collapsed and were replaced by Pentecostal denominations and larger mainstream

communions—Southern Baptists, Southern Methodists, Churches of Christ—
as the new economy transformed country towns into exurbs.

The traditional singers' world of agrarian economy, intergenerational family,
intimate congregation, and civic community has been eclipsed. Most of them no
longer live the old way, yet they continue to believe in its truth and goodness, its
web of relationships, its culture, its sacrality. Only one institution remains
through which to express that sacrality: Sacred Harp singing. And so southern
singers have conferred on it the "connotations and associations" of their entire
traditional culture, loading it with a burden of dislocated sacrality it was never
designed to carry, but which it has proven entirely capable of bearing.

Why new northern singers are drawn to Sacred Harp singing seems at first
more difficult to explain. The cultural divide between northern and southern
singers could hardly be greater. The new northern singers are on the whole
younger, more urban, better educated, more professional, and more secular than
traditional southern singers. They have come to Sacred Harp through academic
or musical exposure, not through families or congregations. Above all, they do
not share the life experience and religious worldview of the rural south so essential to Sacred Harp tradition. How is it, then, that such unlikely people are
drawn to something like Sacred Harp singing and invest deep personal meaning and much of their free time in it?

Again Luckmann's theory of primary and secondary sacrality can provide
some help. It is fair to assume that most northern singers have experienced the
inability of primary religious institutions to sustain a unified worldview and
have taken the further step that Luckmann described of employing secondary
means to access to sacrality as they put together a customized sacred cosmos
for themselves. Since Luckmann wrote, this search for supplementary sacrality
has increased to the point that it is a familiar feature of the secular urban lifestyle
now called postmodern. Most northern singers are baby boomers or younger
and have come to adulthood in full possession of the postmodern sensibility.
This condition does not mean that northern singers are irreligious. Many of
them, in fact, belong to congregations and synagogues, often serving in the
performance of liturgical music. But postmodernity does mean that northern
singers no longer inhabit a traditional religious worldview as southern singers
do. The realm of the sacred itself has become multivocal for northern singers.
Indeed it is the very openness of postmodernity to secondary sacrality that invites northern singers to find it in Sacred Harp.

But how is Sacred Harp meaningful for northern singers? Some, to be sure,
see it exclusively as a musical or cultural activity, but there can be no doubt that
core northern singers, those listed in *Sacred Harp Singings,* have made a much
deeper commitment to the tradition and its community that can only be
termed religious. Monitor Radio correspondent Pat McMurray asked three
long-term members of Norumbega Harmony about the meaning of Sacred
Harp for an April 1992 feature story.[38] Their answers expressed a range of north-

ern sensibilities that offer important clues to the sacrality of Sacred Harp for new northern singers.

Ginnie Ely, a software designer with Digital Equipment and nationally known singer and leader, identified with the southern tradition, especially the intense emotionality and community of local singings in the South. "They get in there and they sing," she said. "They fill the place; people are standing in the windows and the doors, and they shout and they scream and they sing the stuff. Then outside is a permanent table that's huge, and they pile food on this till it's amazing. And you go out, and you eat, and then you go back in and you sing."

Bob Parr, an electrical engineer at MIT, related most strongly to the vocal sound and the poetic imagery of the texts. "Between the very strong harmonies of open fifths and fourths and seconds, and the sound of the vocal production," he said, "you get a sort of buzzing in your head of a strong, primitive sound that has a very powerful feeling. [And] sometimes the words can be actually a very powerful metaphor for life. I find myself singing that way. You get lyrics like 'Death, like an overflowing stream, / Sweeps us away, our life's a dream.' I mean, that's neat, a real head trip."

Sue Turbak, a twenty-year member of the group, used explicitly religious language to express her sense of singing with Norumbega Harmony. "It's their communication with God," she said, "their interaction with one another and their personal relationship with God." Turbak placed special value on the lyrics of Sacred Harp hymns. "This music penetrates my daily life," she said. "I will be walking to work, and there will be a song, one of these hymns, going through my head. And I'll tune into the words, and say, oh, *that's* what it means!" She also stressed the importance of community for northern singing circles. "The singing is [one element]," she continued, "but it's also the community life—getting to know one another. Some of [the singers are] our extended family. Many of us get together outside the group. For some of us it is our spiritual community."

Each of these responses identifies an important element in Sacred Harp's appeal to northern singers. Ginnie Ely's is the most secular on its face, but in naming the power of group singing and the fellowship of traditional southern singers, she marked a vitally important element of postmodern sacrality, what Luckmann called "togetherness." Since the 1960s, postmoderns have increasingly sought effective communities outside of primary religious institutions, often in cultural movements like the folk music revival. Sacred Harp singing, especially in its traditional southern form, provides an extraordinarily intense cultural community to which Ely, like many northern singers, was drawn through folk music and folk dance networks.

Bob Parr's response pointed to singing itself as a vehicle for secondary sacrality. Sacred Harp singing creates a unique sound. The harmony of the tunes is rough-hewn and irregular, its scales are often modal, and the powerful choral sound does indeed create an indescribable "buzz." In folk festival workshop settings, it is not unusual to see people peering through the door and asking,

"What *is* that? I've never heard anything like it before!" Sacred Harp's music and sound has also attracted attention in Early Music players and singers, who rightly see in its dense texture and modal scales vestiges of preclassical styles. A significant proportion of northern singers have come to Sacred Harp through this Early Music route.

There is another important religious aspect, however, to Sacred Harp vocalism that Parr referenced. Sustained singing is an ancient technique for creating altered states of consciousness through hyperventilation, elevated blood oxygen, and cranial and somatic vibration. Sacred Harp singers sing at full volume and extreme range for hours at a time, accruing all of those effects in abundance. These combined with often-striking poetic figures of the text, as Parr noted, can create remarkable experiences even if one does not share the religious worldview of the hymn. The very act of Sacred Harp singing can provide powerful somatic and aesthetic experiences that the most secular singer can appropriate as a secondary expression of sacrality.

Sue Turbak's answer suggested a more direct focus on the spiritual community of northern singers and a more personal religious connection with the texts and tunes. Groups like Norumbega Harmony and the Chicago singers have been singing together for more than two decades. To sing about life, death, sin, and immortality at the top of one's lungs and at close quarters is an act that almost requires self-disclosure. It is virtually impossible to have sung together that way for any sustained period of time and not share other aspects of life with fellow singers. The customary hospitality at northern house singings also enhances social sharing. Close personal ties of the sort Turbak described have developed in all established northern singing communities, especially in smaller performing groups where singings are weekly and the group travels together to concerts and workshops. Norumbega Harmony, for example, takes a winter weekend retreat and a summer beach trip each year specifically to strengthen interpersonal ties through singing, family activities, and shared meals. While such social arrangements cannot equal the generations-long community of traditional southern singers, they supply an analogue to it that sometimes achieves the intimacy of an extended family, a rare experience of "togetherness" in the postmodern northern urban world.

Turbak's comments about the spiritual dimension of Sacred Harp singing reflect the experience of many northern singers. Most of them have some kind of religious background. Although that background no longer supplies what Luckmann would call a primary worldview, it still informs northern singers' appropriation of Sacred Harp's emotionally and doctrinally laden texts. That language can still speak directly to life's meaning for singers like Turbak. Others may experience the words more as a facilitating medium. In his important recent study *Public Worship, Private Faith: Sacred Harp and American Folksong,* John Bealle has suggested that the "open quality" of Sacred Harp lyrics combines with the nonsectarian, informal musical practices of the singing school to create "an extraordinary celebration of ritual unity without explicit doctrinal consensus."[39] For those less comfortable with the hymns' explicitly theological language, the act of singing itself seems to mitigate their uneasiness.

Sacred song makes it possible to sing what we cannot say, and singing adds meanings beyond the verbal sense of the words. When one looks around the hollow square at the annual New England convention and sees singers rapt in song with their eyes closed, some weeping, as they wail out the words of the southern spiritual ballad "Villulia"—"Mercy, o thou son of David, / Thus poor blind Bartimeus prayed, / Others by thy grace are saved, / Now to me afford thine aid"—it is hard to gainsay Sue Turbak's sense that in very personal, postmodern ways this indeed "is their communication with God."

For northern singers, the communal, musical, and spiritual dimensions that Norumbega's members identified come together in varying proportions to produce what might be called a positive displacement of sacrality onto secondary religious institutions, in which new sacred meanings are vested in activities and communities that lie outside primary religious institutions and worldviews. This positive displacement often occurs in a moment of synergy, a realization that Sacred Harp is more than a historical artifact defined by a corpus of texts and tunes, that it is instead an embodied, living tradition replete with powerful ritual and cultural meanings. This "aha" experience frequently takes place at conventions or on visits to the South where the power of the Sacred Harp tradition is fully displayed. Such moments do not usually occur at one's first exposure to Sacred Harp. Mine occurred at the third Birmingham convention in 1983, even though I had been singing Sacred Harp since 1975 in both the South and the North.

What this breakthrough entails is not a religious conversion, but an embrace of the Sacred Harp tradition itself in all of its complex reality. Bealle helpfully calls this web of tradition "the Sacred Harp narrative," a combination of history, commentary, living memory, and experience that surrounds and interpenetrates the text of *The Sacred Harp* and brings it to life as a positive displacement of sacrality for northern singers.[40] Northern singers venerate the singing and its accompanying Sacred Harp narrative but not the evangelical worldview of the rural south that lies behind the music for southern singers. Northern singers simply do not share that worldview. In order to participate authentically in Sacred Harp, therefore, they valorize the procedures of the singing school and its lore through which they, too, can become true Sacred Harp singers. The definitive, indeed only, location where the different displacements of sacrality for northern and southern singers can meet is in the rituals of the hollow square.

South Meets North, North Meets South

No matter how faithful northern singers want to be to all that Sacred Harp means to them, however, their experience of it is not and, I think, cannot be the same as southern traditional singers'. The dislocations of sacrality for northern and southern singers meet and overlap in the hollow square, but they do not fully harmonize. There is an inevitable tension between these two ways of appropriating Sacred Harp, and as the northern revival has exploded in the past twenty years it has fostered some tensions between southern and northern singers. I asked Jeff Sheppard what would have happened if the new northern singers had not appeared. "We would have had the problem of how we would keep it going," he answered, "but now that they have arrived, it seems we've swapped one problem for another."

Southern singers worry most that northerners may detach the music of *The Sacred Harp* from the singing school and its religious and cultural traditions. Their fears are valid, especially as critical editions of Billings and other early American composers, along with reprints of classic shape-note tunebooks, have brought the Sacred Harp repertory into the musical canon of conservatories and university music departments. Performances and recordings by professional choral organizations, and even by tradition-friendly groups like Norumbega Harmony and Village Harmony, objectify the music for new listeners and remove it from the essential participatory context of the hollow square.

Other musical issues can also be a source of disagreement. Northern singers do not sing *The Sacred Harp* the same way traditional southern singers do. Lacking the generations of oral Sacred Harp transmission of the rural South, northern singers generally do not employ the rich array of melodic ornament, rhythmic emphasis, and folk voice that infuses southern singing style. Most northern singers have already been musically trained in high school or college before they encounter Sacred Harp, and they tend to sing what is on the page and to use choral techniques of vocal production and classical tempos in leading.

These differences may seem minor, and they do not seem to trouble southern leaders, but some northern singers insist that Sacred Harp should only be sung southern style. John Bealle has called this view the "transplantation perspective" on Sacred Harp and documented its origin in the folksong revival of the 1960s and 1970s, whose advocates, including some of today's leaders in Chicago and elsewhere in the Midwest, treated forms like Delta Blues and Sacred Harp as virtually extinct musics whose cultural otherness and authenticity could only be recovered by exact performance reproduction.[41]

The most controverted issue is the traditional southern practice of raising the sixth in minor key, which changes the tune to Dorian mode. Some northern leaders have embraced the practice and instruct new singers to observe it. Others reject it, most seem neutral, but northern singers love to debate such issues. The origin and history of the raised sixth was the subject of heated discussions during 1998 and 1999 in Sacred Harp newsletters and on the electronic mail subscription lists for the international FaSoLa network and the Institute for Early American Culture at Williamsburg, Virginia. No final consensus emerged from the debate, but both the scholarly level of the discourse and its cyberspace medium reflected the academic and musical roots of the new north.

Such debates are nothing new for the singing-school tradition. There has always been disagreement among singing masters and tune-book editors about how to sing their music. There is still musical diversity among traditional singers today. Mississippi singers, for example, characteristically set much slower tempos and use the four-beat butterfly pattern of leading much more often than their colleagues in Alabama and Georgia. This healthy diversity holds fair promise for the future of the Sacred Harp even as it strengthened its past. William Billings is justly celebrated for publishing the first great American tune book in 1770, but the more significant historical development was the appearance shortly thereafter of a host of competitors who prevented any monopoly on repertory or performance practice. Musical and stylistic diversity, not uniformity, has produced the fairest fruit of the American singing school. Its truest restoration would embrace the glory of its compositions, the diversity of its styles, and the sincerity of its praise in whatever way the people express them.

A related and more serious problem between North and South has been establishing the "right reasons" for participation by new northern singers. Even when they replicate the singing-school procedures in exacting detail, new northern singers often bring a more recreational attitude to singings, at least at first. This attitudinal difference marks precisely the difference between the negative and positive displacements of sacrality in the two constituencies, and it is a difficult dilemma to solve. As northern leaders have become more familiar with the Sacred Harp narrative and southern singings, they have introduced more seriousness and communal intentionality into their local singings. But because there are always new recruits and brand-new singing locales in the North, there is also an inevitable lag. For traditional singers, it is worse for the singing school standards to be deployed improperly, either willfully or unwittingly, by new northern singers than for it to be ignored, as it is by professional performance groups. While the latter is a regrettable and uncontrollable misuse of the music, the former represents a challenge to the tradition itself.

"We want people to join our tradition and be a part of it," Jeff Sheppard told me, "but we don't want them to come in and try to change us. We want to keep it as pure as we can." Rather than be changed by the Sacred Harp revival, the Sheppards along with Hugh McGraw and Richard DeLong decided to change it. Since 1976 these leaders, most notably McGraw, have performed a remarkable feat in interpreting the Sacred Harp tradition to new northern singers. On countless trips to state and regional conventions in New England, the Midwest, and most recently the West, these missionaries have patiently transmitted the history, techniques, and spirit of Sacred Harp and invited new northern singers to join its fellowship.

Their visits proved extraordinarily effective and soon the flow of visitation reversed direction. New northern singers flocked to Birmingham, then to local southern singings throughout the year. So popular have such visits become that some local southern singings have been overwhelmed, but for Jeff Sheppard they have become the crucial mechanism for properly orienting northern singers. "What we'd really like to do," he continued, "is have a medium-sized singing with fifteen or twenty singers. And the best thing that could happen to ten or so [northern] people, not fifty, is to come to these little southern true home singings and see." It is much easier for traditional singers to host visitors from the North than to travel there. As the northern influx has grown, more southern leaders have joined in as hosts and facilitators, including members of the most eminent Sacred Harp families—Creels, Woottens, Densons, and McGraws.

In the midst of this reconstruction of the Sacred Harp fellowship another crucial development took place, the publication in 1991 of a new edition of the tune book. In the mid-1980s Hugh McGraw was appointed by the Sacred Harp Publishing Company to lead what would be just the fourth general revision of *The Sacred Harp* since 1844. McGraw's music committee included distinguished traditional leaders along with established southern scholars of hymnody and musicology. McGraw's 1991 edition featured entirely new shape-note scores, new rules for singing, impressive scholarship, and first-rate editing and production. While the "McGraw Revision" preserved the order of tunes from the earlier Denson Revision, published in 1936 with supplementary editions in 1960, 1966, and 1971, it replaced sixty little-used tunes with new ones, most of them by veteran leaders from Alabama and Georgia such as John C. Hocutt, as well as tunes by each member of the Music Committee.

The McGraw Revision, however, also made a significant gesture of inclusivity by adding fourteen new tunes written by northern composers like Wesleyan's Neely Bruce, Norumbega Harmony's Glen Wright and Bruce Randall, and Chicago's Judy Hauff, Ted Mercer, and Ted Johnson, all longtime singers who also possessed some professional music training. The McGraw Revision has been universally embraced as the definitive collection for the Sacred Harp tradition and has stabilized its singing network by acknowledging new northern singers and composers in the most meaningful way possible: putting them in the tune book.

The process of integrating new northern singers with the southern tradition has been neither easy nor rapid. During the late 1980s in particular, personality conflicts and policy disputes afflicted the southern leadership. As late as 1993 Jeff Sheppard thought it would be necessary "to agree to disagree and move on from there and get to the music." Shelbie Sheppard concurred. "Until we all get back to the basics of why we're out there," she said then, "I don't think it'll get any better. And I think it'll get worse before it gets better." The situation did get worse briefly after 1993, but in recent years northern acceptance of the singing-school tradition, the growth of interregional visits and friendships, the listing of northern singings in *Sacred Harp Singings,* and the resounding success of Hugh McGraw's inclusive 1991 Revision have made things much better indeed.

As the new century progresses, the unlikely encounter of postmodern northern and traditional southern singers has developed into a flourishing new Sacred Harp fellowship. Each constituency retains its own experience of secondary sacrality in the hollow square, and the presence of northern singers is likely to continue to increase while the older generation of traditional southern singers weakens. Yet the two groups know and understand each other better than they ever have, and they have learned to share the singing-school heritage together. While their modes of secondary sacrality remain distinct, they seem to be moving together in important ways. Northern singers now use evangelical language more freely, southern singers are more comfortable with postmodern quirkiness, and everyone loves the new tunes.

In the past two decades, Sacred Harp has become a remarkable experiment in the public expression of sacred song. It is telling that song has been the medium through which such disparate partners have found common rituals for their respective styles of appropriating the sacred. The principal reason for Sacred Harp's remarkable resurgence is the dedication of its singers to the complex and varied meanings of the tradition. Shelbie Sheppard gave it the best articulation from the heart of the southern tradition that remains Sacred Harp's most enduring heritage. "We are sharing our lives and what this music means to [us] when [we] share it with other folks," she said. "If we have any mission in life, the scripture says not to hide your talents under a basket. It goes back to what Jeff and I have and what we share, be it our home, our talents, our time. But if we can share that and instill into folks the worth of the music, the worth of the tradition, then our talents will not be in vain." They have not been in vain. Their efforts have borne fruit as Sacred Harp singing has endured both the crisis of survival and the challenge of revival to begin the twenty-first century refreshed and renewed as a unique expression of sacred song in contemporary America.

Notes

1. Benjamin Franklin White and E. J. King, *The Sacred Harp* (Philadelphia: B. F. White and Joel King, 1844).

2. In 1997 the church changed hands and is now called the Little Vine Church of All People. The annual singing still takes place there.

3. The best general account of Sacred Harp singing and its culture is Buell E. Cobb Jr., *The Sacred Harp: A Tradition and Its Music* (Athens: University of Georgia Press, 1978).

4. Louis Benson, *The English Hymn: Its Development and Use in Worship* (New York: Doran, 1915), 21–26, and J. R. Watson, *The English Hymn: A Critical and Historical Study* (Oxford: Clarendon Press, 1999), 42–56.

5. Richard G. Appel, *Music of the Bay Psalm Book* (Brooklyn, N.Y.: Institute for Studies in American Music, 1975). See also Zoltan Haraszti, *The Enigma of the Bay Psalm Book* (Chicago: University of Chicago Press, 1956).

6. Thomas Walter, *The Grounds and Rules of Musick Explained* (Boston: J. Franklin, 1721), 2–5. Evans 2303.

7. Walter, *Grounds and Rules of Musick Explained*; John Tufts, *An Introduction to the Singing of Psalm Tunes*, 5th ed. (Boston: Gerrish, 1726). Evans 39856; Alan C. Buechner, "Thomas Walter and the Society for Promoting Regular Singing in the Worship of God: Boston, 1720–1723," in *New England Music: The Public Sphere, 1600–1800*, ed. Peter Benes, The Dublin Seminar for New England Folklife Annual Proceedings, 1996 (Boston: Boston University Publications, 1998), 7–10.

8. Benson, *The English Hymn*, 56–89.

9. Isaac Watts, *A Short Essay Toward the Improvement of Psalmody* in *The Works of the Rev. Isaac Watts, D.D. in Nine Volumes* (Leeds: Edward Baines, 1813), 9:1–26.

10. Donald Davie, cited in John Bealle, *Public Worship, Private Faith: Sacred Harp and American Folksong* (Athens: University of Georgia Press, 1997), 162.

11. Selma L. Bishop, ed., *Isaac Watts: Hymns and Spiritual Songs* (London: The Faith Press, 1962), liii.

12. Ibid., liii–liv.

13. Hugh McGraw, ed., *The Sacred Harp: 1991 Revision* (Bremen, Ga.: Sacred Harp Publishing Company, 1991).

14. Nicholas Temperley, *The Music of the English Parish Church* (Cambridge: Cambridge University Press, 1979), 1:163–80.

15. Edwards, cited in Henry Wilder Foote, *Three Centuries of American Hymnody* (Cambridge, Mass.: Harvard University Press, 1940), 148.

16. James Lyon, *Urania; or a Choice Collection of Psalm Tunes* (Philadelphia, 1761); Evans 8908; Josiah Flagg, *A Collection of the Best Psalm Tunes* (Boston: Revere and Flagg, 1764); Evans 9659.

17. William Tans'ur, *The Royal Harmony Complete* (Newburyport, Mass.: Josiah Flagg, 1767). Evans 11256.

18. Stephen Marini, "Rehearsal for Revival: Sacred Singing and the Great Awakening in America," in *Sacred Sound: Music in Religious Thought and Practice*, ed. Joyce Irwin (Chico, Calif.: Scholars Press, 1983), 84–86.

19. William Billings, *The New-England Psalm-Singer* (Boston: Edes and Gill, 1770); Karl Kroeger, ed., *The Complete Works of William Billings*, 4 vols. (Boston: American Musicological Society and the Colonial Society of Massachusetts, 1981–90), 1:32–33.

20. Allen Britton, Irving Lowens, and Richard Crawford, eds., *American Sacred Music Imprints, 1698–1810: A Bibliography* (Worcester, Mass.: American Antiquarian Society, 1990). In addition to Kroeger, ed., *Complete Works of William Billings*, critical editions of other New England masters have recently appeared, including Richard Crawford, ed., *The Core Repertory of Early American Psalmody* (Madison, Wis.: A-R Editions, 1984); Karl Kroeger, ed., *Daniel Read: Collected Works* (Madison, Wis.: A-R Editions, 1995); David Warren Steel, ed., *Stephen Jenks: Collected Works* (Madison, Wis.: A-R Editions, 1995); and Nym Cooke, ed., *Timothy Swan: Psalmody and Secular Songs* (Madison, Wis.: A-R Editions, 1997).

21. H. Wiley Hitchcock and Stanley Sadie, eds., *The New Grove Dictionary of American Music* (New York: Grove's Dictionaries of Music, 1986), 3:388.

22. Michael Kennedy, *The Concise Oxford Dictionary of Music*, 4th ed. (New York: Oxford University Press, 1996), 490–91; William Little and William Smith, *The Easy Instructor, or, A New Method of Teaching Sacred Harmony* (Philadelphia: n.p., 1801).

23. Modern reprints of classic singing-school collections include Jeremiah Ingalls, *The Christian Harmony* (Exeter, N.H., 1805; reprint, New York: Da Capo Press, 1976); John Wyeth, *Wyeth's Repository of Sacred Music* (Harrisburg, Pa., 1810; reprint, New York: Da Capo Press, 1974) and *Wyeth's Repository of Sacred Music, Part Second* (Harrisburg, Pa., 1813; reprint, New York: Da Capo Press, 1964); Allen D. Carden, *Missouri Harmony* (Cincinnati, 1820; reprint of 9th ed., Lincoln: University of Nebraska Press, 1994); William Walker, *Southern Harmony and Musical Companion* (New Haven, 1835; reprint of 3d ed., Philadelphia, 1854; Los Angeles: Pro Musicamericana, 1966; Louisville, Ky.: University Press of Kentucky, 1987); John G. McCurry, *The Social Harp* (Philadelphia, 1855; reprint, Athens: University of Georgia Press, 1973); James Sullivan Warren, *Warren's Minstrel* (Columbus, Ohio, 1857; reprint, Athens: Ohio University Press, 1984); William Walker, *Christian Harmony* (Philadelphia, 1866; reprint of 1873 ed., Spartanburg, S.C.: A Press, 1979); M. L. Swan, *The New Harp of Columbia* (Nashville, 1867; reprint of 1919 ed., Knoxville: University of Tennessee Press, 1978); Joseph Funk, *Harmonia Sacra, a Compilation of Genuine Church Music*, 25th ed. (Philadelphia, 1832; Intercourse, Pa.: Good Books, 1993).

24. Lowell Mason, *The Boston Handel and Haydn Society Collection of Church Music* (Boston, 1822; reprint, New York: Da Capo Press, 1973); Lowell Mason, *Oration on Church Music* (Boston, 1826).

25. Nora Parker, comp., *Directory and Minutes of Sacred Harp Singings, 1992 and 1993* (Temple, Ga.: Sacred Harp Publishing Company, 1993), i.

26. Shelbie Sheppard, ed., *Sacred Harp Singings, 1998 and 1999* (Glencoe, Ala.: Alabama Sacred Harp Convention, 1999), 245–96.

27. See especially George Pullen Jackson, *White Spirituals in the Southern Uplands* (1938; New York: Dover, 1965), *Spiritual Folksongs of Early America* (1937; Gloucester, Mass.: Peter Smith, 1975), and *The Story of the Sacred Harp, 1844–1944* (Nashville: Vanderbilt University Press, 1944).

28. Irving Lowens, *Music and Musicians in Early America* (New York: Norton, 1964); H. Wiley Hitchcock, *Earlier American Music Series* (New York: Da Capo Press, 1965–82).

29. Word of Mouth Chorus, Larry Gordon, director, *Rivers of Delight*, Nonesuch Records, 1976.

30. See also Zoe Ingalls, "Renewing the American Singing School," an article on Norumbega Harmony, *The Chronicle of Higher Education*, August 16, 1992, v. 38, n. 50, p. 81.

31. Among the finest Sacred Harp field recordings is *The Alabama Sacred Harp Convention*, New World Records 205. Recorded in 1959 by Alan Lomax and released in 1977 as part of his Recorded Anthology of American Music Series, it was reissued on compact disc in 1999. One of the earliest New England revival recordings is Old Sturbridge Singers, *The New England Harmony*, Folkways Records, 1964, with notes by Alan C. Buechner.

32. A. Barrand and C. Moody, eds., *Northern Harmony: A Collection of Tunes by Early New England Composers* (Marlboro, Vt.: Marlboro College, 1980); Anthony C. Barrand, Larry Gordon, and Carol Moody, eds., *Northern Harmony: Plain Tunes, Fuging Tunes and Anthems from the New England Singing School Tradition* (Plainfield, Vt.: Northern Harmony Publishing, 1984).

33. Glen Wright and Susan Mampre, eds., *The Sacred Harper's Companion: A Collection of Hymns and Anthems in Traditional Shape Note System by Contemporary Composers* (Belmont, Mass.: Musica, 1993); Timothy Erikson, ed., *The New Northampton Collection of Sacred and Secular Harmony* (Northampton, Mass.: Northampton Harmony, 1993); Stephen Marini, ed., *The Norumbega Harmony* (Oxford: University Press of Mississippi, 2003); Karen E. Willard, *An American Christmas Harp* (Puyallup, Wash.: Karen Willard, 1994), and *The Eclectic Harmony* (Atlanta, Ga.: Eclectic Harmony Music Committee, 1999).

34. Peter Berger, *The Sacred Canopy: Elements of a Sociological Theory of Religion* (Garden City, N.Y.: Doubleday, 1967), 3–53.

35. Thomas Luckmann, *The Invisible Religion: The Problem of Religion in Modern Society* (New York: Macmillan, 1967), 28–50, 77–114.

36. Benjamin Lloyd, *The Primitive Hymns, Spiritual Songs, and Sacred Poems, regularly Selected, Classified, and Set in Order and Adapted to Social Singing and All Occasions of Divine Worship* (Greenville, Ala.: Benjamin Lloyd, 1841; reprint, Beverly Hills, Calif.: Opal Lloyd Terry and LaVerte Lloyd Smith, 1949).

37. Jeff Sheppard and Shelbie Sheppard, interview with author, Birmingham, Ala., June 16, 1993. All subsequent quotations are taken from this interview unless otherwise noted in the text.

38. Pat McMurray, "Sacred Harp Singing at Harvard," Monitor Radio, April 16, 1992.

39. Bealle, *Public Worship, Private Faith*, 235.

40. Ibid., 132–87.

41. Ibid., 254–56.

CHAPTER 4

"Is It Going to Save Someone?":
The Black Church at Song

The fourth great tradition of American sacred song is that of African Americans and the Black Church. African Americans have been making sacred song on these shores since "before the Mayflower," in Lerone Bennett's haunting phrase.[1] Over the course of nearly four centuries, African American sacred song has developed extraordinary diversity and complexity, its forms ranging from the spirit possession of West African shout still preserved in Afro-Caribbean *vodun* and Santería to the heroic hope of the slave spiritual, from the gospel songs of Thomas A. Dorsey to the transcendental jazz compositions of Duke Ellington and John Coltrane. Reflecting the historic contours of African American experience, this tradition of sacred song has encompassed vast cultural polarities: tribal religion and Evangelical Protestantism, slavery and freedom, rural community and urban world. From these contexts African Americans have created the richest and most original tradition of sacred song in American history.

Yet for all its diversity and creativity, the core of African American sacred song is unquestionably located in the worship of the Black Church. Since the Great Awakening of the mid-eighteenth century, African Americans have turned in overwhelming numbers to the biblicism and emotional spirituality of Evangelical Protestantism and transformed it into their own unique expression of religion through the great black denominations: African Methodist Episcopal, African Methodist Episcopal Zion, and Christian Methodist Episcopal; National Baptist Convention USA, National Baptist Convention of America, and Progressive National Baptist Convention; and the Church of God in Christ and other black Pentecostal communions, who together represent more than twenty million African Americans, over 80 percent of their population. More than any other institution, the Black Church has preserved the African sacred-song heritage and nurtured its transmutation into Christian praise. It is therefore in the music of the Black Church that the meaning of African American sacred song can best be discovered.[2]

Apostolic Church of God

Just below Hyde Park on Chicago's South Side stands an urban no-man's land. Originally the site of utopian structures built for the 1893 World's Columbian Exposition, the district between 59th and 63rd Streets eastward from Martin Luther King Boulevard to Lake Shore Drive now stares vacantly across the Midway at the soaring gothic towers of the University of Chicago. The once-integrated neighborhood was already being abandoned almost thirty-five years ago when I was a student at the university, victim to real estate speculation, white flight, and uncertain plans for the university's relocation. Little has changed since then, except that more housing has been abandoned or demolished and a few new university buildings have been constructed along the south side of the Midway, the great lawn two blocks wide and twelve blocks long upon which the World's Columbian Exposition's famed amusement park originally stood.

The streets here now resemble a war zone. Most of the buildings—a classic Chicago mix of wooden clapboard single homes, brick apartment courts, and concrete gothic apartment houses—are boarded up and covered with graffiti. Other structures have simply been abandoned, their windows shattered and their doors smashed. Especially eerie is the open space. There is a great deal of it, not green but rather covered with bricks and glass, the remains of the wrecking ball. So much has been destroyed that vacant lots actually dominate the urbanscape. The buildings stand as ghostly relics, reminders of a community long since consigned to oblivion.

Along the streets of the neighborhood, churches are almost the only structures that seem to function at all. Ornate but now threadbare edifices of the great black denominations dominate the environment. Once the heart of a thriving community, 63d Street is church row, boasting nearly a dozen early twentieth-century sanctuaries within only a few blocks. But on a beautiful Sunday morning in late April 1994, there was only modest activity in the streets. Small groups of people walked toward the churches, their aging congregations now dwarfed by the very size of their own church buildings.

In sharp contrast to these struggling churches stood Apostolic Church of God, an impressive new brick and glass sanctuary at 63rd and Dorchester Street in the shadow of a crumbling elevated railway. Apostolic is a congregation of the Pentecostal Assemblies of the World (PAW), one of the fastest growing American denominations. Between 1960 and 1998, the PAW has grown from 45,000 to a reported 1.5 million members, reflecting the massive upsurge of charismatic religion across American Christianity in the late twentieth century.[3]

Surrounded by parking lots and urban rubble, Apostolic houses a vibrant congregation of more than fourteen thousand members. This Sunday most of them crowded into the church, filling its four thousand–seat sanctuary to capacity for the 9:30 and 11:00 A.M. and 4:00 P.M. services. Entering through one of the six glazed doors on Dorchester Avenue, I was immediately surrounded by a friendly, vital, and very busy congregation. The standard greeting was not "Good Morning" or "Hello," it was "Praise the Lord" or, more frequently, "Praise Him." These were Christians clearly intent on worshipping Jesus.

I had just enough time before service to drink a cup of coffee in the crowded cafeteria and explore the building. On the main level, a semicircular hallway separated the massive sanctuary from offices and other facilities. An information center stood opposite the main sanctuary entrance, flanked by the Saving Grace Ministries Bookstore, an ample operation filled with Bibles, Christian literature, music, and recordings, including those of Apostolic's live radio Sunday broadcast. Past the cafeteria, offices and classrooms lined one side of the hallway while glass doors opened into a large chapel on the other side. The hallway terminated in a large gathering area and technical facilities for the sanctuary.

I entered the gathering area to encounter Apostolic's sanctuary choir, about 150 strong at the early service, clad in dark crimson robes with the letters "ACG" embroidered in the same color on the left front yoke panel. The choir had completed their warmup under Stuart Wilson, Apostolic's director of music. As Wilson finished his last instructions for the service, he turned the choir over to their chaplain, Evangelist Ivory Nuckolls. After a short prayer and a series of announcements, Nuckolls introduced one of the service leaders who delivered a three-minute exhortation, complete with a scripture text and illustrations, to bring the choir into spiritual focus for its task of "bringing souls to the Lord."

As the choir began forming up for its entrance, I hurried back to the main sanctuary. There I was greeted by an array of male and female ushers dressed in somber navy blue suits, black shoes, and white gloves. Embroidered on their left breast pockets was a light blue cross surmounted by a gold crown of thorns, the denominational symbol of the Pentecostal Assemblies of the World, to which Apostolic belongs. Inside, the sanctuary was completely packed. Folding chairs had become necessary to accommodate worshipers in the aisles and at the rear of the auditorium. An usher assigned me to a chair on an aisle looking straight down into the center of the sanctuary.

The sanctuary was a vast galleried amphitheater fanning out 180 degrees from a two-story-high brick wall, into which had been built a 250-seat choir loft and a second-story baptismal pool. Sculpture groups of the Crucifixion and the Resurrection adorned the walls to each side. A spare pulpit of contemporary design stood before the choir at the center of a shallow stage that stretched across the entire front of the wall. Behind the pulpit a row of twenty-five chairs, including three gothic-style chief seats in the middle, spanned the front of the stage. Men and women dressed in suits and elegant dresses, elders of the church, slowly filled the chairs in anticipation of the service. Some conversed, others prayed, while instrumentalists gathered in a masked pit under the stage.

At 9:30 A.M. sharp one of the senior leaders moved to the pulpit and greeted the congregation. "Good morning, brothers and sisters, welcome to Apostolic Church of God," he said. "Let's rise to greet our pastor and our choir." Suddenly an unseen band in the pit beneath the stage burst forth in a rocking up-tempo gospel chorus, driven by electric organ, electric bass, and percussion, with elaborate piano riffs and swinging trumpet and saxophone pointing. From stage left entered the Reverend Dr. Arthur M. Brazier, minister of Apostolic, vested in the white and red episcopal robes of the Pentecostal Assemblies of the World. As Bishop Brazier moved across the stage to his episcopal chair, the choir entered from the rear of the auditorium. They proceeded marching and clapping down the two center aisles to the front of the sanctuary, around the bottom of the stage and up into the choir loft behind the bishop and the elders. As soon as the choir was in place, it let fly with a high-voltage introit in four parts, beginning a cadenced ritual opening of worship that did not miss a single beat.

> *Choir:* I'm glad to be at service,
>   I'm glad to be at service,
>   I'm glad to be at service one more time.
>   Where Jesus can talk to me, and Jesus will set me free,
>   I'm glad to be at service one more time. [*Repeat*]
>   One more time, one more time,
>   I'm glad to be at service one more time.
> *People:* Applause
> *Leader:* Let the church say "Praise the Lord!"
> *People:* Praise the Lord!
> *Leader:* Let the church say "Thank you, Jesus!"
> *People:* Thank you Jesus!
> *Leader:* Once again we are happy to be back in the house of prayer.
>   One more time.
>   [*Louder*] One more time the Lord has blessed us.
>   [*Louder*] One more time the Lord has smiled upon us.
>   [*Louder*] One more time he woke us up, in our right mind.
>   [*Softer*] One more time, he blessed our souls to be here together.

As the organ softly entered, the leader called the congregation to prayer. He began with praise and thanks to God for his love and kindness and for saving his people, filling them with the Holy Spirit, and blessing their homes "in every way." He prayed for the sick, the poor, and the homeless, asking God to heal and bless them, and to open their eyes. He asked a particular blessing upon this service and Bishop Brazier, praying that the "free course" of God's word would flow in his sermon. After this prayer the organ swelled to a one-fold Amen, then dropped back to play a hymn quietly in the background as Romans 8:28–34 was read antiphonally by the evangelist and the congregation. Again the organ swelled, this time with three virtuoso transpositions of the Amen worthy of any conservatory-trained organist.

After a brief pause a male soloist began to sing, accompanied by piano, bass, and synthesized strings. His lyric was taken from Galatians 2:20: "I am crucified with Christ, nevertheless I live; yet not I, but Christ liveth in me." The piece was an anthem for baritone and chorus in contemporary style, focused much more on melody and harmony than on the rhythmic patterning that had carried the service musically to this point. "I Am Crucified with Christ" was a piece of contemporary Christian music that could be performed comfortably in thousands of American Protestant congregations both black and white and, indeed, in Catholic charismatic services as well.

The offering followed, and as the offertory a tenor soloist, backed by organ, bass, and percussion, launched into "Through It All," a contemporary spiritual ballad with a bluesy chorus in which the choir joined:

> *Solo:* I have many tears and sorrows, have questions for tomorrow,
>   Sometimes I don't know right from wrong.
>   But in every situation, God's given blessed consolation,
>   That my trials came only to make me strong.
> *Chorus:* Through it all, through it all,
>   I've learned to trust in Jesus,
>   I've learned to trust in our God.
>   Through it all, through it all,
>   I've learned to depend upon his word.
> *Solo:* I've been many places, I've seen so many faces,
>   Sometimes I feel so alone.
>   But in my darkest hours, yes those sweet dark hours,
>   Jesus lets me know that I am his own.
> *Chorus:* [Repeat refrain]

At the final line of the next verse, the soloist broke into a brief improvisational exhortation, bringing the song to its emotional high point before it concluded in a final chorus sung by the choir with voiceover by the soloist.

> *Solo:* I thank him for the mountain, and I thank him for the valleys,
>   And I thank him for all the storms he brought me through,
>   But if I never had a problem,
>   I wouldn't know my God could solve them,
>   I wouldn't know what faith,
>   I wouldn't know what believing is,
>   I wouldn't know what confidence in the Lord means!
>   I wouldn't know that he is the El Shaddai! the Almighty God!
>   I wouldn't know what faith in my God could do!

Solo and Chorus: Through it all, through it all,
    We're learning to trust in Jesus,
    I've learned to trust in my God,
    Through it all, [*Solo:* how about you?] through it all,
    I've learned [*Solo:* and I have learned] to depend upon his word.
    Hallelujah, hallelujah!

The service continued with an extended pastoral prayer, again delivered by the leader, who raised up the concerns of the community and asked Jesus' help and blessing. Almost as a responsorial voice of the congregation, a baritone soloist began a contemporarily scored but tightly rocking version of the gospel classic "Give It All to Jesus" for solo, choir, and full band with congas and bongos.

Solo: Heavy burden? Give it to Jesus,
    Aches, pains? He will deliver.
    Sons and daughters, they going astray?
    Don't worry about it. You just pray.
Chorus: Give it all to Jesus,
    Troubles great and small,
    Give it all to Jesus,
    He's the answer to it all.
    He will work it out, for you.

The verse and chorus were repeated more animatedly, with the congregation joining in. The energy built to the end of the chorus, when the choir broke into an unaccompanied choral chant, actually a second set of words for the chorus, over which the soloist improvised:

Choir: No matter what the problem,
    No matter, God can solve it,
    No matter what you need,
    Trust my Lord, he is real,
    He will work it out, for you.

Three times this chorus was sung, each time with more elaborate scoring, more pointed rhythm, and more intense singing. Then came a final, rocking chorus using just the line, "He will work it out for you," with everyone in the building singing and clapping.

Appreciative applause had greeted the earlier songs, but "Give It All to Jesus" evoked an extended period of uplifted hands and cries of "Hallelujah! Thank you, Jesus! He really worked it out!" Exclamations spoken in spiritual tongues, called glossolalia, could also be heard up and down the aisle. The congregation had been spiritually awakened by the alternation of sacred song with spoken prayer and recited scripture.

A break for announcements followed this first charismatic high point, then more music ensued, but of a different character: a choral setting of Psalm 100 in the King James Version (KJV), "Make a Joyful Noise unto the Lord, All Ye Lands." This setting featured triple meter with sections for women in unison as well as two-part chorus, accompanied by piano, bass, trumpets, and synthesized strings. The piece was performed as an anthem, with the congregation listening, not joining in, to triumphal music that sounded a bit like a big production number from Andrew Lloyd Weber's *Godspell*.

The service of prayer and praise ended with the anthem's final words: "Hallelujah! Praise his name for ever and ever!" words that Bishop Brazier took as his cue as he entered the pulpit. "Well, that's what we want to do," he began, "praise his name forever and evermore." Then before even naming his text, Brazier offered a quick reflection on emotion in worship and religious experience that Jonathan Edwards himself would have heartily endorsed. "That's really a part of our worship, blessing God and praising the Lord," Brazier said. "It's a thrilling thing for me to be part of this great movement, this great Pentecostal fervor! People who rejoice in the Lord, and make a joyful noise to the Lord, and who feel the presence of the Lord in their emotions. I don't really think you can come into contact with God without feeling some kind of emotional touch. It may not be like somebody else's, but everybody always feels something."

Bishop Brazier's sermon title was "Where Are the Nine?" It was based on Luke 17:12–19 (KJV), the story of ten lepers healed by Jesus, but only one of whom, a Samaritan, gave thanks and praise to him for the cleansing. Brazier began his sermon with a dramatic account of leprosy as a disfiguring and dreaded disease of the Ancient Near East, which afflicted the ten who pleaded with Jesus for his aid. They must have wondered, Brazier remarked, what to make of his instruction that they show themselves to the temple priests. "I imagine that as these men went, all of a sudden they began to see changes in one another," Brazier continued,

> and as they looked, I can see them seeing one another's hands, and I can see them jumping for joy. But in their rejoicing they neglected the source of their healing. They forgot about Jesus! But one didn't, and one went back. One! One! One went back! These other men they did not go back and fall down on their faces, these other men did not fall down on their knees in adoration and praise. They disappeared from the pages of the New Testament and disappeared into oblivion. Whatever happened to them no one knows, but this one man, who shall remain unnamed, was among this mixed colony of lepers. The one who came back was not Jewish, the one who came back was a Samaritan.

Brazier then launched into what homiletic theory calls the "application" of the text to the lives of his congregation: "I wonder whether there was a certain amount of pathos in the Lord's voice—'were not there ten? Where are the nine?' And I wonder this morning as I look out over this beautiful congregation, is this not the story of so many of us today?" The bishop challenged his congregation to honor the promises they have made to God: to attend church and to offer tithes and gift offerings to Jesus who has heard their pleas and granted their requests just as he heard the prayers of the ten lepers.

At several moments during the sermon the congregation responded with applause and the elders assembled on the dais had urged Brazier on, shouting "Preach!" when he made a resounding point, or "Well?" when he asked a rhetorical question. Overall, the emotional temperature of the congregation had risen considerably to this point in the bishop's oration, but neither he nor it had articulated the emotional and spiritual power that now simmered on the brink of explosive expression. At this moment Bishop Brazier paused, looked out upon his vast congregation, and launched into a classic peroration of Black Church preaching, a rhythmic, impassioned exhortation that brought the community to its feet, applauding, cheering, raising its arms and voices in ecstatic praise:

> O my friends, don't let the Lord ask, *where* are the nine?
> Don't let the Lord have to ask,
> *Where* is that one that I saved from that narcotics addiction?
> Don't let the Lord have to ask,
> *Where* is that woman that I saved from the street?
> *Where* is that man who I took the needle out of his arm?
> *Where* is that man who I broke the cocaine pipe?
> *Where* is that man or woman who I broke that spirit of pride?
> *Where* are they?
> I want you to be able to say like Samuel said, "*Here* am I, Lord!"
> I want you to be able to say as Isaiah said, "Lord, *here* I am!"
> Don't have the Lord ask:
> *Where* are those I have healed?
> *Where* are those whom I have given good jobs to?
> *Where* are those whom I have kept in good health?
> *Where* are those whom I have given strength?
> *Where* are those whose children I have kept safe?
> *Where* are those whom I have saved from catastrophe?
> *Where* are those whom I have comforted in their bereavement?
> *Where* are they?
> *Here* we are Lord! *Here* we are!
> Don't forget what God has done for you, brother.
> Sister, don't forget the Lord.
> Don't forget God in your worship service.
> Don't forget God in your home.
> Don't forget God in your job.
> *Always* praise him!
> *Always* lift him up!
> *Always* magnify him!

> *Always* adore him!
> *Always* thank him!
> Don't ever forget him and what he's done for you.
> You were a leper,
> You were dead in sin,
> But "He raised you up,
> Turned you around,
> Put your feet on solid ground,"
> Washed you and cleansed you,
> Covered you with his righteousness.
> Don't ever forget him!
> Don't ever forget him!

After this verbal explosion Brazier quieted the congregation with an altar call, inviting those who had felt Christ's converting grace to come forward to be welcomed and counseled by the church. The morning service ended quickly with the bishop's blessing and dismissal, followed by an up-tempo postlude by the band. Between services, twelve people were baptized by immersion in the second-story baptismal pool, then the forces of Apostolic Church of God regrouped for another service at 11 A.M., complete with a different sermon from Brazier and different music from Stuart Wilson's choir.

From Africa to America

The service at Apostolic Church of God embodied many classic elements of black church song. No one service or music program can completely express the extraordinary legacy of black church music, but this powerhouse on Chicago's South Side produced a variety of musical and vocal styles through which much of that legacy was expressed, particularly the Holiness and Pentecostal movements of the twentieth century. The story of black church song is a compelling journey from West African roots through Evangelical Protestant hymns and slave spirituals to the gospel songs of the twentieth century that have become the Black Church's most original and enduring contribution to sacred song in America.

The deepest sources of black church song lie in its West African heritage. Tribal peoples kidnapped into American slavery—Yoruba, Ibo, Ashanti, Gabon, Fulani—shared many musical and religious characteristics. For West Africans, music was a powerful spiritual form shared by everyone in the community, a constantly employed medium that accompanied all important events and episodes of life. West Africans inhabited a sacred cosmos grounded in the spiritual power of all entities in nature and presided over by the gods and the ancestors. Traditional forms of religious organization ranged from shamanistic healers and visionaries to organized priesthoods. Above all, West Africans experienced and expressed the sacred cosmos through song and dance, which became the last refuge of their identity when they were brutally torn from their land and sold into American slavery.

In her magisterial study *The Music of Black Americans,* Eileen Southern lists among West African musical practices a vast array of instruments used in accompanying song and dance: drums, bells, gongs, rattles, xylophone, mbira, flutes, pipe, fiddles, and lutes. The sources report a variety of rhythmic figures but uniformly strict observance of regular pulse. West African peoples favored short melodies in modal or gapped scales and harmonic intervals from a third to a fifth below the melody. Songs classically took the form of "call and response," in which soloists sang improvisatory verses or exclamations that "called forth" repeated chants or refrains from the people. From this evidence Southern concluded that "in essence, musical performance [in West African tradition] consisted of repeating a relatively short musical unit again and again, with variation in its repetition."[4]

These deep structures of the African musical past provided the essential foundation of black church song. In the American experience of the slaves, however, those musical and religious structures passed through the filter of Evangelical Protestantism, never to be quite the same. The same Great Awakenings that fostered the Sacred Harp tradition during the late colonial and antebellum periods also reached the slaves. Among the many effects of plantation and camp-meeting revivals was the acquisition by the slaves of classic hymn texts by Isaac Watts, Charles Wesley, and other Anglo-American Evangelical writers. Called "Dr. Watts Hymns," these sacred lyrics have comprised the textual core for virtually all black church hymnals published in America, beginning with *A Collection of Hymns and Spiritual Songs from Various Authors* compiled in 1801 by Richard Allen, founder of the African Methodist Episcopal Church.[5]

One notable aspect of black church performance of "Dr. Watts Hymns" was the preservation of the Puritan practice of lining out, the reading or intoning of each line by a deacon before it was sung by the congregation. In the new postbellum black denominations of the 1870s and 1880s, lining out was transmuted into a sophisticated form of call and response, recalling both West African roots and the slave spiritual. Lining out remained popular in the black Baptist churches until the 1920s. Today "Dr. Watts Hymns" are still widely used, especially in the African Methodist and National Baptist denominational families for whom they comprise the indispensable core of worship music.

Yet "Dr. Watts Hymns" were not used at Apostolic Church of God, nor were hymnals placed in the pews. The huge church on Chicago's South Side sang its faith not according to the mannered hymnal texts and tunes of white Evangelicalism but from memory in songs of suffering and triumph grounded in the slave spiritual and shout, then hammered into new forms of gospel hymn and gospel song by the urban experience of African Americans in the twentieth century. The slave spiritual is rightly celebrated as an extraordinary expression of sacred song in America. As African slaves were gradually Christianized in the antebellum South, they created what E. Franklin Frazier aptly called "the invisible institution" of slave Christianity.[6] Developed on the plantation at remotely located praise houses and bush meetings, slave Christianity was sustained by the preaching of exhorters and the singing of spiritual songs. The condition of slavery cast the spiritual into uniquely polyvocal forms. On one hand the spiritual consistently expressed pious evangelical hopes for "a home in heaven" where the earthly suffering and oppression of the slaves would be transformed into triumphant heavenly life with the Lord. On the other hand, the very same lyrics could express fervent this-worldly hopes for black liberation.[7]

Spirituals focused on biblical accounts of redemptive suffering, especially the Exodus account in Genesis. They created a sacred narrative of slave aspirations to overcome their bondage both in this world and the next. Black theologians, historians, and musicologists—most notably Howard Thurman, Benjamin Mays, James Cone, Albert Raboteau, and Jon Michael Spencer—have shown how the spiritual spoke to the slaves by identifying their plight with Israel in Egypt and appealing to God for justice and freedom. Other important images in slave spirituals derived from the biblical prophets like Daniel and from the sufferings of Jesus in the Christian gospels. The spiritual articulated the tragic experience of slavery through a fusion of biblical imagery with African American musical traditions, frequently cast in minor or modal melodies and persistent rhythmic figures. James Cone classically summarized the religious meaning of the slave spiritual: "The spiritual is the spirit of the people struggling to be free, it is their religion, their source of strength in a time of trouble."[8]

By contrast, the shout expressed the ecstatic side of slave religion in what Southern called "a special service, purely African in form and tradition," that followed formal plantation services in slave praise houses or at outdoor "bush meetings." The editors of the pioneer 1867 collection *Slave Songs of the United States* supplied this account of a praise-house shout: "The benches are pushed back to the wall when the formal meeting is over, and old and young, men and women . . . all stand up in the middle of the floor, and when the [spiritual] is struck up, begin first walking and by-and-by shuffling round, one after the other, in a ring. The foot is hardly taken from the floor, and the progression is mainly due to a jerking, hitching motion, which agitates the entire shouter."[9]

In principle shouts were a subset of spirituals, a part of evangelical slave worship that allowed ample room for charismatic manifestations including ex tempore bodily movements. But in practice shouts reiterated the music of West African ecstatic chant and sacred dance. "In performance," Southern wrote, "a ring spiritual was repeated over and over as the shouters moved around in a circle, often for as long as four and five successive hours. The song thus took on the character of a chant. . . . The tempo of the music and the pace of the circling gradually quickened so that the performance eventually displayed 'signs of frenzy.'"[10] Whereas the spiritual told of slave spirituality through texts modeled from the biblical narrative and melodies derived from both African and American scales, the shout expressed the ecstasy of West African spirit possession through the ceaselessly repeating rhythms of sacred dance.

After Emancipation former slaves organized new Baptist denominations and responded to the appeals of African Methodist missionaries. Both of these traditions enshrined "Dr. Watts hymns," including those of Methodist Charles Wesley, as the foundation of black church song. These new free black communions in the South at first resisted the spirituals of the slave past, but during the 1870s and 1880s they changed their attitude, owing to the efforts of the Fisk Jubilee Singers. Founded in 1871 to raise funds for Fisk University, the pioneer black Baptist college in Nashville, the Jubilee Singers enjoyed great international success after 1875 by adding careful arrangements of spirituals to their programs of European choral classics and "Dr. Watts hymns." Other black college groups soon followed the Fisk formula and for the last quarter of the nineteenth century the Jubilee style maintained an important link between the emerging Black Church and the slave experience expressed through the plantation spiritual.[11]

A vast tide of southern blacks poured into northern cities after Emancipation, reaching a peak during the 1910s and 1920s, providing immense resources for any religious movement that could redefine the relationship between uprooted rural folk and their traditional God of evangelical faith. Grounded in Methodist tradition, the Holiness movement supplied one such definition in claiming that humans could attain what John Wesley had called "entire sanctification," complete freedom from willful sin, as a "second blessing" distinct from the grace received in salvation. Among African Americans the Holiness movement spread quickly into the historic African Methodist Episcopal and African Methodist Episcopal Zion churches and made deep inroads into the new black Baptist denominations of the south.

The Holiness movement found its distinctive mode of sacred song in the gospel hymn, the most popular form of revival music at the turn of the nineteenth century. Introduced by Congregationalist preacher Dwight L. Moody and his Methodist soloist Ira D. Sankey during their 1872 revival campaign in Great Britain, gospel hymns became instantly popular among American Evangelical denominations both black and white. From the sentimental Victorian ballad, gospel hymns borrowed emotional first-person lyrics describing the singer's personal experience of saving grace and moral empowerment. From operettas, glees, and barbershop choral styles they took close harmonies, flatted-seventh chords, and melody-centered settings. From the dance hall they absorbed the rhythms of the waltz and the two-step. Sung to instrumental accompaniment by piano rather than organ, gospel hymns presented a new Evangelical sacred-song aesthetic assembled on the streets of Chicago and at the entertainments of New York.[12]

The Holiness movement produced the first great African American hymn writer, Charles Price Jones, whose hymns and theology would deeply influence the Black Church in the twentieth century. In 1894 Jones, a Baptist minister from Mississippi, experienced a call from God to seek holiness and to write hymns as a way to proclaim its teachings.

> When I first gave myself to the Lord to be sanctified, I had no idea at all of taking up holiness as a fad, or an ism, or a creed, or a slogan of a cult. I just wanted to be personally holy. I just wished to make my own calling and election sure to my own heart by walking with God in the Spirit. One day as I staggered under the weight of this obligation, under the necessity of this ministry, I felt that I must be alone and especially talk to God about it. . . . The Spirit spoke within from the Holy of Holies and said, "You shall write hymns for your people." This He said six or seven times till it was fixed in my mind.[13]

Jones produced more than one thousand hymns, many of them for his pioneer gospel hymn collections *Jesus Only* (1899), *Jesus Only Nos. 1 and 2* (1901), and *His Fullness* (1906).[14] Jones composed his most famous gospel hymn, "Jesus Only," in 1897.

> Jesus only is my motto,
> Jesus only is my song,
> Jesus only is my heart-thought
> Jesus only all day long.
> Then away with ev'ry idol,
> Let my Lord be all to me;
> Jesus only is my Master,
> Jesus only let me see.

In his recent book *Black Hymnody,* Jon Michael Spencer commented on the historic significance of this early black gospel hymn. "Clearly bearing the Holiness insignia of zealous Christ-centeredness," Spencer wrote, "'Jesus Only' interprets what it means to surrender oneself fully to the Lord." The song also classically expressed the West African stress on repetition both textually and musically, now transformed into the gospel hymn medium.[15]

The same year that he wrote "Jesus Only," Jones along with fellow Baptist Charles H. Mason founded the Church of God in Christ (COGIC) as one of the first black Holiness denominations. The Holiness movement's emphasis on entire sanctification, however, soon encouraged more radical claims from those who claimed to have experienced a "third blessing" of glossolalia, or "speaking in tongues," described in Acts 2:1–4 as the bestowal of the Holy Spirit upon the Apostles on the day of Pentecost.

On New Year's Day 1901, white Methodist evangelist Charles Parham began preaching a protracted revival to students at his tiny seminary in Topeka, Kansas. Parham proclaimed the gift of tongues to be a defining sign of true Christianity, and soon "the fire fell," first upon Agnes Ozman, then upon others among Parham's students. Parham called his movement "the Apostolic Faith" and conducted evangelistic tours for several years in the Midwest and Southwest. At Houston Parham encountered William J. Seymour, an enigmatic black radical Wesleyan evangelist who experienced "the baptism of the Holy Spirit" and took the Pentecostal message to the west coast. In April 1906 Seymour began preaching in an abandoned warehouse on Azuza Street in Los Angeles. The Azuza Street revival became the defining episode of American Pentecostalism, driven by singing in tongues and charismatic preaching.

Jennie Moore, the black woman who first received Spirit-baptism in glossolalia at Azuza Street, reported her experience: "When evening came, we attended the meeting [and] the power of God fell and I was baptized in the Holy Ghost and fire. It seemed as if a vessel broke within me and water surged up through my being, which when it reached my mouth came out in a torrent of speech in the languages which God had given me. . . . I sang under the power of the Spirit in many languages. . . . The Spirit led me to the piano, where I played and sang under inspiration, though I had not learned to play."[16]

"Tongue-songs" like Jennie Moore's were quite common at Azuza Street, elemental vehicles of charismatic utterance. On more than one occasion they sang simply: "Jesus, Jesus, Jesus, Jesus / Power, Power, Power, Power" endlessly to a chant melody consisting only of repeated figures on the first and minor third degrees of the scale, supported by driving gospel piano chording and riffs. Many at the Azuza Street meetings reported the musical "perfection" of songs sung in the spirit, performed with spontaneous harmonies offered by "the heavenly chorus" of singers inspired by the individual tongue-singer who first struck up the song. Chicago evangelist William H. Durham captured the extraordinary spiritual effect of this sort of charismatic singing. "I never felt the power and glory that I felt in Azuza Street Mission," he reported, "and when about twenty persons joined in singing [as] the 'Heavenly Chorus,' it was the most ravishing and unearthly music that ever fell on mortal ears."[17]

The Azuza Street revival drew thousands of converts to Pentecostalism, many of whom brought its new teachings and experiences into their own denominations. Pentecostal claims proved highly divisive, however, among black Holiness groups like Jones and Mason's Church of God in Christ. Mason experienced glossolalia at Azuza Street early in 1907 and championed it as the definitive sign of true Christianity, while Jones just as steadfastly rejected the tongues phenomenon. The two leaders eventually broke over the issue, with Jones leading the Holiness minority out of the Church of God in Christ to form the Church of Christ (Holiness). Similar divisions over "the third blessing" or "latter rain" of tongues beset other black and white Holiness churches. Once established as autonomous bodies, moreover, Pentecostal denominations continued to experience conflict and schism. Disputes over the nature of sanctification, musical instruments in worship, baptism by immersion, the Trinity, and church polity repeatedly fractured early Pentecostal denominations.[18]

The most important of these conflicts was the "Oneness" or "Jesus Only" Controversy. In 1916 some early Pentecostals embraced the beliefs, as described by historian Grant Wacker, "that God was one (not triune) and that He had revealed Himself fully in Jesus Christ." Accordingly they taught that the Risen Lord was the Creator and that his spirit was the Holy Spirit. They pronounced baptism in the name of Jesus only, following the command of Peter in Acts 2:38: "Repent, and be baptized every one of you in the name of Jesus Christ so that your sins may be forgiven; and you will receive the gift of the Holy Spirit." The controversy produced a number of Oneness denominations including the Pentecostal Assemblies of the World, incorporated in 1919 under the leadership of G. T. Haywood. Today the integrated but predominantly black PAW is the largest Oneness denomination in America.[19]

Regardless of specific doctrinal formulation, however, denominations like Bishop Brazier's Pentecostal Assemblies of the World affirm the experience of glossolalia as a sign of true Christian faith and apply that standard not only to the tongue-songs and ecstatic utterances of lay members but also to the preaching of ministers as well, manifested in yet another traditional mode of sacred song in the black church, the chanted sermon. Brazier's sermon bore the lineaments of classic evangelical preaching, replete with dramatized retelling of the biblical story, appeal to potential converts, and moral exhortation of the faithful. But in his peroration Brazier employed a different mode of sermonic expression, his language suddenly rhythmic and cadenced, his voice rising in pitch and volume on the first word of each verbal figure. In response, the congregation applauded and fell into spontaneous charismatic praise with body and voice. In those climactic moments Brazier and the people of Apostolic Church of God enacted the primal ritual form of call and response that roots the black church in America to its antebellum and African past.

The chanted sermon is a unique form of sacred song, combining melody, rhythm, call and response, polyphony, rational content, and improvisation.[20] Musicologist William Turner, using a term coined by historian of religion Mircea Eliade, has called the chanted sermon a "kratophany," a manifestation of power rendered through the spoken word and its accompanying gestures. The musicality of the chanted sermon, he argued, supplies a "surplus" of meaning that carries its words far beyond their literal meaning.

The music of black preaching can be understood as a sort of "singing in the spirit," for there is a surplus (glossa) expressed in music which accompanies the rational content (logos) expressed in the words. The rational portion is contained in the formal structure of the sermon which reflects the homiletical soundness and the doctrinal tradition in which the preacher stands. For the glossal portion, the preacher becomes an instrument of musical afflatus: a flute through which divine air is blown, a harp upon which eternal strings vibrate. For the sake of the audience, the preacher becomes an oracle through which a divinely inspired message flows.[21]

Turner traced the roots of such preaching and its glossal "surplus" to traditional African societies in which "the very force of life that pulsates through
individuals and communities is given objective tangible expression in rhythmic
motion and music, and that musical rhythm is the aesthetic signification of the
force sustaining the people." In the slave community, Turner argued, "the surplus of deep stirrings, intensity, and zeal within the African spirit, easily expressed in African languages by means of rhythm, tone, and pitch" were ultimately "deposited in black preaching." Jon Michael Spencer similarly regarded
black preaching as a likely source for the slave spiritual and located its characteristic musicality, its "licks," in several elements including "parallel syntax with
similar word endings, aphoristic iterations, vocal percussiveness, and intonation." Bishop Brazier employed all of these devices at Apostolic Church of God.[22]

Spencer also addressed the question of form and spontaneous creativity in
the chanted sermon. The literary and argumentative forms of the sermon, he
wrote, "concretely capture" kratophanic power, but the effective release of that
power comes through oral improvisation. "When given a word, phrase, or sentence, the preacher can repeat it, vary it, contrast it, or extend it," Spencer observed. "When a word, phrase, or sentence is repeated verbatim, the preacher
can stress the same syllables and words, emphasize other syllables and words,
deliver the material with the same rhythmic pattern, superimpose a different
pattern, or sing the text to the same tune, vary it, or intone a new tune."[23]

Like Bishop Brazier, each preacher in this tradition employs a unique blend
of these verbal and tonal elements. The range of chanted sermon in the Black
Church is therefore immense, and yet a distinctive song tradition is also clearly
identifiable. The primal rhythms, iterations, and intonations of sung preaching articulate the kratophany of African religious heritage as do the polyphonic
responsorial call-and-response acclamations of instruments and people. Historically fused to the beliefs of American Evangelical and Pentecostal traditions,
these performative conventions of the chanted sermon have created a distinctive mode of African American sacred song rich in power and influence.

Gospel Song

During the early decades of the twentieth century the urban congregations of
black Pentecostalism transformed the gospel hymn into something new: the
gospel song. They brought new instruments into worship: tambourine, drums,
guitar, and horns. The percussion of these instrumental bands drove the rhythm
of the shout into black gospel song even as the spiritual informed its melodies
and harmonies. Early gospel songwriters introduced a new freedom of literary
and musical form. Their hymn texts broke out of the classic English meters of
Watts and Wesley and their musical structures shared much with emerging new
secular black music styles including ragtime, blues, and jazz. Among early black
gospel songwriters Charles Albert Tindley (c. 1851–1933), the great Philadelphia

United Methodist preacher and singer, deserves pride of place owing to his classic songs written before World War I, including two of his most popular, "We'll Understand It Better By and By" (example 12 on page 344) and "Stand by Me."[24]

Horace Clarence Boyer has described Tindley's transformation of the white gospel hymn into black gospel song as a three-part development.

> In the first place, [Tindley] concentrated on texts that gave attention to such important concerns of Black Christians as worldly sorrows, blessings, and woes, as well as the joys of the afterlife. Second, he placed many of his melodies in the beloved pentatonic scale and left a certain amount of space in his melodic line and harmonic scheme for interpolation of the so-called blue thirds and sevenths. [Finally,] he also allowed space for the inevitable improvisation of text, melody, harmony, and rhythm so characteristic of Black American folk and popular music.[25]

Gospel songs spread quickly through the black churches. Though resisted at first by the older mainstream denominations, even the musically conservative National Baptist Convention eventually gave its endorsement to the new style by publishing in 1921 a collection of gospel hymns and songs called *Gospel Pearls*. This paperbound volume served black churches for decades as the definitive gospel songbook, much as Sankey's *Gospel Hymns* had functioned for gospel hymns in white communions.[26] The same year also marked the emergence of Lucie E. Campbell (1885–1963), the dominant musical force in the National Baptist Convention from 1930 to 1962 and composer of "He Understands; He'll Say, 'Well Done'," which Horace Clarence Boyer has called "the second most popular gospel song in all Black Christendom."[27]

In the same watershed year of 1921 Thomas A. Dorsey (1899–1999) began writing gospel songs for the choir of Chicago's Morning Star Baptist Church. After a successful but troubled career as a piano blues man, Dorsey, widely regarded as the father of the gospel song, was appointed choral director in 1932 of Pilgrim Baptist Church in that same city, a position he retained for more than forty years. Of more than five hundred songs he published, Dorsey's most popular works included "If I Don't Get There," "We Will Meet Him in the Sweet By and By," "There'll Be Peace in the Valley," and "Take My Hand, Precious Lord" (example 13 on page 346), the most popular black gospel song ever written.

> *Chorus:* Precious Lord, take my hand,
> Lead me on, let me stand—
> I am tired, I am weak, I am worn.
> Through the storm, through the night,
> Lead me on, to the light,
> Take my hand, Precious Lord,
> Lead me home.

When my way grows drear,
Precious Lord, linger near,
When my life is almost gone,
Hear my cry, hear my call,
Hold my hand lest I fall,
Take my hand, Precious Lord,
Lead me home.

When the darkness appears
And the night draws near
And the day is past and gone,
At the river I stand,
Guide my feet, hold my hand,
Take my hand, Precious Lord,
Lead me home.

In *The Rise of Gospel Blues,* Michael Harris has recently analyzed "Take My Hand, Precious Lord" as a turning point in black church song. According to Harris the power of the song, written in 1932 as Dorsey grieved the deaths of his wife and son, lies in a mixture of musical and spiritual dimensions. First, Dorsey worked within the constraints of evangelical hymnody by appropriating a well-known hymn tune, "Maitland"—published in 1844 by George N. Allen as a setting for Thomas Shepherd's 1693 hymn text "Must Jesus Bear the Cross Alone"—as the melodic basis for "Precious Lord." But Dorsey also made crucial technical changes to Maitland. He reversed the sequence of verse and refrain and supplied original lyrics that shifted the emphasis in the song from the expository presentation of traditional evangelical hymns to the exhortative urgency of black preaching he had learned from the enormously popular recorded chanted sermons of Rev. W. M. Nix. Ultimately, however, the compositional crisis of "Take My Hand, Precious Lord" manifested Dorsey's most important achievement: "He found at last a way to speak as forthrightly with his gospel blues as he had so routinely done with his lowdown, secular blues," Harris wrote. "Whereas previously he had only been able to cower away from sorrow in his gospels, he had always been able to cry out about it in his blues. With 'Take My Hand, Precious Lord,' Dorsey allowed himself to wail, to get 'lowdown,' to purge—rather than just soothe—his grief."[28]

This spiritual and musical fusion of gospel hymns and blues marked the emergence of the gospel song, which Dorsey developed, organized, and managed during his long career. Dorsey performed as a soloist on several gospel recordings during the 1930s and collaborated closely with the two most famous female black gospel singers of the 1940s and 1950s, Roberta Martin and Mahalia Jackson. He also organized the first women's gospel quartet. This dimension of Dorsey's career highlights the increasing importance of performers and public performance in popularizing the new gospel song style. Singing evangelists, soloists, and quartets began touring during the 1920s, performing at church benefits, revivals, and song contests. At first black gospel singers sang in the Jubilee style of close harmony and slow tempo, but through figures like Dorsey they absorbed urban black musical culture and their performances became more vocally unrestrained and rhythmically driven. After World War II these influences culminated in the career of Dorsey's protégé Mahalia Jackson, whose first hit gospel song, "Move On Up a Little Higher," was written not by Dorsey but by William Herbert Brewster (c. 1897–1987), his great contemporary who also penned Clara Ward's greatest hit, a version of the spiritual "How I Got Over." Jackson's extraordinary soprano range and blues inflections permanently fixed the gospel vocal style and her popularity on records, radio, and television brought gospel song into America's musical mainstream.[29]

Of perhaps even greater long-term significance was the parallel rise of gospel quartet singing, which Dorsey pioneered for women at Pilgrim Baptist. Itself a synthesis of shape-note singing, sung preaching, increasing vocal range, and call and response, the quartet style grew steadily in popularity and musical complexity from the first recordings during the 1920s to postwar LPs by the Mighty Clouds of Joy, the Dixie Hummingbirds, the Five Blind Boys, and the blues-influenced Staple Singers. In the late 1950s, gospel soloists and quartet singers employing electric guitars and the rhythm-and-blues performance style successfully crossed over into the black secular music market and eventually into pop and rock. Successful crossover artists from this "sanctified" style—many of them assisted by composer and music publisher Kenneth Morris (1917–88), author of the enormously popular 1945 gospel song "Yes, God Is Real"—established gospel song as a constituent element of American popular music and gospel singers as a perennial recruiting ground for broader-market black music artists.[30]

Thomas Dorsey served yet another crucial function in the rise of gospel song with his role as leader of gospel choirs and choir organizations. In 1931 he organized what Eileen Southern has called "the world's first gospel chorus" at Ebenezer Baptist Church in Chicago. Several years later he and gospel singer Sallie Martin formed the National Convention of Gospel Choirs and Choruses, whose vast annual meetings featured the newest and best in gospel performance. Since the Second World War, the gospel choir has emerged as an increasingly powerful stylistic and performance influence. Through the 1950s and 1960s, Clara Ward and James Cleveland perfected the gospel choir sound and made it the most popular style in black congregational song. Paul Oliver in *The New Grove Dictionary of American Music* has described the gospel choir style as featuring a singer using "growl effects contrasted with shrill pure notes, extemporizing to [the choir's] energetic vocal accompaniment." With the 1969 crossover hit recording of "Oh, Happy Day" by the Edwin Hawkins Singers, whose leader was a minister of music in a Church of God in Christ congregation, the gospel choir sound reached the top of the pop charts. Since then, as Jon Michael Spencer noted, Pentecostal choirs—notably the Brooklyn Tabernacle Choir and New Jersey Mass Choir—and famous singing families like the Hawkinses (Edwin and

Walter), the Crouches (Andrae and Sandra); and the Winanses (BeBe and CeCe) have moved into the forefront of black gospel music.[31]

Make a Joyful Noise

Virtually all of the major elements of black church sacred song were to be found in the music program of the Apostolic Church of God, expressed in a sophisticated contemporary performance style. Apostolic's minister of music in 1994 was Stuart Wilson, a young black church musician who after less than two years had molded its music program to new standards of professionalism appropriate for its weekly radio and television broadcasts, while also sustaining the church's evangelistic message and spirituality. I interviewed Wilson to discover what went into the extraordinary sacred-song performances I had experienced there. The answer, I learned, began and ended with Arthur M. Brazier, pastor of the church and bishop in the Pentecostal Assemblies of the World. Brazier oversees every aspect of his remarkable ministry with a quick, discerning eye. Music is no exception. The bishop, Wilson reported, is "extremely particular" about what is sung in his church.[32]

But the day-to-day selection and preparation of sacred song at Apostolic are handled by Wilson himself. The thirty-three-year-old director of music was hardly an unlikely choice for the job in 1993. Wilson is a fourth-generation church musician whose father and mother both served in the music ministry at Christ Temple Cathedral Church of Christ, Holiness in Chicago. His father was organist at Christ Temple Cathedral, his mother a pianist and singer there. Wilson's four brothers consist of two keyboard players, a bass player, and a violinist. His mother gave him piano lessons in the family home, where frequent jam sessions developed the technical and improvisational skills of all the brothers. At the age of ten, Wilson began piano study at Roosevelt University under Phyllis Hill. His keyboard excellence won Wilson a scholarship to Jackson State College in Jackson, Mississippi, but he majored in accounting and experimented for several years with a career in that field.

Finally resolved on a music career, Wilson, like Dorsey and a host of black church musicians, first played house parties and clubs, but soon he experienced a spiritual conviction to enter the music ministry of the church. "The real turning point," he recalled, "was when my mother passed in May 1990. Before she died she passed the mantle of her music ministry to me. I remember it was 4:30 P.M. on May 30, 1990. She gave me a clear mission to undertake music ministry full-time." For a year, Wilson took on his mother's responsibilities at Christ Temple Cathedral, then "the Lord led me to another church, Liberty Baptist in Chicago." He served two years at Liberty as organist and eventually minister of music. In retrospect Wilson saw those years at Liberty as preparation for his ministry at Apostolic. "I never could have done Apostolic without it," he said. "It was a training ground. The old church was too familiar; Liberty was Baptist, not quite the same thing. It was different from my teaching and Liberty was larger, with larger problems."

Wilson's first contact with Bishop Brazier came at a meeting in which the young musician sought a role in Apostolic's 1992 Christmas concert. Wilson did not get that job, but at the interview Brazier mentioned a new position opening at the church as minister of music. "He wanted someone with spiritual background, musical background, being able to orchestrate, direct, play, a little bit of everything," Wilson reported, "and it sounded like something I wanted to do." Wilson was undergoing a vocational crisis at Liberty and later sought out Brazier's counsel. Gradually it became clear that Wilson and Apostolic would be a good match. After several more meetings, visits to Apostolic's worship, and much prayer, Wilson decided to leave Liberty and join Apostolic. "It was the teaching of Bishop Brazier that made the difference," Wilson said. "His teaching and the [Holiness] teaching of Christ Temple Cathedral where I came from have some traditional differences, but it's much the same thing. The Lord was definitely in the plan. Coming from the outside to a church that size, when you have people who are already there, it was a big step for me, one that was a leap of faith."

As minister of music at Apostolic, Wilson's main functions are "to direct and teach the sanctuary choir, direct the morning services, make sure that musicians are adequately prepared to present music, whether that means scoring out parts or going over it with the ones who do not read, and also to oversee the music operations of the church. We have a women's choir, a men's choir, a teen choir, and a children's choir, each with its own leader." Supporting these vast choral forces, 250 voices in the Sanctuary Choir alone, and more than 500 voices overall, is a sixteen-member instrumental staff: "We have four keyboard players in the pit right behind the bishop," Wilson reported, "a bass player, a lead guitar player, three percussionists, four trumpet players, two saxophone players, and a flute player."

Sanctuary Choir rehearses on Tuesday evenings. Sprinkled liberally through the rehearsal are some songs the choir knows cold, the "twenty or so" songs, Wilson said, "the people really love and we could do blindfolded." This core repertory proceeds from Brazier's own discernment. "One of his favorite songs is 'Behold the Man,'" Wilson told me. "When they first learned 'Behold the Man,' Bishop would ask for that quite a bit. Of course the more you sing it, the more the congregation starts to take to it. And what happens is his favorites become their favorites." The Sanctuary Choir rehearses within earshot of Brazier's office, and he regularly makes his presence felt. "He listens to rehearsals," Wilson said. "He may not come out all the time. He may come out to say something to the choir at the end or at the middle. But if he hears something in his office that he has some question about, he says 'we need to hold off on that.'"

Brazier is clearly a hands-on pastor who has established stringent standards for music selection at Apostolic. "Ask Bishop about a song," Stuart Wilson said, "and he'll ask you 'is it going to save someone?' You can argue about trivial questions for years to come, but there are people who need to be saved." Brazier and Wilson sharply criticize repetitive "praise songs," popular in the Charismatic movement of the 1970s and 1980s, as well as commercialized gospel songs produced to compete in the pop market. "There are a lot of songs out that are just repetitive and are commercial," Wilson said, "but we don't do anything like that. Bishop is extremely particular about the message of the song. It has to have a definite story, a definite meaning. Something that speaks to the majesty of God, his son Jesus, his grace, his mercy, and his love for us. Nothing that is just repetitive. There may be songs that the congregation may love and say 'why don't you all do this song?' But that doesn't really force us to use it."

Brazier and Wilson apply the central tenet of the Holiness and Pentecostal movement, giving over one's entire life to the promptings of the Holy Spirit, to all dimensions of sacred song. Following the mandates of 1 Corinthians 14:15 to "sing with the spirit and with the understanding also," and of Ephesians 5:19 to "be filled with the Spirit, . . . singing and making melody to the Lord in your hearts," they submit their worship to spiritual discernment and the communal union that it brings. Such a strategy can be disruptive, but Wilson understands it as a matter of his spiritual accountability to Jesus as a minister of the gospel.

In Wilson's choice of soloists, for example, discernment entails "almost letting people get mad at you if they aren't chosen, because I take my responsibility seriously, and the Lord's not going to hold them accountable for my responsibility. I just tell them the Spirit leads me in that direction, and I can't do anything if they get upset." In observing this mandate Wilson follows the lead of his mentor, Bishop Brazier. "He's had people upset with him," Wilson said of Brazier, "but his attitude is 'I have to go where the Lord leads me, not with what people think. Because when I stand before the judgment seat, I'm held accountable. No one's going to be there to answer for me.'"

The same principles of being led by the Spirit and pastoral accountability make for a close collaboration between Brazier and Wilson. "I meet with the bishop every week just to touch bases with him, usually on Tuesday of our rehearsal," Wilson reported, "because he is ultimately responsible for the flock, and I want to make sure that we're always on the same page and working together." This spiritual collaboration expresses itself in a way unique to Pentecostal worship. Unlike the careful coordination of sermon text and service music typical of many Christian congregations, Wilson and Brazier wait upon the Spirit to bring forth the most spiritually efficacious combination of preaching and sacred song. Wilson prepares service music before Brazier knows what his sermon texts will be. Even the sequence and content of the service itself is improvised under the Spirit's leading.

"Sometimes I'll know [the texts] before service," Wilson said, "or sometimes not before he takes it. Sometimes the TV room will call, like when it's the 150th Psalm. When he reads it, the musicians answer with the song 'Praise ye the Lord.'" But typically pastor and music minister rely on the Spirit to fit sacred song and sermon. "Usually the Lord sees fit to coincide," he remarked. "There was a [sermon] that was on the Prodigal Son and we sang a song 'His Grace Was Greater' by the Brooklyn Tabernacle Choir, and the words are: 'I was like the prodigal who wanted his own way.' And it just so happened it fit perfectly. And we hadn't planned it or anything! The Spirit just led that way. And that's usually how it goes."

Often the choir doesn't know what it will sing until Wilson calls the song in the midst of the service itself.

> We'll rehearse something on Tuesday, but [the choir] doesn't even know what we're going to sing on Sunday. Bishop [is] a very organized person and he'll say, "what are you going to sing?" and I say, "I don't know." He'll ask "how are you going to do it Sunday?" and I'll say "I don't know! You know the Spirit leads." You hate to say that to your pastor, but you really don't know. The Spirit might tell you that someone may need [a particular song] that day, and the Spirit may say "This song." And it just so happens that it works.

Spirit Possession and Signifyin(g)

Given the vast array of musical forms through which the Black Church has expressed its faith, the question arises whether any elements of religiousness fuse them into a distinctive tradition. Interpreters of the Black Church agree that such commonality exists at the level of lyrical content. While grounded in the Evangelical Protestant lyrics of "Dr. Watts hymns," black church song has maintained a persistent focus on those aspects of the Christian message that have had the most compelling meaning for African Americans. For a hundred years, scholars from W. E. B. Du Bois to Howard Thurman and James Cone to Jon Michael Spencer have identified those themes as African American expressions of faith and hope in their condition of suffering. Slavery, poverty, oppression, and struggle have been the historic legacy of African peoples in America. Their sacred songs have therefore addressed Christianity's capacity to heal, transform, and remedy that legacy and the powers that impose it. Themes of exodus both personal and communal, of prophetic vision and courage, of Jesus as healer and guide, of the Holy Spirit as real and efficacious presence in the world, and of God's kingdom of justice and peace both now and in the hereafter have suffused black church song from its beginnings. The songs of Chicago's Apostolic Church of God testify to the enduring presence of these biblical and spiritual emphases.[33]

Recent interpretation, however, suggests that the religious meanings of black church song extend beyond lyrical content in at least two further dimensions: the enduring power of spirit possession and an improvisational style of speech and song given the label "signifyin(g)" by its leading theorists. Both of these elements have served the Black Church in negotiating its tragic and deeply conflicted way in the New World, and both of them were abundantly present in the worship at Apostolic Church of God.

Spirit possession is a mode of religious experience in which the subject's soul and body are believed to be directly controlled or subsumed by the sacred powers. It is characterized by an ecstatic state, often induced by rhythmic song or dance, that produces apparently involuntary behaviors ranging from violent bodily movement and glossolalic utterance to a condition of unconsciousness or sleep. After these charismatic episodes, the possessed return to everyday consciousness and report dramatic encounters with the sacred powers including heavenly journeys, visions, instructions, and prophecies.[34]

Spirit possession is an ancient phenomenon, most familiar perhaps to Western culture in the Delphic oracle and Dionysiac rites of the Greeks. It predated the classical Mediterranean world. This earlier form survives today in shamanism, a mode of religiousness characteristic of archaic peoples and practiced in tribal religions throughout the world, including those of Africa, Asia, and the Americas. In shamanism holy persons, healers, and other "masters of spirits" known generically as shamans undertake an arduous vision quest that eventuates in their travel in trance to the spirit world where the ancestors and totemic deities supply them with objects, songs, and rituals through which spirit possession can be renewed and sacred powers exercised in the world. In West African tribal religions, spirit possession occurs in many different forms, including initiation rites and neophyte rituals, as well as the regular worship of initiates. In his massive 1982 study *Music and Trance,* French ethnomusicologist Gilbert Rouget listed seven characteristics of possession trance: movement, noise, in company, crisis, sensory overstimulation, amnesia during trance, and no hallucinations.[35]

Traditional tribal religions of West Africa, including spirit possession, traveled with slaves to the New World. Slavery imposed a crushing oppression upon the Africans that eliminated most of their cultural traditions. Spirit possession, however, survived. In colonies like Haiti, Cuba, and Brazil, relatively dense and homogeneous patterns of slave settlement and the syncretistic capacities of Catholicism permitted the retention of West African spirit possession along with its generic deities and ritual music. These West African features eventually melded with Catholicism to produce the still-flourishing Afro-Caribbean spirit possession religions of vodun, Santería, and candomblé respectively.[36]

In the American South a more diversified and dispersed West African population, along with a vigorous system of social control and slave distribution, visited more radical destruction on African cultures than in the Caribbean and Latin America. The musical consequence of American slavery was, in Jon Michael Spencer's telling phrase, "the drum deferred," the official prohibition of drum and shout on the plantation. While that prohibition was not entirely effective, the principal musical medium for sustaining spirit possession and its traditional gods certainly went into eclipse.[37]

Spirit possession survived, ironically enough, through the Evangelical Protestantism introduced to slaves by their white masters. One of Evangelicalism's central tenets was that the Holy Spirit cleanses the regenerate human soul and "dwells within" it. During the Great Awakening this teaching promoted the experience of charismatic gifts among both white and black converts. By the late eighteenth century, West African spirit possession had blended with the evangelical style of charismatic spirituality in the slave community. This potent combination laid the foundation for the reemergence of charismatic gifts and "sanctified" music in the Black Church after Emancipation.[38]

Most interpreters of spirit possession have emphasized its social function in providing religious empowerment for victims of political oppression. That has certainly been the case in the African American experience. Slave revolutionaries Gabriel Prosser, Denmark Vesey, and Nat Turner were Methodists who claimed that angels had appeared to them proclaiming the day of liberation, and after the collapse of Reconstruction in 1877 the Black Church took up the agenda of God's justice for African Americans, which it has never relinquished.[39] Appropriate as this emphasis on the political effects of spirit possession has been, it has nonetheless tended to minimize the religious meaning at the heart of charismatic experience.

Spirit possession is the most radical kind of religious experience, a direct, nonmediated contact with sacred power itself. To know the sacred absolutely and internally is a human reality that transcends all other cultural imperatives. Such an experience certainly breeds inspiration and confidence to overcome political oppression but, more important, it relativizes every form of social structure and cultural control and relocates spiritual and cultural authority within the ambit of the self. The sacred powers can authorize the individual to defy even the constraints of the very religious tradition that they manifest.

This sort of radical authority is especially relevant to our inquiry given the African American experience of cultural loss and betrayal. Caught between the destruction of their African identities and the profoundly ambivalent message of Evangelical Protestantism that promised them freedom in heaven while denying it on earth, African Americans could depend on received cultural and religious traditions only at the greatest peril. What they required was the authority to make their own religious and cultural reality. Spirit possession, still resonant with West African heritage and legitimated by Evangelicalism, helped to provide that authority. When the historic opportunity to make their own world finally arrived after the Civil War, the most original and enduring achievement of African Americans was the production of a unique religious culture. The first generation of emancipated African Americans created the Black Church and the second infused it with the spirit possession and charismatic manifestations of the Holiness and Pentecostal movement. The Black Church today continues to voice the freedom of the African American soul through the powers of the spirit.

The radical experience of spirit possession in black religion has always been expressed through music. Gilbert Rouget has denied that any particular melodic scale or instrumentation has intrinsic powers of spirit possession, but found that repetition of figures with gradual acceleration and breaks or abrupt changes in rhythm "recur frequently" enough that they might well be regarded as "universal of possession music."[40] In the primal African ring shout, for example, endlessly repeated melodic phrases and rhythmic patterns provided the indispensable grounding for spirit manifestations and associated movements. Virtually every African American form of sacred song has sustained that connection between musical repetition and spirit possession.

Another melodic element of black sacred song, however, overlies the incessant repetition of musical and rhythmic figures and exemplifies a protean form of African and African American cultural expression. In musical terms it is best thought of as improvisation. In its broadest and most penetrating theoretical sense it has been identified by Henry Lewis Gates Jr. as "signifyin(g)." In his 1988 study of African American cultural expression, *The Signifying Monkey*, Gates presented a powerful new theory of literary interpretation and rhetoric grounded in African and African American mythic, poetic, and fictive texts. Gates argued that African American literature is fundamentally figurative rather than argumentative, rooted in a tension between speaking and writing that produces metaphors whose power lies in indeterminacy and ambiguity.[41]

In classic West African thought, Gates wrote, "the text is not fixed in any determinate sense," but rather is "in motion," fraught with interpretive license, contextuality, displaced meanings, and open-endedness. African Americans appropriated this deep structure of symbolic expression, Gates argued, to create a tradition of "signifyin(g)," "a double-voiced utterance" that comments on antecedent texts "by tropological revision or repetition and difference." For Gates, the genius of African and African American literary expression consists in the ever-changing creativity of signifyin(g), a rhetorical practice that both recapitulates and revises traditional narrative and poetic figures in a playful and freeing style.[42]

Gates's concept of signifyin(g) opened the way for new theoretical thinking about African American musicality and meaning. In *The Power of Black Music*, Samuel A. Floyd recently applied Gates's interpretive perspective to the canon of African American music, including much of the Black Church's sacred song. Floyd argued that the same modality of "repetition and difference" Gates found in African American literature also applies to music. "Gates's figures and tropes point to the musical work as performance or oration," Floyd wrote, "as rhetorical, symbolic object." For Floyd, "the master trope" of black music is call and response, rooted in the West African ring shout and permutated through four centuries of African American experience. "In African-American music," he wrote, "musical figures Signify by commenting on other musical figures, on themselves, on performances of other music, on other performances of the same piece, and on completely new works of music. Moreover, genres Signify on other genres: ragtime on European and American dance music; blues on the ballad; the spiritual on the hymn; jazz on blues and ragtime; gospel on the hymn, the spiritual, and blues."[43]

Gates and Floyd suggest a different kind of sacred song expression than what we have yet encountered. While Native American, Chicano, and Sacred Harp varieties of sacred song possess widely divergent styles and religious functions, in all of these traditions sacred song articulates previously defined mythic and ritual meaning. For Native Americans both music and language serve the larger communal experience of identity through sacred dance. In the Chicano tradition music "sets" or accompanies holy language, while for Sacred Harp singers the act of singing embodies secondary sacrality, not primary religious identity. But if Gates and Floyd are right, sacred song is itself a primary mode of black church religiousness through the improvisatory practices of call and response.

Many commentators have observed the powerful effect of music on spirit possession. Most of them have interpreted repeated rhythmic and melodic figures as a sort of trigger mechanism or gateway for altered states of consciousness. In African American tradition, however, the improvisatory qualities of sacred song seem not so much to trigger spirit possession as to articulate the very qualities of sacrality itself. According to Gates and Floyd, African American sacrality is dynamic in essence: the sacred is expressed by the inspired free play of speakers and singers across literary and musical texts, not by the fixed performance of the texts themselves. That freedom should be the essential quality of sacrality for African Americans is neither surprising nor dubitable given their tragic historical experience. What is critically important for our inquiry, however, is that African Americans have employed sacred song not as a medium to embody the sacred powers or a setting of holy language or an occasion for secondary sacrality, but rather as a manifestation of the free play and vitality inherent in the sacred itself.

The process can be well illustrated by the Brooklyn Tabernacle Choir's rendition of the classic gospel hymn "What a Friend We Have in Jesus" in their 1991 recording *Live with Friends*.[44] The original hymn, an 1855 text by Joseph Scriven set by Charles Converse in 1868, has enjoyed immense popularity among Evangelicals, Fundamentalists, and Pentecostals for more than a century. "What a Friend" features a repetitive form, A1–A2–B–A3, typical of gospel hymns and gospel songs (example 14 on page 348).

The gospel hymn's reiterated initial musical figure supplied the grounding form for the Brooklyn Tabernacle Choir version. Choral arranger Carol Cymbala transformed the A figure into a syncopated choral chant, called a "vamp," with a vigorous gospel piano accompaniment that roughly followed the rhythmic and harmonic structure of the original. Over this matrix the soloist presents a line that plays off the vamp and moves to blue melodics and syncopated dance rhythm. Technically it is, just barely, a version of "What a Friend." As sacred song, however, it is pure signifyin(g), a call-response utterance that transforms the original version and then plays a new variation over it (example 15 on page 349).

In African American tradition, and especially in Pentecostal communions like Bishop Brazier's Pentecostal Assemblies of the World, the Holy Spirit "bloweth where it listeth," it comes and goes freely according to its own will. This free-dom, even caprice, of the sacred so familiar to African Americans from their Evangelical and Pentecostal heritage was grounded more deeply, according to Gates and Floyd, in the West African traditions of Esu and Elegba, gods who likewise played with human destiny.

From this interpretive perspective, black church song expresses the playful and spontaneous nature of the sacred directly through its most characteristic mu-sical form of call and response. The improvising voice of calling soloist over the endlessly reiterated responding figure of the people articulates not only the presence of sacred power but also its very nature and form of being. The insis-tent voice of the free call "signifies" against the fixed textual and musical forms of the song to draw the people into the sacred presence. Both call and response are necessary to articulate this spiritual reality because the sacred can neither be captured by form nor be experienced without form. It is the spiritual free-dom of the calling voice, in improvised utterance over against and yet in har-mony with the fixed form of choral communal response, that most authenti-cally manifests the sacred for the Black Church and roots its liberating faith in the performance of sacred song.

This inspired balance of freedom and form in African American sacred song has enabled the community to transform biblical texts into spirituals and to render "Dr. Watts hymns" into gospel songs. In the broadest sense, black church song has appropriated the symbology of Evangelical Protestant hymnody as a formal ground of religious expression and then, by signifyin(g) upon those forms, reasserted through improvisatory song the freedom of the Spirit asserted by both the African and the American religious traditions living in the black people of the United States.

Notes

1. Lerone Bennett Jr., *Before the Mayflower: A History of Black America*, 6th ed. (New York: Pen-guin, 1993).

2. The most recent comprehensive account of the Black Church is C. Eric Lincoln and Lawrence H. Mamiya, *The Black Church in the African-American Experience* (Durham, N.C.: Duke Univer-sity Press, 1990). For a useful survey of music practice in the contemporary Black Church, see J. Wendell Mapson Jr., *The Ministry of Music in the Black Church* (Valley Forge, Pa.: Judson Press, 1984).

3. "Christian and Jewish Religious Membership in the United States, 1960–1995," <http://www.publicpurpose.com>; Eileen W. Lindner, ed., *Yearbook of American and Canadian Churches, 2002* (Nashville: Abingdon Press, 2002), 348.

4. Eileen Southern, *The Music of Black Americans,* 2d ed. (New York: Norton, 1983), 16.

5. Richard Allen, *A Collection of Spiritual Songs and Hymns from Various Authors* (Philadelphia: John Ormrod, 1801).

6. E. Franklin Frazier, *The Negro Church in America* (New York: Schocken, 1964), 1–19.

7. Southern, *Music of Black Americans,* 168.

8. James Cone, *The Spiritual and the Blues: An Interpretation* (New York: Seabury Press, 1972), 32.

9. Cited in Southern, *Music of Black Americans,* 169.

10. Ibid., 170.

11. Ibid., 221–27. For the classic account of the Fisk Jubilee Singers, including sixty song scores, see G. D. Pike, *The Jubilee Singers of Fisk University* (Boston: Lee and Shepard, 1874).

12. Sandra S. Sizer, *Gospel Hymns and Social Religion: The Rhetoric of Nineteenth-Century Revivalism* (Philadelphia: Temple University Press, 1978), 3–49.

13. Cited in Jon Michael Spencer, *Black Hymnody: A Hymnological History of the African American Church* (Knoxville: University of Tennessee Press, 1992), 101.

14. Charles Price Jones, comp., *Jesus Only* (Jackson, Miss.: Truth Publishing, 1899), *Jesus Only Nos. 1 and 2* (Jackson, Miss.: Truth Publishing, 1901), and *His Fullness* (Nashville: National Baptist Publishing Board, 1906)

15. Spencer, *Black Hymnody,* 114.

16. Jon Michael Spencer, *Protest and Praise: Sacred Music of Black Religion* (Minneapolis: Fortress Press, 1990), 155.

17. Ibid., 159.

18. On early Pentecostal history see Edith W. Blumhofer, *Restoring the Faith: The Assemblies of God, Pentecostalism, and American Culture* (Urbana: University of Illinois Press, 1993), and Grant Wacker, *Heaven Below: Early Pentecostalism and American Culture* (Cambridge, Mass.: Harvard University Press, 2001).

19. Wacker, *Heaven Below,* 6–7, 88, 187–88; Charles Edwin Jones, *A Guide to the Study of the Pentecostal Movement* (Metuchen, N.J.: Scarecrow/ATLA, 1983), 678–82.

20. Spencer, *Protest and Praise,* 227.

21. William C. Turner, "The Musicality of Black Preaching: A Phenomenology," *Journal of Black Sacred Music* 2, no. 1 (Spring 1988): 22, 29.

22. Ibid., 26; Spencer, *Protest and Praise,* 231–32.

23. Spencer, *Protest and Praise,* 238.

24. Ibid., 212–14.

25. Horace Clarence Boyer, "Charles Albert Tindley: Progenitor of African American Gospel Music," in *We'll Understand It Better By and By: Pioneering African American Gospel Composers,* ed. Bernice Johnson Reagon (Washington, D.C.: Smithsonian Institution Press, 1992), 53–78.

26. Spencer, *Black Hymnody,* 85–88.

27. Horace Clarence Boyer, "Lucie E. Campbell: Composer for the National Baptist Convention," in *We'll Understand It Better By and By,* ed. Reagon, 81–95.

28. Michael W. Harris, *The Rise of Gospel Blues: The Music of Thomas Andrew Dorsey in the Urban Church* (New York: Oxford University Press, 1992), 239.

29. Paul Oliver, Max Harrison, and William Bolcom, eds., *The New Grove Gospel, Blues, and Jazz* (New York: Norton, 1986), 199–204; Horace Clarence Boyer, "William Herbert Brewster: The Eloquent Poet," in *We'll Understand It Better By and By,* ed. Reagon, 211–31.

30. Oliver, Harrison, and Bolcom, eds., *New Grove Gospel,* 201; Ray Allen, *Singing in the Spirit: African-American Sacred Quartets in New York City* (Philadelphia: University of Pennsylvania Press, 1991), 19–49; Horace Clarence Boyer, "Kenneth Morris: Composer and Dean of Black Gospel Music Publishers," in *We'll Understand It Better By and By,* ed. Reagon, 309–28.

31. Southern, *Music of Black Americans,* 453; Oliver, Harrison, and Bolcom, eds., *New Grove Gospel,* 201; Spencer, *Protest and Praise,* 217–21.

32. Stuart Wilson, telephone interview with author, June 21, 1995. All subsequent quotations are taken from this interview.

33. See Cone, *The Spiritual and the Blues,* 20–107; W. E. B. Du Bois, *The Souls of Black Folk* (New York: Gramercy Books, 1994), 3–11, 192–203; Howard Thurman, "Deep River," in Thurman, *For the Inward Journey* (Richmond, Ind.: Friends United Meeting, 1984), 199–240.

34. I. M. Lewis, *Ecstatic Religion: An Anthropological Study of Spirit Possession and Shamanism* (Baltimore: Penguin Books, 1971), 37–65.

35. Gilbert Rouget, *Music and Trance: A Theory of the Relations between Music and Possession* (Chicago: University of Chicago Press, 1985), 11. The classic study of shamanism is Mircea Eliade, *Shamanism: Archaic Techniques of Ecstasy* (Princeton, N.J.: Princeton University Press, 1964).

36. See Leslie Demangles, *The Faces of the Gods: Vodou and Roman Catholicism in Haiti* (Chapel Hill: University of North Carolina Press, 1992); Joseph M. Murphy, *Santeria: African Spirits in America* (Boston: Beacon Press, 1993); and Robert A. Voeks, *Sacred Leaves of Candomble: African Magic, Medicine, and Religion in Brazil* (Austin: University of Texas Press, 1997).

37. Spencer, *Protest and Praise*, 135–52.

38. Albert J. Raboteau, *Slave Religion: The "Invisible Institution" in the Antebellum South* (New York: Oxford University Press, 1978), 243–65.

39. See Douglas R. Egerton, *Gabriel's Rebellion: The Virginia Slave Conspiracies of 1800 and 1802* (Chapel Hill: University of North Carolina Press, 1993); James Sidbury, *Ploughshares into Swords: Race, Religion, and Identity in Gabriel's Virginia, 1730–1810* (New York: Oxford University Press, 1997); Eric Foner, *Nat Turner* (Englewood Cliffs, N.J.: Prentice-Hall, 1971); John Lofton, *Denmark Vesey's Revolt* (Kent, Ohio: Kent State University Press, 1983).

40. Rouget, *Music and Trance*, 78–94.

41. Henry Louis Gates Jr., *The Signifying Monkey: A Theory of African-American Literary Criticism* (New York: Oxford University Press, 1995).

42. Ibid., 3–88.

43. Samuel A. Floyd Jr., *The Power of Black Music: Interpreting Its History from Africa to the United States* (New York: Oxford University Press, 1995), 95, 236.

44. Brooklyn Tabernacle Choir, *Live with Friends,* Word CD 701 9170 609, 1991.

CHAPTER 5

Klezmorim and Sephardim:
The Jewish Music Revival

The Jewish tradition of sacred song is perhaps the most complex and diverse in contemporary America. Rooted in the worship of ancient Israel and two millennia of synagogue liturgy, this immense and august tradition first arrived in America during the 1650s. Sephardic Jews expelled from Spain and Portugal in the late fifteenth century emigrated first to Recife, Brazil, then to the Dutch North American colony of New Netherland. These Sephardim brought a tradition of sacred song rendered in a medieval Judeo-Spanish vernacular called Ladino. In 1654 they organized Congregation Shearith Israel on Manhattan Island, the oldest synagogue in America. Later in the colonial period, major Sephardic communities also developed in Philadelphia, Newport, and Charleston. Into antebellum times this Sephardic heritage of Hebrew melody, cast in Islamic and Gregorian styles, dominated the sacred song of America's synagogues.[1]

During the decades bracketing the Civil War, however, American Judaism was dramatically transformed by the arrival of liberal Reform Jews from Germany, led by Cincinnati rabbi Isaac Meyer Wise (1819–1900). Emigrating to America in flight from the failed Socialist Revolution of 1848, Reform Jews carried the Romantic musical culture of Berlin and Vienna, especially the style of Felix Mendelssohn, grandson of Moses Mendelssohn (1729–86), one of Reform's principal founders. In 1857 Wise published the first American synagogue liturgy, *Minhag America*, which outraged traditional opponents by its abandonment of Hebrew and its modernistic translations that seemed to depart from biblical and Talmudic formulations. Musically, Wise was just as radical, calling for the installation of organs in synagogues, the composition of Protestant-style chorale hymns to replace traditional synagogue songs, and new settings of the cantorial service in the Romantic musical style. Preeminent in new American Jewish centers like Cincinnati, Pittsburgh, and Chicago and dominant in the rising industrial cities of New York, Philadelphia, and Boston, the Reform movement became the most important influence on American Jewish liturgical music after the Civil War.[2]

Yet another variant of Judaism's global musical tradition appeared in the United States around 1900, brought by Jewish emigrés from Eastern Europe known as Ashkenazim. These Jews spoke Yiddish, a medieval Judeo-German vernacular, and performed distinctive liturgical and folk music born of centuries resident in Poland and Russia. The Ashkenazim brought new varieties of Judaism to America, most notably the Orthodox. From its original base in New York City, Orthodox Judaism grew by 1900 to challenge the earlier Sephardic and Reform constituencies in America.

In the twentieth century, two important indigenous American Jewish movements emerged and a small but influential community of Hasidim took firm root. The Conservative movement, a middle path between Reform and Orthodox, was organized in 1887 with the founding of the Jewish Theological Seminary in New York. During the 1930s Reconstructionism gathered around founder Mordecai Kaplan's writings that interpreted Judaism as a civilization rather than a religion alone. In addition, the Holocaust brought mystical Hasidic sects to America as they fled the destruction of the ghettos of central Europe. Each of these varieties has employed its distinctive approach to sacred song. Conservatives have combined the Romantic musical tradition of Reform with important elements of Orthodox synagogue song, while Reconstructionists have underscored the importance of the Jewish folk-song heritage in worship and community education. The Hasidim's distinctive tradition of joyful sacred song has remained largely hidden from public view until quite recently. Today, Conservative and Reform each account for 40 percent of America's religiously affiliated Jews, while the Conservative and Hasidic communities have enjoyed the greatest growth in recent decades.[3] At the same time, nearly half of America's Jews are "secular" or not affiliated with any of these denominations, creating a highly complex cultural and religious demography.

Synagogue Song

Despite enormous theological, musical, historical, and cultural differences that subsist among these religious communities of American Judaism, they all adhere to the same essential liturgical forms for worship in the synagogue. The most important of these forms are the ritual calendar, the standard Sabbath prayer and praise service, the cantillation of scripture, and the singing of special liturgical poems suitable for particular worship occasions.

Like other great religious traditions of the world, ancient Israelite liturgy developed a ritual calendar based on the agricultural cycle of planting, growth, and harvest, along with particular feasts and festivals of transcendent religious importance. The Jewish High Holy Days occur during the harvest month (usually September by the Gregorian calendar): Rosh Hashanah, the new year celebration during which the *shofar*—the sacred ram's horn—is blown to announce the renewal of the Holy One's love and protection of the people of Israel, and Yom Kippur, the day of atonement and reconciliation with the Holy One and the community that occurs ten days after Rosh Hashanah. Also central to the Jewish liturgical year is the springtime observance of Pesach or Passover, the week-long commemoration of Israel's exodus from Egyptian slavery. Lesser holidays include the celebrative occasions of Purim, Succoth, and Hanukah.

Jewish sacred song flowers brilliantly during these special holy days, but its more regular and universal expression occurs in the sabbath song of the synagogue. Ancient Israelite worship centered in sacrificial rites at the Jerusalem temple that featured psalms and hymns performed by a priestly chorus and orchestra. In local synagogues or houses of assembly, however, psalm and hymn singing was more modestly performed without instrumental accompaniment. After the destruction of Jerusalem and the Second Temple by the Romans in 70 C.E., rabbis of the Jewish Diaspora preserved the ancient psalmody while developing a new form of worship based in praise, scripture reading, and prayer.[4] In his classic book *Jewish Liturgy and Its Development*, A. Z. Idelsohn divided synagogue Sabbath worship into two basic elements of prayer (*tefilla*) and praise (*shevah*). The tefilla, also known as *amida*, is based on the Eighteen Benedictions (*Shemone Esre*) of ancient usage. Typical Sabbath worship excises many of these prayers, but the canon of eighteen traditional prayers, actually nineteen since the second century C.E., continues to govern liturgical practice. Idelsohn flatly stated that "there is no service without the *amida*."[5]

The praise portion of synagogue Sabbath worship includes three distinct elements: morning benedictions, verses of song (*Birchoth Hashahar*), and the *Shema* and its three benedictions. The Shema is the high point of synagogue Sabbath worship, the supreme expression of Jewish sacred identity, sung or recited by rabbis, cantors, and congregations. It begins: "Hear, O Israel: The Lord is our God, the Lord alone. You shall love the Lord your God with all your heart, and with all your soul, and with all your might. Keep these words that I am commanding you today in your heart. Recite them to your children and talk about them when you are at home and when you are away, when you lie down and when you rise. Bind them as a sign on your hand, fix them as an emblem on your forehead, and write them on the doorposts of your house and on your gates" (Deut. 6:4–9).

In traditional practice, all of these standard prayers, hymns, and blessings are sung or chanted in the synagogue either by a rabbi or by a specially trained cantor. The great antiquity of these liturgical melodies and their universal distribution among even the most far-flung Jewish communities led Idelsohn to postulate their origin in pre-exilic Israel.[6] Idelsohn's interpretation still retains great authority, but ethnomusicologists like Amnon Shiloah have recently challenged it, arguing instead that the corpus of Jewish liturgical song was inevitably shaped by the cultures in which Jews of the Diaspora have lived for nearly two millennia. Of special influence, Shiloah argues, was Islam, host to the most important Mediterranean Jewish communities for centuries.[7]

The scripture portions for Sabbath worship are sung in synagogue by the rabbi, employing a style called cantillation. Rabbinic tradition ascribes the practice of cantillation to the times of Ezra the Scribe and Israel's restitution after the Babylonian captivity in the sixth century B.C.E. (Neh. 8:8). Whatever its historic origin, Shiloah defines cantillation as "a simpler, freer structure than ordinary vocal music, closer to solemn declamation than to structured, organized singing. Although on occasion this music may be ornamented with rich vocalizations, its form and flow are subordinated to the text and it is clearly adapted to the syntax and punctuation, the natural rhythm and melodic nature of the text being sung. Thus in this type of presentation, the word has absolute priority."[8]

As sung in synagogue, these texts are freely intoned on one note, ending with a cadential formula. Changes in pitch or in accent and the incidence of pauses and rests are dictated strictly by the literary and intellectual qualities of the sacred text, not by melodic considerations. Of particular importance to cantillation of the biblical text is a complex system of twenty-six kinds of accents still in universal rabbinic use, originated by Aharon Ben-Asher in the early tenth century at Tiberias on the Sea of Galilee and known as the Tiberian tradition. In essence, cantillation presents a tenth-century manner of reading the sacred text by means of vocal and gestural suggestion. "In one sense [cantillation] was construed as a means of revealing the more profound significance of the text," Shiloah wrote, "and in another it was viewed as a musical device intended to facilitate comprehension." Cantillation's overall function in the synagogue service, then and now, is to sharpen the congregation's sense of the scripture portion by signaling its literary structure, theological emphasis, and emotional tone according to the forms of the Tiberian tradition.[9]

One literary and musical element above all others has provided new texts and melodies for synagogue worship over the centuries: the liturgical poem, or *piyyut,* introduced by the fifth-century Palestinian rabbi Yosi ben-Yosi. The biblical prayers and hymns of the ancient Sabbath service inevitably invited further elaboration by rabbinic and cantorial leaders, whose poetic expressions gradually took on standard form. The earliest *piyyutim* from Palestine and Iraq were unrhymed, blank verse Hebrew poems that relied on powerful strophic and acrostic forms for ritual acceptance in the synagogue.

During the ninth and tenth centuries, however, the center of Hebrew poetic expression shifted first to southern Italy and then to Spain, where, as Shiloah noted, "for the next five hundred years, the piyyut blossomed with a direct affinity to the various forms of Arabic poetry."[10] In Iberia, Sephardic piyyutim developed a rich variety of meters that often demanded sung responses by the congregation. After the expulsion of Jews from Spain in 1492, the composition of piyyutim continued to flourish in Sephardic Jewish centers like Yemen, Tunis, Morocco, and Aleppo, while Ashkenazic rabbis of central Europe contributed yet another distinguished tradition of piyyutim that was readily incorporated into their tradition of Sabbath worship.

Perhaps the greatest piyyut of all is the poem *Lecha dodi,* "Come, my Beloved, to meet the Bride; let us welcome the Sabbath," composed in 1529 by Solomon Alkabetz (1505–c. 1572) at Safed (Zefat) in northeastern Palestine, then a great center of rabbinical interpretation and Jewish mysticism:

"Observe" and "Remember," in a single command, the One God announced for us. The Lord is One, and His name is One, for fame, for glory, and for praise.

Chorus: Come, my Beloved, to meet the Bride; let us welcome the Sabbath.

Come, let us go to meet the Sabbath, for it is a source of blessing. From the very beginning it was ordained; last in creation, first in God's plan.

Shrine of the King, royal city, arise! Come forth from your ruins. Long enough have you dwelt in the valley of tears! He will show you abundant mercy.

Shake off your dust, arise! Put on your glorious garments, my people, and pray: "Be near to my soul, and redeem it through the son of Jesse, the Bethlehemite."

Bestir yourself, bestir yourself, for your light has come; arise and shine! Awake, awake, utter a song: the Lord's glory is revealed upon you.

Be not ashamed nor confounded. Why are you downcast? Why do you moan? The afflicted of my people will be sheltered within you; the city shall be rebuilt on its ancient site.

Those who despoiled you shall become a spoil, and all who would devour you shall be far away. Your God will rejoice over you as a bridegroom rejoices over his bride.

You shall extend to the right and to the left, and you shall revere the Lord. Through the advent of a descendant of Perez we shall rejoice and exult.

Come in peace, crown of God, come with joy and cheerfulness; amidst the faithful of the chosen people come, O Bride; come, O Bride.[11]

Lecha dodi ushers in the sabbath service everywhere in the Jewish world. This text and its musical settings have been studied intensively to establish the basic structure of Jewish sacred song, but with inconclusive results. In his monumental ten-volume *Thesaurus of Hebrew-Oriental Melodies* (1914–32), Idelsohn sought to demonstrate the unity of global synagogue music by citing three structurally similar settings of *Lecha dodi* collected from the eastern Mediterranean, the Portuguese community in London, and the Sephardic community of northern Italy. Recently, however Idelsohn's long-accepted claim has been challenged. Mark Slobin's survey of contemporary American cantorial practice, for example, revealed the complexity of local synagogue usage, with ninety-three cantors recording 184 different melodies for this text. In his 2000 study *The Lord's Song in a Strange Land,* Jeffrey A. Summit found quite different tunes and liturgical contexts for *Lecha dodi* in five Boston area Jewish communities. Amnon Shiloah estimated as many as two thousand different melodies for *Lecha dodi* worldwide.[12] Six settings published by Slobin will serve to illustrate the musical and stylistic diversity of *Lecha dodi* in America (example 16 on page 352). Slobin's selections were based on a musical survey he sent to American hazzanim in the late 1980s. The first two melodies, closely related Romantic tunes from the early nineteenth century by Sulzar and Lewandowski, were the most popular, followed by a composite melody of unknown origin and an anonymous Hasidic tune. The last two settings represent alternative tunes sung to the poem at different liturgical seasons.

On any Friday evening or Saturday of the year, American synagogues of every description resonate to sacred cantillation and melodies set to ancient prayers, hymns, scripture readings, and piyyutim. This musical articulation is the primary form of sacred-song experience for observant American Jews, regardless of their denomination. Synagogue song today is carefully managed by a cantorate whose standards of taste and performance are informed by rigorous training and close professional association. The cantorate first emerged in the seventh century C.E., when synagogues began to hire special prayer leaders and sacred singers called *hazzanim.* The *hazzan's* original task was to sing the piyyutim. According to Slobin, the complex rhyme and meter of piyyutim gave rise to specialists who were valued for their performance of that genre, along with other special texts whose musical demands exceeded the talent of the typical rabbi.

Through a millennium of liturgical history, hazzanim acquired an ever-growing repertory along with an ambiguous standing in Jewish religious culture. On one hand, as Slobin reports, among the Sephardim "legendary prowess made the position of hazzan the most permanent and continuous synagogue office, one which underwent relatively few changes after the Middle Ages." Yet Ashkenazic hazzanim on the whole held a Bohemian sort of reputation, appreciated for their musical skill yet suspected because of their irregular training and lack of professional discipline.

Slobin grants the hazzan a vital role in the preservation and development of Jewish sacred song, rooted in his ability as a *bricoleur,* a transformer of traditional texts and musical expression. "Since to be a hazzan [is] to be a master of texts," Slobin wrote,

the cantorate lies close to the core of [traditional Jewish] culture, particularly
the *expressive* culture, which, roughly defined, means the aesthetics of everyday life. . . . What this culture particularly values is commentary, interpretation, exegesis—the reworking of sacred texts as a daily and life long activity—
that may be linguistic, musical, or even, in the case of handicrafts, material,
snowballing its way through history, enlarging through gradual accretion, as
well as varying from place to place at any given time.[13]

By the seventeenth century, hazzanim had become trusted bearers of Jewish
sacred-song traditions. In America, Sephardic rabbis and hazzanim faithfully
maintained their musical heritage for two hundred years. Beginning in the 1840s,
however, the success of the Reform agenda produced a precipitate decline among
traditional hazzanim. While urban Reform congregations mounted impressive
modern music programs and hired professional operatic cantors, the ancient
synagogue repertories and performance styles suffered neglect. The status of the
traditional hazzan in America had reached a low point by the 1870s, when
cantorial performance of the Ashkenazic rite suddenly burst on the scene, borne
by a vast tide of more than two million Jewish immigrants between 1882 and
1924, most of them Orthodox from Poland and Russia.

Slobin depicts the period from 1880 to the 1940s as the era of the "star hazzan,"
a time when great Orthodox cantors from central Europe established new standards of liturgical excellence for leading synagogues throughout America. The
first was Poland's Chaim Weinshel, hired by New York's Anshe Suvalk Congregation. Other noted Orthodox cantors included Seidel Rovner, Moshe Koussevitsky, Pierre Pintchik, Adolph Katchko, and Gershon Sirota. The advent of the
Victrola phonograph made recorded cantorial performances widely available
in America. Yosele Rosenblatt, "the Jewish Caruso," made classic recordings on
78 RPM discs that enjoyed great commercial success and synagogue influence,
especially during the 1930s.[14]

Since World War II a new generation of Reform, Reconstructionist, and Conservative cantors has maintained the Romantic style through cantorial training programs at Hebrew Union College in Cincinnati, the Reconstructionist
Seminary of America in Philadelphia, and the Jewish Theological Seminary in
New York, while a steady supply of Orthodox hazzanim has flowed from Yeshiva
University in New York. Synagogue music today enjoys a higher general standard of musical performance than at perhaps any other time in American Jewish history. New settings of synagogue texts have continued to appear from the
pens of distinguished composers like Herbert Fromm and Samuel Adler, while
many Reform, Reconstructionist, and Conservative congregations have incorporated traditional Ashkenazic or Sephardic settings in their worship services.[15]

The most dramatic area of musical renewal in American Jewish culture since
1975, however, has taken place outside of the synagogue, in a realm of music that
blends together the sacred dimension with the lived experience of everyday life

in traditional Old World communities. This renewal has been marked most clearly by the vigorous and unprecedented revival in America of two quite different historic forms of Jewish music: the klezmer music of popular Ashkenazic culture in nineteenth-century central Europe and the Sephardic song of medieval Mediterranean Jewry. These two examples reveal more pointedly than synagogue song the complex meanings of music and Judaism for contemporary American Jews. It is from them that the most is to be learned about the Jewish music revival in contemporary America.

Schlemiel the First

On a warm, wet evening in early May 1994, I traveled to Harvard Square in Cambridge, Massachusetts, for a performance by the American Repertory Theater (ART). Housed in the brick-and-Bauhaus theater complex of Harvard University's Loeb Drama Center, ART has for more than twenty years brought distinguished dramatic productions to the greater Boston community. ART founder and director Robert Brustein has presided over a wide array of dramatic works from Aeschylus to Shakespeare, baroque pageantry to Japanese *kabuki*, Ibsen tragedies to Philip Glass operas. Outside the theater, the forsythia and dogwood were still blooming. Inside, the crowd was abuzz in anticipation of a theater event that even Brustein had never before attempted.

The production was the world premiere of *Schlemiel the First*, coproduced by the ART and Philadelphia's American Musical Theater Festival. Billed as "the first klezmer musical," *Schlemiel* is based on a play by Isaac Bashevis Singer (1904–97), the Polish American Jewish writer and 1978 Nobel laureate whose works, including collections of tales and stories like *Zlateh the Goat and Other Stories* (1966) and *The Fools of Chelm and Their History* (1973), represent perhaps the last great flowering of Yiddish literature.[16] The music, written by Hankus Netsky with lyrics by Arnold Weinstein, blends klezmer music, the traditional celebration music of central European Ashkenazic and Hasidic Jews, with the song traditions of Yiddish theater and folk culture.

The character of Schlemiel arose in seventeenth-century Yiddish folklore and appeared in many published collections of folk tales. *Peter Schlemihl* (1814), a comic novel by Adelbert von Camisso, gathered together many traditions about the bumbling, gullible, but ultimately good-hearted figure, the common man of Yiddish folk culture.[17] Sholem Aleichem (1859–1916), a Russian Jew born Solomon Rabinowitz, brought Schlemiel into American Jewish theater and literature. Aleichem was the preeminent Yiddish writer of his generation whose bittersweet novels, plays, and short stories of Jewish life in Russian *shtetls* were widely read and produced. Largely through Aleichem's efforts, Yiddish was established as a canonical literary language. His Schlemiel stories inspired Singer and other writers to carry Yiddish literature forward, even as his founding of the Yiddish Arts Theater in New York around 1910 gave a vital impulse to the

production of Yiddish drama and musicals that survived late into the twentieth century.[18] Singer's play, commissioned by Brustein in 1974 for the Yale Repertory Theater, casts Schlemiel as the beadle (sexton) of the synagogue in Chelm,
a legendary city of fools from Yiddish folklore.

In Singer's version, Schlemiel is a hopelessly simple yet honest man, accompanied through life by his complaining though faithful wife, Tryna Ryzta. When
faced with an exceedingly fine question about the Talmudic Law, Chief Rabbi
Gronam Ox and the sages of Chelm send Schlemiel to find the answer by consulting with rabbinic authorities in Warsaw. On his journey through the mountains, however, Schlemiel is turned around by a disgruntled gremlin named
Chaim Rascal and returns to his hometown of Chelm believing it is Warsaw.
Amazed at the similarity between the great capital and his hometown, Schlemiel
doggedly pursues his commission, consulting with Ox and the other rabbis
about the answer to their own question. For their part, Ox and the rabbis try to
interpret the remarkable similarity between this pilgrim and their own beadle,
Schlemiel. So similar are the two men that Ox eventually declares the visitor to
be "Schlemiel the Second," entitled to the marital rights of Schlemiel the First,
who is currently on a journey to Warsaw. Chaos and tomfoolery ensue, with
Schlemiel eventually reunited with Tryna Ryzta, who learns that her husband,
though hardly a heroic figure, is genuinely loyal and loving.

This is hardly the stuff of high drama, but it is a good yarn by any standard.
When brought off by a spirited cast assisted by traditional costumes of Yiddish
theater and a spectacular score, the wisdom of Singer's scenario comes to vibrant
life. Act 1 weaves the story of Schlemiel's commission to Warsaw, highlighted by
his autobiographical song "A Beadle with a Dreydl," in which he describes how
his life is fated like the toss of the traditional Jewish children's toy top. Tryna Ryzta
regales the audience with a comedic lament about her life with Schlemiel. The
first show-stopper, however, is "We're Talking Chelm," a brilliant number sung
by Gronam Ox and the Sages of Chelm. Arrayed in the earlocks and black
longcoats of eighteenth-century Ashkenazim and Hasidim from central Europe,
Ox and his colleagues caper about the stage, singing a sprightly song that extols
their own putative intellectual excellence as leaders of the great city of Chelm.
The Sages of Chelm continue to entertain with a wonderful rendition of the great
Yiddish theater song, "Roumania, Roumania," a traditional *doina* by Aaron
Lebedeff, that sends Schlemiel off on his paradoxical pilgrimage.

In act 2, Schlemiel, Tryna Rytza, and the Sages all ponder through song the
mysteries of how there could be a second Schlemiel in their midst so like the
first. Tryna Rytza realizes that she really does love and respect Schlemiel the First,
while Schlemiel concludes that his old life was the best life. It remains only for
the Sages to discover that Schlemiel the Second *is* Schlemiel the First and to
congratulate themselves in another rave-up titled "Wisdom." The show ends
with a reprise of "We're Talking Chelm" for the entire cast.

A generation ago, *Schlemiel the First* might have been considered an inappropriately satirical product of cheeky avant-garde artists or perhaps dismissed as just another Yiddish musical with an audience restricted to New York City's Jewish community. Since 1994, however, it has played to sold-out houses in Cambridge, Philadelphia, and New York. At the end of the ART premiere performance, a sizable part of the crowd descended on the Klezmer Conservatory Band in the pit clapping enthusiastically to the dancing rhythms of the fourteen players on clarinet, violin, trumpet, trombone, bass, banjo, piano, and drums. When the music finally ended, the happy patrons applauded, whistled, and exited in high excitement.

The driving force behind the show's music is Hankus Netsky, chairman of the Jazz Studies Department at the New England Conservatory of Music. *Schlemiel* is the outgrowth of Netsky's extraordinary success as founder in 1980 of the Klezmer Conservatory Band, one of the leading ensembles in the contemporary American revival of traditional central European Jewish music. I interviewed Netsky about a month after seeing *Schlemiel*. I had hoped to learn something from him about his experience with *Schlemiel* and the klezmer revival. Not only was I enlightened about those projects, but as this genial and gifted musician spoke with me for nearly two hours, his conversation opened a unique perspective on the history of Ashkenazic music in America and how his work figures in the Jewish tradition of American sacred song.[19]

First, about *Schlemiel*. "The Schlemiel thing is very funny," Netsky said. "[The Klezmer Conservatory Band] did this concert at the New England Conservatory in December 1992, and we played about twenty-five minutes, just one set. But out of that one set we got one hundred nights of work for the band. Since then we've done two tours with Joel Grey, and *Schlemiel* will keep going. Just from people who saw us at that one show!" After Grey, brilliant star of *Cabaret,* chose the band to play for his 1993 Yiddish revival touring show *Borscht Capades,* he began promoting it to friends, including Robert Brustein. "[Brustein] finally saw us at the 125th Anniversary of the Conservatory concert in 1993," Netsky recounted. "Why? Because Joel Grey invited him. [Without Grey] I don't know if [Brustein] would ever have gotten out of his world, which is a very different world from ours."

But "get out" Brustein did, making a connection between Singer's play and Netsky's music. Brustein told the story in the ART playbill:

> This musical version of *Schlemiel* was conceived one sleepless night after I had attended a benefit performance at Jordan Hall featuring the Klezmer Conservatory Band. The vibrating klezmer music had started up my heart and bubbled my blood, and I was determined to find a theatre vehicle that might transport these rhythms onto the stage of the Loeb. Around four in the morning, a play popped unto my head that we had staged at Yale during the mid-seventies entitled *Schlemiel the First.* . . . It was a long, unstructured, somewhat unwieldy, but oddly ingratiating dramatization of [Singer's] Chelm stories, and it seemed to me exactly the right text for the Yiddish intonations of a klezmer musical.[20]

Brustein quickly assembled the creative team of Netsky, lyricist Arnold Weinstein, and director David Gordon. "A process of close collaboration ensued," Brustein wrote in his program notes, "beginning in late summer [1993] and continuing well into late winter, until the cutting, rewriting, and restructuring of the text, and the matching of the music and lyrics, were completed to everyone's satisfaction." After an "arduous casting process" in the early spring of 1994, *Schlemiel* was ready for its world premiere. Brustein offered a Jewish culinary metaphor for his production along with a heartfelt tribute to its late author: "*Schlemiel the First* is an entirely homegrown musical banquet which we have endeavored to make as appetizing as the latkes and kasha consumed by its characters. It has given all of us great pleasure to prepare it for you, and we hope it suits your palate. It is offered partly in tribute to the memory of Isaac Bashevis Singer, a great Yiddish-American writer, whose impish mastery of folk humor, mischief making, whimsy, and demonology continues to bring us such enduring delight."[21]

I asked Netsky about the traditions of Yiddish theater referenced in *Schlemiel*, as well as his own responsibility to Singer's text as a composer. *Schlemiel* represents a revival of this Yiddish literary and theatrical tradition, a powerful new production that invokes the cultural world of Ashkenazic Jewry before the Holocaust. It is deeply moving to American Jewish audiences. In our interview I asked Netsky about the power that *Schlemiel* seemed to generate in such a diverse audience. His response began with the creative team. "These folks all were Jewish. It gave us all something to channel that Jewishness into. I think that's the key," Netsky observed. "If you find the right way to channel your Jewish identity, yes, people who may not have found it before might find it now. It might not be the religion as it was presented by their parents or by the symbolic offering once a week, but in this case it's through a theatrical medium, or writing, or through music."

To its creators, then, *Schlemiel* became a vehicle for recovering and reencountering Jewish identity. "I think everyone working with the show experienced some kind of cultural rediscovery," Netsky said. "I find that [experience] more significant than the idea of just taking Jewish music and Jewish theater [as the basis for a production]. I mean, that's been done for years." This same "recovery of Jewish identity" manifests itself even more powerfully in the two most notable aspects of the contemporary Jewish music revival, klezmer and Sephardic. Both of those movements, in turn, illuminate important dimensions of how sacred song figures in the larger world of American Judaism.

The Klezmer Revival

Hankus Netsky's interest in the klezmer music of Hasidic Judaism began with his family, his neighborhood, and his religious surroundings. "I grew up very attracted to traditional Jewish culture in the Mount Airy district of Philadelphia," he said. "My father was in the upholstery supply business, which was basically the rag business. He would take me to work to sort rags with these old guys hearing about the old country. When I was about seven or eight years old, a rabbi moved in very nearby to lead this real Hasidic congregation. I had no idea what that was. But even though I was only seven or eight years old, I was already a musician. So that when someone donated a Torah scroll, I was the one who played the procession."

Hasidic Jews like Netsky's neighbor Rabbi Isaacson were part of an eighteenth-century mystical Jewish sectarian movement founded by the Russian sage Israel ben Eliezer (c. 1698–1760), known as the Baal Shem Tov or "Master of the Good Name [of God]." As much legendary character as historical figure, the Baal Shem became the subject of many Yiddish folktales teaching his spiritual message of purity of heart, joyfully ecstatic worship, and adherence to God's law in every aspect of human life. The early followers of the Baal Shem formed communities around their local spiritual leaders, called *tzaddiks,* who built the Hasidim ("the pious ones") into a tightly knit separatist movement grounded in a synthesis of mystical interpretations of rabbinic teaching and Yiddish folk beliefs. Hasidism exploded across the Jewish *shtetls* and ghettos of central Europe in the mid-eighteenth century, at one point influencing more than half of European Jewry before a liberal reaction weakened its impact after 1780.[22]

The Hasidim developed a rich body of music for Sabbath services and special occasions like weddings and circumcisions. Musicians who played festive songs and dances at the latter kind of celebrations were called *klezmorim* ("music makers"); their music came to be known as "klezmer." Fashioned from Jewish and Yiddish dances and folk tunes, klezmer employed the vernacular instruments of central European ghetto culture—violin, cello, clarinet, and *hackbrett* (dulcimer)—in a distinctive style that was celebratory, rhythmic, even comedic, yet with a pervasive modal tonality that recalled ancient origins and memories of persecution.[23]

Netsky's exposure to klezmer music in Mount Airy was sporadic at best, however, and the Protestant-style Reform music he heard on the radio held little interest. What did draw him to Jewish music was the sacred song of his family's Conservative synagogue. "Our synagogue choir was very traditional," he recalled,

> no organ, just [vocally] accompanying the cantor in singing things that went back centuries. [We also sang] the classic nineteenth-century composers. Our cantor, Joseph Levine, was a real authority and the student of Abba Weisgal, who was a great cantor in Baltimore. The cantors always encouraged me to learn what they were doing. I was very interested in that, and I would go to synagogue and sing in duets. I would lead services and learn the chants. So through the synagogue I was exposed to people who helped me discover many interesting things.

The Conservative movement's strong commitment to Zionism and the nation of Israel supplied Netsky with yet another powerful Jewish music tradition. "Israeli dances: that's what I was raised on! For the younger generation, someone like me had two choices: I could go to arts and music camp to do what I loved, or I could go to a camp that would teach me how to go to Israel. But it was not my culture." He did not take the Israel route, but Netsky was nonetheless richly provided with a broad range of Jewish music traditions by the time he was ready for college.

Synagogue worship and Israeli song were the characteristic musical influences on Netsky's generation, so strong that as a young man he did not know much about klezmer music even though his own extended family was deeply versed in it. "It was strange because my grandfather and two of my great uncles and two of my uncles played [klezmer] in their careers. There was lots of music around in my family. I could find a book of the stuff, but I didn't know how it really sounded, how it worked. Only once or twice, when I would go to hear my uncle's band and they'd be playing a bar mitzvah or something, and be playing an old-fashioned [tune], and I'd be excited. But then they'd go to something else."

Netsky discovered klezmer at the New England Conservatory through his mentor, Ran Blake, the great Third Stream jazz theorist, teacher, and artist. "Blake encouraged me," Netsky said. "He would get mailings about klezmer and I would go down to [the performances]. I told him about my interests in this music and from then on he looked out for me." Only then did Netsky begin to research his own family for klezmer roots. "I had one relative still around from the old generation who was willing to talk with me," Netsky recalled. "It was my grandfather's brother Sam, then in his late seventies. I had this photo of my grandfather's band on my wall and I wondered what they sounded like and what they played. So I called my Uncle Sam and I said, 'Let me come over and you can tell me about this.' And he told me stories for hours about what it was like to play. Then he brought me upstairs, and it turned out he had all of these 78 recordings of this music."

Uncle Sam, a dentist who had given up his musical career in the 1930s, first played records of novelty performances, star turns by famous Yiddish players, but Netsky didn't like them at all. "Then he got into the authentic stuff, and I just realized that this was it! This is what I had been looking for all my life! He had hundreds of records of Yiddish theater and klezmer. So I brought my tape recorder back the next day and recorded everything I could, and talked with him more about it. It turns out he had played with some of the people on the records. He still had every note of music he'd ever learned. He'd made records and told me lots of stories. He really got me initiated."

In 1980, Netsky experienced another musical epiphany that triggered his professional interest in performing klezmer music. "I went to a jam session at the Philadelphia home of Nick Maloney, a prime mover in the Celtic music revival.

I was so turned on I couldn't believe it! In every room people were learning tunes on all the pipes and playing all of these different instruments. And I said to myself, 'My God, I have all this klezmer music, I can do the same thing!' And that's what I did."

Back in Boston Netsky organized klezmer jam sessions and classroom performances. Eventually one of the players suggested that the group organize a concert of Jewish music for the larger New England Conservatory community. Netsky planned a diverse program of traditional and original religious music, along with a concluding set of klezmer. Preparation for the concert brought major changes to the ensemble, now billed as the Klezmer Conservatory Band. "I had to fill out the band with a few other instruments to make it sound like the records my uncle had," Netsky recalled. "[Eventually] I assembled a four-teen-piece band. We learned pieces directly from the records, and I worked with them on the ornamentation."

Their first concert in February 1980 brought extraordinary results for the new Klezmer Conservatory Band. "At the end of the concert when we played this klezmer music, the audience really went wild! I had no idea why, but here we were in Boston and nobody had played the stuff here for years apparently, so they really went nuts. They gave us an encore, but we didn't have any more pieces. They wanted to hire us right away for more concerts, but we only knew three songs. Suddenly we had a new career! All of a sudden I realized there was this huge gap to be filled, and I was stuck with a fourteen-piece band!"

The rest is history. Garrison Keillor, host of National Public Radio's popular program *A Prairie Home Companion,* solicited listeners to find music groups to perform on the show during its 1980 New England tour. Netsky sent a tape of the first concert to Keillor, who selected the band for one of the broadcasts. So powerful was the audience response to klezmer tunes that the band played on the show five times within a matter of weeks. They made a recording with Vanguard Records, then quickly moved on to a better contract with Rounder Records. Sales skyrocketed and by 1983 the Klezmer Conservatory Band was on tour, first nationally, then internationally, including a tour of Germany. "It just took off on its own without any hype at all," Netsky said. "Whenever we played, the word just sort of got around and people would call us." This spontaneous surge of popularity led to one big break after another, and eventually to *Schlemiel.* Nor was the Klezmer Conservatory Band's experience unique. New York bands like The Klezmorim and Kapelye, organized a few years earlier, also enjoyed a similar pattern of concert and recording success.[24]

What accounts for this extraordinary response to klezmer music? As Netsky understood it, more is involved in the revival than simple cultural appropriation or nostalgia. A basic reason why the postwar generation of American Jews now embraces klezmer, he ventured, is because it was denied them when they were growing up. "[Klezmer] was very deliberately withheld," Netsky said.

You look at the history up to 1924, the first generation, not wanting to be seen as greenhorns, drops every vestige of [Jewish culture] that they could by the Second World War, in which of course the community is wiped out. At which point Israel is starting to be reborn. Then an entire generation in the 1950s and 1960s is being taught that this [traditional] culture is gone and forgotten, and let's forget about it anyway because it represented weakness and passivity. Israeli culture is all that we should care about.

Postwar American Jews raised under such religious and cultural principles might naturally enough encounter klezmer in the 1980s and 1990s as an alien yet intriguing form of Jewish culture to be explored and enjoyed. Such a relative deprivation theory, however, does not completely account for the intensity of the contemporary embrace of klezmer, as Netsky readily admitted. There's more to it, he observed, including the diverse roots of the Jewish music revival itself. "You do have to think about the history of that renewal," he insisted. "You have to take the success of the broadway show *Fiddler on the Roof* as crucially important, and you have to take the Havurah movement seriously, where people took religion seriously on their own terms, completely outside the structure of any synagogues, and that led to many things that we do."

Fiddler on the Roof, the immensely popular 1965 Broadway hit by Jerry Bock and Sheldon Harnick, marked a fundamental change in the public expression of Jewish culture in America by presenting the traditional Orthodox world of the central European peasant shtetl in an exuberantly positive light.[25] Slobin has commented on the importance of this production for American Jews as an expression of ethnic subculture successfully designed to be acceptable to the larger American "superculture." Slobin wrote:

> In building *Fiddler on the Roof*, its creative team turned to Hasidic celebrations as a source of material for dance and to the old, unaccompanied, meditative *nign* tune as an inspiration for the ethnic tinge that the Broadway sound needed to set off the show—just listen to Tevya's "yob-a-dob-a" in "If I Were a Rich Man." Because the creators of *Fiddler* were Jewish, the construction of this Broadway landmark proceeded from an internal discussion of how subcultural codes and messages might successfully be built into the supercultural space.

At a single stroke, *Fiddler* took traditions of Yiddish theater and Hasidism that had been marks of minority subcultural identity known only to traditional Jews and celebrated them in a popular theatrical form available not only to more cosmopolitan Jews but to non-Jewish Americans as well. *Fiddler* opened the cultural door through which klezmer would step a decade later.[26]

If *Fiddler* set the musical path for the klezmer revival, the Havurah movement supplied klezmer's first non-Orthodox, non–Hasidic Jewish constituency. The Havurah movement, meaning "fellowship community" in Hebrew, developed in the late 1960s and early 1970s as "small, intense, highly participatory, informal worship [groups] . . . influenced by Martin Buber's neo-Hasidism and by Eastern philosophy, [which strove] to re-create communities that felt Jewishly authentic, spiritual, and antimaterialistic." Harvard sociologist David Riesman once described the Havurah founders to Netsky as young Jews who "felt estranged from American society, as exemplified by the Vietnam War and mass culture, and from the Jewish community, as exemplified by what they considered to be its inauthentic bureaucratic institutions." Havurah members shared and celebrated the diversity of traditional Jewish culture. In the early 1970s, for example, sabbath services I attended at Havurah Shalom, "the movement's model independent havurah," included an eclectic mix of Israeli folk songs, traditional synagogue songs, and Hasidic dances performed to klezmer music.[27]

By 1980 these renewal forces had created a growing constituency for traditional Jewish music, including klezmer. Since then it has simply exploded onto the international music scene. By any measure, the popular response to klezmer has been extraordinary. Radio, video, concerts, and recordings have brought klezmer a growing non-Jewish audience in America and especially in Europe, where Slobin has reported a large, eclectic, and enthusiastic European constituency for the music from Madrid to St. Petersburg. Slobin's recent book, *Fiddler on the Move: Exploring the Klezmer World,* interprets the meaning of klezmer for this non-Jewish audience primarily as "a heritage music" rather than as a mode of sacred song and religious culture.[28] Slobin cites culture theorist Barbara Kirshenblatt-Gimblett on the definition of heritage music. "While it looks old," she wrote in her 1998 book *Destination Culture: Tourism, Museums, and Heritage,* "heritage is actually something new. Heritage is a mode of cultural production in the present that has recourse to the past." Kirshenblatt-Gimblett further distinguished between traditional music, "that is part and parcel of a way of life," and heritage music, "that has been singled out for preservation, protection, enshrinement, and revival."[29]

From this perspective klezmer, celebratory ritual music from a central European Jewish culture that was systematically destroyed more than a half-century ago, cannot possibly be traditional music for contemporary non-Jewish Americans. Instead they embrace it as heritage music. They select klezmer, much as contemporary Germans consume Native American powwow and ceremonial songs, from a range of lost, marginal, or exotic music cultures that have been captured and re-presented through performance media. Heritage music is not quite world music, however, which is the commercial appropriation, presentation, and often mixing together of musical elements derived from traditional cultures. Heritage music advocates invest different meaning in their music experience than world music consumers do because the "preservation, protection, enshrinement, and revival" dimensions of heritage invite its audience into what Kirshenblatt-Gimblett calls "a second life" in an imagined cultural world.[30]

Slobin sees klezmer as a heritage music comprised of overlapping "clusters" or "constellations" of cultural meaning that range from "a political and ideological game of public relations and prestige" when it is presented at, say, an Israeli cultural celebration, to the Italian "enthusiastic free-spirited response" that "seems in another space altogether, having to do with expanding musical horizons, more involved with taste than politics." Klezmer has perhaps the greatest range of meaning of any heritage music, Slobin argues, especially for non-Jews: "Non-Jews have a multiple, fragmented consciousness about the Jews, as any example of music contact, like . . . a Berlin audience going to a klezmer event, will show. There are no other heritage musics that can draw an audience from motives ranging from sheer show biz through expiation of your grandfathers' sins." But none of these heritage meanings for non-Jews, he concludes, can tap the unique reservoir of significance that klezmer holds for its core Jewish constituency.[31]

The religious significance of American klezmer has been created by its Jewish audience. The reasons for klezmer's appeal are as complex as the history of American Judaism itself, but one fact above all is clear. The postwar generation of American Jewish liberals, who once explicitly rejected Yiddish traditions as obsolete remnants of a past best forgotten, has suddenly turned to its historic heritage for religious and cultural meaning. Regardless of the particular paths they have taken, urban and suburban liberal Jews across denominational differences have since 1980 embraced klezmer music as a powerful expression of their identity. For some, the fact that the music remains distanced on concert stage or compact disc makes it more easily approachable. For others, klezmer calls forth celebration and dance: they want it live and they hire the band for weddings and for bar and bat mitzvahs. Regardless of how the music is performed and heard, the klezmer revival has reached a new generation of American Jews for which it possesses novelty, historic resonance, and sacred meaning that it had lacked for their parents.

Few of the new klezmer enthusiasts become Hasidim or even Orthodox. Their religious trajectory has instead followed the more modest path leading from Reform and Reconstructionist to Conservative synagogues. Since 1980 these three denominations, historically the most characteristically American expressions of Judaism, have all gravitated toward a more traditional ritual sensibility and an openness to every expression of Jewish culture. Through efforts like those of Netsky and the Klezmer Conservatory Band, klezmer has reappeared in concert form at precisely the right time to attract that sensibility and to propel traditional Hasidic celebrative music to unprecedented popularity among American Jews and Gentiles as well.

The Sephardic Music Revival

As significant as klezmer has been for the Jewish music revival, however, it is only part of a still larger encounter of contemporary American Jews with their musical heritage. After klezmer, the most important Jewish music movement in America today is the revival of medieval Sephardic sacred song. The story of the Sephardic renewal supplies a necessary complement to klezmer for understanding how sacred song is transforming contemporary American Judaism.

On a sweltering Wednesday morning in early June 1994 I interviewed Judith Wachs, founder and artistic director of Voice of the Turtle, one of America's leading Sephardic revival groups, at her shaded Victorian house in Cambridge, Massachusetts. Over lemonade we talked about the origins and significance of the Sephardic music revival. Since 1978 Voice of the Turtle, or simply "Turtle" to its friends, has been a major vehicle of the Sephardic music revival. At the beginning, however, Wachs had had no inkling that she was about to embark on a major cultural and religious enterprise. "When I started," she said, "this was all a mystery to me. I didn't know Spanish, I didn't know [Sephardic] culture, and I didn't know where this was leading."[32]

Wachs's first exposure to Sephardic music occurred as a member of Quadrivium, Boston's pioneer Early Music ensemble founded by the late Marlene Montgomery. At a Quadrivium rehearsal in 1977 a visiting singer named Aviva brought some Sephardic songs and sang them to the group. "She sang this song in Ladino," Wachs remembered, "but I didn't know it. I said to Aviva, 'What is that? Was your father a cantor?' Because she was singing in a cantorial style, in the chanting mode with ornamental flourishes of the vowels and with [religious] feeling. She said, 'It is a Sephardic song.' I said, 'What does that mean?' She said, 'Oh, the Jews that live in Spain.' And that did it."

Wachs was fascinated by the music and mystified by the existence of an ancient Jewish music tradition that she had never known. Her surprise was genuine, because she possessed a rich background in Jewish music. "I, who grew up in the Ashkenazic tradition, and had an extensive Hebrew and religious education, had no idea [what Sephardic tradition was]. We came from a super-Orthodox family in Brooklyn. My grandfather was an Orthodox rabbi, and many of my uncles were Orthodox rabbis. My father was a passionate aficionado of cantorial music. Not only did he enjoy it personally, but it was spread out through any living space that I was in at all times."

Wachs's father collected early recordings by the great cantors of central Europe. The elder Wachs saturated his family's environment with old 78 RPM recordings, exhorting everyone within hearing distance to appreciate Ashkenazic cantorial artistry that receded ever further beyond audible clarity with each submission of soft vinyl disc to blunted Victrola needle. "[My father] would hear one scratchy section of a piece and say, 'Oh, that's Pintchik,' or 'Oh, that's Rosenblatt,'" she remembered. "And if there was a particular passage that he really loved, he would crank it up, and you would hear in the background this incredible voice. He'd say 'do you feel it?'"

Wachs's early sacred-song experience also included frequent visits to live cantorial performances, including Moshe Koussevitsky and other star hazzanim. Wachs credited this home musical environment for shaping her own musical and spiritual sensibilities. "My ears were saturated with those cantorial voices," she remembered. "Basically I loved it then and I still love it now. I would have loved to think that I could become a cantor when I was a kid, but I was a girl. And a girl was not a cantor. That was the end of that discussion. The girl is not a boy, it was as simple as that, and therefore a girl is not a cantor."

Wachs finally got her chance to be a cantor at that 1977 Quadrivium rehearsal where she first heard the music of what for her was a lost heritage of Jewish sacred song. Curious about the music and its traditional culture, she began serious research. She eventually found two collections of Sephardic songs edited by Yitzak Levy, one of liturgical melodies and one of folksongs.[33] Wachs gathered a small group of musicians from Quadrivium—Derek Burrows, Lisle Kulbach, and Jay Rosenberg—to join her in exploring the new scores. Crucial to her experiment in medieval Sephardic music was the mentoring of Marlene Montgomery. "Marlene had taught us to get off the page," Wachs remembered, "and what we did is take that [Sephardic] stuff and play around with it. What she taught us was to take the notes of music and to be instruments and to hear what the music was."

Armed with Montgomery's embodied sense of song, Wachs moved deeper into the texts, scores, and cultural contexts of Sephardic music. At first she and her colleagues, now beginning to perform as Voice of the Turtle, had no idea how to perform the music they had found. "Yitzhak Levy put all of the ornamentation [into the scores]," Wachs said. "They were songs that had no tempo markings. I thought they were just meant to be sung slowly as ballads. We sang beautiful sad songs and no one knew what they meant." This well-meaning but literal approach to the music soon elicited some helpful hints from Turtle's earliest audience. "People came to us early on," Wachs recalled, "and said, 'why is everyone so sad? We're not so sad, we also like to laugh!' So we got a clue." That clue led Wachs to explore not only the historical and ethnographic context of Sephardic sacred song, but its performance practice in traditional communities as well.

Wachs's search for authentic Sephardic music and culture took her during the mid-1980s to Portugal, Spain, Turkey, Rhodes, Morocco, and Israel. She learned that despite significant formal and regional differences, a coherent Sephardic song tradition had survived from medieval times. "The Sephardic Jew who is from Rhodes and those whose heritage is from Morocco [seem] miles apart in celebration of how they did things," she observed. "[But Sephardic variants] are not really so far apart, because the center core is the Jewish religion. The thread of communal organization is similar among their communities as it was in Spain."

The songs Wachs collected at these sites spoke not of the prayers and hymns of the synagogue service, but rather of everyday existence interpreted by and saturated with sacred symbolism—a realm of religious folksong and especially of women's religious folksong. Wachs met many female traditional singers like Flory Jagoda, a Bosnian-born Holocaust survivor, who revealed to her the traditional Sephardic world and women's folksong performance in it. "I listened to many of these women," Wachs recalled, "and I said of them, what an incredible cantor she would make. Then I said to myself, what do you mean she *would* make, in subjunctive case? This woman *is* a cantor."

The fundamental insight that women served as custodians of sacred folksong outside the synagogue opened a stunning new perspective on the religious, cultural, and historical meaning of the songs that Wachs had so assiduously collected among Mediterranean Sephardim. Her experience with living songs and singers led her to explore the role of women's social networks in traditional Sephardic communities. "It was very interesting to me," she remarked, "to see what in fact the women did to contribute to the cohesion of the Jewish community, what they were able to preserve of the roots of the heritage whether sacred or secular, and how the secular which has been preserved is a metaphorical treasure chest of the sacred. A lot of the 'secular' turns out to be metaphorical hymns to God. The Beloved and the Bride, and other allusions of the Song of Songs, for example, you hear jumping out of these songs."

At our interview, Wachs cited a Turtle favorite to illustrate how male-performed synagogue song was complemented by the informal but no less important rituals of women's community. "Somebody made up a story about how it was when Joseph's brothers sold him, how it was when Potiphar's wife tried to seduce Joseph, how all her friends invited to the feast were so entranced with how handsome Joseph was that, when they were served their trays of dessert with knives, they cut themselves and their blood ran. Now isn't that fabulous, isn't that just absolutely fabulous?"

The song is a *coplas* from Rhodes, named for the succession of rhymed couplets that comprise its literary form and dictate its melodic structure. But how is such a song sacred? Coplas are songs that refer to some biblical text and expand upon it in the style of the *Midrash*, the vast collection of commentaries upon and elaborations of the Hebrew scriptures compiled during the first seven centuries of the common era. For the Sephardim, coplas functioned as a kind of women's musical midrash sung in the community outside of the synagogue. In this case the scriptural reference is quite explicit, Genesis 39, but what the song contributes is an extracanonical expansion of the heroic figure of Joseph and an amplification of the feeling tone of the seduction episode from a woman's perspective. The song makes the biblical story present by charging it with quite understandable human feelings of attraction and awe that might be experienced if one of the woman singers were to meet Joseph. It is not a theological interpretation of the story, to be sure, but it is hardly a nonsacred or nonreligious one.

At the other end of the Sephardic song spectrum stand songs developed in Spain under the Inquisition, in which singers referenced the survival of Jewish liturgical practices through lyrics deeply encoded with ritual symbolism. Wachs explained an example of such an encoded Passover song from sixteenth-century Spain that recalls "The Twelve Days of Christmas" as well as table songs from the

Seder or Passover Haggadah service. "What did you do to hide the fact that you were celebrating Passover [under the Inquisition]?" she asked rhetorically.

> I can tell you how from one very specific perspective, from one little song that goes: "what did the *duenna,* the lady of the house, eat during the third night of Passover?" She eats four hens and five whatevers, six suckling lambs, eight ovens full of bread, ten thousand bottles of raki. It just goes on and on! This song is said to be one of the code songs that were sung by the Jewish *conversos,* who were forcibly or voluntarily converted, who were practicing Catholics but also believing Jews. So they constructed this song on the same poetic structure as some of the table songs that you sing at the Seder, where you tell the story of the Flight from Egypt. If you can't do the whole Seder because it's too dangerous, and you can't sing all the songs because your servants have been instructed to watch you, then you sing "What did the Lady of the Passover eat on the third night?"

From this extraordinary corpus of Sephardic songs, Judith Wachs and Voice of the Turtle selected a repertory to perform for American audiences. Their performance principles followed the living music dictates of their mentor, Marlene Montgomery. "If the song came from Turkey," Wachs remembered, "we would use Turkish instruments. And we had to sing in this funny scale sung by a man who doesn't sing it the same way twice! And there aren't two versions of this song, so you can't cross-reference it. So we listen to Marlene. She's always speaking to us: just listen to the music, and do what it tells you. And basically, we follow our tastes when we can't resolve it."

This performance approach has brought occasional criticism for some of Turtle's performances as lacking historical authenticity, but Wachs delivered a clear and substantive response to it: "It's the same question in medieval music where you use this note or that note and there's always an expert who says do it this way or that," she said, "but there is no such thing as correct or pure [for this music], because this is all Dianic, it has to do with what [women] did. And you can't say they didn't do it, because the song gives you the evidence."

Turtle performances mix this experimental musicality with what Wachs called "a schematic focus" in programming that teaches audiences more than just musical meanings. For example, a Hanukah concert will always have celebrative songs that counterpoint more sober and reflective offerings. One of Turtle's most popular Hanukah offerings is "Vayhí miqéts burmuelos con miel," a Ladino song from Jerusalem (example 17 on page 354).

> Vayhí miqéts burmuelos con miel
> Par'ó los hazía Yoséf se los comía
> Par'ó al caño, Yoséf al baño
> Par'ó al bet ha-ha-yím
> Yoséf a los qiduxim.

"And it was at the end"; Burmuelos with honey:
Pharaoh made them, and Joseph ate them,
Pharaoh fell into the river, and Joseph went to the bath,
Pharaoh went to the cemetery, and Joseph went to the wedding!

Of this song Wachs commented that "it is a parody of the text in the Bible read on the Sabbath of Hanukah in the synagogue [Genesis 41], where Joseph interprets the dream of the Pharaoh. It begins with the [first phrase of the] actual biblical text, but quickly it becomes a story of making and eating *burmuelos* [traditional fried-dough holiday treats], and then of Pharaoh's downfall and Joseph's triumph." The song pulls together the women's world of Hanukah preparations with a telescoped paraphrase of the holiday synagogue text being read and studied by the community's men. Through Wachs's commentary, Turtle's audience gains an insight into the lived religion of medieval Sephardim expressed unexpectedly through song.[34]

Such enjoyable songs are a staple of Turtle's Hanukah concerts, but Wachs also programs more sobering offerings to drive home the larger meanings of the holiday. "[The concerts] will [also] have Hebrew songs from one of the Psalms of David that was sung by Jews from Saloniki," Wachs noted, "a community that was devastated by the Holocaust, very few of whom had gotten out."

This kind of mixing exemplifies Wachs's approach to performance and interpretation. "I provide extensive concert notes," she said, "and at the performance I say here's what you're hearing: the song that Judah the Maccabee sang at the rededication of the Temple. The word in Hebrew for rededication is *hanukah*. Very few people know this. What we're remembering is the history that happened at the time of the Maccabees and the Greeks. Suddenly our audiences are getting, through the vehicle of Sephardic music, the broadest dimensions of the celebration of a holiday."

Voice of the Turtle has found a large and enthusiastic audience for its unique repertory of Sephardic sacred song. But why have their performances and recordings met with such an intensely favorable response? Wachs readily allows that part of Turtle's audience is American Sephardic Jews who simply enjoy hearing their historic folksong corpus being performed. This sector of Turtle's constituency, she believes, is very small, perhaps 5 to 10 percent. Who are the rest of that audience, and why are they drawn to Turtle's music? Wach's answer was strikingly similar to Hankus Netsky's about klezmer: "The rest of the audience contains a high number of people whose religious background is Jewish but who do not practice in established communities," Wachs said. "They don't belong to a synagogue, and the extent to which they observe is very patchwork. It is sort of an existential observance, they observe it when they feel it. We are purveyors of music to people who are Jewish, for whom—and this had been told to me directly to my face—we provide their sense of Jewishness in a way that allows them to identify with it differently from the identity that their parents had with their Jewish religion."

Asked about why such "existential observants" find Sephardic song so compelling, Wachs had a ready answer. "The way we have chosen to present concerts," she said, "is based not so much upon the fact that this is Sephardic tradition, but that this music has such tremendous dimension in terms of its ability to provide access to historical, biblical, liturgical, and cultural manifestations of what it means to be Jewish."

Pressed for a more analytical assessment, Wachs said that Turtle's concerts provide a living aural access to the particularities of Jewish life in times and places long since lost to American audiences and yet still surviving through the ensemble's meticulous research and enthusiastic performances. "The dimension of Jewish history, Jewish liturgy, Jewish daily life, Jewish poetry, and Jewish allusion—the metaphors that people dealt with and heard on a daily basis, the literary and musical mechanisms for historical access to their daily life—is what we are trying to present in a concert."

While the revival of Sephardic song is certainly the center of Turtle's performance agenda, it is part of a much larger project of using sacred song to open their audience to the spiritual power of distant Jewish traditions. "Once you open up—and song is a way of opening up—what is more spiritual than having access to the old spirit of how people practiced their religion?" This sensitive multidimensional approach has led American Jewish audiences of all persuasions to embrace Voice of the Turtle, and the Sephardic tradition of sacred song, as a vital and authentic expression of Jewish identity.

Powers of the Paraliturgical

The revival of music traditions like Sephardic and klezmer has created a powerful response among a significant segment of American Jews today. In what sense, however, can that response be understood as religious? The experiences of Judith Wachs and Hankus Netsky point to a broader set of issues that inform the Jewish music revival and its religious meaning. The first of these is the placement of the music in Jewish religious culture. Rather than occupying the formal worship context of the synagogue, klezmer and Sephardic belong to a realm best described as paraliturgical, music and song that accompanied celebrations on the periphery of formal liturgy or imbued everyday activities with religious symbolism and sensibility. Klezmer performed these functions at circumcisions, bar and bat mitzvahs, and weddings as Sephardic did for holidays and the world of women's work.

This paraliturgical placement is highly significant. "Existentially observant" Jews, many of them not affiliated with synagogues, have championed the klezmer and Sephardic revivals because they find something religiously meaningful in these musics and songs that have at most an indirect reference to the synagogue liturgy. The combination of such paraliturgical distancing with the historically diverse Jewishness of these music traditions has made a powerful religious impact on contemporary American Jews. In the several American religious cultures we have examined thus far, such an appropriation of sacred song could only have been described as displacement, the dispersal of sacred meaning away from primary religious institutions onto alternative cultural forms. In the case of the klezmer and Sephardic revivals, however, paraliturgical distance seems to have had the opposite effect. The very nonliturgical and quotidian qualities of these musics have enhanced rather than weakened their traditional religious significance.

This sacralization of paraliturgical music and song raises the vexed question of where or even whether it is possible to draw a line between the religious and ethnic dimensions of Jewish culture. While every religious community is defined by its cultural traditions, Jews possess perhaps the most complex understanding of the relationship between religion and ethnicity. As an ancient people, they hold in common an extraordinary body of sacred texts and historical experience from the Ancient Near East. But they have also experienced nearly two millennia of dispossession and dispersion, so that to be Jewish has also been to live out the traditions of the ancient heritage in a strange land and to incorporate at least some of that strange land's own culture into Jewish life. Thus it is possible to argue that to be Jewish is both a religious identity and an ethnic one.

One of the most important ongoing debates in the history of American Judaism has involved precisely this question of whether Jewish identity is at base religious or ethnic and to what extent that identity, however defined, should be preserved in the New World. The Reform movement has since the mid-nineteenth century followed an intentional assimilation strategy that divested Jewish worship and ethnic culture of many of its central European Ashkenazic characteristics, though this emphasis has diminished in recent decades. Mordecai Kaplan's Reconstructionist movement has taken the alternative view that in its essence Judaism is an evolving civilization, all of whose contemporary cultural forms possess inherent religious value. Conservatives in turn have argued for the centrality of the rabbinic tradition while taking a moderate view of the ethnic identity and civilization claims. It is safe to say that few other issues have been more disputed in American Jewish intellectual history or are more contentious today.[35]

Recently, a musical version of this debate has emerged around the interpretation of paraliturgical musics like klezmer and Sephardic. The received opinion has been that of A. Z. Idelsohn who in 1929 offered an interpretation of what he called "Jewish folk-song" as inseparable from religion: "Life as the Jew visualized it," he wrote, "has no room for what is commonly denominated 'secular.' This spiritual nationality brought forth a folk-song as distinctive as the people itself. Just as to the Jew religion meant life and life religion, so to him sacred song has been folk-song, and folk-song, sacred song." For Idelsohn, all Jewish folksong is by definition sacred song because it and everything Jewish is intrinsically religious.[36]

Idelsohn's brilliant scholarship sustained his interpretation through three generations, but recently Amnon Shiloah has offered a broader sense of Jewish folksong that takes issue with the religious absoluteness of Idelsohn's position and argues instead for its irreduceably humanistic nature. "In actual fact, the situation as we know it is much more complex," Shiloah wrote. "Among the thousands of familiar folksongs, . . . Jewry has songs that express all conceivable tenors and hues of normal human activities and describe the entire gamut of upheavals that constitute the experiences one is likely to undergo in this world."[37]

At stake between these two views of Jewish song is the status of the sacred as expressed in community singing. Hankus Netsky and Judith Wachs took their own nuanced positions on these matters. Netsky saw the religious dimension as intrinsic to all of Jewish culture, "Religion has to be in the background," he said, "it's so much a part of the culture that you can't avoid it," including klezmer. Netsky also took issue with Mordecai Kaplan, arguing an imperative to preserve the historical traditions of Judaism. "Kaplan's philosophy is brilliant," he said, "but he missed such an important dimension. His idea is that Judaism is an evolving religious civilization, but that's not the point. Judaism has a history and a culture, and you've got to look back at what evolved before."

Judith Wachs took a somewhat more cultural view of the question, judging her traditional Sephardic songs as genuinely sacred and yet expressive of precise historic conditions and traditional cultural practices. "The repertory with which I deal," she said, "reveals a cultural mosaic, the dimensions of that [Sephardic] culture with reference not only to the strict orthodox observation of religion as practiced in the synagogue, but it also gives you the building blocks of the quotidian culture, the teeny manifestations of what was done on a daily basis, how it was done, and when was it done."

Both Netsky and Wachs appear to endorse Shiloah's open-ended humanistic sense of Jewish sacred song in interpreting their respective genres. The way in which klezmer and Sephardic may be religious for contemporary American Jews, however, raises still further questions. If the revival of these paraliturgical musics has acquired sacred meaning as a function of ethnic or cultural identity, then Shiloah's view can be sustained. If, on the other hand, the klezmer and Sephardic revivals have a religious explanation, then Idelsohn's claim still has merit.

Mark Slobin has provided a helpful framework for interpreting how the klezmer and Sephardic revivals might be understood as ethnic or cultural musical expressions. In *Subcultural Sounds*, Slobin outlined a process whereby the "micromusics" of ethnic "subcultures" interact with the dominant Western "superculture" of Euro-America through "intercultural" dynamics of "industry, diaspora, and affinity." Slobin set the Jewish music revival in these cultural dynamics as an example of what he calls "reevaluation." "Over time," he wrote, "new perspectives cause a reordering of group priorities, a changed understanding of what is 'authentic,' what represents 'us' best to outsiders, what sells best to a new generation of listeners, or what is now 'ours' that once was 'theirs.' Such shifts often accompany significant social change in the superculture or a particular historical moment in the life of the subculture."[38]

Slobin sees the rise of klezmer, and by extension the Sephardic revival, as a function of the integration of Jews into the American superculture during the 1960s and their consequent freedom to draw their own musical and cultural boundaries. He wrote, "It is hard for me not to believe that this sort of unbuttoned ethnic music-making by young Jewish-Americans is tied to the fact that for Jews, ethnic boundaries are now erected more from the inside out than from the outside in. You don't have to be as careful with your daily life if no one is peering in the window. You might dust off some skeletons in the closet, or reconsider your embarrassment at the way your old relatives behave."[39]

At least as important for the American Jewish community's sense of ethnic identity, however, was the enormous impact of the Six Days War of 1967 which threatened the survival of the State of Israel. Many observers have interpreted the renewal of interest in Jewish traditions by American Jews during the 1970s and 1980s as a response to the 1967 war. The Yom Kippur War of 1973 only reinforced the search for spiritual, historical, and cultural roots. Guided by the novels of Chaim Potok, Irving Howe's influential 1976 book *The World of Our Fathers*, and the neoconservative editorship of Norman Podhoretz at the bellwether journal *Commentary*, cosmopolitan American Jews since the mid-1970s have reexamined the imperative of assimilation and found it wanting. Their explorations into the spiritual, historical, and cultural roots of Jewish tradition have yielded a significant shift to Conservatism, which during the 1990s became the largest Jewish denomination, and with a small but steady flow of converts to Orthodoxy and Hasidism.[40]

More broadly, cosmopolitan American Jews since 1973 have embraced a range of Jewish cultural forms from pre-Holocaust Europe and the global Diaspora, including klezmer and Sephardic music. The first klezmer revival recording, for example, was released in 1977 by Lev Liberman's New York band, the Klezmorim, while Voice of the Turtle performed its first Hanukah concert in 1978. Hankus Netsky commented on the process:

> What's happened with the recent generation of Reconstruction and Reform is exactly that they're saying, "yes, we're an evolving religious civilization, but we've thrown out way too much of our heritage and we should reclaim it." The significant thing is [that] we rediscovered [klezmer] without a nostalgic feeling. This Yiddish culture took a thousand years to develop. It represented, and still does, a way for the Jews to transcend the environment, the same way the blues did for urban blacks, the same way the slaves sang spirituals. It was the Jews' way out of the miserable conditions they were going through, and when I hear it, it's these old ragged self-taught musicians playing this music that is just so otherworldly.

The Jewish music revival then can be fairly understood as a matter of ethnocultural development, in Mark Slobin's terms a reevaluation, one of those boundary shifts "that often accompany significant social change [at] a particular historical moment in the life of the subculture."

But this interpretation does not explain the religious processes at work in the Jewish music revival. The ethnocultural view indicates when and why the revival has occurred, but not how this paraliturgical music has accrued such powerful religious meanings. Many factors are involved, of course, but another concept from the history of religions offers perhaps the most helpful clues to this elusive religious phenomenon. It is the concept of "repristination," literally "the action of returning to an original state," that historians of religion have identified as a fundamental part of human religiousness. According to this view of religion, beliefs become efficacious when they are performed, when they are re-presented to believers. Myths are recited or sung or danced or enacted and thereby gain their unique power over hearts and minds. In these performances, believers "return" to the times and events depicted in the myth and experience the sacred cosmos as it was at its origins. Repristination refers specifically to the psychological and spiritual process through which this identification of the believer's self with the sacred realm occurs.[41]

Something like this process of repristination, I think, occurs for contemporary American Jews at klezmer and Sephardic revival concerts. The difference between those concerts and traditional synagogue ritual consists not so much in the informality of the concerts as in their historical and symbolic referents. The synagogue service recalls worshipers to their sacred origins in the biblical narrative. Revival concerts recall audiences to locations in the postbiblical history of diasporic Jews: the medieval Sephardic communities of the Mediterranean basin and the Ashkenazic world of pre-Holocaust central Europe. According to the repristination concept, these locations and their musics have attained mythic status as new elements of the Jewish sacred narrative. By hearing and understanding Sephardic and klezmer music, contemporary American Jews are able to transport themselves into new dimensions of their religious origins and create an identification with Jewishness that, for some, even the synagogue service cannot supply.

How do klezmer and Sephardic music facilitate this process of repristination? The sheer factuality of these musics in the first instance reminds American Jews of a past distant from them in time and space. More religiously important, however, is the historic and symbolic status of the communities that produced these musics. Both the Iberian Jews who produced the classic Sephardic repertory and the central European Ashkenazim who created klezmer were victims of religious persecution, exile, and genocide. Their histories recapitulate and extend the sacred tragedy of Israel from Egyptian slavery, Babylonian captivity, and Roman diaspora into the medieval and modern periods. Given the renewed search of American Jews for religious and cultural rootage, it is not difficult to understand how for them klezmer and Sephardic music might resonate with more than simply historical or ethnic significance.

The most powerful element in the religious repristination of klezmer and Sephardic musics, however, is the sheer experience of sacred-song performance. The perceptual immediacy of song performance combined with music's ability to transcend time by sounding the same now as when first composed, makes it a unique medium to express religious meaning from the distant past. Knowing about klezmer or Sephardic music is not at all the same as hearing it. A performance of these musics can bring their religious worlds to life and convey them with a power sufficient to spark religious repristination.

This musicoreligious power returns the listener not only to the primal worlds of medieval Sephardim and early modern Ashkenazim but also to the living process of oral transmission that preserved the music for listeners today. Judith Wachs commented on the sacrality created by centuries of Sephardic oral transmission. "The power of music is a power different than other kinds of power," she said. "When a song comes down through the centuries, it has been weeded. People have said, 'I like that song' many, many times, from different backgrounds, centuries, and times, coming from different places, socially, intellectually, spiritually. This therefore is an education, spiritual folk music out of time that they have handed down through the centuries. And it's astonishing how powerful it is when you hear it."

Re-presenting such music through performance to its contemporary inheritors is an act capable of repristinating that audience back to the time and place of the music. The response of American Jewish audiences to klezmer and Sephardic manifests precisely the characteristics of the repristinating experience: the music itself gains access to their emotions and thoughts in a new way that renews and transforms their awareness of their most fundamental spiritual and religious identity.

Liberal and moderate Jews today—members of Reform, Conservative, and Reconstructionist communities as well as their "existentially observant" counterparts in American urban centers—are placing a special premium on developing their Jewish identity. For them, the recovery of klezmer music and Sephardic song is an extraordinary experience, a transforming repristination that brings them back into the sacred world of the Jewish past and makes that sacrality alive and available to them today. The songs of the Sephardim and the music of the klezmorim possess unique capacities to create this distinctively Jewish sense of transcendence. The Jewish music revival presents yet another way in which song and the sacred combine and create. Judith Wachs said, "American Jews must ask, 'Who speaks to me?'" For many at the beginning of the twenty-first century, the answer to her question is the unlikely tandem of the klezmorim and the Sephardim.

Notes

1. For the standard account of American Jewish history, see Howard M. Sachar, *A History of the Jews in America* (New York: Knopf, 1992).

2. Mark Slobin, *Chosen Voices: The Story of the American Cantorate* (Urbana: University of Illinois Press, 1989), 36–49.

3. The most widely used general survey of Judaism in America is Nathan Glazer, *American Judaism*, 2d ed. (Chicago: University of Chicago Press, 1989).

4. Abraham Zvi Idelsohn, *Jewish Music in Its Historical Development* (New York: Henry Holt, 1929), 7–21.

5. Abraham Zvi Idelsohn, *Jewish Liturgy and Its Development* (New York: Henry Holt, 1932), xv.

6. Idelsohn, *Jewish Music*, 24–100.

7. Amnon Shiloah, *Jewish Musical Traditions* (Detroit: Wayne State University Press, 1992), 31–33, 53–56, 125–27. See also Shiloah, *The Dimension of Music in Islamic and Jewish Culture* (Brookfield, Vt.: Variorum/Ashgate Publishing, 1993).

8. Shiloah, *Jewish Musical Traditions*, 87.

9. Ibid., 101.

10. Ibid., 111.

11. David A. Teutsch, ed., *Kol Haneshamah: Shabbat Eve*, trans. Joel Rosenberg (Wyncote, Pa.: Reconstructionist Press, 1989), 48–54.

12. Abraham Zvi Idelsohn, *Hebraisch-orientalischer Melodienschatz* (Leipzig: Breitkopf und Hartel, 1914–32), English trans., *Thesaurus of Hebrew-Oriental Melodies* (New York: KTAV Publishing House, 1973); Shiloah, *Jewish Musical Traditions*, 22; Jeffrey A. Summit, *The Lord's Song in a Strange Land: Music and Identity in Contemporary Jewish Worship* (New York: Oxford University Press, 2000), 33–104; Slobin, *Chosen Voices*, 198–201.

13. Slobin, *Chosen Voices*, 7–9.

14. Ibid., 50–89.

15. See Herbert Fromm, *On Jewish Music: A Composer's View* (New York: Bloch, 1978).

16. Isaac Bashevis Singer, *Gimpel the Fool and Other Stories* (New York: Noonday Press, 1957), *Zlateh the Goat and Other Stories* (New York: Harper and Row, 1966), *The Fools of Chelm and Their History* (New York: Farrar, Straus, and Giroux, 1973), and *The Collected Stories of Isaac Bashevis Singer* (New York: Farrar, Straus, and Giroux, 1982).

17. Adelbert von Camisso, *Peter Schlemihl*, trans. Leopol von Loewenstein-Westheim (London: J. Calder, 1957).

18. Sholem Aleichem, *Tevye the Dairyman and The Railroad Stories* (New York: Schocken, 1987), *Tevye's Daughters* (New York: Crown, 1944), *The Old Country* (New York: Crown, 1946), and *The Adventures of Mottel, the Cantor's Son* (New York: H. Schuman, 1953); Irving Howe and Ruth Wisse, eds., *The Best of Sholem Aleichem* (New York: Simon and Schuster, 1979). See also Maurice Samuel, *The World of Sholem Aleichem* (New York: Knopf, 1943); and Ken Frieden, *Classic Yiddish Fiction: Abramovitsh, Sholem Aleichem, and Peretz* (Albany: State University of New York Press, 1995).

19. Hankus Netsky, telephone interview with author, June 6, 1994. All subsequent quotations are taken from this interview.

20. Robert Brustein, "Schlemiel the First," American Repertory Theater *Playbill*, Spring 1994.

21. Ibid.

22. Martin Buber, *Jewish Mysticism and the Legends of the Baal-Shem* (London: Dent and Sons, 1931); Dan Ben-Amos and Jerome R. Mintz, *In Praise of the Baal Shem Tov: The Earliest Collection of Legends about the Founder of Hasidism* (New York: Schocken, 1970); Abraham Joshua Heschel, *The Circle of the Baal Shem Tov: Studies in Hasidism* (Chicago: University of Chicago Press, 1985); Murray J. Rossman, *Founder of Hasidism: The Quest for the Historical Baal Shem Tov* (Berkeley: University of California Press, 1996).

23. Idelsohn, *Jewish Music,* 455–60.

24. Mark Slobin, "Fiddler Off the Roof: Klezmer Music as an Ethnic Musical Style," in *The Jews of North America,* ed. Moses Rischin (Detroit: Wayne State University Press, 1987), 98–103.

25. Jerry Bock and Sheldon Harnick, *Fiddler on the Roof: Vocal Score* (New York: Times Square Music, 1965).

26. Mark Slobin, *Subcultural Sounds: Micromusics of the West* (Hanover, N.H.: University Press of New England, 1993), 97.

27. Summit, *The Lord's Song in a Strange Land,* 43; Riv-Ellen Prell, *Prayer and Community: The Havurah in American Judaism* (Detroit: Wayne State University Press, 1989).

28. Mark Slobin, *Fiddler on the Move: Exploring the Klezmer World* (New York: Oxford University Press, 2000), 11–35.

29. Barbara Kirshenblatt-Gimblett, *Destination Culture: Tourism, Museums, and Heritage* (Berkeley: University of California Press, 1998), 7.

30. Ibid., 8.

31. Slobin, *Fiddler on the Move,* 34–35.

32. Judith Wachs, interview with author, Cambridge, Mass., June 9, 1994. All subsequent quotations are taken from this interview.

33. Yitzhak Levy, *Antologia de Liturgia Judeo-Espanola* (Jerusalem: Editorial Instituto del Cante, 1980), and *Chants Judeo-Espanol,* 4 vols. (Jerusalem: World Sephardi Federation, 1959–73). More recent collections of Sephardic song include Susana Weich-Shahak, *Judeo-Spanish Moroccan Songs of the Life Cycle* (Jerusalem: Jewish Music Research Centre, 1989), and Alberto Hemsi, *Cancionero Sefardi* (Jerusalem: Jewish Music Research Centre, 1995).

34. Translation from Voice of the Turtle, *Circle of Fire* (1987), Songs of the Sephardim 5, Titanic Ti-159.

35. Glazer, *American Judaism,* 90–98; Mordecai Kaplan, *Judaism as a Civilization* (1931; reprint, New York: Thomas Yoseloff, 1957). See also Emanuel S. Goldsmith and Mel Scult, *Dynamic Judaism: The Essential Writings of Mordecai M. Kaplan* (New York: Schocken, 1985).

36. Idelsohn, *Jewish Music,* 357–58.

37. Shiloah, *Jewish Musical Traditions,* 158.

38. Slobin, *Subcultural Sounds,* 95.

39. Ibid., 96.

40. Chaim Potok, *The Chosen* (New York: Simon and Schuster, 1967), *The Promise* (New York: Knopf, 1969), *My Name Is Asher Lev* (New York: Knopf, 1972); Irving Howe, *World of Our Fathers* (New York: Harcourt Brace Jovanovich, 1976).

41. Mircea Eliade, *The Myth of the Eternal Return* (New York: Pantheon, 1954), 49–92, and *The Sacred and the Profane: The Nature of Religion* (New York: Harcourt, Brace, and World, 1959), 68–115.

Sacred Song and
Contemporary
American Religion

New Music of the Spheres: From the New Age to Neo-Paganism

The first part of this book has examined sacred song in America's most enduring religious traditions. Such an analysis, however, does not address the protean richness of popular religion that has also characterized American religiousness since colonial times. In this second part, accordingly, we will turn to the roles of sacred song in religious communities and movements that have flourished during the last decades of the twentieth century. Only by complementing sacred song's functions in traditional communities with its roles on the innovative edges of our religious culture can a sufficiently balanced view be gained of sacred song in contemporary America. We begin with the New Age, one of the most characteristic American religious movements of the late twentieth century.

"Live Maine Women Folk Sat"

The Grand Auditorium in Ellsworth, Maine, population 5,975, is an art deco performance hall and movie house. The 500-seat theater's full stage, pit, and wings permit it to host live shows as well as films. It is the Grand's facade, however, that has made the theater an object of endearment to this small port town on Maine's central coast. Swathed in blue and orange neon, the marquee is a 1930s classic, supported by decorated Corinthian columns and the original glassed-in ticket booth. When the theater was threatened by declining business and possible demolition during the 1980s, local residents and summer friends organized successfully to preserve it. The Grand now plays to solid houses with a mixture of first-run films and local concerts. It is the sort of place that people love and simply refuse to let go, where a generous cross-section of the community still gathers to hear local artists perform.

One such concert filled the Grand on the Saturday evening of a mid-August weekend in 1994. I thought the marquee was a bit unclear on the attraction. "Live Maine Women Folk Sat" it announced proudly but somewhat uncertainly. Inside, Maine WomenFolk, a regional consortium of feminist musicians, played to a full house. Young dulcimer virtuoso and composer Barb Truex presented a series of original works for electric dulcimer, electric violin, and trumpet. Julia Lane, Celtic harper and singer, followed Truex. Anne Dodson sang a set of traditional and original folksongs. The final performer was flutist and composer Kay Gardner from Stonington, an ancient fishing town on the southern end of Deer Isle.

Entering to enthusiastic applause, Gardner, a statuesque middle-aged woman dressed in matching aqua tie-dyed shirt and pants, bounded barefoot onto the stage bearing a platinum flute. Immediately she broke into a soaring, haunting melody sung with the instrument's remarkable tone and vibrato. The melody was not tuned in a major or minor key but rather in some sort of modal or non-Western scale. The melody also abandoned the regular tempo and rhythmic pulse of Western music. Instead, Gardner's song spoke of Native American flute and Indian *raga*. The eloquent utterance lasted perhaps five minutes, weaving a joyful spell that was greeted by enthusiastic applause. Gardner, clearly enjoying herself, took a bow and joked that she had just returned from Michigan and hasn't had time to change clothes. "This is what they're wearing out there, believe it or not!" she laughed.

Gardner told a brief story about her next piece, "Waterfall Improvisation." She said that some years ago she began composing flute improvisations to express her experience of specific natural places. Recently she had gone to South America and composed "Waterfall" while visiting a cataract in the Amazon jungle. The piece was meant to be heard along with the sound of that or some other waterfall, but since it was difficult to get one into the Grand Theater, she asked the audience to close their eyes and imagine the sound of their favorite waterfall. In a brief guided meditation, she focused our attention on flowing water and sparkling light and invited us to enter into spirit of the waterfall. Then she began to play her improvisation on the Peruvian pipes, a five-note instrument that Gardner endowed with percussive speech and breathy tone. The song shimmered over the utterly silent audience and then was gone. Still louder applause followed.

For her last piece, Gardner introduced two female colleagues, a pianist and a cellist, friends from Stonington with whom she played regularly. The three colleagues had prepared *Lunamuse,* one of Gardner's earliest major compositions. Gardner explained that the work requires a drone, and since no drone instrument was handy, the audience would have to provide it. Sounding a note on her flute, Gardner asked us to intone it on the vowel "Ah," keeping the tone steady yet unforced and taking plenty of time for sustained breath. Several hundred Mainers and summer people in the Grand Auditorium proceeded to sing softly, setting up a three-octave vocal drone. Once the tone was established, Gardner and friends performed *Lunamuse,* a one-movement flute trio reminiscent of the style of Maurice Ravel or Eric Satie. The addition of the drone, however, transformed the piece, creating an uncanny experience of harmonic spiraling as the music moved through a sequence of modal melodies and tunings. Singing the drone also engaged the audience directly in the piece as co-performers. When it concluded, everyone applauded in affirmation of their own individual and collective experience as well as the trio of players on stage.

Maine WomenFolk 1994 concluded with all of the artists, led by Anne Dodson, singing and playing the Appalachian folk hymn "Bright Morning Stars Are Shining." A long ovation followed this last number. The crowd filed out slowly. All of the performers had shared original works with us and spoken powerfully about nature and spirit, love and truth. Chatting afterwards in low tones, the artists mingled with friends and neighbors, everyone sharing their responses to the musical and spiritual visions of the evening. Eventually the Grand Auditorium went dark, its momentary community of sound and sensibility dissolved into the cool air and starlit sky of a Maine summer night.

This unassuming little concert Down East was in one sense simply an annual gathering to hear local women musicians perform some of their own works. In another sense, however, it was one piece in a nationwide mosaic of similar music events that take place coast to coast and border to border. These events, loosely organized into an annual round, present the music of a new and distinctively American religious movement popularly called "New Age." And despite her relaxed demeanor on her home stage, Kay Gardner is one of the most important musical and intellectual leaders of that movement.

The New Age and Its Music

While the term *New Age* recalls its origins in the 1960s, today participants in most so-called New Age movements reject the term, preferring to be identified by their own specific communities or practices. By whatever name, however, a new American spiritual movement emerged from the Age of Aquarius, manifested itself in a myriad of forms during the 1970s, and coalesced into the New Age movement of the 1980s. The high point of the movement to date has been the Harmonic Convergence of August 1988, a rare alignment of the sun, moon, and planets celebrated as the beginning of a millennial era of higher consciousness. The New Age lost some momentum during the 1990s, owing in part to negative public reaction to "channeling," a psychic phenomenon in which ancient spirits are believed to speak through present-day mediums, and to the fatal futurism of the Heaven's Gate movement. Despite these setbacks, however, New Age ideas and practices continue to thrive in countless ashrams, witch covens, crystal and holistic healing groups, esoteric Christian centers, Sun Dance and Sweat Lodge societies, radical ecology cadres, and feminist Neo-Pagan communities across America.

Historian of American religion Catherine Albanese has supplied one of the best accounts of the New Age in her book *Nature Religion in America from the Algonkian Indians to the New Age*. Albanese interpreted the New Age as one of many North American religions that have located the sacred in the realm of nature. She called the New Age a "recapitulating piety," a religious movement that incorporates spiritual concerns and practices already well precedented in the American experience. Albanese described the New Age as a contemporary amalgam of "different denominations of the religion of nature" including Native American beliefs and rituals, "Puritan" nature literature, radical environmentalism, Goddess religion, and "vibrational medicine."[1]

What could be the sacred song of such an eclectic movement? The answer is as multifaceted as the New Age itself, a broad spectrum of styles that nonetheless share some fundamental musical elements. At one end of that spectrum stands Paul Winter's 1982 *Missa Gaia/Earth Mass,* a masterpiece of New Age ecological consciousness that celebrates the sacredness of land, sky, and sea. The score, dedicated to St. Francis of Assisi "in the year of his 800th birthday," combines Winter's saxophone combo with solos and ensemble settings of texts from the Bible, the Roman Catholic Mass, and evangelical Protestant hymns, along with recorded whale utterances and organ compositions in late Romantic style. Winter, veteran soprano saxophone jazz man turned ecological liturgist, presented *Missa Gaia* regularly during the 1980s to sellout crowds at New York's Episcopal Cathedral of Saint John the Divine. His more recent, similarly eclectic Winter Solstice concerts now play to packed houses at Saint John and Washington, D.C.'s National Cathedral. It is fair to say that, on the East Coast at least, Paul Winter's celebrative works have been the single most important musical expression of New Age spirituality.[2]

The other extreme of the New Age music spectrum emerged at the other end of the continent, in California. West Coast New Age musicians have concentrated more on music as healing and meditation than on Winter's cosmological celebrations. In the early 1970s Steven Halpern, a keyboard musician with a Ph.D. in physiology, began researching biofeedback, esoteric cosmology, and ancient Hindu music-healing. In the album notes to his acclaimed 1975 recording *Spectrum Suite: A Meditational Environment* for piano and flute, Halpern described the purpose and technique of his music: "The selections are designed to resonate specific areas of the body in a consecutive, and uplifting, manner. The overall flow of this album quiets the mind and body more effectively than other music—a fact verified via biofeedback measurements and Kirlian photography. The title comes from the album's format—an entire uninterrupted side which relates the seven tones of the musical scale and the seven colors of the rainbow to the seven etheric energy sources (chakras) in our bodies."[3]

Other popular recordings by Halpern soon followed, including *Zodiac Suite: A Cosmic Attunement* (1976) for electric piano, electric violin, bamboo and alto flutes, chimes, bells, and wind effect, and *Starborn Suite* (1977) for piano and string ensemble, recorded in part at Findhorn, Scotland's famed New Age community. Halpern's work during the 1970s pioneered the contemporary practice of musical healing in America, which has become one of the New Age's most popular and widespread movements. His theory of music and healing, published in 1979 as *Tuning the Human Instrument,* has had lasting impact on New Age music. Proposing "the non-frantic alternative" to hypertense life in contemporary America, Halpern called on readers to change their "soundscape" by eliminating the static of radio and television and replacing it with sustained tones designed to stimulate the seven *chakras* or energy centers of the body as taught by *kundalini* yoga.[4]

Somewhere near the center of the New Age musical spectrum, between Paul Winter's cosmological celebrations and Steven Halpern's musical healing, stand the movement's most successful artists, George Winston and Carlos Nakai. Winston's piano compositions and solo recordings for Windham Hill Records have enjoyed extraordinary popularity since the release of *December: Piano Solos* in 1982. That album was the first in a now-classic series of meditations on the seasons which established Winston as a front-rank New Age artist. Influenced by baroque and classical keyboard works, minimalist composer Philip Glass, and jazz pianist Keith Jarrett, Winston's compositions feature repeated rhythmic and melodic figures with very simple harmonic development. Since *December,* Winston has produced dozens of recordings and performed hundreds of sold-out concerts. His style has also attracted a number of similarly minded performers who eventually joined him as fellow "Windham Hill Artists," creating with their recordings a readily identifiable and commercially successful style of New Age music.[5]

R. Carlos Nakai, a Navajo/Ute flute player and composer, has soared to New Age fame through his recordings for Canyon Records of what David McAllester calls "the new genre of Indian message songs."[6] Nakai's first success came with his 1983 recordings *Changes,* a collection of traditional Native American melodies including "Zuni Song," "an embellishment of a melody [sung] at sunrise to greet the beginning of the day" (example 18 on page 355). Nakai characterized "Zuni Song" as supplying "a soothing, restful atmosphere. The artist paints by it. The psychiatrist employs it to provide an aura of pleasantness and peacefulness. It can help solve the cares of the day during a time of meditation."[7]

Since 1983 Nakai has made twenty-seven recordings, including *Cycles* (1985), later used by Martha Graham as the score for her ballet *Night Chant,* and *Ancestral Voices* (1992), finalist for the 1994 Grammy Award in the "Best Traditional Folk Music" category.[8] Most of Nakai's work consists of original and improvised songs in traditional Native American style. He records with complex synthesizer techniques that evoke Native American sacred sites like the Grand Canyon and supplies spiritual commentaries for his compositions like this poem for *Journeys* (1986):

> At birth we embark on a good journey
> seeking a destination of happiness.
> The journeys on our life-road
> facilitate development of our
> emotional, mental, physical, and
> spiritual states-of-being into a
> way of true power and wisdom.
> The Heart-center power, expressed as
> happiness and love will guide us
> upward on a path away from frustration,
> bitter toil and travail.[9]

With the enormous rise of popular interest in Native American traditions during the 1990s, Nakai's flute songs have become virtual anthems for New Age spirituality, played ceaselessly on the sound systems of homes, cars, and bookstores and shops wherever New Age style or substance obtain.

Winter, Halpern, Winston, and Nakai well represent the variety and illustrate the important common elements of form and style that characterize New Age music. New Age music is minimalist in conception and design. Unlike almost every other major kind of American sacred music, the New Age employs tone alone, musical sound itself, as a sacred medium. While virtually all sacred-song traditions join tone to text, New Age artists and theorists emphasize the intrinsic spiritual qualities of tone over against the priority of sacred texts. Not surprisingly, therefore, all of these pioneer New Age artists are instrumentalists rather than vocalists. Their music inclines quite strongly to melodies built on nondiatonic scales, using everything from Chinese pentatonic scales and Indian ragas to Greek modes and blues scales. Many of their compositions are solo works that possess no harmonic parts, or ensemble pieces with quite simple harmonic structures.

These characteristics of New Age music differ sharply from the varieties of sacred song discussed in part 1 of this book. Even the spirit-possession music of African Americans, which sometimes borders on wordlessness, is markedly different in style from New Age sacred sound. This stylistic difference expresses the religious distinctiveness of the New Age. While both African American spirit-possession and New Age spirituality entail a direct personal experience of the sacred, historians of religion have categorized the contrast between them as the difference between trance and ecstasy. Whereas in trance the individual is possessed by a supernatural entity in an intensely ritualized communal context, ecstasy is a solitary meditative experience of entry into the divine being.

In his study *Music and Trance: A Theory of the Relations Between Music and Possession* (1980),[10] ethnomusicologist Gilbert Rouget offered this theoretical summary of these opposite spiritual modalities:

Ecstasy	Trance
immobility	movement
silence	noise
solitude	in company
no crisis	crisis
sensory deprivation	sensory overstimulation
recollection	amnesia
hallucination	no hallucination

While few historic religions follow this theoretical typology exactly, Rouget's scheme would be widely accepted by historians of religion. They would also generally categorize New Age phenomena, most of which feature individual meditation techniques, as occupying the ecstasy side of the ledger. There are certainly New Age exceptions to this rule like Wiccan rituals and Matthew Fox's esoteric Christian "techno-mass" celebrations since 1996 in the San Francisco Bay area, but Rouget's typology adequately marks the religiousness of the New Age.[11]

Rouget's musical conclusion following from his categorization, however, was far more controversial. Rouget stated flatly that "as it has just been defined, [ecstasy] never makes use of [music] at all. There is an inherent incompatibility between the practice of ecstasy and music."[12] Rouget takes a quite narrow view of ecstasy, equating it almost exclusively with monastic mysticisms of the Christian and Buddhist traditions. Ecstatic mysticism has indeed flourished historically in such disciplined institutional contexts, but one major significance of the New Age lies precisely in its emergence as an eclectic, nonmonastic, laicized popular ecstatic movement. Moreover, because New Age spirituality is often practiced at home or in groups where sound systems are readily available, the movement has created music genres that can be either performed or listened to by practitioners. It can be argued persuasively that these qualities mark the New Age and its music as a profoundly American religious movement, its diverse, decentralized, personalized, and technologized character reflective of religious and cultural patterns deeply ingrained in American identity in the twenty-first century.

New Age music also differs from traditional sacred song in its heightened ideological function. In New Age communities, musical tone is experienced and understood as a direct manifestation of the sacred rather than simply as an aid to meditation. Ideas about how sacred sound and song work upon human beings have become central elements of New Age belief. Steven Halpern's esoteric theory of sound and health, for example, appeared early in the movement's history and has contributed mightily to its metaphysics as well as to its meditational practices. More recent writings like theosophist Don Campbell's *The Roar of Silence: Healing Powers of Breath, Tone, and Music* and Joy Gardner-Gordon's *The Healing Voice: Traditional and Contemporary Toning, Chanting, and Singing* have extended the range of musico-metaphysical teaching to include the human voice as an instrument of vibrational healing. Such a role for sacred sound in the fundamental metaphysical and moral teachings of a religious movement is extremely rare in modern times. New Age music has, in fact, become the most important example of sacred song's role in a formal belief system in American religious history.[13]

Singing the Goddess: Wiccans and Neo-Pagans

Given the diverse and fluid nature of the New Age movement, accurate estimates of its constituencies are notoriously difficult to make. By any measure, however, women's spirituality is one of the most important elements in New Age religion. Women's spirituality emerged quickly in the feminist movement of the 1960s and 1970s. Spurred by the discovery of shared life experience in consciousness-raising groups, early feminist singers like Holly Near and Meg Christian wrote songs and lyrics appealing to women to create their own counterculture in a patriarchal world. Women's music festivals became occasions for experiments in community and culture making. Meanwhile in theological circles, a new generation of women scholars mounted a feminist critique of traditional Christianity and Judaism. Since 1980 the most radical of these critics, most notably Mary Daly, have called for an autonomous "womanchurch" to address the spiritual needs of the majority gender. At the same time, cultural feminists like Carol Christ reclaimed the Goddess worship of ancient India, the Mediterranean, and the Near East. Perhaps most controversially, organized witchcraft appeared in American public culture during the 1960s as the Neo-Pagan Wiccan movement and has grown vigorously since.[14]

These many strands of women's spirituality are interwoven in a continuum of movements and organizations. Of those strands, the most fully developed religious cultures have been the Goddess and Wiccan movements. Since 1980, these two manifestations have become increasingly fused into Neo-Paganism. According to Margot Adler's pioneering account *Drawing Down the Moon,* the single leader who has done most to unify Neo-Paganism has been the seer and writer Starhawk. "There are some," Adler wrote in 1986, "who have estimated that Starhawk's book *The Spiral Dance* has *alone* created a thousand women's covens and spiritual groups." Fifteen years later, that number may have doubled.[15] Born Miriam Simos in 1951, Starhawk was raised in a Jewish household in the San Francisco Bay area, became interested in feminism and witchcraft at UCLA in the late 1960s, and was initiated into the Craft in 1972 by Hungarian hereditary witch Z. Budapest at Venice, California. After launching a promising career as a novelist, Simos/Starhawk was in 1976 elected leader of the Covenant of the Goddess, a legally incorporated religious organization formed by Bay Area witches. Three years later she published *The Spiral Dance.*[16]

Starhawk claimed that witchcraft is "the Old Religion" of the West, a thirty-five-thousand-year-old mythological cycle of "the Mother Goddess, the birthgiver who brings into existence all life; and the Horned God, hunter and hunted, who eternally passes through the gates of death that new life may go on." She emphasized the fifteen-hundred-year compatibility of the Old Religion with Christianity, only to be shattered by the systematic persecution of witches by Catholics and Protestants from 1484 through the seventeenth century. After an "age of disbelief" from 1700 through 1950, "the Craft, today, is undergoing more than a revival, it is experiencing a renaissance, a re-creation," according to Starhawk, spurred by women who are "actively reawakening the Goddess."[17]

That female deity is not to be confused with the transcendent male gods of Western tradition. Instead, "the Goddess is not separate from the world—She *is* the world, and all things in it." Though for Starhawk the Goddess is important for men as a source for healing their internal division "into a 'spiritual' self that is supposed to conquer their baser animal and emotional natures," the female deity holds primal power for women. "The image of the Goddess inspires women to see ourselves as divine, our bodies as sacred, the changing phases of our lives as holy, our aggression as healthy, our anger as purifying, and our power to nurture and create, but also to limit and destroy when necessary, as the very force that sustains all life. Through the Goddess, we can discover our strength, enlighten our minds, own our bodies, and celebrate our emotions. We can move beyond narrow, constricting roles and become whole."[18]

To call forth and ritualize the empowerment of women through "the rebirth of the Ancient Goddess Religion" was the task Starhawk undertook in *The Spiral Dance.* Her account of the Craft's beliefs, organization, and practices has become canonical for the New Age. Part of the book's great appeal, however, has been its provision of ritual texts and techniques from the Craft: sixty-one exercises including "rhythm play," "group breath," "power chant," and "womb chant"; twenty-five "invocations, chants, and blessings"; seven spells; eleven herbal charms; and three "myths": "Creation," "The Wheel of the Year," and "The Goddess in the Kingdom of Death."

As Starhawk reported, the women's spirituality movement has produced its own sacred song, hymns to God the Mother, mantras and yogic healing drones, Pythagorean paeans to Greek and Roman goddesses, and Wiccan chants to the Earth Goddess. Among the most influential theorists, composers, and performers of women's sacred song is Kay Gardner. Her 1984 recording *A Rainbow Path* has become a classic of New Age women's spirituality and her 1990 book *Sounding the Inner Landscape* a landmark interpretation of music healing.[19] Her career has embodied the most important elements of the women's spirituality movement and its music since the 1960s.

Cosmographer of Sound

On the morning after her concert at the Ellsworth Grand, I interviewed Kay Gardner in her yellow clapboard Victorian house overlooking Stonington Harbor on the southern tip of Maine's Deer Isle. At our interview I learned not only about Gardner's understanding of sacred sound and healing music, but also about her pilgrimage from midwestern housewife and mother to intellectual and spiritual leader of the Neo-Pagan community. Gardner grew up in a musical family. Both parents were amateur musicians who loved folksongs "from different cultures and countries." Her own music-making began with piano lessons at the age of four. Slow to read notation, she memorized the lessons played by her teacher and then reproduced them. As an eight-year-old she added the flute to her musical training. Her parents and teachers encouraged Kay to compose and improvise on both instruments. When she was ten, the family moved from New York to Ohio, where she soon encountered her life's musical vocation: "The first time I saw a conductor, I decided that was what I wanted to be. I had seen one [woman] high school band director, so I thought if I want to conduct, I have to be a band director. So I went to the University of Michigan to become a band director, mainly because I had never seen or heard of a woman orchestral director, so I had no role model."[20]

Gardner did not complete her degree at Michigan. "I flunked out," she said, "because some of the music education courses were so stupid, I just refused to go." Instead she married, bore two children, and for eleven years raised her family. After her divorce, Gardner returned to musical studies at SUNY–Stony Brook where she took a master's degree in flute performance under Sam Barron. Gardner's creative release, however, was tied more to her encounter with her own sexuality than to her musical studies. After taking her degree, Gardner came out as a lesbian. "That was one very important thing," she said, "because when I came out, my creativity started again. I just opened up totally to who I really was on the deepest level, and the music started flowing."

Gardner moved to New York City where in 1973 she joined a lesbian feminist band called Lavender Jane. Together they made music history. "We put out the very first recording of lesbian feminist music," she reported. "It wasn't my music, but I helped produce it and played flute in it and wrote the arrangements." The success of Lavender Jane gave Gardner her first commercial opportunity as a composer. "My very earliest music was orchestrated original folksongs that I had written in the [modal scales]," she said. "So I wrote a lot of songs and arranged them for alto flute and string quartet."

Gardner's search for a feminist musical aesthetic was also tied to her lifelong quest for spiritual meaning. "I had been brought up as a Christian Scientist," she said, "with a father who was an MIT man, very scientific, and Mom was totally metaphysical. I dropped that religion, I couldn't relate to it. I just wanted to go to church with my Catholic friends because there was incense. Then I decided I couldn't be inside a building. It wasn't right because God/Goddess, all that is, is in nature and outdoors. I really related to neo-paganism because it's an earth religion. So I was initiated in Wiccan tradition." She began practicing as a witch in 1968 and, like Starhawk, was formally initiated into the Craft by Z. Budapest in 1975.

Gardner's personal synthesis of music, sexuality, and Wiccan spirituality bore its first fruit in 1974 with the composition of *Lunamuse,* the work for flute, piano, cello, and drone she performed at the Ellsworth Grand concert (example 19 on page 356). "I wrote *Lunamuse,*" Gardner remembered, "as I was traveling as a minstrel throughout New England with a sister performer whose name is Jerri Ann Hinderly. It was literally written in circle dancing under the full moon. We would stop at various women's communities in New England, and this piece was in progress at that time. So whenever there was a full moon, I would sing the melody while I played the accompaniment, just a nice ostinato on the guitar. When I got back to New York City, I made a composition out of it."

Lunamuse appeared as a track on *Mooncircles,* Gardner's first solo recording in 1975.[21] Though highly successful, *Lunamuse*'s feminist spirituality also proved controversial. She remembered:

> *Lunamuse* was a circle dance, a pagan celebration, and I was given a lot of flack for it because it was not politically correct. Back in 1975, women's spirituality was something we weren't supposed to do because it wouldn't make social change. I believed it would, and so I was in trouble for that. I was really writing what came to be called New Age music before it got to *be* New Age music! Which is basically music that is concerned about the environment, celebrates world spirituality. It wasn't just a women's thing, but I was coming from it very deeply as a feminist, and I was bringing that to it.

The composition also marked a watershed in Gardner's stylistic and theoretical development. "With the audience droning and with all the repetition in it and the modal theme—sort of a mixture of blues and Phrygian mode, and in a cyclical form—that was the very first piece to announce the style I would be writing in for the next twenty years." In Gardner's view, her Neo-Pagan spirituality came first, triggering her musical expression; only later did she become aware of her music's healing power. "Many folks who listened to *Lunamuse* said it was healing," Gardner recalled, "but at that time 'healing' was a word I did not use a lot. And I thought, well, what makes a piece of music healing? From there I began my studies of healing."

Those studies were decisively shaped by a 1976 internship with Antonia Brico, the legendary pioneer conductor of the Denver Symphony, and her spiritual discoveries in that city. With Brico, Gardner realized her musical ambition to conduct and compose at the highest professional level. From the kundalini ashram where she lived, Gardner learned that she had probably experienced "the rising of kundalini" in 1971, a surge of enlightenment proceeding upward through the eight chakras or energy centers of the central nervous system: root (base of the spine), belly, solar plexus, heart, throat, brow, crown, and the transpersonal point directly above the crown. "It happened just as I was leaving the marriage in 1971 and the whole thing was very spontaneous, because I had not been studying with a guru." The realization that yogic traditions explained her experience interested Gardner in Hindu ideas of the body and of music. "That's when I got the idea for a piece called *A Rainbow Path*," a suite of movements intended to stimulate the energy of each *chakra*. Gardner completed and recorded *A Rainbow Path* in 1984. The album consists of eight flute meditations with drone, similar in style to *Lunamuse*, the tonic of each ascending up the scale to stimulate the chakras in vertical succession.[22]

A Rainbow Path represented Gardner's movement from feminist Wiccan–based music to a broader and more Eastern-influenced concept of healing music grounded in her yogic training. Gardner's timing was again perfect. During the mid-1980s many New Age movements had embraced Steven Halpern's eclectic theory of music as healing vibration. *A Rainbow Path* brought that theory squarely into women's spirituality, where it found a vast new audience. "I recorded *A Rainbow Path*," Gardner noted, "and everything took off for me." The album remains her bestseller almost twenty years after it was first released.

After several solo flute meditation albums, Gardner returned to healing music with a more specific agenda. "I wrote [and in 1987 recorded] a piece called *Viriditas*, which is a play on Hildegard of Bingen's term, written specifically for people with AIDS. Because it was in the key that touches the heart and lung area which affects the immune center, it was a piece that was for a specific disease." Gardner spent the late 1980s and early 1990s writing *Sounding the Inner Landscape* and producing an accompanying recording "that explains the book as a meditation, not as a lecture." Most recently Gardner has turned to classical Western music forms, including an oratorio for orchestra and women's chorus titled *Ouroboros (Seasons of Life)*, as well as exploring world music in her performances and recordings.

Gardner's career to date has embodied and expressed many dimensions of the women's movement and its developing spirituality. "I've been riding the wave right along," she said, "from the women's movement for the first recording I did, to *A Rainbow Path* and the new spirituality, and now I don't know where this oratorio goes. Who knows? I'm on a crest. I know where I have to be." In reflecting on the shape of "the wave," Gardner was quick to point out the essential role played by the women's community. "I started out in the women's community," she said, "because I was scared to go out in the general community. I really was. I didn't have enough self-confidence in the early days, and I really needed a support community." Sometimes that support was more uncritical than Gardner required. "They didn't know who I really was, they were just excited to see a woman out there. They would have clapped if it had been rotten! But hopefully it wasn't rotten, and they were educated along with me as I was getting more strength and more confidence, and so I kind of took a community of listeners right along with me."

Though Gardner has pursued an intense performing and composing agenda, her following has responded most to "the solo flute stuff," which is fine with her. "You know, I can whip that off in no time, [because] it's improvisation. I just let it flow through in whatever setting I'm in, whether it's the Amazon, or if I'm in England, or wherever these sacred sites are that I record at. But I need it all. I love the improvisation, I love having an instrument that's like part of my body so that I don't have to think when I play. And that's the flute for me, just letting it flow."

But as at the Ellsworth Grand concert, Gardner also loves to mix acoustical instruments and let the natural sound vibrations work on the audience. Gardner spoke forcefully about the importance of live sound presented without amplification or filtering. "I want the audience to listen," she said simply. "I don't want an engineer to determine what they can hear. I feel this is just being re-spectful to the audience." Her audiences have returned that respect by making Gardner one of the most popular New Age sacred music artists. Her influence lies, however, in more than her performing career alone. During recent years, Kay Gardner has also emerged as a leading theorist of healing music who teaches it as the foundation for New Age spirituality.

"When I auditioned for the master's program in flute at Stony Brook," Gardner recalled, "they told me my vibrato was really slow. I've measured it now, and my vibrato is right between the alpha and theta state of brain waves. Which makes it very meditative, and which also explains why that [kind of] music would interest me, because it's my own inner rhythm." This remark character-izes her orientation as a theorist of New Age music. For Gardner, musical praxis and intuitive knowledge have always preceded theoretical reflection. "The in-tuition comes first," she said, "like Einstein and his theories, you know, you get the idea first and then you have to take years to intellectually back it up. So that is actually what I have been doing [since 1976]."

Gardner's reflections on music and the human body reached even deeper into her personal past. Ironically, it was her response to Christian Science that first moved Gardner to explore the importance of the body. "One thing I had trouble with as a Christian Scientist was the constant denial of the body," she observed. "The body didn't exist and we're totally spirit. Well I'm sorry, we exist and we're here, and we're here for a reason, and in order to be whole we have to recognize the physical along with the spiritual, the mental, and the emotional."

Gardner's musical, intellectual, and spiritual journey finally issued in her sys-tematic theory of "music as medicine" published as *Sounding the Inner Land-scape*. The book marked Gardner's emergence as a teacher of divinity as well as a musical force in the New Age movement. The text has become a New Age clas-sic and a prime example of how music and sacred song have shaped the move-ment's beliefs. Gardner's theory rested on the claim that music and the body are part of a larger physical universe which is governed by laws of vibration. Whether represented macrocosmically by Plains Indians as "the medicine wheel" or microcosmically in Hindu kundalini yoga as the doctrine of the chakras, sound is understood in most religious traditions as possessing unique power to link the sacred and the human. Combining the spinning quality of sacred sound in the medicine wheel with the capacity of pure tone to radiate "etheric" energy and auras of colored light from the chakras, Gardner envisioned music as a sacred entity that embodies and expresses "the spiral dance" of being itself.[23]

Sounding the Inner Landscape placed great significance in the musical theories of ancient Greek philosopher Pythagoras of Samos. In the fifth century B.C.E. Pythagoras discovered that what we hear as distinct musical tones bear a precise physical and mathematical relationship to one another. He established that the ratios of the lengths of vibrating strings corresponded to the relative tones they produced. For example, if the fundamental tone or tonic of a vibrating string sounds at middle C, dividing that string exactly at its midpoint will produce a tone one octave above middle C. To sound the string at one-third of its length will produce a tone at the interval of a fifth, on the G an octave and a half above middle C. Smaller simple fractions of the string length—one-fourth, one-fifth, and so on—will produce additional tones that establish the seven notes of the scale (62–67).

From these physical phenomena Pythagoras deduced that all possible degrees of tone are included in the vibration of the fundamental tone. One tonic generates all possible overtones, called "harmonics." He also established seven principal modes of seven tones each (plus the octave), beginning on each degree of the scale. Pythagoras named the modes after peoples of ancient Greece: Ionian, Aeolian, Dorian, Phrygian, Lydian, Lesbian, and Locrian. Significantly, Pythagoras also assigned moral and emotional attributes to each of these modes. Phrygian, for example, denoted a fiery quality (129–36).

For Gardner, this Pythagorean tradition linked the seven degrees of the Greek modal scale to physical reality and the seven different modes to spiritual reality. Applying that linkage to kundalini teachings about the powers and qualities of the chakras, she associated the healing centers in the human spinal column and brain with the natural system of harmonics and the spiritual qualities of the traditional Greek modes. From these and other eclectic correlations, Gardner constructed a cosmology that placed the tones of the chromatic scale in a correspondent relation to other elements of the universe including colors, vowels, chakras, auras, the endocrine glands, gems, fragrances, and "esoteric attributes" such as vitality, passion, and insight. In Gardner's view, sacred song manifests these correspondences and thereby connects the human to the physical and the divine (example 20 on page 357).

Proceeding from this cosmological ground, *Sounding the Inner Landscape* addressed the musico-sacral properties of chant, harmonics, rhythm, harmony, melody, and form. The central message of the book was that music's connection of the physical to the metaphysical can be used for healing. Toning and chanting with the proper scales to the rhythms of heart and breath, Gardner claimed, could retune the energy of bodily organs as well as the human soul. The remainder of the text explained how various elements of music accomplished these effects.

The fundamental element in healing music for Gardner is the drone. "Used as a tonic," she wrote, "and I mean this both musically and medically, the drone becomes the bed upon which all the other healing music elements rest. The drone is the basis of healing music in that each tone that is sounded for a long period of time will touch the physical body in a specific area" (28). The healing effects of tone are not limited, however, to these primary drone resonances. Gardner also found great healing power in the harmonic overtones that occur above a sustained tone. "The phenomenon known as harmonics (overtones)," she wrote, "is the most elusive and yet inherent element of *all* music. The steps of a stairway from the physical body to the spiritual 'bodies' (auras), harmonics are the sounds in healing music which bring to balance the entire human organism, from the physical body on through all of the auric bodies." When a tonic is "struck" with healing intent, each ascending layer of the aura simultaneously vibrates to the "unstruck" sound of each ascending overtone. When music is simple enough to feature a drone sound for a long period of time, the resulting overtones make their presence felt on every auric level (60–73).

Gardner's own music combines drone and harmonics with melody, which she calls "the heart and soul of music." As a flutist she finds melody to be her natural mode of musical expression, but her advocacy of melody is also grounded in a historical interpretation of how Western music has lost its healing power. "When we moved away from the primacy of melody after 1600," she said during our interview, "when the bass line determined what the melody would be, that's when we moved away from the healing element of music. Melody does something that harmony does not do. I really believe it touches us very deeply, to the depths of the soul. It's a heart thing, and we lost that in compositional music."

In the traditional music of India, Gardner has found a style that combines the healing powers of drone and its harmonics with those of melody. Based on modal scales called ragas, Indian music consists of an ever-changing melody woven around a never-ceasing drone. "There is no harmony per se," Gardner said of this music, "but the harmony is in the harmonics and the relation of the melody to the drone." The analogous form in Western sacred music is Gregorian chant, built on the Greek modes. "I'm writing Gregorian chants, in a sense, because they had the drone and the parallel fifths going along, which was just listening to the harmonics in the environments in which they were singing. Those long beautiful melodic lines, this is where it's at, this is what people are hungering for. Also it's the old tuning they're hungering for. It's beautiful. That's why people are buying chant albums."

Indeed, one of the most successful sacred music albums of the 1990s worldwide was *Chant*, a selection of Gregorian chants performed by the Benedictine monks of San Domingo de Silos in Spain.[24] Chant—toning with the human voice—is for Gardner the form of healing music par excellence. "The human voice," Gardner wrote, "is the most powerful and effective musical instrument, or tool, for holistic healing of the human organism. Whether it is one's own voice or the voices of others, a healing vocal sound touches us not only in our bodies but in our souls as well."[25]

For Gardner, however, healing involves more than simply toning. It also requires the right intent through purity of heart and proper visualization of the healing. "If the intent behind the music is pure," she argued in *Sounding the Inner Landscape*, "if it is created to heal, or if it is spiritually inspired, it will have a healing or inspiring effect on the listener. The first and most important element in healing music, then, is the intent with which it is created and the intent with which it is presented. Intent begins and ends the circle of musical healing."[26]

Gardner has taught her cosmology of music along with toning and meditation techniques in countless workshops since the 1970s. Thanks to her work and that of Steven Halpern, Don Campbell, and other sacromusical leaders, these teachings are quite widespread in the New Age movement. But Gardner adds yet another important and distinctive element to her teaching and composition: her calling as a Wiccan priestess of music.

Priestess of Music

"I consider myself a priestess of music," Gardner said, "and this is a sacred path I'm taking." That path arose from her early experience of women's spirituality and Wiccan Neo-Paganism. "The way I got into [Wiccan] celebrations was through women's spirituality," she recalled, "which in the beginning was Dianic, meaning it was women only, and for many years I worked with women only. In our ritual, music and sound are used all the time." Gardner offered an evocative description of the Wiccan liturgies in which her musical and spiritual vocation developed.

> There's a whole section of the ritual where we will sing chants and things to welcome everybody, and chants of the seasons, especially considering the ritual season we are celebrating. Then there will be a time where we raise energy, and in that raising of energy it's kind of a group drone that keeps getting higher and higher naturally, until it's almost howling, almost an animal kind of thing, that just raises the energy so that we're ready to do our psychic healing work or whatever work we're doing. Spells we call them, prayers others would call them. So sound is extremely important in our ritual and also chanting. And we end with chanting and drumming. There's a lot of drumming and with untrained drummers you're going to get heartbeat rhythms. There's one in particular x-xx-xxx / x-xx-xxx / x-xx-xxx that you always hear. So much drumming and carrying on; it's much wilder than the western church.

Gardner received the title "priestess of music" from Z. Budapest at her 1975 Wiccan initiation. Although the musician was humbled by this designation, she admitted, "there are several of us in the women's music movement that I would consider priestesses, because the work that they are doing is trying to awaken the listener, [trying to be] transformation artists. I want to explore how does [music] make you feel, where does it take you in your deepest soul? That's the role I see myself as fulfilling for the women's community and for the community at large."

Gardner's most important activity as priestess of music, in her view, is composing. While most of her compositions have been for solo flute or small ensembles, Gardner's recent major composition, *Ouroboros,* is a ground-breaking oratorio for orchestra, chorus, and soloists based on the ancient Celtic calendar of pagan holidays as they relate to the ages of women. Each holiday in the annual spring-to-winter calendar is represented by solos for females of increasing age—8, 13, 21, 34, 55, and 89 years—with a women's chorus handling chants for the larger cycle of birth, death, and rebirth. "It's modal," Gardner said of the musical style of *Ouroboros,* "because my expression is modal. Some parts are based on Hindu ragas and celebrating the chants. There is a solo for the voice, then an orchestral interlude, and then a chant. The chant would be a chant of passage, a Neo-Pagan chant that can be lifted and used for specific rituals of passage."

Before *Ouroboros,* Gardner did not use words, preferring to employ the power of musical sound alone to achieve spiritual effects. "We don't need to use words," she said, "we can just bring the listener to a place, and we don't decide where the place is or anything. If we let universal consciousness flow through us as we're creating, then whoever hears it is going to be able to tap into it as well." *Ouroboros,* however, required original texts expressing the complex cyclical meanings of women's lives. So Gardner held a competition through women's publications to find a poet for the oratorio, guided again by her spiritual and musical experience. "A poem must sing to me," she said. "I put the words up on the piano, and I play the words. If a poem sings I have absolutely no trouble setting it. It almost sets itself. And so I found two wonderful poets. I could have used just one, but one of them seemed better at the chant, at the short form, with rhymes and lines. The other had this beautiful expression that just flowed and was much better for the solo passages."

With its Wiccan chants, Celtic women's narrative, and large-scale instrumental and choral forces, *Ouroboros* is a significant creative departure for Gardner. It appears to be, in the terms we have used to interpret New Age music, a shift from ecstatic to trance, from sustained tonal metaphysics to rhythmic, texted, communal celebration. To the extent that *Ouroboros* is a Neo-Pagan utterance rather than a kundalini-based meditation, Gardner does indeed seem embarked on a new stylistic turn. But regardless of the style and substance of a given work, Gardner approaches musical creativity in the same way, as an explicitly spiritual event.

"Composition is a sacred act," she said. "People are going to have spirit through the music, *if* the music is written with pure intent, and not just an intellectual exercise." To that end, she employs specific rituals and meditational techniques in her method of composition, including prayer and altar building. "I have an altar here next to the piano that I always build before I write a piece, with things that will bring me to meditating on whatever subject I'm writing upon. Actually it's a statement of intent. When I build an altar I honor earth, air, fire, water, and spirit, the five basic things. I honor that and ask for guidance that I may be clear and open as a vessel, as a conduit, really, for that energy to flow through me and into the music."

Gardner's composition altar for *Ouroboros* included a series of postcards painted by a woman artist to represent the stages of life expressed in the composition. "I would have one of her postcards there for each season I was writing about," Gardner reported, "along with other things like that. And I usually have a statue of Saraswati, Hindu goddess of music and harmonics, who's my inspiration. She's all over my house. I use her as an inspiration just to call on her as a focus point for me."

For *Ouroboros* as for her untexted music, Gardner placed herself within the processes and metaphors about which she is writing. If, as in this work, she is writing about metaphors for the seasons of the year and of life, she will compose the several sections of the work only at the appropriate times. "I worked on *Ouroboros* through the year as the seasons came," she recalled, "and the seasons represented each movement. Winter Solstice being birth, I wrote at that time of year. Then I wrote the next movement at mid-winter, and then to the equinox and all through the year, finishing it on Halloween, which is the high holy day for pagans." The same method of immersion into musico-sacral time and space applies to Gardner's use of Hindu ragas which, she explained, "were written for particular times of the year and of the day."

Gardner was pleased with the results of her spiritual and musical disciplines in *Ouroboros* at its premier performance at the 1994 National Women's Music Festival in Bloomington, Indiana.[27] Her criterion of judgment was not the technical excellence of the performance, but its spiritual impact on its intended audience. "After the performance of this oratorio," she reported, "about a third of the audience just stayed and wept, because it touched them. There's never been anything for women. We've got [Richard Strauss's] *Ein Heldenleben* [A hero's life] and that kind of stuff [for men], but what is there for women?" This calling to write music for women's spirituality, however, does not make Gardner or her music radically separatist. Rather, she regards herself a "humanist" who composes for all in a unique female voice. "What I'm writing is for everybody," she said, "but I am the language of my music. I may strive to have universal consciousness flowing through me, but it's flowing through me as a woman, a woman with a specific musical language."

Gardner resists any easy labels of her work beyond calling it "healing music" or "women's spirituality," although she does acknowledge that she is among the most classically trained composers of women's music. "I've always had trouble with labels," she commented. "At the beginning no one knew what the hell to call my music. And women's music, how do you categorize that? There's all kinds of styles. It's hard to categorize music at all. They do that for the record bins, really. Who's to say what's classical and what's folk? And if it has an improvisational element, is it jazz?"

One label Gardner wants to move beyond is "New Age," in large measure because of what she considers the unauthentic commercial intention of most so-called New Age music. Quick to exempt figures like Paul Winter, Steven Halpern, George Winston, and Carlos Nakai from this judgment, Gardner nevertheless insisted that "a lot of New Age music is schlock. Terrible stuff. All of a sudden this stuff was being sold, so everyone went out into their garage, got their home studio going, got the sound of some crickets over there, and a little ocean over here, and oh wow a river! Hey a river, that would be good, that would sell!"

More important than these labels and judgments of the past, for Gardner, is the spirit and music of the future. With its oratorio form and classical orchestra, *Ouroboros* has marked an important new departure in Gardner's sacred-music vocation. Since 1995 she has written a number of larger-scale compositions, including spiritual choral works on texts by Robert Frost, Henry David Thoreau, thirteenth-century Sufi mystic Hafiz, and Starhawk; two orchestral pieces—"Century March" for the millennial celebration and "Lament for the Thousands" commemorating the September 11, 2001, terrorist attacks on New York and Washington, D.C.—and "Three Sumerian Hymns to Inanna" for chorus and instrumental ensemble.[28] At the same time, Gardner has become deeply engaged in world music because of its potential to shape global awareness. "I'm really interested in the artists who are incorporating or influenced by music of different cultures. That's where I think it's moving, because communication has brought us much closer to different cultures. I mean, there's just a million things we can do now: the whole world's just opened up. And this is the direction I think all music is taking. We're moving into world consciousness." This world-music interest has produced two collaborative recordings, *OneSpirit* with percussionist Nurudina Pili Abena and *The Shaman's Cave* with Native American singer Brooke Medicine Eagle.[29]

From the Age of Aquarius and the Harmonic Convergence to the New Millennium, New Age spirituality has always contained a large dollop of eschatological expectation. As the new millennium develops, Wiccans have joined other New Age seers in dedicating themselves to ushering in the culminating era of human history. As spiritual teachers they are inspired by the potential of world music, much of which employs the drone and modal scales, to bring spiritual unity and social harmony to the planet. As priestesses of music, Kay Gardner and her Wiccan colleagues embrace that vision as their vocation. "Right now we're all

SACRED SONG IN AMERICA

in a state of flux with the end of the millennium," Gardner said. "It's a huge state of flux. New things are happening all the time. Many of us who are now considering themselves elders in the women's music movement have quit their jobs. I'm moving out of performance a lot and into teaching, because performance is fun, but I am here to teach."

Gardner is drawn to the millennial future by the bright hope of a new eon of human enlightenment and peace. With characteristic verve she embraces that future as one who has already traveled far down the path of women's spirituality and its sacred song. She is more than ready for the rest of the journey. "We see ourselves moving but we don't know where we're going," she reflected. "We all seem simultaneously to know that we are moving into this new time. The world is in a state of flux, and there's something, to use a line from *West Side Story,* there's 'something coming, don't know what it is, but it is gonna be great.' I don't know what it will be, but I'm here to pick up on the vibes of it and go!"

Notes

1. Catherine Albanese, *Nature Religion in America from the Algonkian Indians to the New Age* (Chicago: University of Chicago Press, 1990), 194.

2. Paul Winter, *Missa Gaia/Earth Mass,* Living Music LD 0002, 1982; *Solstice Live: A World Music Celebration of the Winter Solstice,* Living Music 01048–81525–2, 1993; *Celtic Solstice,* Living Music 01048–81529–2, 1999. In San Francisco, creation theologian Matthew Fox has presented a related form of "techno-cosmic masses" since 1995, though Fox's events are more explicitly liturgical than Winter's and feature recorded music including rap and hip-hop. See Matthew Fox, *The Coming of the Cosmic Christ: The Healing of Mother Earth and the Birth of a Global Renaissance* (San Francisco: Harper and Row, 1988), and *Creation Spirituality: Liberating Gifts for the Peoples of the Earth* (San Francisco: HarperSanFrancisco, 1991).

3. Steven Halpern, liner notes to *Spectrum Suite: A Meditational Environment,* 1975; reissued as audio CD, Steven Halpern, *Spectrum Suite: Music for Meditation and Inward Peace, Inner Peace Music,* ASIN B000031UU, 1994.

4. Steven Halpern, *Tuning the Human Instrument* (San Rafael, Calif.: Halpern Institute, 1979), 161–68.

5. George Winston, *December: Piano Solos,* Windham Hill Records WH-1025, 1982.

6. David P. McAllester, "The Music of R. Carlos Nakai," in R. Carlos Nakai and James Demars, *The Art of the Native American Flute, with Additional Materials by David P. McAllester and Ken Light* (Phoenix, Ariz.: Canyon Records Productions, 1996), 79.

7. Ibid., 83.

8. R. Carlos Nakai, *Cycles: Native American Flute Music,* Canyon Records CR-614, 1985; and Nakai and William Eaton, *Ancestral Voices,* Canyon Records CR-7010, 1992.

9. R. Carlos Nakai, *Journeys: Native American Flute Music,* Canyon Records CR-613, 1986.

10. Gilbert Rouget, *Music and Trance: A Theory of the Relations between Music and Possession* (Chicago: University of Chicago Press, 1985), 11–12.

11. Stephen Marini, "Rock Masses," in *The Encyclopedia of Contemporary American Religion,* ed. Wade Clark Roof (New York: Macmillan, 1999), 619–20.

12. Rouget, *Music and Trance,* 11–12.

13. See Don G. Campbell, *The Roar of Silence: Healing Powers of Breath, Tone, and Music* (Wheaton, Ill.: Theosophical Publishing House, 1989); and Joy Gardner-Gordon, *The Healing Voice:*

Traditional and Contemporary Toning, Chanting, and Singing (Freedom, Calif.: The Crossing Press, 1992).

14. Rosemary Radford Ruether, *Woman-Church: Theology and Practice of Feminist Liturgical Communities* (San Francisco: Harper and Row, 1985); Carol Christ and Judith Plaskow, *Womanspirit Rising: A Feminist Reader in Religion* (San Francisco: Harper and Row, 1979); Carol Christ, *The Laughter of Aphrodite: Reflections on a Journey to the Goddess* (San Francisco: Harper and Row, 1987), and *Rebirth of the Goddess: Finding Meaning in Feminist Spirituality* (New York: Routledge, 1997).

15. Margot Adler, *Drawing Down the Moon: Witches, Druids, Goddess-Worshippers, and Other Pagans in America Today,* rev. and expanded ed. (Boston: Beacon Press, 1986), 228.

16. Starhawk [Miriam Simos], *The Spiral Dance: A Rebirth of the Ancient Religion of the Great Goddess,* 10th anniversary ed. (San Francisco: HarperSanFrancisco, 1989), 17, 22–23.

17. Starhawk, quoted in ibid., 18.

18. Starhawk, *Spiral Dance,* 22–24.

19. Kay Gardner, *A Rainbow Path,* Ladyslipper LR-103, 1984; *Sounding the Inner Landscape: Music as Medicine* (Stonington, Maine: Caduceus Publications, 1990); *Sounding the Inner Landscape,* Ladyslipper, ASIN: B00000JN7X, 1999.

20. Kay Gardner, interview with author, Stonington, Maine, August 16, 1994. All subsequent quotations are taken from this interview unless otherwise indicated in the text.

21. Kay Gardner, *Mooncircles,* Urana Records, WWE-80, 1975.

22. Gardner, *A Rainbow Path.*

23. Gardner, *Sounding the Inner Landscape,* 1–29. Subsequent page references can be found in the text.

24. The Benedictine Monks of San Domingo de Silos, *Chant,* Angel CD 55138, 1994.

25. Gardner, *Sounding the Inner Landscape,* 34.

26. Ibid., 8.

27. Kay Gardner, *Ouroboros (Seasons of Life),* Ladyslipper LR-115, 1994.

28. Kay Gardner, electronic mail to author, June 21, 2002.

29. Kay Gardner and Nurudina Pili Abena, *OneSpirit,* Ladyslipper LR-113, 1993, and Brooke Medicine Eagle and Kay Gardner, *The Shaman's Cave,* Ladyslipper BME-13, 1993.

CHAPTER 7

Contested Praise:
A Tale of Two Hymnals

Hymnals are the single most important publication of America's churches. They have been the mainstay of denominational and independent religious publishing houses since the eighteenth century. Only Bible translations rival hymnals in religious and commercial importance. Hymnals, however, function as far more than just collections of sacred music. John Wesley, founder of the Methodist movement, offered the classic definition of the hymnal as "a little body of practical and experimental divinity."[1] He meant by this phrase that hymnals should address every dimension of religious life. This all-embracing character of hymnals helps account for their controversial nature as well as their perennial popularity. While scholars debate the intricacies of biblical narrative and systematic theology, the living belief of the church is inscribed in the words it sings and the melody it makes to God. It is no exaggeration to say that hymnals are the preeminent public expression of American Protestant sacred song and denominational identity.

The hymnals of the major denominations share a core of hymn texts that preserve in sacred song the formative historical episodes in American Protestantism. The First and Second Great Awakenings (1726–55 and 1799–1844) created a common evangelical theology of personal salvation and moral reform that was shared broadly by America's largest Protestant denominational families: Methodist, Baptist, Presbyterian, Disciples of Christ, and Congregationalist. These denominations also embraced a common hymn repertory based on the poetical works of Congregationalist Isaac Watts, Methodist Charles Wesley, and a host of their successors and imitators. This is the same hymnodic tradition shared by *The Sacred Harp* and other antebellum tune books and it has been well preserved through the twentieth century.

This evangelical textual corpus was greatly expanded by the gospel hymns of Fanny J. Crosby and other postbellum evangelical writers. Especially popular among Fundamentalists and Pentecostals, gospel hymns appeared during the 1870s revivals of Dwight L. Moody and his gospel singer Ira D. Sankey and spread quickly under their evangelistic successors like Billy Sunday and Sam Jones.[2] During the same period, Protestant liberals wrote a countervailing body of Social Gospel hymns fervently exhorting the church to embrace an imperative for social reform.[3] A small number of Social Gospel hymns migrated into more conservative denominations and were incorporated into the evangelical and gospel hymn core, while more gospel hymns entered the hymnody of mainline Protestant liberals. Whether to maintain this corpus of classic hymns and how to do it has become the crucial issue in contemporary American Protestant hymnody.

At the end of the twentieth century, the inclusive language movement mounted a radical new challenge to these traditional texts. Drawing on feminist and liberation theologies, proponents of inclusive language demanded that hymn texts be revised to eliminate gender distinctions, racial references, class differences, and military images wherever possible, and especially to supply less exclusively masculine and patriarchal language for God. The roots of this sacred-song reform movement lie in pioneering theological works of the 1960s and 1970s, including Harvey Cox's *The Secular City,* Mary Daly's *Beyond God The Father,* and Rosemary Radford Ruether's *New Heavens, New Earth.*[4] These writers spoke of a religious world in which boundaries of gender, race, and class could be overcome in an inclusive vision of Christianity as an embodied and pluralistic community of God.

During the 1980s and 1990s, inclusive language reformers applied these theological imperatives not only to newly written hymn texts but also to the classic texts of American hymnology. English poet Brian Wren's 1984 hymn collection *Bring Many Names* and his 1989 book *What Language Shall I Borrow?* sparked a vigorous renewal of hymn text writing in the inclusive mode on both sides of the Atlantic. By the 1980s American hymnists like Ruth C. Duck, Michael G. Bausch, Carol Doran, and Thomas H. Troeger had produced collections of inclusive-language hymns and worship resources.[5] But the inclusive-language project has also brought controversy to every mainstream American Protestant denomination. That controversy reveals with striking clarity the importance of sacred song in the realms of religious belief and ecclesiastical institution, arenas in which its influence is often overlooked.

Almost every major American Protestant denomination has produced a new hymnal since 1980. Two of the new denominational books, the Southern Baptist Convention's *Baptist Hymnal* (1991), and the United Church of Christ's *New Century Hymnal* (1995), illustrate the impact of the inclusive language controversy and the process of how hymnals get into the pews. Other examples could serve the purpose just as well, including *The Hymnal, 1982* of the Episcopal Church, *The Presbyterian Hymnal* of the Presbyterian Church (U.S.A.) (1990),

The Chalice Hymnal of the Christian Church (Disciples of Christ) (1995), and most notably *The United Methodist Hymnal* (1989), which made national headlines when thousands protested its inclusive language–induced removal of "Onward Christian Soldiers."[6] The Southern Baptist Convention (SBC) and the United Church of Christ (UCC), however, offer a classic comparison and contrast of denominational and hymnological circumstances in contemporary American Protestantism. An examination of their recent hymnal experiences reveals the range of contemporary American Protestant responses to the inclusive-language controversy. The experience of both denominations, moreover, affirms the enduring importance of hymnody as an often-contested medium of doctrinal expression and institutional control.

Contrasts between the SBC and the UCC are more obvious than comparisons. At nearly 16 million adult members, the SBC is America's largest Protestant denomination, while at 1.375 million communicants the UCC is one of the smallest major denominations.[7] The SBC is technically a fellowship of more than 42,000 congregations primarily in the Southeast and Southwest, who retain a great deal of local and regional autonomy. The Convention itself exists to coordinate mission and educational functions for its member congregations and has very little constitutional power of its own. The UCC, on the other hand, is a 1957 federation of separate denominations geographically concentrated in New England and the Midwest. The Congregationalists—of New England Puritan origin—and the Evangelical and Reformed—of Pennsylvania German Calvinist ancestry—are the senior partners in the merger, which has sought to establish genuine union on difficult issues among historically and geographically diverse traditions. The sharpest contrasts between SBC and UCC, however, are theological. The SBC is the great bastion of evangelical conservatism and fundamentalism in America, while the UCC is the standard-bearer for American Protestant liberalism.[8]

Important similarities also subsist between the two denominations, though these often go unnoticed. Historically, both have been marked by the influence of Evangelical Calvinism and the Great Awakenings that have regularly punctuated the history of American religion since the mid-eighteenth century. The SBC and UCC are, in fact, historical cousins. The churches that eventually formed the SBC in 1844 can be traced to radical evangelical Separate-Baptists of Connecticut who broke away from the Congregationalists during the Great Awakening in the 1740s, embraced believer's baptism, and immigrated to North Carolina during the 1750s. This common bloodline is still visible today, especially in the institutional organization of the two communions, both of which honor the autonomy of local congregations, employ regional associations to approve candidates for ministry, and support a large but decentralized church bureaucracy. All of these denominational similarities and differences came into play in the tale of their two hymnals of the 1990s.[9]

Ridgecrest

Every summer, a stretch of Interstate 40 twenty miles west of Asheville, North Carolina, becomes the center of church music in Protestant America. Within twenty winding miles through the Blue Ridge Mountains, the superhighway leads to conference centers of three of the nation's largest and most important denominations: Lake Junaluska Conference Center of the United Methodist Church, Montreat Conference Center of the Presbyterian Church, and Ridgecrest Conference Center of the Southern Baptist Convention. Between them, these three denominations represent 30 million members.

Montreat, Junaluska, and Ridgecrest are multipurpose, year-round church resorts, used by their denominations to host diverse gatherings of the ecclesiastical infrastructure. Laid out over acres of mountain coves and meadows, they include summer cottages, dormitories, assembly halls, gift shops, dining rooms, research libraries, colleges, athletic facilities, boys' and girls' camps, bridle and nature trails, and, of course, chapels-in-the-woods. At each of these locations, ministers and lay leaders from the denomination gather for weeklong special training and educational programs ranging from mission and youth to senior citizens and church finance.

One of the highlights of summertime on Carolina's church conference row is Music Week, when thousands of ministers of music, choir directors, church organists, and other church-music workers gather for five days of seminars, master classes, concerts, and worship. This is the time when church-music folk renew their collegial networks and learn about new trends and publications in church music. Seeking to learn about music in the nation's largest Protestant denomination, I went to the 1993 Church Music Leadership Week at Ridgecrest. There I found a new understanding of how American Protestant music is created, performed, published, and promoted. I also learned about the potentially heated issues that simmer beneath the apparently placid surface of even the most traditional denominational hymnals.

The pre-stressed concrete pillars and glazed entryway of Pritchell Hall, the heart of Ridgecrest, defy the stereotype of Southern Baptists as antediluvian conservatives. Instead Pritchell's high-vaulted lobby, built in the 1960s, proclaims a powerful modern American religious community intent on gathering believers to rehearse and increase their faith. I arrived at Pritchell in the late morning of June 24, 1993, for an interview with Terry York, project director for the 1991 edition of *The Baptist Hymnal*. A receptionist directed me to the program director's office in nearby Spilman Auditorium, Ridgecrest's 2,500-seat assembly hall. I found York in a small suite of cream-colored cinder-block offices located in the classroom wing of Spilman.

From these three cramped rooms the leaders of the Church Music Department of the Southern Baptist Sunday School Board coordinated a large and complex program. During Church Music Week 1993, a teaching staff of thirty-five church-music professionals offered seven separate instructional tracks for all levels of SBC church-music leadership from the experienced minister of music and organist/choir director through the Sunday school and congregational ranks. Each track followed a strenuous daily schedule of four class periods, daily worship at 11 A.M., and featured concerts at 3:30 and 7:45 P.M. Except for meals, there was no scheduled free time between Monday afternoon and the concluding Friday brunch.

The highlights of each day were the morning worship service and the special concerts. The 1993 concerts included the Oklahoma Baptist All-State Choir, four concert/dramas presented by noted congregational choirs, the Conference Band and Orchestra, and a performance of Vivaldi's *Gloria* by the Oratorio Chorus. The worship services were, if anything, even more diverse. Each service featured a particular musical style: gospel, traditional hymns, praise songs, or contemporary works. Thursday worship, which I attended, featured traditional hymns performed in heroic high-romantic style by the Oratorio Chorus and Conference Orchestra. With 150 voices and an eighty-piece orchestra supporting a congregation of 2,500 trained musicians, the sound was as glorious as it was massive.

On that Thursday morning Terry York bounded onto the stage of Spilman Auditorium to greet the SBC's assembled musicians to the final worship service of Church Music Week. It was an appropriate role for the forty-three-year-old manager of the Field Services Section of the Sunday School Board's Church Music Ministries Department, who may know more SBC music leaders than any other person in the denomination. Church Music Weeks in June at Ridgecrest and in July at the SBC's companion conference center in Glorietta, New Mexico, "are probably the most high-profile things that our section puts together," York said. "One week in each location, we have about 2,600 people on campus for the sole purpose of music leadership training."[10]

It is the day-to-day work of York's Field Service Section, however, that best reveals the importance of church music for America's largest Protestant denomination. Headquartered in the nine-story Centennial Tower in downtown Nashville, the Baptist Sunday School Board is the central institution of the Southern Baptist Convention, renamed LifeWay Christian Resources in 1998. LifeWay is the largest religious publisher in the world. LifeWay's mission statement dedicates the agency to "assist local churches and believers to evangelize the world, develop believers, and grow churches by being the best worldwide provider of relevant, high-quality, high-value Christian products and services."[11]

In 1992 the agency published and distributed 72 million pieces of church literature. The Church Music Department alone publishes four quarterly journals: *Glory Songs*, "easy choir music for volunteer and part-time music directors and the members of their church choirs"; *Handbells for Directors and Ringers*, articles and pieces for handbell ensembles; *Contemporary Praise*, "choral music in a contemporary style for adult and youth choirs"; and *The Church Musician*, a top-of-the-line glossy production containing one hundred pages of articles and interviews along with a portfolio of a dozen or more hymn arrangements.

York's Field Services Section includes seven field consultants who conduct regional conferences and workshops, promote Church Music Department publications, and ascertain recent musical trends in SBC congregations. "My section is responsible for going out to the churches and interpreting the [SBC] materials," York said, "and then coming back to tell the materials sections [who produce the publications] how it's going and saying what else would they like to have. We like to be the eyes and ears of the [Church Music] department and we do that with varying degrees of success." This intense interaction with state conventions and local congregations is necessary because the denomination's polity permits vigorous competition for the SBC church-music dollar. Although the SBC mandates publication of its own music materials, individual congregations are autonomous, left entirely free to buy the denomination's music or not. "The closer we stay tuned in to what the Southern Baptist churches are saying," York said, "the better chance we have of producing what they want, and they buy it when we connect. If we don't hit the target, they go somewhere else."

This carefully countervailing approach to musical matters will not come as a surprise to those who know the Southern Baptist Convention. While Southern Baptists can engage in vicious doctrinal and institutional conflict, as they have since the fundamentalist takeover of the denomination during the early 1980s, their normal mode of ecclesial behavior is characterized by a sensitive balance of local autonomy and denominational loyalty, a balance perfectly illustrated by the church music program from Ridgecrest to the quarterlies to the field consultants. The system gets results. Although a significant proportion of SBC congregations exercise their freedom to choose alternative music from independent publishers like Hope Publishing Company of Grand Rapids, Michigan, and Word, Incorporated, of Waco, Texas, millions of members remain loyal to Church Music Department materials and, above all, to *The Baptist Hymnal.*

The Baptist Hymnal

The 1991 edition of *The Baptist Hymnal* has been the fastest-selling hymnal ever published in the United States. The Sunday School Board received nearly 500,000 advance orders for the book, and during its first year alone the new hymnal sold 1.135 million copies. By the summer of 1993 total sales stood at nearly four million copies and grew steadily to more than five million in 2001.

American Protestant denominations have regularly revised their hymnals, but it does not happen all that often. The SBC, for example, issued only four official hymnals in the twentieth century, including the 1956 first edition and the 1975 revision of *The Baptist Hymnal.* Impetus for the 1991 edition came from the Church Music Department during the early 1980s. York said, "We became aware that there was a lot happening in Christian music, some of it initiated by Christian artists—Keith Green, Sandi Patti, those types—some just by the new English renaissance in hymnody, the Brian Wrens and so on. Congregations were bringing it into their worship experience by one means or another. At the same time it was not hard to see that in the existing hymnal there were some hymns that were being used and some hymns that were being ignored."

The Church Music Department's proposal to commission a new hymnal was approved by the 1985 annual convention. York and general editor Wesley L. Forbis designed an ambitious three-pronged research agenda for the project. The first move was to ascertain what the church was, in fact, singing. "We went to a scientifically represented sample of a thousand-something churches that represented urban, rural, and all the geographic and ethnic range," York said, "and we simply asked them what they were using from their hymnals and [did they] use individual hymns seldom, never, or frequently." The survey received a statistically significant response from the churches and was used to construct the initial hymnal database. A second, simpler hymnal questionnaire was distributed to all delegates at the 1986 SBC annual convention and to every congregation in the denomination. Finally, the ninety members of the Hymnal Committee were solicited for their own preferences.

The research phase took one year to complete. "We took all of that information," York reported, "and mixed it up in a computer, and it produced for us a two-volume report about what we now could document, what we could begin with: a tremendous diversity of worship styles and music styles in the SBC." Translation of the data and selecting the hymns took an additional three years. In the selection process, York and Forbis were guided by what might be called the principle of infradenominational inclusivity. "The challenge was to take all of this diversity in worship style, ethnicity, geography, and all that goes into it," York recalled, "to come up with one book to exemplify, to model the unity: one volume that contains all this diversity." To achieve that new balance, little-used hymns from the 1975 *Baptist Hymnal* were dropped, thereby providing space for new materials. The order of the old book was preserved, so that "Holy, Holy, Holy" was still hymn number 1 and "Amazing Grace" was still hymn number 330. Although the new edition contained 15 percent new material, the finished product still closely resembled its successful predecessor.

New lyrical and musical material was the most challenging area for the editors. Forbis and York aggressively sought out the latest trends in SBC sacred song, again using a multiple strategy. "One approach," York recalled, "was just to let Southern Baptists know we were about this project and things came in unsolicited. We answered every letter, every phone call." The project also included a New Materials Committee. "Their job was to search, search, search," York reported. "We probably looked through at least 50 hymnals, many currently in use by Southern Baptists. We searched anthem literature that we knew had been popular in Southern Baptist churches. Could that anthem be rewritten in hymn form and come back in that way? We looked under every rock,

behind every bush, to find material that people wanted to sing, and were singing in their churches."

All new material was subjected to the same selection and review procedures
as were traditional texts and tunes. "Every hymn in the new hymnal went
through the same process," York reported. "I don't care if it was 'Holy, Holy,
Holy'/ Nicaea, it went through the same process. And that way we could say to
the SBC constituency honestly that every note, every syllable had been reviewed
in the same way, and that proved to be a very solid thing." The even-handed-
ness of the selection process gained the confidence of the denomination for the
hymn project even before the book appeared. "The process was set up," he said,
"so that anyone could call me at my office and say, 'what happened to such and
such a hymn? I submitted it' or 'I hear it had been submitted.' I had a computer
that I was using that could call up every hymn that we were using and tell them
exactly what the status was."

Forbis and York also sought outside advice on the hymnal project. Carlton
Young, editor of the 1989 *United Methodist Hymnal,* gave the SBC leaders access to Methodist deliberations, including a close look at the "Onward, Christian Soldiers" flap and the potential dangers of hymnal editing. York minimized
the importance of that controversy. "Frankly," he said, "I believe that whole
episode was distorted and blown out of proportion by the press beyond what
actually happened." Perhaps so, but the spectacle of a major American Protestant denomination's hymnal committee excising a traditionally popular hymn
and then being taken to task by tens of thousands of their coreligionists must
have supplied a cautionary tale to the Southern Baptist editors.

The principal theological reason for which the United Methodists' Hymnal
Committee had removed "Onward, Christian Soldiers" was the inclusive-language claim that the text was too militaristic. Like the SBC, United Methodists
had not approved an inclusive-language standard. Unlike the SBC, however, the
Methodists possessed a strong inclusivist wing whose influence was manifest in
the dispute over W. S. Gilbert's famous text. York compared the politics of hymn
texts in the two denominations. "They are very similar [to us] in many aspects,"
he rightly stated, "but there are enough differences in what we knew about Baptists and, how can I say this, what they would accept, that I think we avoided
some of the problems [the Methodists] had." Yet inclusive language was an issue among some Southern Baptists, and the SBC hymnal leaders paid careful
attention to it, particularly for newly written hymns they considered.

The editors began with the core of consensus SBC favorites, granting the fact
of virtually universal use by the faithful as a theological priority over inclusive-
language concerns. "Hymns we considered to be in the spiritual memory bank
of our worshipers were left alone," York reported. "We did not touch them."
Forbis noted that the questionnaire had shown "almost unanimous agreement
as to some 225 hymns that should be retained."[12] Another 200 were popular
enough to include in "the spiritual memory bank." All of these texts were as-

sessed by subcommittees for musical and doctrinal adequacy; all were carried over into the new hymnal without editorial revision.

Hundreds of other traditional but not exceptionally popular hymns fell under a rigorous and quite conservative theological, poetic, and historical test. "If the exclusive language was an issue," York said, "[or] if archaic language was an issue, [or] if other language concerns were an issue; and then if the poetry could stand a change; and if the historical integrity of the hymn was not imposed upon, [then] some changes would be considered." The most liberal linguistic evaluation for *The Baptist Hymnal* was applied to new hymn texts. "For new hymns being composed," York stated, "we were very careful that the inclusive issue be there and that archaic language be considered."

On militaristic language, however, Southern Baptists were adamant. "We felt that Southern Baptists know the difference between acknowledging spiritual warfare—'put on the whole armor of God' [Eph. 6:13]—and promoting and pushing people into the armed forces to go into battle," York said. "We gave credit for Southern Baptists to know the difference and we weren't afraid of militaristic language."

Following these editorial principles, Forbis, York, and the Hymnal Committee made what appears to have been an effective selection. The 1991 edition of *The Baptist Hymnal* has been embraced like no other SBC hymnal. Clearly the membership recognizes itself theologically, textually, and musically in this collection. The book accomplished its task, York reiterated, by including as much of the diversity of Southern Baptist worship practice as possible. "Of course we couldn't put all of any one of those diversities in there," said York, "but we did our best to get the best of that diversity and a representative amount in there. And if I may say so, I think we pulled it off."

One may fairly ask just how diverse can Southern Baptists have been in 1991, let alone today? While the impetus for the new hymnal came from Church Music Department professionals with a genuine concern for worship inclusivity in the denomination, it is also true that the timing of the new book coincided with what Southern Baptists call "The Controversy." Riding a wave of reformist zeal for "biblical inerrancy" and the imposition of strict standards of doctrinal orthodoxy and moral teaching, the denomination's fundamentalists took control of the Convention's elected offices, bureaucracy, and educational institutions during the early 1980s. Since then, the new SBC leadership has demanded conformity to increasingly contentious theological and moral teachings. This policy has produced both substantial growth and the polarization of the denomination, including the organization of new "moderate" seminaries and church fellowships.[13]

While much of the fundamentalist program had not been formulated in 1985, its initial emphasis on scriptural authority, doctrinal orthodoxy, and denominational unity may clearly be detected in *The Baptist Hymnal*. "Before the process of planning the hymnal project ever began," editor Wesley Forbis wrote in the book's preface, "it was recognized that a scripturally based hymnal reflecting distinctive doctrinal concepts would strengthen unanimity among Baptists." To that end, "the Theology/Doctrine Committee faithfully reviewed every line of the 4,000 plus hymns considered for inclusion; only those judged theologically sound were recommended for inclusion." Even the hymnal's original goal of unity through diversity was ultimately trumped by doctrinal orthodoxy. "While seeking to include a broad diversity of hymnic forms and styles," Forbis wrote, "it was determined that in keeping with the dynamic of Southern Baptist churches, the topical organization of the hymnal, its musical contents, and worship aids should reflect the Scripture distinctives as reflected in the *Baptist Faith and Message.*"[14]

The 1991 hymnal used the revised 1963 version of the Baptist Faith and Message, the denomination's confessional statement first adopted in 1925. The impact of such a formal doctrinal standard on the organization of the book was unmistakable. The editors completely revised the theological interpretation of the hymns. They removed the 1956 edition's twelve substantive categories—General Worship, God the Father, Jesus Christ the Son, The Holy Spirit, The Word of God, Salvation, The Christian Life, The Church, The Kingdom of God, Missions, Social Betterment, The Immortal Life—and replaced them with just four: The Glory of God, The Love of God, The People of God, The Witness of the People of God. They also added a "Plan of Salvation" titled, "How to Become a Christian," which tells how by providing seven "basic facts from the Bible: 1. God loves you. 2. You are a sinner. 3. Sin separates you from God. 4. You can't save yourself. 5. God sent His Son Jesus to remove the sin barrier. 6. You can receive Jesus Christ through faith. 7. Through prayer you can trust in Jesus Christ."[15]

Such changes hardly amount to hymnodic brainwashing, but such a program of uniformity was entirely absent from the 1956 and 1975 editions of *The Baptist Hymnal,* which were widely used outside the SBC. Earlier Baptist hymnals in the South also presented a hymnody notable for its interdenominational and theologically diverse character. The 1991 hymnal marked a historic move toward the theological standardization of SBC hymnody in a denomination that has been staunchly anticreedal and has loudly proclaimed the absolute competence of the individual to discern the content of faith through personal encounter with God and the scriptures.[16]

The Baptist Hymnal vigorously pursued John Wesley's goal for hymnals by providing "a little body of practical and experimental divinity" for Southern Baptists. It also embraced the Methodist founder's insistence on one specific and exclusive formulation of Christian faith and practice. *The Baptist Hymnal* thereby showed, on the fundamentalist side of this tale of two hymnals, how hymnody in contemporary America can become a medium for denominational politics and theological partisanship. In an utterly different denominational and theological context, the same can be said for the United Church of Christ and *The New Century Hymnal.*

The New Century Hymnal

If *The Baptist Hymnal* is an example of hymnal making that does not threaten denominational worship styles, *The New Century Hymnal* (1995) of the United Church of Christ is by contrast an example of a hymnal designed to test the limits of a denomination's liturgical practice and indeed its own self-understanding. The story of the controversial UCC book begins with the origin of the denomination itself in 1957. After the union the two major UCC partners, the Congregationalists and the Evangelical and Reformed Church, continued to publish their own hymnals. The 1958 edition of *The Pilgrim Hymnal* and the Evangelical and Reformed *Hymnal* of 1940 recorded steady sales even after the appearance in 1974 of *The Hymnal of the United Church of Christ,* the new denomination's first official hymnal. By 1990, more than thirty-five years after its ecclesiastical union, the UCC still lacked a single hymnal shared by most of its constituents.[17]

An even more important impetus for the new hymnal was the UCC's support of inclusive language. As early as 1973 the General Synod, the denomination's plenary governing body, voted that "all newly printed materials (including worship books and services, hymnals, curricula, books, journals, and magazines, personnel matters and documents) published or used officially by the agencies of the United Church of Christ will be written (or rewritten when revised) to make all language deliberately inclusive." In 1977 General Synod IX directed that inclusive-language guidelines be developed and authorized "the creation of a new official hymnal which would follow the guidelines to intentionally inclusive language." *Inclusive Language Guidelines for the Use and Study of the United Church of Christ* appeared in 1980 and remains the definitive standard for linguistic inclusivity in the UCC.[18]

Originally designed as a study aid for UCC writers, editors, clergy, and laity, the *Guidelines* defined gender and racial language bias and applied remedies for it to traditional language about God, the church, and people in scripture, hymnody, and official UCC documents. "If women and ethnic racial groups are to be acknowledged as full human beings and partners with men and white people in the fullness of Jesus Christ," the *Guidelines* said, "we must, as a church, confront language bias and as a church act as a continual force for human liberation, salvation, and healing" (1).

The *Guidelines* dealt directly with the issue of hymn and worship language. "The worship life of the people of God is the coming together of the whole people—male and female, young and old, black, brown, yellow, red, and white. It is a whole people worshipping not just an anthropomorphic God but a whole God." The document specifically encouraged lyricists and composers to move in four new directions:

1. Write new hymns that reflect sexual diversity and images of racial diversity;
2. Use hymns and verses within hymns that are inclusive in language and im-

agery; 3. Be sensitive to the use of color as a normative statement in hymns, such as "cleanse us Lord, whiter than snow" (the beauty of the rainbow demonstrates the powerful beauty of many colors); 4. Use hymns, songs, and prayers that reflect the cultural pluralism that affirms differing racial and ethnic groups' experiences of God in history. This will help all of us to name God through many particular realities. (12)

The *Guidelines* promoted an immediate shift to inclusive-language worship by supplying an appendix listing acceptable hymns from the hymnals most used by UCC members in three categories: those that were "free from sexist bias," those "with masculine language referring to Jesus" but otherwise free from sexist language, and those "without sexist language except for one or more stanzas."

The inclusive-language hymnal project was finally authorized in 1989 by General Synod XVII and assigned to the Board of Homeland Ministries, an independent agency of the UCC and administrator of Pilgrim Press, the denomination's publishing house. Work began with the appointment of a representatively diverse Hymnal Committee of thirteen members chaired by James Crawford, Senior Minister of Old South Church, Boston. Like the Southern Baptists, the UCC Hymnal Committee undertook a thorough research effort to ascertain what local congregations were singing. The committee agreed to consider the contents of the 1940 Evangelical and Reformed *Hymnal*, the 1958 *Pilgrim*, and the 1974 UCC *Hymnal* as their initial text and tune database. "In the summer of 1990 and 1991," Crawford recounted at an interview in his study overlooking Copley Square, Trinity Church, and the Boston Public Library, "we sent research questionnaires to every church in the denomination, asking them what they had sung in those last twelve months. So, over the course of the twelve months we got complete data."[19] The UCC's questions about textual quality and representative diversity were precisely the same ones asked by the Southern Baptists.

Thus prepared, the Hymnal Committee "went through all of those hymns and took every one," Crawford said, "and the major questions were: What will we use and what won't we use? What's good and what's not good? What are the ones the people in Gettysburg, Pennsylvania, never sing and the people in Boston, Massachusetts, never sing? What has to be in there for Gettysburg, what has to be in there for Boston? And so that was [how we formed our] basic canon for the [new] book." The Hymnal Committee also solicited original texts and freely reassigned tunes for hymn texts both old and new. Crawford commented that "there are some texts that are just brilliant, but which have been given up over time, or maybe even recently, because their tunes don't seem to reflect that brilliance. So we would get into some of those, and sometimes we would give a new text to an old tune."

By 1991 the committee had produced a set of five "theological affirmations" to govern its hymn selections, later revised in February 1992. The affirmations supported "praise of the One, Sovereign, Triune God, who in infinite mystery is always more than doctrine can describe"; God's creation of "people of all ages, tongues, races, genders, and abilities" in the divine image; a call "to glorify God with the earth's resources"; recognition of "the interdependence of love for God and love for neighbor"; and inclusive-language reform. "We rejoice in providing a rich variety of metaphors for singing of God and inclusive words for singing of people," the committee wrote, "words which all people can sing."[20]

Not content simply to add new hymns and new inclusive-language translations of non-English hymns, the Hymnal Committee decided to revise the UCC's own canonical hymns to meet its theological affirmations and literary norms. "We sent them out," Crawford said bluntly, "because the metaphors needed changing and the committee was not a bunch of poets." The results were prepared and sent to a board of eighty-four readers representing the widest possible range of UCC diversity. It is fair to say that the inclusive translations and revisions were of mixed quality and, on the whole, aggressive in character. The committee itself, however, had little trouble accepting the wholesale removal of archaic language, the degendering of the Trinity, and the pan-gendering of the faithful in traditional hymn texts.

Reflecting upon his committee's work, Crawford expressed a sanguine belief that it would produce genuine change in the UCC. "My own hope," he said at our interview, "is that this book is just not another step along the evolutionary curve, that it really is a breakthrough book. We have convinced ourselves that the nature of our metaphor is so important, that where aesthetics came into conflict with justice, we chose justice, especially given our history and our tradition of using primarily if not exclusively male metaphors for God and for Christ. We sought at every step and in every word to discover if we could broaden the metaphor."

Crawford and his committee viewed the new hymnal as an instrumentality through which gendered images of the divine would be strictly balanced both in the collection as a whole and within individual hymns. They hoped that through general use in the denomination, the hymnal's melding of old and new metaphors and images for the sacred would eventually eliminate the problems of sexism from the liturgical expression of the church. Crawford spoke passionately to the issue: "My own feeling is that down the road, when the male metaphors have been sufficiently relativized and [when] there are enough female metaphors that point to the same reality, the male metaphors, which we will no longer have used exclusively, will be in use comfortably again, and in fact will be freshened."

Beyond such metaphorical "freshening," Crawford pressed for a new understanding of hymnic language itself. "Not only [will metaphors] be freshened, we will understand that that's all they are—metaphors!" he enthused. "Pointers toward something! And not confuse the metaphors for the reality, which is what we're always doing. We're confusing the vessel with the treasure. We have done this in many, many cases; and that's why this book is going to shake people up. So you will discover in this book a significant breakthrough. This is not an evolutionary move; there are dramatic changes in metaphor that point to the same reality, but use different words."

Bearing high the banner of these inclusivist aspirations, the Hymnal Committee pressed on toward its goal of producing a preliminary sampler from the new book to be presented at the 1993 UCC General Synod XIX in St. Louis. Somewhere along the way, however, the process began to splinter over the committee's decision to eliminate the word "Lord" altogether from *The New Century Hymnal.* The hymnal project had received early and weighty cautions about such a strategy. The 1980 *Guidelines* had warned about this very terminological issue, pointing out that "the word 'Lord' is particularly difficult as it often symbolizes the word 'Yahweh,' for God, which the Jews never called by name directly. Therefore, Yahweh did not symbolize the patriarchy of God as much as it symbolized the unapproachable majesty of God."[21] In the months leading up to General Synod XIX, some African American and Hispanic leaders in the UCC objected to the removal of "Lord" and "Señor" from their traditional hymn texts, while representatives of more conservative UCC regions voiced concern that the inclusive editing process had gone too far.

A struggle eventually developed within the Hymnal Committee over the metaphors that referred to God and to Jesus as the Christ. After a myriad of positive and consensual inclusive-language decisions, the committee finally divided on the question of whether "Lord" was a gender-based term or not. "'Father' we could handle okay," said Crawford; "we found ways to neutralize that or relativize that somehow, but 'Lord' was another ballpark." As major denominational leaders began to line up informally on both sides of the issue, Crawford and a solid majority of the Hymnal Committee stood firm for rejecting "Lord" as an unacceptably gender-based metaphor for God and Jesus. Differences in rhetorical taste had suddenly become a matter of accounting for basic belief.

"I must [remark] personally here," Crawford said, "at the number of people I have heard on the other side in this fight, [who] tell me that so far as they were concerned, the word 'Lord' is not a gender-based metaphor. I don't believe that. I know a lot of people who don't believe that either." Many other UCC members, however, including some of Crawford's Hymnal Committee colleagues, disagreed. At the committee's March 1993 meeting in Orlando, Florida, three of its thirteen members, "key people who had made tremendous contributions to the process," resigned in protest over eliminating the word "Lord" from *The New Century Hymnal.* Crawford readily acknowledged the sincerity of the dissenting minority and the effectiveness of their protest. "They were very sincere about it. In Orlando we just stopped. There wasn't anything we could do."

For the dissident committee members, the theological issues surrounding the term "Lord" were the most weighty. "There was a person from Illinois," Crawford recalled, "for whom the word 'Lord' in her Evangelical and Reformed tradition was absolutely the sine qua non [of faith]: 'Jesus is Lord.' There was another woman from Texas and a man from Iowa who felt very much the same way." Some on the committee were ambivalent about the issue while others, including Crawford, "believed we had to find another term that would continue to express the sovereignty of Christ, and to confess essentially that Christ is Lord, even of the term 'Lord.'"

The dissenting member from Texas appealed the "Lord question" to the General Synod XIX meeting in St. Louis in June 1993, obtaining a resolution from the Southwest Conference asking to restructure the hymnal so that it would better reflect the diversity of the denomination. According to Crawford, this first resolution was designed to create a quota system for unrevised traditional hymns from each UCC constituency along with a smattering of new inclusive-language materials—a package quite like *The Baptist Hymnal*. Crawford and the Hymnal Committee immediately objected to the resolution as an abdication of the denominational goal of inclusivity.

Crawford formulated the crucial difference between the two sides with an aphorism: while the dissenters hoped "that everybody would be able to sing *some* of the hymns in the book," the Hymnal Committee was committed "to make it possible for everyone to sing *every* hymn in the book, whether or not they felt comfortable with it." Put another way, the dispute was about two different understandings of inclusivity, the dissenters holding that it meant maximal diversity of hymn text style while the committee insisted that it required the linguistic reform of every text. As the dispute widened to denomination-wide proportions, other editorial approaches were suggested, such as printing each hymn twice on facing pages, once in its original form and once in its inclusive-language revision. Crawford and the Hymnal Committee rejected that suggestion as another form of quota that permitted congregations to avoid confronting their own inclusive-language guidelines when applied to sacred song.

Meanwhile the three resignations from the Hymnal Committee brought swift reaction from the denominational leadership. In the spring of 1992 the UCC Board of Homeland Ministries dissolved the Hymnal Committee and appointed a new six-member editorial board that included Crawford. In taking over the project, the new editorial board reaffirmed the theological principles and editorial work of its predecessor. The new editors also produced *The New Century Hymnal: A Sampler,* a collection of forty-one hymns carefully selected from the prospective hymnal, along with representative psalter materials and other worship resources.[22] The *Sampler* was to be distributed in 1993 at General Synod XIX as a kind of combined progress report and defensive tactic. Armed with advance copies of the sampler, Crawford and the other editors "were assigned to some particularly tricky [regional] synods in order to interpret the book." Shortly before General Synod XIX convened, however, the Southwest Conference proposed a new resolution mandating that the word "Lord" be restored to the hymnal in texts where it originally appears.

The ensuing debate surprised Crawford in its response to the inclusive-language criteria. "The thing that startled me," he recalled, "was my debate with pastors or theologians who were shocked that we would dare to throw out the first confession of the Christian church: Jesus is Lord. I have tried to persuade them that to relativize the word is not to set aside the sovereignty that stands behind it. It is to indicate that the sovereignty is not necessarily tied up in the gender of whoever is sovereign." Here was a substantive theological answer to hymnal critics who denied that "Lord" was a gendered term. Crawford summarized the pro-hymnal position in a memorandum to the General Synod, pressing the case that the UCC's inclusive-language guidelines required a truly non- or transgendered term for the divine sovereign to be employed in the hymn texts of *The New Century Hymnal*.[23]

In St. Louis, hymnal advocates scored an early victory. At a preliminary hearing, the General Synod's hymnal committee voted 44 to 4 against the Southwest Conference resolution to restore the word "Lord" and recommended that the resolution be voted down in plenary session. On the Synod floor, however, the Southwest Conference resolution passed overwhelmingly. "We were ecstatic [after the hearing]," Crawford remembered, "but General Synod did not have the same advantage [of small group deliberation] the committee had. People got up and reacted [to the "Jesus is Lord" issue], and we lost two to one." Pro-hymnal forces were astonished at this crushing reversal, but all was not lost. "[Homeland Ministries Vice-President Thomas E.] Dipko got up and said that General Synod cannot tell the Board of Homeland Ministries what to do," Crawford reported. "He was absolutely shocked and stunned like the rest of us were. But it was his inimitable style that carried the day." More accurately, Dipko enabled the Board of Homeland Ministries, an independent agency whose project was the new hymnal, to play another day.

Inclusive-Language Editing

As sheer sacred song, the renovated texts of *The New Century Hymnal* certainly have been changed. A good illustration is English Calvinist Robert Robinson's classic 1758 hymn, "Come, Thou Fount of Every Blessing." *The Baptist Hymnal* and *The New Century Hymnal* both use "Nettleton," its most commonly associated tune, from John Wyeth's *Repository of Sacred Music, Part Second* (1813) to set Robinson's text. *The Baptist Hymnal* also uses "Warrenton" from the 1844 edition of *The Sacred Harp* as a second tune setting. The theological and editorial issues raised by inclusive language, however, lie with the alternative published versions of the hymn text.[24]

Robinson's original follows, as printed in *The Baptist Hymnal*, with words italicized that are altered in *The New Century Hymnal*:

> Come, *thou* fount of every blessing,
> Tune my heart to sing *Thy* grace;
> Streams of mercy, never ceasing,

Call for songs of *loudest* praise:
Teach me some melodious sonnet,
Taught by flaming tongues above,
Praise the mount! I'm fixed upon it,
Mount of *Thy redeeming* love.

Here I *raise my Ebenezer;*
Hither by Thy help I'm come,
And I hope, by Thy good pleasure,
Safely to arrive at home:
Jesus sought me when a stranger,
Wand'ring from the fold of God;
He, to rescue me from danger,
Interposed his precious blood.

O to grace how great a debtor
Daily *I'm constrained to be!*
Let *Thy* grace, *Lord,* like a fetter,
Bind my wand'ring heart to *Thee:*
Prone to wander, *Lord, I* feel it,
Prone to leave the God I love;
Here's my heart, *Lord,* take and seal it,
Seal it for *Thy courts above.*[25]

The *New Century* version of this hymn is titled "Come, O Fount of Every Blessing" and alters seventeen of its twenty-four original lines. The alterations are italicized:

Come, *O* Fount of every blessing,
Tune my heart to sing *your* grace;
Streams of mercy, never ceasing,
Call for songs of *endless* praise.
Teach me some melodious sonnet,
Sung by flaming tongues above.
Praise the mount; I'm fixed upon it,
Mount of *God's unfailing* love.

Here I *pause in my sojourning,*
Giving thanks for having come,
Come to trust, at every turning,
God will guide me safely home.
Jesus sought me when a stranger,
Wandering from the fold of God,
Came to rescue me from danger,
Blessed body, precious blood.

O to grace how great a debtor
Daily *I am drawn anew!*
Let *that* grace *now,* like a fetter,
Bind my wandering heart to *you.*
Prone to wander, *I can* feel it,
Wander from the love I've known:
Here's my heart, *O* take and seal it,
Seal it for *your very own.*[26]

The revisions in this hymn are for the most part skillful, tasteful, and poetically apt. Other classic hymns were treated rather more severely in *The New Century Hymnal.* "Come, Thou Fount" is a good illustration of the inclusive-language dilemma precisely because it is not an extreme example. But is the revised version of this hymn, one of the most popular in all of Protestant Christianity, theologically and spiritually the same? Should it be? Or are inclusivists correct that its theological substance and poetic rhetoric should be changed to accommodate a vision of Christian faith blind to gender, race, class, and condition?

The first revision seems simple enough: change "thou" in the first line to "O." The change scans perfectly, it is euphonic with the original, and it preserves the note of petition voiced in the poem's first line. But why change the title line in the first place? The revision illustrates the inclusivist imperative to eliminate archaic hymn language, specifically the "thees" and "thous" of early modern sacred rhetoric. In this case, "thou" was deemed too distancing a term for modern singers, while "you" might be too intimate and revisionist, hence "O," a neutral alternative that eliminates the archaism with little negative side-effect. The traditionalist counter to this editorial judgment is that God is sufficiently other and transcendent to require address specifically in the second-person plural, which only "thee" and "thou" can still render, albeit in an old-fashioned sort of way. The archaic critique easily carried the day in the Hymnal Committee: the "thees" and "thous" are gone from this and every other lyric in *The New Century Hymnal.* There are seven other instances of "thee," "thou," and "thy" in Robinson's hymn text. All were eliminated, replaced mostly by "you" and "your."

The most thorough single revision occurs in the second verse. The first four lines have been almost entirely rewritten and the last two lines of the eight-line stanza have been significantly changed. The archaic language criterion has clearly been applied to the first part of the stanza. Robinson's reference to the Ebenezer, the stone set up by Samuel to commemorate the Israelite victory over the Philistines at Mizpah (1 Sam. 7:12), is now obscure to most UCC members. A change certainly seems warranted, and while the new version sacrifices the specific biblical reference, it carefully retains the original's sense of spiritual pilgrimage guided by God's providence.

Revisions to the second half of the hymn are based on other, more controversial inclusive-language principles. The one reference to Jesus by the masculine pronoun is eliminated. "Lord" is excised three times as a term of address to God in prayer and replaced twice by recasting the line and once by "O" as an exclamation. These changes appear at first to be largely cosmetic, removing as they do only one-syllable words. But in three cases their removal entails a complete reworking of the line and an inevitable alteration of original meaning. Whereas changes in the first half of the poem are quite faithful to Robinson's explicit theology, these and several others in the second half are not as consonant with the eighteenth-century Calvinist's views.

In the last two lines of the second verse—"He, to rescue me from danger, / Interposed his precious blood"—Robinson stated poetically the doctrine of substitutionary atonement, according to which Christ freely accepted death as punishment for humanity's sin in order to save it from eternal damnation. *The New Century Hymnal*'s rendering—"Came to rescue me from danger, / Blessed body, precious blood"—certainly praises the rescue and the rescuer, but it elides Robinson's explicit reference to substitutionary atonement. This elimination of Jesus' "interposing precious blood" is difficult to justify on inclusive principles alone. It is rather a theological alteration reflective of the UCC's long intellectual struggle with the doctrine of the atonement. The precise nature and meaning of Christ's death on the cross has been one of the most controverted doctrines in the history of most UCC constituencies. Liberals, who for the most part have won those battles, have removed the atonement from the theological center of UCC thought, and now from Robinson's hymn.[27]

The same editorial process may be seen in the treatment of the third verse, in which Robinson expressed what Reformed Protestants have always called the doctrine of free grace, the tenet that the atoning grace of Christ's sacrificial death was voluntarily undertaken, freely offered by him to the faithful, sovereign in its effect, and unmerited by human works. Robinson's original third verse presented four metaphors for the human experience of grace: debtor, prisoner, wanderer, and gift. Believers are "daily constrained" by their debt to Christ's grace because they continue to sin and stand in need of further mercy. They therefore plead to be bound in chains as a prisoner to the sovereign grace that they require. Original and committed sin promotes the grave temptation for believers to depart from saving grace, but in Robinson's rendering that very grace convinces them to offer themselves back as a gift for God's disposal at the Last Judgment.

The New Century Hymnal produces a different account of free grace. The metaphor of the believer as sinful debtor has been changed to one of grace as a gravitational force that "daily draws" her. The second image of bondage to grace survives pretty well, but under the third metaphor the believer is now prone to wander from "the love I've known" rather than from "the God I love." Finally, the last metaphor of God's grace as gift has been changed to describe the believer as already God's possession rather than to exalt God's sovereign and merciful act of redeeming judgment. None of these changes are formally heterodox, but they neither convey Robinson's original theological sense nor improve his poetry. The new version of lines 5 and 6, in particular, substitutes a weak noncadential repetition of "wander" for Robinson's much stronger repetition of "prone" as the first word of each line.

Why bother to make such extensive editorial changes in a vastly popular and noncontroversial traditional hymn? The editors' agenda seems in this case to have moved beyond the mandates of the *Inclusive Language Guidelines* to a vigorous assertion of liberal and liberationist theologies and to correct Robinson accordingly. Was that their mandate? These theological and institutional issues became the central points of an argument that has accompanied *The New Century Hymnal* since its publication.

The New Century Hymnal Controversy

Despite its rough treatment at the 1993 General Synod, *The New Century Hymnal* finally appeared in July 1995 published by the Pilgrim Press in two editions, one denominational and one ecumenical. The book complied with the Synod's ruling on the "Lord" question, at least so far as titles and first stanzas were concerned, but the aggressive program of inclusive-language reform begun with the *Sampler* continued unabated in the completed book. In his introduction to the hymnal, Crawford wrote:

> Every text underwent careful scrutiny of its metaphors and pronouns that refer to God, Christ, and the Spirit. Why the scrutiny? Because for nearly two millennia these words have tended toward exclusively masculine characterization bearing painful consequences, especially for women. Every effort was made to ensure that all hymns spoke to and for all of God's people, equally. This resulted in the examination of language from racial, ethnic, and sociocultural perspectives, and the review of language that could be diminishing to people with physical disabilities. Consideration was also given to imagery to assure that it relate to the scientific understandings of a coming generation.[28]

Not surprisingly, the new hymnal generated significant conflict in the denomination and provoked a series of critical responses from the national media. A February 1996 *Newsweek* article by religion editor Ken Woodward sounded the alarm. Woodward duly reported that "many of the lyrics have been altered to meet contemporary views on equality, nonviolence, and acute social sensitivity," but he questioned the commitment of the hymnal editors to the uniqueness of Jesus as God's "only begotten son." Calling the editors "hymn doctors" who employed feminist and androgynous expressions to avoid "using male pronouns for God," Woodward quoted senior UCC theologian Willis Elliott's judgment that "what we're being asked to celebrate [in *The New Century Hymnal*] is the advent of a new religion." In his conclusion, Woodward also took issue with the hymnal's wholesale revision of favorites like Katharine Lee Bates's "America the Beautiful" and the African American spiritual "Steal Away."[29]

Woodward's *Newsweek* article prefigured more detailed and substantive objections. John Ferguson, professor of church music at St. Olaf College, reviewed the hymnal for the spring 1996 issue of *Prism,* the leading in-house journal of the UCC. While praising the production values and helpful features of the book and endorsing the inclusive-language principle in general, Ferguson concluded that *The New Century Hymnal* is "an appropriate attempt to address gender difficulties in language addressing God [that] got out of hand. [It] goes too far, is too radical in its approach to God language, especially in the revision of traditional texts. In its attempts to be gender neutral, it has narrowed the possible range of options for God's people to use in describing and addressing the Trinity."[30]

The same issue of *Prism* heightened the debate by carrying pro-hymnal articles by the book's editor Arthur G. Clyde and by Daniel L. Johnson, a Hymnal Committee member and minister of the Evangelical United Church of Christ in Godfrey, Illinois. Clyde defended the selection of the hymnal's texts on ecumenical, biblical, and historical grounds. Its employment of the Common Lectionary, a collection of weekly scripture texts shared by most mainline Protestants, "demonstrates this most basic objective," Clyde wrote, "that *The New Century Hymnal* be rooted in the scriptures." Clyde also argued that today's inclusive language alterations in essence follow the historic Protestant principle of "worship in the vernacular." "In its language of rediscovered and expanded metaphors," he wrote, "this book strives to enrich understanding of the texts of our heritage for their renewed use by this generation and generations to come. These, along with carefully selected texts of this age, are what *The New Century Hymnal* will carry into the next era."[31]

Daniel Johnson's essay, "A Hymnal We Produced," took a more defensive tone. After reviewing the hymnal's development process, documenting the denomination's consistent endorsement of inclusive language, and identifying five different ideological "filters" that have informed hymnals of the UCC's constituencies in the twentieth century alone, Johnson insisted that *The New Century Hymnal*

> is not an eccentric new curiosity, nor is it an interloper foisted on us by strangers from outside the circle of Christian orthodoxy. It is a new work of and for the United Church of Christ, created from within the covenants and commitments that continue to shape the denomination we are still in the process of becoming. It is we, no one else, who created *The New Century Hymnal.* We ourselves must accept the responsibility for its faults and its strengths, and critics should stop the nonsense of accusing its creators of ignorance, heresy, or villainy.[32]

By far the most thorough criticism of *The New Century Hymnal* has been mounted in *How Shall We Sing the Lord's Song? An Assessment of The New Century Hymnal,* a collection of essays edited by Richard L. Christensen, a UCC minister and professor of church history at Phillips Theological Seminary, Tulsa,

Oklahoma. The book was published by the Confessing Christ movement, one of several traditionalist fellowships in the UCC. The volume included Ken Woodward's original *Newsweek* article; an exchange of hostile letters between Woodward and Andrew Lang, staff writer for the UCC Office of Communication in Cleveland; pro and con essays by Daniel Johnson and Willis Elliott; an alternative account of the editing process by David B. Bowman, a disaffected member of the original Hymnal Committee; and a background piece on the hymnal's major controverted doctrines by Gabriel Fackre, Abbott Professor of Systematic Theology Emeritus at Andover Newton Theological School.

The most substantive and detailed criticism in the volume came from Christensen himself in his essay, "The Language of Faith and *The New Century Hymnal*." "The question for the UCC in regard to *The New Century Hymnal* is simply this," he wrote, "does [it] give expression in fresh and imaginative ways to the faith with which the prophets and martyrs, alongside the communion of saints in each generation, have sought to bear witness to the astonishing love of God in Jesus Christ, for the wholeness (shalom) of our fractured world?" Christensen's concern was not with denominational politics or factional strategies, but with one of the most fundamental questions that can be asked of any religious expression: is it, in fact, orthodox? After weighing evidence, Christensen answered his own question in the negative. "Many of the language changes made either changed the meaning of the hymn text," he concluded, "or served to obscure or ignore crucial elements of the Christian faith."[33]

Building on the earlier critiques by Woodward, Elliott, and Bowman, Christensen attacked *The New Century Hymnal* for misunderstanding and then virtually abandoning the doctrine of the Trinity. "The idea seems to be that father language promotes male dominance," he wrote. "This is a gross misapprehension of the formulation of the doctrine of the Trinity and the Church's teaching about it. The common teaching of the Church over the centuries has been that the three persons of the Trinity are co-equal, co-substantial, and co-eternal. Properly taught, there is no dominant-subordinate element to the Trinity, but mutual self-giving" (23).

Christensen accused the hymnal of Arianism, the fourth-century heresy that subordinated the Son and the Spirit to the Father in order to preserve the oneness of God. Condemned in 325 C.E. at the Council of Nicaea, Arianism reappeared among Reformation Protestants and played a prominent role in the Unitarian Controversy of the eighteenth and early nineteenth centuries that permanently divided the Congregationalists in 1824. Christensen's criticism implied that at long last the Congregationalists and their UCC partners of the Reformed heritage had given up the doctrinal affirmation upon which their historical identity had depended. The Arians had finally won.

Pursuing this trinitarian line of criticism, Christensen also rejected the hymnal's positions on the Lord question and the maleness of the Messiah. On the Lord question, "there seems to be a strange notion alive in the Church that we can have no hierarchical images at all, no transcendent power superior to us," Christensen wrote. "If there is no truth that comes from beyond us and transforms us, then there is no hope of transcending our circumstances, and true equality and genuine freedom go out the window. The issue is not whether or not to have a lord, but which one" (27). The idea that eliminating "Lord" will help to prevent sexism and abuse, Christensen said, "is terribly naïve. It is not language that causes abuse, but the sinful nature of human beings" (28). The hymnal's "refusal to use male terms for Jesus," furthermore, amounts to a denial of Incarnation, committing "the ancient heresy of Docetism" that "makes Jesus less than fully human" and renders Jesus "a kind of universal principle instead of the concrete historical discloser of the living God" (30).

For Christensen, these failures entailed far more than a rhetorical disagreement. They amounted to nothing less than the loss of Christianity's fundamental intellectual and moral message. "This is not just a nitpicking argument concerning fine distinctions between words," he wrote. "If we lose the co-equality of the persons of the Trinity, we lose the very mandate in Christian tradition which calls us to a co-equal life together in community, that is, we lose one of the basic elements of the faith that informs our concern for justice in society" (26).

Christensen pressed his critique to its logical conclusion, insisting that inclusive-language reform is grounded ultimately not in an enlightened Christian liberationist theology, but in the interpretation of religion as psychological projection pioneered by nineteenth-century German philosopher Ludwig Feuerbach and his heirs, including Marx and Freud. "When someone says 'I cannot call God Father because of my experience with an abusive father,'" Christensen wrote, "that is a negative projection of experience onto God. The problem here is that in Jesus Christ, we see that this is precisely not who God is. In Jesus Christ, the negative images from one's own experience can be crucified and we can discover the mercy and freedom given to us through the loving God" (31). Christensen warned that anyone who uses gender language for God, male or female, grounded exclusively in their personal experience makes the error of "worshiping a god of his or her own desires and not the living God revealed in Jesus Christ" (31). Such worship, he insisted, amounts to solipsism at best, and atheism at worst.

The outcry over *The New Century Hymnal* reached its peak in 1997 with the publication of Christensen's book, but there is still widespread discomfort with the hymnal among both clergy and laity. What had begun in 1989 as a consensus commitment by the UCC to an inclusive-language hymnal became by 1993 a heated debate on the Lord question and then, after the hymnal's publication in 1995, a bitter dispute over the historical and theological limits of inclusive-language reform itself. For more than twenty-five years the UCC had stood as the foremost liberal Protestant champion of inclusive language. It had approved inclusive-language standards for church documents, preaching, worship, and scripture translation with little opposition. Hymns were a different matter, however, and the UCC's debate over *The New Century Hymnal* revealed important dimensions of sacred song's role in religious culture.

Experience, Tradition, Identity

The editorial decision to revise traditional hymn texts radically seems to have challenged the historic identity of the UCC's constituencies in a way that other changes in worship and teaching did not. Three dimensions of that challenge stand out most clearly. First, the revisions were received by many as a rejection of their own experience of Christian nurture. This is what Southern Baptist Terry York referred to as the "spiritual memory bank" issue. Hymns are the most familiar and frequently repeated texts of Christian religious culture. Because they are set to music and sung, hymns have a textual fixity not open to the sort of interpretive multivocality that a scripture passage possesses through preaching and theological writing. The simultaneously oral and aural, musical and literary qualities of hymns make their meaning more fixed, and more complexly fixed, than biblical passages. It is not only the poetry itself but also the sound of the sung hymn that lodges in the memory and casts up a host of recalled meanings over time.

Most American Protestants carry a group of signature hymns in their minds that return them to scenes of Sunday school, summer camp, youth fellowship, revival, church community, and family celebrations. Historians of religion call this return to origins the process of repristination, a reentry into the pure, constitutive moments of sacred experience. To alter the language of a repristinating medium like hymnody is to question the purity of the sacrality they express. When such a signature hymn is altered at all, many respond that they did not learn it that way, or it was not sung that way when they were young. This discomfort expresses their sense that a change in the hymn text somehow invalidates their lived experience of it. A radical revision like *The New Century Hymnal*'s invites the response that one's entire life experience of the faith has been questioned.

Interference with this repristinating function of sacred song can spark a struggle over the proper definition of the religious tradition itself. That is precisely what happened in this case, as Christensen's collection amply illustrates. Such a struggle can take many forms, but the UCC followed historical form in posing the issue as a matter of right teaching. All of the UCC's constituencies share the Reformed heritage of rigorous systematic theology dating to Calvin himself. For them, true faith has always been predicated on knowing the correct formulation of Christian doctrine.

It is not surprising, then, that Christensen and the other critics attacked *The New Century Hymnal* on doctrinal grounds, accusing the book and its editors of betraying foundational beliefs of Christianity including the Trinity, the divinity of Christ, and the Incarnation, and embracing historic heresies including Arianism and Docetism. The intensity and extremity of this doctrinal reaction by critics points to the crucially important role that hymns play in the articulation and teaching of doctrine. The critics objected as much to the apparently arbitrary, unsystematic, and ill-considered doctrinal nature of the hymnal's revisions as to the particular new teachings it has implanted in traditional hymn texts.

The critics' call for a reformulated standard of orthodoxy, however, encountered a third dimension of UCC identity. As a federation of different historic communions, the denomination is permanently and irreducibly diverse in matters of specific doctrinal formulation. No matter how close they may be as heirs of the Reformed tradition, the sister churches have consistently opted to maximize their freedom of doctrinal interpretation. The ideal of diversity within unity has guided the UCC since its formation in 1957, and supporters of *The New Century Hymnal* have been quick to claim it in their defense. Daniel Johnson and other defenders cited the openness of the hymnal-making process while editor Arthur Clyde pointed up the ecumenical and biblical foundations of the hymn collection. David Bowman, on the other hand, cited the same criterion to argue that *The New Century Hymnal* ultimately became the polemical project of a small group of Homeland Ministries leaders and not a fair expression of the denomination's true unity and diversity. This procedural dimension of the controversy has been especially troubling to denominational critics and shows how sacred song has the power to undermine the institutional self-definition of a religious tradition as well its doctrinal standards.[34]

Despite the rough treatment *The New Century Hymnal* has received, however, Jim Crawford remains undeterred in his pursuit of liturgical language that all Christians can sing. "As [Christians] come to understand these aspects of the nature of religious language as analogous, parabolic, metaphoric, they will say, 'Oh, is that all? I thought my faith was at stake, but obviously it's not. You've just enabled me to say the same thing in a different way.'" Crawford stakes much of his hope for the hymnal on the new generation of mainstream American Protestant ministers. "I do believe," he says, "that this is a hymnal with a sensitivity to texts and metaphors and theological perspectives that will appeal not only to a large sector of the UCC, but to an increasingly large sector of men and women [from other denominations] who will be graduating from seminaries and who will bring it with them [into their ministries]." If Crawford is right, *The New Century Hymnal* will make a quantum leap in UCC lay comprehension of sacred song's language and theology. If he is wrong, the book will join a distinguished line of reforming hymnals whose reach has exceeded their grasp.

Hymnals may be consensual or innovative, but they have always constituted major public expressions of American Protestant beliefs and spirituality. And when created by denominations, they also become occasions for institutional and theological controversy. The new SBC and UCC hymnals occupy opposite ends of a spectrum created by the problem of diversity and inclusivity, the most important issue in twenty-first-century American Protestantism. *The Baptist*

Hymnal is about as representative of its denominational constituency as a hymn collection can be, and by design. For its editors, inclusivity meant the inclusion of all hymnodic styles present in the sprawling Southern Baptist denomination. Yet even this minimally inclusivist goal fell afoul of exclusivist imperatives for biblicism, orthodoxy, and unity mandated by the SBC's new fundamentalist leadership. When finally published in 1991, the hymnal presented itself not as an inclusive expression of diverse worship styles but rather as an exclusivist vehicle for increasing denominational unity.

The developers of *The New Century Hymnal*, on the other hand, took a corrective posture toward their denomination's sacred song, and they have encountered strong reaction to their work that graphically illustrates sacred song's ability to define religious experience, historic tradition, and community identity. In this case the hymnal committee discovered that a long-affirmed UCC imperative for inclusive language did not necessarily extend to the lyrics the denomination sings in worship. *The New Century Hymnal* has received nothing but praise for its inclusion of culturally diverse musical and textual materials. The argument has come over how to interpret the inclusive-language imperative for traditional hymn texts. The hymnal editors were surprised by lay insistence on preserving the term "Lord" as a symbol for God and Christ and simply stunned by the claim of critics that their radical inclusive-language editing amounted to theological exclusivism, not to mention heterodoxy. When the inclusive-language imperative was applied to the UCC's own hymnal, it was perceived by many in the denomination as an exclusionary effort by a partisan group of editors to remove or weaken historic expressions of the faith.

In both the UCC and the SBC, attempts at hymnic inclusivity became occasions for arguments about exclusivity. These ironies reveal both the power of hymnody as a shaping force for belief and practice in contemporary American Protestantism and the delicate balance that obtains between denominational leaders and the laity when the faith is publicly expressed through new hymnals. In the end, the judgment of history on these two hymnals will depend on the laity's reaction to them.

By the beginning of 2002 at least some results were in, and they too point up the difficulty of interpreting sacred song's protean role in religious culture. Over its first seven years, *The New Century Hymnal* had sold over 350,000 copies. That number is dwarfed by *The Baptist Hymnal*, which topped five million in sales during 1999, but these numbers can be deceiving. The UCC is one-tenth the size of the Southern Baptist Convention and far more diverse. *The New Century Hymnal*'s sales represent nearly one-quarter of the denomination's membership. After seven years *The Baptist Hymnal* had sold 4.5 million copies, or 28 percent of the SBC membership. It is fair to say that, relatively speaking, the two hymnals have performed roughly equally in terms of sales. UCC critics cite dissatisfaction with the new hymnal among congregations who bought it in advance, but sales of the other two UCC hymnals, *The Pilgrim Hymnal* and the

Evangelical and Reformed *Hymnal,* had dwindled to a few hundred copies per year before they went out of print in 1998. As a publishing venture, at least, *The New Century Hymnal* seems to have been nearly as representative a denominational publication as *The Baptist Hymnal.*

If there is anything that this tale of two hymnals teaches, it is that sacred song is a profoundly stabilizing force in Protestant religious culture. The deeply traditional Southern Baptist Convention realized this and created a new hymnal with as few innovations as possible to increase its unity under new fundamentalist leadership. Given the ceaseless focus on unity and uniformity in today's SBC, however, it is entirely possible that a new and even more narrowly defined hymnal will be required, one that attempts to define the orthodox core of SBC hymnody. Such a fundamentalist initiative would doubtless generate a "moderate" response in hymnody as it has in the creation of new seminaries and church fellowships, thereby sustaining the traditional cycle of polarized unity that has characterized the SBC since 1845.

In its own way, however, the United Church of Christ also followed its own traditions in producing and responding to an inclusive-language reform hymnal. Fractious praxis was the hallmark of mainline liberal denominations in the last century. Communions like the UCC are long used to furious political, cultural, and theological controversies that eventually resolve into mutual recommitment to the larger liberal cause. The UCC's argument over *The New Century Hymnal* has been in every way typical of earlier contests over denominational union and inclusive language itself. Regardless of the issue, so long as dissidents are free to protest and are given a fair hearing, the UCC's principle of diversity in unity remains intact and so does its denominational identity. *The New Century Hymnal* likely will continue to have a conflicted legacy, but in the contested praise of its new hymnal the United Church of Christ has reaffirmed its most essential identity and demonstrated the indispensable role of sacred song in creating and maintaining it.

Notes

1. Franz Hildebrandt and Oliver Becker, eds., *A Collection of Hymns for the Use of the People Called Methodists,* vol. 7 of *The Works of John Wesley.,* ed. Frank Baker (Oxford: Clarendon Press, 1983), 74.

2. Nathan O. Hatch, *The Democratization of American Christianity* (New Haven: Yale University Press, 1989), 125–61; Sandra S. Sizer, *Gospel Hymns and Social Religion: The Rhetoric of Nineteenth-Century Revivalism* (Philadelphia: Temple University Press, 1978), 20–50.

3. Henry Wilder Foote, *Three Centuries of American Hymnody* (Cambridge, Mass.: Harvard University Press, 1940), 309.

4. Harvey Cox, *The Secular City* (New York: Macmillan, 1967); Mary Daly, *Beyond God the Father: Toward a Philosophy of Women's Liberation* (Boston: Beacon Press, 1973); Rosemary Radford Ruether, *New Heaven, New Earth: Sexist Ideologies and Human Liberation* (New York: Seabury Press, 1975).

5. Brian Wren, *Bring Many Names* (Carol Stream, Ill.: Hope Publishing, 1985), and *What Language Shall I Borrow?: God-Talk in Worship, A Male Response to Feminist Theology* (New York: Crossroad, 1989); Ruth C. Duck and Michael G. Bausch, eds., *Everflowing Streams: Songs for Worship* (New York: Pilgrim Press, 1981); Ruth C. Duck, ed., *Bread for the Journey: Resources for Worship* (New York: Pilgrim Press, 1983), and *Flames of the Spirit: Resources for Worship* (New York: Pilgrim Press, 1985); Carol Doran and Thomas H. Troeger, *New Hymnal for the Life of the Church: To Make Our Prayer and Music One* (New York: Oxford University Press, 1992); Thomas H. Troeger, *Borrowed Light: Hymn Texts, Prayers, and Poems* (New York: Oxford, 1994). For a recent inclusivist statement on many of the issues addressed in this chapter, see Brian Wren, *Praying Twice: The Music and Words of Congregational Song* (Louisville, Ky.: Westminster John Knox, 2000).

6. Wesley L. Forbis, ed., *The Baptist Hymnal* (Nashville: Southern Baptist Sunday School Board, 1991); Arthur G. Clyde, ed., *The New Century Hymnal* (Cleveland: Pilgrim Press, 1995); Episcopal Church, *The Hymnal 1982* (New York: Church Hymnal Corporation, 1985); LindaJo McKim, ed., *The Presbyterian Hymnal: Hymns, Psalms, and Spiritual Songs* (Louisville, Ky.: Westminster/John Knox Press, 1990); Daniel E. Merrick and David P. Polk, eds., *Chalice Hymnal* (St. Louis: Chalice Press, 1995); and Carlton R. Young, ed., *The United Methodist Hymnal: Book of United Methodist Worship* (Nashville: United Methodist Publishing House, 1989).

7. Eileen W. Lindner, ed., *Yearbook of American and Canadian Churches, 2002* (Nashville: Abingdon, 2002), 349, 358, 389.

8. See John Lee Eighmy, *Churches in Cultural Captivity: A History of the Social Attitudes of Southern Baptists* (Knoxville: University of Tennessee Press, 1972); Gregory A. Willis, *Democratic Religion: Freedom, Authority, and Discipline in the Baptist South, 1785–1900* (New York: Oxford University Press, 1997); Paul Harvey, *Redeeming the South: Religious Cultures and Racial Identities among Southern Baptists, 1865–1925* (Chapel Hill: University of North Carolina Press, 1997); and Dennis L. Johnson and Charles Hambrick-Stowe, *Theology and Identity: Traditions, Movements, and Polity in the United Church of Christ* (New York: Pilgrim Press, 1990).

9. Clarence C. Goen, *Revivalism and Separatism in New England, 1740–1800: Strict Congregationalists and Separate Baptists in the Great Awakening* (New Haven: Yale University Press, 1962), 1–67.

10. Terry York, interview with author, Ridgecrest Conference Center, Ridgecrest, North Carolina, June 24, 1993. Further quotations are taken from this interview.

11. Charles Willis and Linda Lawson, "LifeWay Christian Resources Proposed as Sunday School Board's New Name," Baptist Press news service, Sept. 16, 1997.

12. Forbis, ed., *Baptist Hymnal*, vii.

13. See Nancy T. Ammerman, *Baptist Battles: Change and Religious Conflict in the Southern Baptist Convention* (New Brunswick, N.J.: Rutgers University Press, 1990); and David T. Morgan, *The New Crusades, the New Holy Land: Conflict in the Southern Baptist Convention, 1969–1991* (Tuscaloosa: University of Alabama Press, 1996).

14. Forbis, ed., *Baptist Hymnal*, viii.

15. Walter Hines Sims, ed., *Baptist Hymnal* (Nashville: Convention Press, 1956), vii–viii; Forbis, ed., *Baptist Hymnal*, xiii, 667.

16. Arthur L. Stevenson, *The Story of Southern Hymnology* (Salem, Va.: A. L. Stevenson, 1931), 142–64.

17. Ethel Porter and Hugh Porter, eds., *The Pilgrim Hymnal* (Boston: Pilgrim Press, 1958); Evangelical and Reformed Church, *The Hymnal* (St. Louis: Eden Publishing House, 1941); United Church of Christ, *The Hymnal of the United Church of Christ* (New York: United Church Press, 1974).

18. United Church of Christ, *Inclusive Language Guidelines for Use and Study in the United Church of Christ* (New York: United Church of Christ, 1980), 3.

19. James Crawford, interview with author, Old South Church, Boston, June 6, 1994. All subsequent quotations are taken from this interview unless otherwise indicated in the text.

20. United Church of Christ Hymnal Committee, "Theological Affirmations," unpublished memorandum, 1992.

21. *Inclusive Language Guidelines*, 4.

22. United Church of Christ, *The New Century Hymnal: A Sampler* (Cleveland: Pilgrim Press, 1992).

23. James Crawford, "An Approach to *The New Century Hymnal*," July 14, 1993, memorandum to United Church of Christ General Synod XIX, St. Louis, Mo.

24. John Wyeth, *Wyeth's Repository of Sacred Music, Part Second* (Harrisburg, Pa.: John Wyeth, 1813); Benjamin Franklin White and E. J. King, *The Sacred Harp* (Philadelphia: B. F. White and Joel King, 1844).

25. For more information on Robinson's text, see "Come, Thou Fount of Every Blessing," in John Julian, *A Dictionary of Hymnology* (London: John Murray, 1892), 252.

26. "Come, O Fount of Every Blessing," *The New Century Hymnal*, 429.

27. See H. Shelton Smith, *Changing Conceptions of Original Sin: A Study in American Theology since 1750* (New York: Scribner, 1955).

28. James Crawford, "Introduction," *The New Century Hymnal* (Cleveland: Pilgrim Press, 1995), x.

29. Kenneth Woodward, "Hymns, Hers, and Theirs," *Newsweek*, February 12, 1996, 52.

30. John Ferguson, "The New Century Hymnal: A Review," *Prism: A Theological Forum for the UCC* 11, no. 1 (Spring 1996): 38–39.

31. Arthur G. Clyde, "The New Century Hymnal: A Theological and Liturgical Expression," *Prism: A Theological Forum for the UCC* 11, no. 2 (Spring 1996): 27–35.

32. Daniel L. Johnson, "A Hymnal We Produced," *Prism: A Theological Forum for the UCC* 11, no. 1 (Spring 1996): 4–10.

33. Richard L. Christensen, "The Language of Faith and *The New Century Hymnal*," in *How Shall We Sing the Lord's Song?: An Assessment of The New Century Hymnal*, ed. Richard L. Christensen (Centerville, Mass.: Confessing Christ, 1997), 3, 23. Subsequent page references can be found in the text.

34. David B. Bowman, "How Diminished Were 'We'?" *Prism: A Theological Forum for the UCC* 11, no. 2 (Spring 1996): 13–16.

CHAPTER 8

Mormons and Music: Maintaining and Mainstreaming Sectarian Identity

One sacred singing ensemble stands above all others in America: the Mormon Tabernacle Choir. This legendary group of 320 singers has performed Sunday broadcasts of "music and the spoken word" on the CBS radio network live from Salt Lake City every week since July 1929. At more than 3,500 programs and still counting, the broadcast is America's longest-running religious media presentation of any kind. The choir has made more than one hundred recordings, rendering a vast repertory of American and European church music with its characteristically massive sound and precise diction. The ensemble has earned five gold and two platinum records and two Grammy Awards. Tours to Europe during the Cold War brought the choir to the first rank among America's cultural ambassadors. On the evening of July 4, 1976, the choir's performance at the Lincoln Memorial was broadcast live to the nation on network television. Three U.S. presidents have hailed the Tabernacle Choir as "a national treasure."

No other sacred-music organization in America can approach this level of achievement. It is fair to say that the Mormon Tabernacle Choir has been the paramount public expression of sacred music in America in the second half of the twentieth century. As such, the choir demands close attention and analysis. But there is much more involved here than simply the story of how one sacred-music ensemble achieved extraordinary fame and influence. Beyond its international acclaim, the choir is a vital institution of one of America's most controversial and least-understood religious groups, the Church of Jesus Christ of Latter-day Saints (LDS), its adherents popularly known as the Mormons.[1]

Founded by Joseph Smith (1805–44), Mormonism is based on the Book of Mormon, published by Smith in 1830 as a translation of an ancient text that corroborated and amplified the accounts of the Bible.[2] The Book of Mormon tells the story of Israelites who fled from Babylonian captivity and sailed to the New World, raised a civilization here, and eventually divided into two hostile nations, the believing Nephites and the apostate Lamanites. The account details the appearance and ministry of the risen Christ among the Nephites, their eventual genocidal defeat by the Lamanites, and the deposit of their sacred records by Mormon, the last Nephite prophet, at the Hill Cumorah near what is now Palmyra, New York, where Smith lived. Smith claimed that an angel named Moroni appeared to him, revealed the location of the engraved plates along with ancient "seer stones" for translating it, and proclaimed him the prophet who would restore the true church of Christ and build the kingdom of God on earth.

During his fourteen-year ministry, Smith gained thousands of converts who joined his quest to reestablish Zion. After gathering his followers and leading them on a pilgrimage of persecution from New York State to Nauvoo, Illinois, Joseph and his brother Hyrum were murdered in Carthage, Illinois, on June 27, 1844. Brigham Young succeeded Joseph as the Mormon leader and led the Saints on the Great Trek of 1846–47 to Utah, where he established their American Zion.[3]

Latter-day Saints accept Joseph Smith's Book of Doctrine and Covenants as a divinely inspired collection of declarations and revelations for establishing God's kingdom in the last days. It is from this text that Mormons find their most important warrant for sacred song. Doctrine and Covenants 25:12 reads: "For my soul delighteth in the song of the heart, yea, the song of the righteous is a prayer unto me, and it shall be answered with a blessing upon their heads." Mormons take this passage as a divine imperative for the Saints to promote sacred song. In every music context I encountered among them, from church authorities to the choir to independent "alternative" composers and performers, this passage was cited as scriptural justification for music-making. The church interprets the prophet's text to mean that any true act of sacred singing, whether the work was written by a Mormon or not, brings a blessing not only for the singers, but also for those who hear it.

This imperative, however, opens up many possible stylistic approaches to sacred music. Therein lies the central tension in LDS music: what music qualifies as "the song of the righteous" and what does not? The question is not merely theoretical or rhetorical. The classic example of its very real significance is the choir itself. Its mission has been controverted in the LDS community since before the beginning of the radio ministry. At issue has been the precise balance between the choir as an agent of explicit LDS evangelism on the one hand and its role as an institution that has proven uniquely effective in gaining acceptance for the Mormons in an otherwise hostile national culture.

Mormons bear a complex heritage of radicalism, sectarianism, communalism, persecution, polygamy, and patriotism. They have been suspected, feared, and resisted by American Protestants—and the U.S. government—for much of their history. That such a community of religious outsiders could produce a choral organization that became synonymous with American national identity almost defies explanation. That the vehicle for such cultural integration has been sacred song says much about the power of religious music in American national identity. That the choir continues to encounter tensions within the community about its role as a "national treasure" offers a unique window on the complexity of the church's identity and its music.[4]

Rehearsal with the Tabernacle Choir

March 24, 1994, brought a raw, wet, windy early spring evening to Salt Lake City, Utah. Through the good offices of Associate Director Don Ripplinger, I had obtained a rare opportunity to participate in a rehearsal of America's most celebrated sacred choral ensemble, the Mormon Tabernacle Choir. After a hurried walk through the cold drizzle to Temple Square, I was welcomed by a friendly, spare man with an umbrella who ushered me into the choir members' door of the Mormon Tabernacle, within whose fabled acoustics the choir has rehearsed and broadcast to its worldwide audience.

Soon a choir member—the tenor section leader, it turned out—descended the stairway and welcomed me warmly to the Tabernacle and the rehearsal. He escorted me into the loft and asked what part I wanted to sing. I requested second tenor and was ushered toward my assigned seat. The rehearsal had almost begun, but before I could find my seat, Don Ripplinger, whom I had interviewed earlier that afternoon, graciously introduced me. A rustle of cordial applause accompanied me to a front-row seat, center-right of Dr. Ripplinger, with clear sight lines to organist John Longhurst at the console of the Tabernacle's legendary Aeolian-Skinner pipe organ.

The Mormon Tabernacle is as famous as the choir that performs in it. Completed in 1867 under the supervision of Brigham Young, the Tabernacle is an oval-shaped sacred space 250 feet long, bisected by a central aisle and flanked on both sides by rows of pews. Now seating more than 6,000 people, the Tabernacle was one of the largest and best designed concert halls of its day. The most notable architectural aspect of the Tabernacle is its unusual proportion of sidewalls to dome. The brick sidewalls of the Tabernacle are only one story high, pierced frequently by windows. A ten-row gallery supported by slender columns masks the sidewalls. A four-story dome surmounts this low ring of brick and glass. The dome, a remarkable tapered barrel-vault held together by wooden pegs and rawhide thongs, creates the extraordinary acoustical qualities of the Tabernacle. From the back entrance of the Tabernacle one can hear the sound of a pin dropped on the organ console at the opposite end of the building, hundreds of feet away.

The other major feature of the Tabernacle is its massive Aeolian-Skinner pipe organ. Built in 1948, the organ voices 11,000 pipes in 188 stops. The instrument's heroic sound has provided a constant presence in choir broadcasts and recordings.[5] The choir sits in twelve steeply pitched rows at the apsidal end of the building, flanking the massive pipes of the organ. For rehearsals, choir members sit in 107 clusters of three singers to a part, arranged so that each group of three is entirely surrounded by singers on other parts. This configuration requires that each cluster be able to carry its own part independently while hearing all the other musical lines being sung immediately around it.

At the rehearsal Don Ripplinger sat on a high conductor's seat at the center of the platform, his music neatly arranged on a music stand. A tall, lean man with silver hair and scholar's reading glasses, he rested easily on his perch as he fastened a microphone around his neck in order to be heard clearly by the massive wall of singers facing him. My seat turned out to be a prime viewpoint from which to observe not only the interaction of conductor Ripplinger and organist Longhurst, but also the operation of the Tabernacle's state-of-the-art recording system. I could also see the sound technology station, a hooded desk with computer and screen positioned just stage right of the organ console. A man with headphones sat in front of the desk monitoring instructions from Ripplinger along with those from a recording engineer somewhere out of sight.

Promptly at 7:30 Ripplinger called the rehearsal to order. He took command with the ease of a man who has been associate conductor of this ensemble for nearly twenty years. He announced a lengthy agenda for the two-hour rehearsal. The choir would look at some new music, prepare for the next two Sunday broadcasts, Palm Sunday and Easter Sunday, rehearse special music for the upcoming General Conference of the church, and also review choruses from the Berlioz *Requiem* for a forthcoming performance with the Utah Symphony. Ripplinger called first for an arrangement of "The Church's One Foundation," published in 1866 by Anglican Samuel S. Stone and set to Samuel S. Wesley's 1864 tune "Aurelia." A universal favorite of Protestant America, though not printed in the current LDS hymnal, this hymn would be performed for the broadcast the first Sunday after Easter. We took up the piece, a rather straightforward arrangement of the classic hymn and its associated tune. Before we had finished all the verses, however, several members raised questions about the exact words of the text. Some plenary discussion ensued before Ripplinger determined what we would sing at least for now. As we proceeded, he stopped occasionally to tune a chord and to try different voicings in the arrangement.

After a full run-through of the hymn, there was a pause for announcements. Notice was given of a golf tournament for interested members during the upcoming weekend, along with information about visiting performers and a call for mandatory rehearsals next Tuesday and Thursday to prepare music for the LDS General Conference, the much-anticipated semiannual gathering of the church leadership in the Salt Lake Tabernacle to deliver counsel to the whole church membership. Following the announcements, Sister Carol Crist, a choir member, prayed from the podium, giving thanks "for the opportunity we have to participate in this ministry of music" and "for the caring and love we feel for each other."

Next up was the "Alleluia" from Jean Berger's *Brazilian Mass,* a mid-twenti-eth-century work that has been a staple of American church and school choirs for decades. As Ripplinger led the choir through Berger's undulating rhythms, he shouted out directions over the singing. "Chant, baritones!" he cried, "keep it steady and rhythmic! Sopranos, you don't need to drive it so hard!" After answer-ing many queries from the singers and correcting fine points of intonation and rhythm, Ripplinger said, "Let's give it a whirl. Let's tape it." The piece came off fairly well. In the coming week Ripplinger would diagnose the recording with exacting detail and prescribe further interpretive corrections at the next rehearsal.

The rehearsal had begun to gain some momentum, but I was frankly surprised by what I heard. Instead of the vocal power, burnished tone, and precise dic-tion that had made the choir world-famous, it produced uncertain entrances, sloppy diction, and rather less-than-perfect tuning. These musical impressions made me wonder just what the state of the choir had become. As the rehearsal proceeded, however, I began to realize the significance of a fact I had known but never fully appreciated: the Mormon Tabernacle Choir is entirely volunteer. Although many members have studied privately or in school, and there are some exceptional voices in the ensemble, virtually all of the singers are true amateurs.

Later I asked Ripplinger how today's choir compares with the past. He stated flatly that the choir's general musical technique and dynamic range is better than ever before. The sound "is more refined now than it's been," he said. "For years it was just raw power. Now it's both." He laid these improvements down pri-marily to the improving quality of each year's recruits, which he in turn attrib-uted to better music education among Mormons in general. "Where else are you going to find a choir of this size," he asked rhetorically, "that meets on a regu-lar basis and sings a repertoire that is probably as varied as any musical organi-zation there is? We just jump from one stylistic thing to another. We jump from Disney to Berlioz in the same night or in the same rehearsal. It's a phenomenal organization."

New choir members are selected twice a year by an application process open to all LDS members between the ages of thirty and fifty-five. Openings occur because of a strictly enforced policy that singers may only serve for twenty years. In fall 1993, 28 retirements were announced, an unusually high number; 112 applications were received for those places. Applicants provide comprehensive information about their musical background. If they make the first cut, they are invited to supply an audition tape. Conductor Jerold Ottley and Ripplinger, his associate, review the tapes and conduct final interviews and auditions with promising candidates.

Bill Grant, a rock-solid second tenor with whom I sat, is a typical member. When admitted to the choir in 1988 at the age of forty-six, Bill had never sung in an ensemble larger than his local congregational choir. After joining, he be-gan to take voice lessons to improve his vocal technique and sight reading, but he readily admitted that he is not an accomplished musician. Bill drives about an hour and a half each way every Thursday night to rehearsals and every Sunday morning to the broadcasts at the Tabernacle, and he practices the assigned music faithfully at home on other evenings of the week. He told me that being a member of the choir was a wonderful privilege and that touring with it in Israel during 1993 was "the experience of a lifetime." Such people have always been the bedrock of the Mormon Tabernacle Choir, otherwise ordinary folk who happily and humbly give their time and talent to the choir's ministry of music.

The entire choir operation is self-financing except for the salaries of the conductor and associate conductor, the Tabernacle's three organists, the librarians, and the secretarial staff, who are paid directly by the church. When they gather for weekly rehearsal on Thursday nights, their only regularly scheduled meeting, these 320 singers will have learned all newly assigned music on their own. Many of them have never heard how the score they have studied should sound. Like choir members in churches of every denomination all across America, they must start from scratch, and at the beginning of their rehearsal they sound much like everyone else, only bigger. As Ripplinger directed the choir in a first reading of Bach's famous Good Friday chorale "O Sacred Head Now Wounded," the logic of the rehearsal process became increasingly clear. The initial rehearsal music is unfamiliar to the group, good for warming up, settling down, learning the score, and getting in a vocal groove. As the singing continues, the choir encounters music increasingly familiar to it. By the last hour or so of such a rehearsal, the ensemble gains full stride, confident and ready to perform on Sunday.

So it was that raw March evening. The break between new and more familiar music was formally marked by the admission of the general public to the rehearsal at 8 P.M. Even on this inclement occasion, visitors filled two-thirds of the Tabernacle's seats. During warmer weather, the place is packed every Thursday night. Most of the visitors were Latter-day Saints, but the worldwide reputation of the choir, the Aeolian-Skinner organ, and the Tabernacle itself also drew tourists intent on hearing this remarkable sacred sound live. Such popularity means that three-quarters of every rehearsal occurs before a large live audience. Needless to say, such circumstances promote closer attention and better performance by the singers.

Ripplinger greeted the audience with characteristic Mormon warmth and extolled the choir's dedication. "To show you the kind of commitment it is for them," he said, "last year they were here 151 times during the year. It's a wonderful, wonderful group of people to work with. They do it because they love to sing, they love to share the songs with the people they sing for."

By now it was 8:15, time for the serious business of the rehearsal. Welcoming the audience had given the singers a nice break. Now Ripplinger turned to "O, for the Wings of a Dove" for soprano soloist and chorus, from Felix Mendelssohn's *Elijah*, a popular Romantic oratorio recorded and frequently performed by the choir. The conductor worked the piece hard despite the presence of the audience. When the sopranos missed their first cue, for example, he taunted them: "You get a chance to sing all alone for these people and you blow it!" Similarly, he corrected the men's parts and exhorted the whole group to respond to the composer's indications: "Feel the beauty of this passage as it crescendos with each entering part." As the choir prepared to tape, Ripplinger relaxed them with his conductor's wit: "Stand in the noble posture: both legs crossed! I'll think of some good calisthenics for Sunday morning!" The taping went well. A substitute soloist did a wonderful job; audience and choir joined in enthusiastic applause for her work.

Ripplinger quickly worked through an arrangement of the traditional American white spiritual "Jesus Walked This Lonesome Valley." There was another taped take, but without warning the choir made a quantum leap in its singing. The score was quite simple, but the choir was finally ready to sing as only it can. The clean diction, precise ensemble, gorgeous tone, and heartfelt expression were suddenly present, and they remained so throughout the rest of the rehearsal. Wild applause from the Tabernacle audience followed "Jesus Walked." Next, the choir delivered the same kind of performance of a familiar setting of the Prayer of St. Francis, and again the audience responded enthusiastically. Ripplinger announced that "the 'Hallelujah Chorus' will be on Sunday's broadcast, but we will not do that tonight." His message was greeted with loud but good-natured groans from the now-rapt audience.

Next on the rehearsal program was a series of four readings of works familiar to the choir but not sung recently. First was an elaborate choral arrangement of the traditional Easter hymn "Jesus Christ Is Risen Today," set to the 1817 tune "Llanfair" by Robert Williams. After a somewhat rocky rendition Ripplinger asked, "How many of you were sight-reading that?" When many new members raised their hands, he cracked, "those of you who do know it, would you sing it now?" Laughter and a much better performance followed. Ripplinger then called for Charles Gounod's "O Divine Redeemer," and during a strong rendition he commented, "You're getting much, much better with consonants!" The banter continued through an arrangement of the African American spiritual "Were You There?" and the "Sanctus" from Gabriel Faure's *Requiem*.

The rehearsal culminated with the singing of three great choruses from Hector Berlioz's *Requiem:* "Dies Irae," "Rex Tremendae," and "Tuba Mirum." The Berlioz *Requiem* justly ranks among the most massive, taxing, and extraordinary works for orchestra, chorus, and soloists. The choir had performed the *Requiem* during its 1993 Israel tour but apparently not since then. Ripplinger stopped the singing briefly at several points to clarify aspects of the highly complex score. For the audience, however, the three choruses were a treat not only because of the vocal demands capably performed by the choir, but also because organist John Longhurst finally cut loose the Tabernacle Organ, mostly muted during earlier pieces, to play the thundering accompaniment of Berlioz's mighty score. At the conclusion of the "Rex Tremendae" rehearsal ended to huge applause from the Tabernacle audience.

The singers exited quickly as did the audience. I buttonholed Don Ripplinger to ask a few technical questions about the choir's organization and audition policy, but my first remark voiced the basic impression I had received throughout the evening. "The most striking aspect of this rehearsal," I said to him, "was not so much its uniqueness, but quite the opposite: this is exactly the way a chorus rehearsal is supposed to be." Don laughed and confirmed my comment as a compliment, which it emphatically was.

At this rehearsal I learned that the choir's achievement is not the result of some special or esoteric genius, but rather the consequence of its rigorous adherence to the standard norms of American choral practice. The Mormon Tabernacle Choir is not an illusion; it is, in fact, the archetype for the American church choir in the twentieth century. The organization possesses the qualities that every choir director and singer seeks: superb musical leadership, dedicated and talented singers, an extraordinary organ, outstanding organists, and a remarkable performance space that amplifies whatever the ensemble can achieve. The choir is therefore able to realize the kind of sacred song that other American church choirs can only hope to attain.

When such an accomplished and spiritually sensitive standard of performance has been made available by radio and television to every American household for more than a half-century, the choir's national acclaim comes as no surprise. What does surprise is the controversial reception of the choir's success among the Latter-day Saints themselves. While church authorities have embraced, and indeed promoted, the development of the choir as an evangelistic and patriotic instrument, some LDS leaders have questioned not only the selection of repertory but also the larger strategy of aligning the choir with American nationalism. In this matter much more than sacred song is at stake. The contest about the choir's proper role crystallizes with particular urgency the question that has faced the Saints since their beginnings in 1830: how to reconcile their sectarian religious identity as the people of God with their desire to participate fully in the American political and cultural process? What is Caesar's and what is God's?

The Tabernacle Choir and Mormon Legitimation

Two related elements of religious culture help to explain the choir's success: legitimation and civil religion. Emile Durkheim, French founder of the sociology of religion, first elaborated the concept of legitimation in the late nineteenth century. Durkheim argued that religious beliefs and rituals give sacred authority and stability to the power relationships of society. Religion in this sense makes already existing social arrangements sacredly legitimate. A generation later Max Weber countered that religion could also transform entrenched social structures, delegitimate an old social order, and legitimate a new one.[6]

Both Durkheim and Weber assumed a homogeneous traditional society in which a single set of religious beliefs and institutions legitimated a coherent and integrated social system. In religiously plural societies like America's, however, legitimation takes several different forms. The diversity and competition of religious groups make it impossible for any one of them to perform the legitimation functions of traditional societies. Radical sectarian groups, on the other hand, often reject the dominant social system altogether and use their religious beliefs and institutions to create a separate identity for themselves. In his book *Religious Outsiders and the Making of Americans*, R. Laurence Moore has offered this view of sectarian identity to interpret the early Latter-day Saints.[7]

If they encounter too much hostility or if they want to moderate their separatism, sects can seek to legitimate themselves by adopting mainstream religious and cultural beliefs and practices. A sect that appears less deviant and threatening is likely to be accepted and indeed might well become more successful. Beginning with H. Richard Niebuhr's landmark 1929 study *The Social Sources of Denominationalism*, scholars have shown that American sects have often taken this legitimation strategy and improved not only their membership and institutional strength, but their social status as well.[8]

Since 1890 the Latter-day Saints have pursued a generally positive legitimation strategy, cutting back significantly on their separatism. The genius of that strategy has been to use American civil religion as a vehicle for their sectarian legitimation. First labeled by Jean-Jacques Rousseau in *The Social Contract*, civil religion is another kind of religious legitimation: an array of mythic beliefs, rituals, and symbolic institutions that infuse government and nation with sacred authority and meaning.[9]

American civil religion combines transcendent ideals and a national mythos with the practical morality necessary to make the constitutional order work. These elements lend sacred legitimation to the American government and social system. In his classic 1968 study *The Broken Covenant: American Civil Religion in Time of Trial*, Robert N. Bellah located these legitimating functions of civil religion in what he called the "superstructure" of republican theory and the "infrastructure" of democratic political practice. Following Western political philosophy from Plato and Aristotle to Rousseau and Montesquieu, the founders believed that a republic could succeed only if the people were bound together by a set of metaphysical ideas and moral values that created the conditions necessary for civil society. Absent such a "superstructure," they thought, a republic's rule of law would collapse under the corrupting pressures of self-interest and factional rivalry.[10]

In Bellah's view, the founders provided America's fundamental superstructural statement in the Declaration of Independence, which affirmed "self-evident truths" including the existence of God, human equality at birth, and divinely endowed "inalienable rights" to "life, liberty, and the pursuit of happiness." Bellah argued that these superstructural beliefs gradually developed into a sacred narrative of American history and destiny that was shaped by "times of trial" during which the nation's purpose was tested and redefined. The most important of these times was the Civil War, but other critical periods have also contributed to the accretion of civil religious symbols and narratives. Especially important to superstructural beliefs, in Bellah's analysis, are the themes of sacrifice and moral responsibility and the idea of America as "God's New Israel" charged with a mission to redeem the world through the spread of democracy. Important ritual elements also attend American civil religion, most notably a sacred calendar of national holidays and an extraordinary ritual center of monuments and memorials in the nation's capital.[11]

Bellah's "infrastructural" function of civil religion lies in what he called "the creation of citizens" through the constitutional order and the political process. The Constitution created a liberal political order of maximal freedom, protected rights, and limited government. It is one thing to proclaim rights and liberties, however, and quite another to have them honored in practice by the people. As John Adams observed in 1788, "we have no government armed with power capable of contending with human passions unbridled by morality and religion. Our constitution was made only for a moral and a religious people. It is wholly inadequate to the government of any other."[12]

The "morality and religion" that Adams and the other founders so frequently invoked was not a matter of doctrinal formulation or denominational identity but rather the moral discipline of fairness, tolerance, and commitment to the common good that makes it possible for constitutional institutions to withstand contentious, litigious, factional, and self-interested political behavior. In Bellah's view, the observance of that moral discipline in the rough-and-ready world of electoral, legislative, and judicial politics creates citizenship, the infrastructural glue of civil religion that holds together the American regime.[13]

This civil religion has also provided one of the most important avenues of acceptance for the Latter-day Saints by wider American society. Uniquely among American religious outsiders, the Mormons have embraced civil religion, the primary sacred legitimator of the political order, to assert their own legitimacy as Americans. Since 1890 LDS leaders have single-mindedly sought to convince their fellow Americans that the Saints are culturally mainstream and politically committed to the nation's values and purpose. The principal public vehicle for this complex legitimation strategy has been the Tabernacle Choir, and it has been extraordinarily successful at its appointed task.

It is difficult today to appreciate just how hostile the relationship between the Latter-day Saints and American society was for nearly a century after the publication of the Book of Mormon in 1830. Popular agitation against Smith's proclamation of a new scripture and a restored Zion hounded the Latter-day Saints from New York to Ohio, from Missouri to Illinois. Public authorities were also active players in religious persecution of Smith's followers. Missouri Governor Lillburn Boggs exiled the Mormons from that state in 1838 on pain of death. Six years later, when the Saints resisted armed attacks on their new settlement at Nauvoo, Illinois, Joseph Smith and his brother Hyrum were arrested for treason despite their authorization from the state to raise a militia for their self-defense. Their imprisonment at Carthage, Illinois, led directly to their eventual murder by an uncontrolled mob.[14]

The debacle at Carthage resulted in the succession of Brigham Young as president of the church. Young determined that the Saints would find their Zion further west on the American frontier and led the first of many Mormon parties west on an epic seventeen-month trek that ended in the valley of the Great Salt Lake behind the Wasatch Mountain Range. Almost immediately Young sought to gain admission of the Mormon commonwealth to the Union as "the State of Deseret." In 1850, only three years after Mormon settlement began, the federal government declared Deseret to be "Utah Territory," while conceding to Young the office of governor of the territory. Two years later, however, Young and the LDS leadership ratified the practice of polygamy as a revelation given by God to Joseph Smith. Unremitting opposition ensued from federal authorities, eventuating in a proclamation of "a state of substantial rebellion" by President James Buchanan in 1857. Inconclusive armed conflict during a brief "Mormon War" was followed by increasingly severe federal laws against Mormon polygamy passed by Congress in 1862, 1882, and 1887. Brigham Young died in 1877 still defiant on the polygamy issue. One of his successors, Wilford Woodruff, finally announced a command of God to ban polygamy as a precondition to Utah's obtaining statehood in 1892.[15]

In this context of political confrontation the Mormon Tabernacle Choir organized in 1863, taking up residence in the completed Tabernacle building four years later. Although its official task has always been to provide sacred music for Tabernacle services, missionary training, and church meetings like the General Conference, the choir's most important role since the 1890s has been to craft a new public image for Mormonism. The prohibition of polygamy set the stage for a more affirmative presentation of the church and the 1892–93 World's Columbian Exposition in Chicago provided the choir's first great opportunity.

Conductor Evan Stephens led the choir to second place in the exposition's 1893 choral competition. With the First Presidency of the Church in attendance, the choir impressed the judges, the crowd, and the press alike. The St. Louis *Globe Democrat,* for example, praised the "spirit of enthusiasm" of the amateur ensemble which "more properly rendered the [sacred] selections than could have been done by professional skill alone." Mormon authorities also noted the effectiveness of the choir's new outreach. Joseph F. Smith, nephew of the prophet, wrote his wife that the singing "has done more good than five thousand Sermons would have done in an ordinary or even in an extraordinary way."[16]

This auspicious beginning did not quell anti-Mormon sentiments, which reached a new high in 1903 with accusations of polygamy, eventually proved false, against Utah senator Reed Smoot. Within the LDS community, moreover, the growing popularity, travel, and public exposure of the choir brought suspicions of sexual impropriety against its members. In this troubled situation Stephens and the choir embarked on a controversial twenty-three-city tour in 1911. Despite Protestant-sponsored boycotts, poor planning, and a $20,000 loss, the choir impressed eastern and midwestern critics and gained a vitally important hearing by President William Howard Taft and a select group of congressional members.

At the same time the choir took a pioneering role in the development of recording technology. While the ensemble had apparently been recorded as early as 1900, its first professional effort was released in September 1910 by the Columbia Phonograph Company of New York. The selections revealed Stephens's popular approach to repertory. They included four Mormon hymns and four opera choruses along with "America," "The Star-Spangled Banner," Victor Herbert's "Gypsy Sweetheart," and Handel's "Hallelujah Chorus." The sessions produced the first commercially successful sacred-music recordings in America and gave the choir a powerful new medium to promote a mainstream image for the church (155–57).

Anthony Lund succeeded Evan Stephens in 1916. He immediately released nearly one hundred singers and reconstituted the choir to pursue the choral techniques and repertory of his German musical training. When the process for making recordings through microphone signals on vinyl discs was invented in 1927, the Victor Company came to Salt Lake City to record the choir in the Tabernacle. The combination of new recording and reproduction technology, Lund's selection of more classical works, his European performance standards, and the Victor Company's highly successful advertising established the choir as a leading public interpreter of sacred music in America (158).

In 1927 the choir also experimented with radio, providing small ensembles for primitive studio broadcasts on KSL, the NBC affiliate in Salt Lake City. Encouraged by these results, KSL station manager Earl J. Glade proposed to NBC a network religious program featuring live Tabernacle broadcasts of the choir. Although conductor Tony Lund was highly skeptical of radio's ability to provide enough fidelity to capture the choir's sound, he reluctantly agreed to Glade's proposal. At 3 P.M. on Monday, July 15, 1929, the first live choir broadcast was beamed from the Salt Lake City Tabernacle (158–59). In 1932 CBS purchased KSL and the choir broadcast, following the advice of Stanley McAllister, one of the network's vice-presidents and a Mormon. Dr. Harvey Fletcher, a gifted Mormon engineer for Bell Laboratories, assisted Glade, McAllister, and the choir in technical production for the CBS network link.

Under CBS the program took shape as a weekly Sunday offering of "music and the spoken word," featuring the choir, the great Tabernacle organ, and the homilies of Richard Evans, one of the twelve Mormon Apostles advising the First Presidency of the Church. Lund and Evans perfected the broadcast as a vehicle for Mormon legitimation. Lund and his 1935 successor, J. Spencer Cornwall, consistently selected well-known works from mainstream sacred composers— Bach, Handel, Mozart, Mendelssohn, Gounod, Stainer—while Evans delivered dignified and literate sermons designed more for moral edification than for

Mormon doctrinal advocacy. By the time radio entered its golden age during the Great Depression, the Tabernacle broadcast had become the bellwether religious program heard and enjoyed by millions.

During this time of radio ascendancy, the Mormons continued to explore their interest and expertise in audio technology with the choir very much in mind. Harvey Fletcher, one of the fathers of television, was also the principal developer of stereophonic recording and the long-playing phonograph record. In 1940 he presented a public demonstration of stereo at Carnegie Hall in New York City. For the occasion Fletcher prepared three series of recordings: orchestral, instrumental, and choral. The orchestral works were performed by Leopold Stokowski and the Philadelphia Orchestra, the nation's premier instrumental ensemble. The two instrumental recordings featured the Tabernacle organ with Tabernacle organists Alexander Schreiner playing Bach's *Prelude in D Major* and Frank Asper performing Widor's *Toccata in F.* The choral recordings were made by the choir in the Tabernacle, singing "Lift Thine Eyes" from Mendelssohn's *Elijah,* "Hear My Supplication" by Archangelsky, and the great Mormon hymn "Come, Come, Ye Saints." Fletcher's demonstration was a great success, catapulting the choir and the Philadelphia Orchestra to first priority as performing artists for the new generation of commercial recording.

World War II provided the crucial opportunity for the choir to become the voice of American nationalism and civil religion. In 1944 the choir performed on Dmitri Tiomkin's soundtrack for an Army propaganda film, "The Battle of San Pietro," and received a Peabody Award honoring fifteen years of the Sunday broadcast. At the death of President Franklin D. Roosevelt in April 1945, the choir prepared a memorial program in just a few hours and performed it movingly to the nation live on 143 CBS network stations. This presentation, perhaps more than any other, positioned the choir in national memory as the voice of the American people. For the next three decades, church leaders aggressively seized this unique yet not altogether riskless opportunity to make the Mormon Tabernacle Choir into a national cultural, as well as religious, institution (161–62).

The first postwar LDS President, David O. McKay, embodied the new Mormon image. Young, sophisticated, urbane, and financially successful, McKay represented a major departure from Mormonism's traditionally patriarchal style of leadership. McKay assigned the choir to an ambitious program of public performance. Its first venture was to record in 1952 for Cinerama, the pioneering motion-picture projection process that also created the first stereophonic film soundtrack. In 1955 the choir undertook an extensive and vastly successful tour to Europe. Widely hailed in the press, the choir emerged from its European tour as one of America's premier cultural ambassadors in the Cold War era. McKay himself summarized the synergy of agendas at stake in the tour when he said at its conclusion, "The money spent is the best investment we have ever made in spreading goodwill for Utah, the United States, and the Church" (162–63).

McKay relieved Spencer Cornwall as choir conductor late in 1957 and appointed Assistant Conductor Richard P. Condie as his replacement. Condie quickly negotiated a joint recording contract with Eugene Ormandy and the Philadelphia Orchestra. Although Ormandy voiced some doubts about the choir's abilities after his first rehearsals with them, Condie speedily corrected the technical problems and after their recording of Handel's *Messiah,* the Philadelphia maestro declared the choir "best in the world." Public response matched Ormandy's judgment: *Messiah* and a second album titled *The Lord's Prayer* enjoyed remarkable sales. As a single release, the choir/orchestra version of "The Battle Hymn of the Republic" sold nearly a half-million copies in 1959. The albums and the single still rank among the most popular religious recordings ever made (163–64).

For its work with the Philadelphia Orchestra, the choir won two 1959 Grammy Awards. Laudatory national publicity followed, along with frequent appearances on network television. But church authorities had not lost sight of the overriding purpose for the choir's activities. Lester Hewlett, director of the national tour that followed the Grammy Awards, gave unusually candid voice to the choir's evangelistic agenda in a letter to Michigan's Mormon governor, George Romney. "Our only reason for going out like this and spending several hundred thousand dollars," he wrote, "is to break down prejudice so that our missionaries can get entrance into more homes" (164).

Following a double agenda of legitimation and musical excellence, McKay and Condie aggressively pursued the choir's popularity. CBS stereo recordings poured from the Tabernacle while the choir sang at the presidential inaugurations of Lyndon Johnson and Richard Nixon. In 1962 the choir performed at Mount Rushmore on the first live global television broadcast via satellite. Between 1962 and 1974 Condie and the choir undertook six international tours and also sang at six World's Fairs. As recording revenues and national acclaim grew, however, critics within the LDS community voiced doubts about the choir's direction. Joseph Fielding Smith, for one, thought there was too much strain on members' families and commented on public television in 1970 that the choir was touring "too much for its own good. The Choir was not organized to travel around the world. I think they are overdoing it" (165).

Richard P. Condie's loyalty to classic Christian music had brought the Mormon Tabernacle Choir to the pinnacle of commercial, critical, and national acclaim by 1972. Yet he had also succumbed, perhaps inevitably, to church and CBS pressure to program ever more popular music for the choir's broadcasts and recordings. An exhausting 1973 European tour weakened choir morale while new objections to Condie's repertory circulated among the church leadership. In September 1974 newly elected Mormon President Spencer Kimball retired Condie and appointed his popular assistant Jay Welch as the new choir conductor. Shortly before Christmas of the same year, however, Welch resigned suddenly for what he called "personal reasons" and musical leadership devolved on

Dr. Jerold Ottley, Welch's unproven assistant. Shortly after Ottley's appointment, Don Ripplinger was retained as his assistant (165–66).

The choir's nationally televised U.S. bicentennial performance may well have been its high-water mark as an expression of America's civil religion. Since then, its radio audience has diminished, its television appearances have declined, and its recording contracts have been canceled. Ironically enough, the conservative ascendancy of the 1980s did not especially benefit the choir. Instead, by the mid-1980s its national constituency seemed increasingly limited to the World War II generation, along with listeners and patrons who still valued the repertory of Christian and patriotic choral music that the ensemble continued to promulgate with consummate excellence.

In 1988 CBS, now owned by Sony Corporation, severed its relationship with the choir and refused to sell its historic master tapes to the church. Between 1989 and 1992, Decca produced albums of inspirational selections with the choir and soloists Frederica von Stade and Kiri Te Kanawa. Most choir recordings in the 1990s, however, were released by Bonneville Communications, an official LDS production and distribution agency. At present, the remarkable run of choir recordings continues unabated, but its passage from corporations with global distribution capacity to a church-run agency signals not only a contraction in the choir's market but also the assertion of greater church control of every aspect of the ensemble.

During this period of transition, old questions about the appropriate role and repertory for the choir reemerged. The key issue was how specifically Mormon the choir's calendar and repertory ought to be. Some in the community demanded absolute purity of LDS beliefs and practices. "They regard the choir as a Church choir, as their choir," Ripplinger told me, "and we sometimes get static from [them] because they don't think we are doctrinal enough in some of the things that we do, or that we are not proselytizing enough or that we are not direct-gospel-message-minded enough."[17]

The associate conductor was quick to add that the choir indeed holds its ecclesial role as its first priority. "The choir *is* first and foremost a church choir," he said, "we perform at church functions, and that's what we do above all else." In fact, the choir is something like the LDS equivalent of the Vatican choir at St. Peter's in Rome, an ensemble that performs for the public but whose most essential task is to serve the church's liturgical demands at the highest level. Nonetheless, for at least some Mormons the question remains whether it is better for the choir to approach the task of evangelism in its traditionally general way or to be more specifically Mormon in musical identity and performance activity. And there is the rub for the choir: in order to maintain and further its historic mission, members and leaders must interact with the public in ways that seem worldly and yet also broaden its outreach. Church critics of the choir, Ripplinger said, "don't comprehend the other roles that the choir has."

The first of these is the legitimating power of the choir's extraordinary success in becoming part of the symbology of American civil religion. "We're con-sidered a national treasure," he said, "and we're viewed [that way] although people know our Mormon roots and sponsorship because of the way we try to approach things. They look upon us as a national choir, their choir. We've been an ambassador for this country, officially on a number of occasions and unofficially wherever we go. When we travel the world we're finding out that [same] feeling exists throughout the world. And we are [also] a recording choir."

Ripplinger also affirmed the importance of evangelism to the choir's activi-ties. "Our use and our value to the church is to reach out, to soften hearts, to open doors, to make people look differently upon something they might have had questionable views about. There isn't any question that [the evangelistic] element is there." Speaking from theological conviction as well as experience, Ripplinger made the case for the choir's broad approach to evangelism. "You cannot be nar-row and sectarian in what you do," he said, "and expect to have people look at you like they look at the Tabernacle Choir." The broadcast set the pattern. "It's not a Mormon-centered program," Ripplinger noted, "it's an inspirational pro-gram that has inspirational music that will reach all kinds of people at all kinds of levels of musical sophistication. That three minute sermon is generic in that is applies to everyone in terms of how we ought to live and the things we ought to do." He credited Spencer Cornwall and Richard Evans with the "humanitar-ian" values and beliefs that imbued the early decades of the broadcast, "and this formula has simply carried on." It is a formula and a theological perspective to which Ripplinger, for one, is fully committed: "Either you view humanity as brothers and sisters, or you don't," he said, "and I do."

Beyond the issue of evangelistic style stands the still more difficult question of the choir and American nationalism. After a half-century's effort to legiti-mate the church as an American religious institution, the choir today has lost much of its official public sponsorship. The choir now appears to be more a private religious musical organization than a public one. The familiar image of the choir as "a national treasure," and as civil religious legitimator for Mormon-ism, seems a bit out of focus for the church's vision of the twenty-first century. Yet the choir maintains its popularity and artistic momentum, especially inter-nationally, and its blend of patriotism and piety deeply informs its own sense of mission. I asked Don Ripplinger to speak to the choir's unique combination blending of civil religion, religious faith, and musical art. "I can only do it from my own point of view," he replied, "and that is that I am an American. But in the same sense I'm a child of God like everyone else is. I'm a member of the church, I respect and love all other people no matter who they are or where they are, and it just all fits together for me. I can't separate them. Otherwise you limit your influence, you limit what you can do. That vision is tubular; it goes no-where. [There] must be more."

Since my original visit, a number of important changes have taken place, but the choir's overall mission seems to move ahead unaltered. Ripplinger retired in

1995 and Ottley followed in 1999 after a tenure exceeded only by the legendary Evan Stephens (1890–1916). Craig Jessop, appointed in 1995 to succeed Ripplinger as associate director, was named director of the choir in 1999. Under Jessop two new musical organizations have formed. Since 1999 the Temple Square Chorale, under the direction of Mark Wilberg, has served as the training ground for future choir members. The laborious annual application process and the ad hoc musical training of choir candidates has been replaced by what amounts to a junior ensemble through which Wilberg brings singers up to the performance standards of the choir while carrying out their own successful concert schedule. Also in 1999 the choir founded its own instrumental ensemble, the Orchestra at Temple Square, under the baton of Barlow Bradford. Wilberg and Bradford also hold concurrent appointments as associate directors of the choir.

These changes have enhanced the choir's musical independence and reshaped its public agenda. While still recording works like Handel's *Messiah,* the choir no longer relies on performance alliances with professional music institutions like the Philadelphia Orchestra or the Utah Symphony. Now it brings its own orchestra. Organization of the Orchestra at Temple Square also marks an important stylistic shift for the choir. While the Tabernacle organ and its association with classic Christian repertory remains the signature symbol of the choir, the ensemble has moved decisively into the orchestrated anthem style of contemporary sacred-music composers like John Rutter, under whom Jessop studied.[18] This style is increasingly popular in the South, Midwest, and West, where it is not unusual for large urban and suburban evangelical churches to mount music programs with full concert choirs and orchestras. The choir seems to have taken the task of becoming the style leader for this kind of sacred song.

The choir's musical and stylistic reorganization reflects important developments in its agenda of public legitimation. Following its 1987 Emmy Award–winning program, *Christmas Sampler,* the choir entered the holiday television market in earnest with a series of *Christmas at Temple Square* concerts broadcast on PBS and released as recordings. These broadcasts display the new symphonic style of the Temple Square ensembles and, more important, renew the choir's role as the musical celebrant of the nation's holidays and public faith. In January 2001 the choir's public image received another major boost when George W. Bush, following his father's 1988 lead, invited the ensemble back to Washington to sing at his presidential inauguration.

At this writing, the choir's double mission to be the preeminent performer of sacred song for both the church and the nation seems to be on track. Its ability to perform without the assistance of non-Mormon music organizations, along with direct church control of its recording commitments, has tied the choir more firmly to Temple Square and its role as sacred-song leader for the national LDS community that gathers weekly at the Tabernacle. At the same time, the choir's new style signals the weakening of its traditional commitment to popular Christian classics and the embrace of contemporary genres promoted at Ridgecrest,

Montreat, and Lake Junaluska on North Carolina's church music row. In exchanging standard concert repertory for the contemporary anthem style, the choir has acknowledged the passing of its World War II radio audience and aligned itself with powerful evangelical and pentecostal denominations, like the Southern Baptist Convention, that share many of the church's moral teachings and political goals.

In this sense the choir's musical legitimation strategy is now less public and more ecclesial than it was throughout the twentieth century. Yet in another sense the choir today promotes a more specific public agenda for the church than ever before. Now secure in its acceptance by a new generation of evangelicals and cultural traditionalists, the church has charged its choir to become both more specifically identified with the Latter-day Saints and also the unrivaled voice of sacred song for conservative America. Whether it is prepared for that difficult task will be the constituting question facing the choir and its new leadership for the foreseeable future.

Hymns of the Restoration

The Tabernacle Choir has been so successful in representing Mormonism to the public through music that it came as something of a shock for me to learn about the enormous extent and diversity of Mormon musical culture. In interviews with scholars, artists, and church authorities I discovered that music plays an extraordinarily important role in Mormon identity quite apart from the Tabernacle Choir and its special mission. Mormon music culture in recent decades has been defined primarily by the tension between increasingly conservative standards mandated by church leadership and emerging new forms of LDS music including Mormon pop and avant-garde styles.

Music is one of the most important elements of traditional LDS worship and in the 1990s it received great emphasis from church authorities. One widely quoted church leader put it this way: "we need better music and more of it, and better preaching and less of it." Of ten rubrics in the official standards for the weekly Sacrament Meeting, six involve music, most of it sacred song: prelude, opening hymn, sacrament hymn, special music or intermediate hymn, closing hymn, and postlude. Responsibility for these liturgical requirements is borne by local volunteers who fill up to twenty-two music offices allowed in local congregations or "wards."

These staffing demands, however, have created some problems for LDS congregational music. The task of finding, at least in principle, a music adviser, music chairman, music director, organist or pianist, choir director, choir organist, choir president, choir secretary, choir librarian, and four choir section leaders for each ward, along with enough singers for an adequate choir and music leaders for ward auxiliary organizations like Relief Society and Primary and Youth Programs would be a daunting challenge even for a congregation of several hundred members. Given that many LDS wards are tiny communities, some located in remote settings, and that newly missionized congregations tend to be quite small, the church faces a very real shortfall in its musical resources.

Ironically enough, the problem lies at least in part with the very success of the Tabernacle Choir. Ron Staheli, choir director at Brigham Young University in Provo, acknowledged the choir's achievement but also noted a downside to the choir's popularity. The downside, he said, is that "on the local level, people will feel that the music program is taken care of already by the choir." This attitude leads to a kind of benign neglect of ward music that results in "great diversity of quality in programming out there, much of it very weak. In some cases there is no music at all for worship!" The key to a strong local music program, he insisted, is the individual congregation's ability to mount its music based on its own amateur and volunteer musicians. Staheli said that while "choir music has been given a great deal of play as a church obligation by the leadership, for the most part it is perceived as an add-on."[19] His BYU colleague Michael Hicks concurred, remarking that in practice one or two leaders, sometimes musically untrained, can dictate a ward music program according to their own taste and effectively disregard church guidelines.[20] For a religion characterized by disciplined institutional uniformity, this is a troubling circumstance.

LDS seriousness about hymnody extends back to the very beginning of the movement and proceeds directly from the revelations of Joseph Smith. According to Doctrine and Covenants 25, Smith delivered a revelation from God in July 1830 instructing his wife, Emma, a new convert, "to make a selection of sacred hymns, as it shall be given thee, which is pleasing unto me, to be had in my church." This special vocation, along with others given to her in the revelation, seems to have influenced her to embrace the movement. In any event, Emma Smith's work, *A Collection of Sacred Hymns for the Church of the Latter-day Saints,* appeared in 1835 at Kirtland, Ohio. As the original and inspired hymnal of the church, the *Collection* has maintained a unique place in LDS hymnody and has reached new prominence recently.[21]

The *Collection* contained ninety hymns, at least fifty of them by British Evangelical poets, including seventeen by Isaac Watts, and about forty by Mormon writers. Most prominent among the latter were the hymns of William Wines Phelps, whose work closely followed Evangelical literary models, paraphrasing and freely borrowing phrases from Watts and the others. Two other official collections also appeared during the prophet's lifetime. Known as "the Manchester hymnal"—produced in England in 1840 by Orson Pratt, John Taylor, and Brigham Young—and "the Nauvoo hymnal," edited by Emma Smith and published there in 1841, these two works along with the *Collection* comprise the classical canon of LDS hymnody. Notable later LDS hymnals include *Sacred Hymns and Spiritual Songs* (1887) and its musical companion *Latter-day Saints Psalmody* (1889), *Songs of Zion* (1908), *Latter-day Saint Hymns* (1927), and *Hymns: The Church of Jesus Christ of Latter-day Saints* (1948).[22]

The current LDS hymnal, *Hymns of the Church of Jesus Christ of Latter-day Saints* (1985), draws texts and tunes from all of these sources, along with new works since 1950. The new book reflected the leadership's shift to a simpler concept of hymnody. For example, the editors sharply reduced the number of "choir hymns," hymn arrangements made by Tabernacle Choir conductors like Evan Stephens that lent a more accomplished performance quality to traditional hymn tunes and harmonizations. The 1985 hymnbook restored most of the traditional settings for these hymns. In 1989 the church went still further in defining the essential core of LDS hymnody by issuing *Selected Hymns,* a collection of sixty hymns that must appear in every LDS hymnal.[23]

Selected Hymns begins with "Come, Come, Ye Saints" by William Clayton (1814–79), the most popular and widely known Mormon sacred song, sung as a stirring anthem of identity in church meetings and recorded many times by the Tabernacle Choir (example 21 on page 358).

Come, come, ye Saints, no toil nor labor fear;
But with joy wend your way.
Though hard to you this journey may appear,
Grace shall be as your day.
'Tis better far for us to strive
Our useless cares from us to drive;
Do this, and joy your hearts will swell—
All is well! All is well!

Why should we mourn or think our lot is hard?
'Tis not so; all is right.
Why should we think to earn a great reward
If we now shun the fight?
Gird up your loins; fresh courage take.
Our God will never us forsake;
And soon we'll have this tale to tell—
All is well! All is well!

We'll find the place which God for us prepared,
Far away in the West,
Where none shall come to hurt or make afraid;
There the Saints will be blessed.
We'll make the air with music ring,
Shout praises to our God and King;
Above the rest these words we'll tell—
All is well! All is well!

And should we die before our journey's through,
Happy day! All is well!
We then are free from toil and sorrow, too;

With the just we shall dwell!
But if our lives are spared again
To see the Saints their rest obtain,
Oh, how we'll make this chorus swell—
All is well! All is well![24]

Typical of LDS hymnody in its appropriation of nineteenth-century evangelical and adventist hymnody, "Come, Come Ye Saints" is set to a version of an Anglo-American folk tune widely used in antebellum tune books including *The Sacred Harp*, where it appears in a different key and rhythm as "All Is Well" to lyrics from an 1842 camp-meeting collection, *Revival Melodies* (example 22 on page 360).[25]

In a religious community that has experienced extraordinary growth in foreign missions over the past twenty-five years, the musical mandate of *Selected Hymns* illustrates the deep importance that church leadership attaches to hymnic uniformity. In the preface to *Selected Hymns,* the First Presidency voiced its expectations about music at the ward level. "We hope to see an increase of hymn singing in our congregations," the Presidency said. "We encourage all members, whether musically inclined or not, to join with us in singing the hymns. We hope leaders, teachers, and members who are called upon to speak will turn often to this hymnbook to find sermons presented powerfully and beautifully in verse."[26]

Partly in response to the perception of weakening musical discipline and partly in pursuit of a more distinctive LDS musical identity, church authorities issued a *Church Music Handbook* late in 1993, their first general music guideline since 1974. The fifteen-page document "outlines the full music program for stakes and wards," the church's bishoprics and local congregations respectively. It contains sections on "The Purpose of Church Music," "Appropriate Music for Church Meetings," "Music for Church Meetings," "Choirs," "Obtaining and Using Music," "Pianos, Organs, and Keyboards," "Music Callings," "Music Training," and "Church Music Materials." Each of these rubrics is in turn broken down into numerous subheadings.[27]

It is the style of LDS pronouncements to be brief in length and imperative in tone. The *Church Music Handbook* is no exception. For example: "Applause following musical selections is generally not appropriate in the chapel. Any exceptions should be approved by the bishop or stake president in charge of the meeting." The *Handbook* is also studded with quotations from important church leaders, especially Elder Boyd K. Packer, a member of the Quorum of the Twelve Apostles and perhaps the leading policymaker in current LDS music. Among his aphorisms: "Music can set an atmosphere of worship which invites the spirit of revelation, of testimony. . . . The Spirit does not ratify speech nor confirm music which lacks spiritual substance."[28]

The fundamental message of the *Handbook* is simple: officially approved hymns are to be the foundation for all LDS church music. The "General Guideline for Appropriate Music for Church Meetings" states the policy forcefully: "The hymns of the Church are the basic music for Latter-day Saint meetings and are standard for all congregational singing. Hymns are also encouraged for prelude and postlude music, choir music, and special selections. If other musical selections are used, they should be in keeping with the spirit of the hymns of the Church. Texts should be doctrinally correct."[29]

Michael Moody, director of the LDS Music Division in 1994, explained to me the importance of "hymns of the restoration" for Mormonism. "Our leaders talk a lot about hymns of the restoration," he said,

> and always musicians joke: well, what *is* a hymn of the restoration? It's a piece of music, the music and text of which capture the feeling of what we call the restored gospel, meaning that Christ's church has been brought back again to earth. And a hymn of the restoration is really just a hymn that captures that feeling. [It does] not necessarily proclaim the restored gospel, it could be a borrowed Protestant hymn. But there is a body of music that characterizes this [quality] that we have embraced, it's become characteristic, and it seems to carry a spirit with it.[30]

This imperative that worship music should express the spirit and proclaim the message of the restored gospel, buttressed by the Mormon theology of music as itself efficacious for inspiration and testimony, has led church authorities to place increasing emphasis on hymns in all church meetings. "Our leaders are very determined to maintain that body of music," Moody commented, "and to use it as a standard of contemporary church music policy in general."

Although it is an official pronouncement of the church, the *Handbook* has been greeted with significant resistance by those stake leaders and ward congregations who have been able to provide better than normal instrumental resources for their worship. Moody noted, "One of the real controversial issues is the fact that we have discouraged the use of brass in the sacrament meeting, and that's been a real topic of discussion. I think we've moved it from the specific to a general principle. Instead of saying specifically don't play brass, now we say generally, instruments with a prominent or less worshipful sound, such as most brass and percussion, are not appropriate for Sacrament Meetings. Then they really have something to understand."

Many currents of sacred song flow through Mormonism today. Traditional hymnody is ascendant, but many less-traveled roads have been explored by LDS composers and performance groups in recent decades, especially in the area of music for young people. The church has always been deeply committed to transmitting its faith to its children through song. Early on, children's musical training was provided by folk singing in the home and church singing schools, the first of which Joseph Smith himself organized at Kirtland, Ohio, in 1836. In 1878, however, Eliza Snow organized the Primary Mutual Improvement Association for musical training of the very young. Two years later Snow provided a very eclectic tune book for the Primary Association, but it was soon replaced by the all-Mormon *Deseret Sunday School Union Music Book* (1884) and its successor the *Deseret Sunday School Union Song Book* (1891). The Primary Association continues to be the cornerstone of children's musical training and the church regularly issues new collections for it like *Sing with Me!* (1969) and *Children's Songbook* (1989), which tells young singers: "Someday you will be leaders of the Church and the world. What you learn from these songs will help you to be faithful and to serve righteously. The good feelings the songs bring will give you happiness and courage and will help you to remember that you are children of God."[31]

Mormon youth music has a more complex recent history than songs of the Primary Association. Despite relentless denunciations of early rock music by church leaders, Mormon youth had embraced it by the late 1960s. Given the long LDS heritage of accommodation to mainstream musical styles in hymnody and the Tabernacle Choir's repertory, it was perhaps inevitable that Mormons would find a way to incorporate rock into their religious culture. The earliest vehicle for that rapprochement was the Osmonds, the singing Mormon family whose soft-rock concerts, recordings, and television shows enjoyed national popularity during the 1970s. Although the Osmonds employed their notoriety to further Mormon evangelism, especially in their 1974 recording *The Plan*, and their squeaky-clean image became a favorite target of secular critics, some LDS leaders continued to condemn any association of the restored gospel with the "terrestrial garb" of rock music.[32]

Another front in the LDS appropriation of popular music opened in 1973 with the southern California Mormon rock stage show *Open Any Door*. Youth pageants had long played an important role in Mormon religious education, but *Open Any Door* translated this pageant tradition into the rock/pop vernacular. Mormon television and film composer Lex de Azevedo's 1975 show *Saturday's Warrior* perfected the form. Immensely popular among the entire Mormon membership, *Saturday's Warrior* "began to be quoted alongside scriptural canon in church meetings and to be credited with drawing young Mormons to greater faithfulness," according to BYU music historian Michael Hicks. Summarizing the impact of Azevedo's show on the LDS community and its leadership, Hicks wrote, "The success of *Saturday's Warrior* spawned dozens of imitations and gradually convinced church leaders that elements of rock could be used for religious, if not liturgical, purposes."[33]

In the past two decades, still other forms of popular Mormon music have appeared. The most successful artists of this genre are composer Janice Kapp Perry and lyricist Joy Saunders Lundberg, who have created enormously popular cantatas, pageant scores, and songs for young people including *The Savior of the World: A Sacred Cantata* (1980), *I Walk by Faith: Values for Youth* (1985), and *For the Strength of Youth: LDS Standards in Song* (1993).[34] Their scores have been copyrighted by the church and recorded by Prime Records, an LDS corporation. "I Walk by Faith" is a good example of Perry and Lundberg's highly successful style (example 23 on page 361). The collection of ten songs is based on the LDS's Seven Values for Young Women: faith, divine nature, individual worth, knowledge, choice and accountability, good works, and integrity. The title song offers a summary of the Seven Values in a popular ballad style that owes more to the Broadway musical than to traditional Mormon hymnody.

At the other end of the compositional spectrum, composers like Provo's Kurt Bestor are creating film scores for Hollywood even as they pursue a creative music identity that they consider categorically Mormon. There is even "Mormon pop," promoted by popular groups like Afterglow who provide soft-rock songs about supposed courting rituals of young Saints in "the pre-mortal life," a realm of spiritual being before incarnation described by Joseph Smith.

On the whole, the church has maintained a benevolent posture toward these new expressions of Mormon pop. It would seem unwise to pursue a different course at the beginning of the twenty-first century in America. But, in fact, the church is quite willing to prescribe categorical standards for church song despite the influence of popular fashion. "We revere authority," Michael Moody told me, "so [if there is] conflict, then people will bow to authority and it will maintain a certain order. We don't vote. The priesthood says 'This is how we want it,' and the musicians say 'Fine, I see it from a little different perspective, but this is what you want,' and it works."

Yet Moody acknowledged that musical change is inevitable for the Latter-day Saints. "My own philosophy," he said, "is that no arm is strong enough to stay the tide of mass movement in terms of their musical preference and that it will evolve." Musical development is a divine imperative for the Saints, but the prophet also mandated standards for worship music that must not be breached. "There has been an evolvement," Moody acknowledged, "but if you can maintain that traditional liturgical group of hymns and teach the new generation to love and appreciate those, then the other [forms are] an enhancement."

For the Church of Jesus Christ of Latter-day Saints today, the watchword for sacred song is increased fidelity to Mormon tradition and especially to "hymns of the restoration." Yet the church continues to support efforts of the Tabernacle Choir to legitimate Mormonism in American culture at large and to encourage experimentation in new forms of sacred song for youth. Some critics in the church question the wisdom of this multidirectional policy, but in this essential matter of worship and devotional life, the leadership takes the long view. As Michael Moody told me, "one of our leaders said 'the church is like a ship moving forward in a slow steady course.' We are not quick to jump in one direction or another. If someone's down here bailing water, they may think the ship is sinking, but in reality it is a small matter that will be dealt with."

Notes

1. In 2001 the church announced that the terms "LDS" and "LDS Church" were not to be used by the membership. The community's full name or "The Church of Jesus Christ" were now to be standard. Nonmembers, of course, are not bound by such pronouncements; standard historical and scholarly usage will be retained here.

2. James B. Allen and Glen M. Leonard, *The Story of the Latter-day Saints,* 2d ed. (Salt Lake City: Deseret Book Company, 1992), and Leonard J. Arrington and Davis Bitton, *The Mormon Experience* (New York: Knopf, 1979), are the best recent surveys of Mormon history.

3. Jan Shipps, *Mormonism: The Story of a New Religion* (Urbana: University of Illinois Press, 1985), 109–29. This is the most important recent study of the Latter-day Saints' formation and early history.

4. For the intellectual and cultural background of the Latter-day Saints, see John Brooke, *Refiner's Fire: The Making of Mormon Cosmology, 1644–1844* (New York: Cambridge University Press, 1994), and R. Laurence Moore, *Religious Outsiders and the Making of Americans* (New York: Oxford University Press, 1986).

5. Charles Jeffrey Calman, *The Mormon Tabernacle Choir* (New York: Harper and Row, 1979), 92–93.

6. Emile Durkheim, *The Elementary Forms of the Religious Life: A Study in Religious Sociology* (New York: Macmillan, 1915); Max Weber, *The Protestant Ethic and the Spirit of Capitalism* (New York: Scribner, 1958).

7. Moore, *Religious Outsiders,* 25–47.

8. H. Richard Niebuhr, *The Social Sources of Denominationalism* (New York: Henry Holt, 1929).

9. Jean-Jacques Rousseau, *The Social Contract and the Discourses* (New York: Dutton, 1950), 129–41.

10. Robert N. Bellah, "Civil Religion in America," in *Religion in America,* ed. William G. McLoughlin and Robert N. Bellah (Boston: Beacon Press, 1968), 3–23; Bellah, *The Broken Covenant: American Civil Religion in Time of Trial,* 2d ed. (Chicago: University of Chicago Press, 1992), 173–80.

11. Bellah, "Civil Religion in America," 21–27.

12. Ibid., 5.

13. Bellah, *The Broken Covenant,* 180–82.

14. Arrington and Bitton, *The Mormon Experience,* 44–82.

15. Ibid., 176–205.

16. Michael Hicks, *Mormonism and Music: A History* (Urbana: University of Illinois Press, 1989), 152–53. Subsequent page references appear in the text.

17. Don Ripplinger, interview with author, Salt Lake City, March 19, 1993. All subsequent quotations are taken from this interview.

18. Nicolas Slonimsky, *Baker's Biographical Dictionary of Musicians,* 8th ed. (New York: Schirmer Books, 1992), 1564–65.

19. Ron Staheli, interview with author, Brigham Young University, Provo, Utah, March 20, 1993.

20. Michael Hicks, interview with author, Brigham Young University, Provo, Utah, March 21, 1993.

21. Emma Smith, ed., *A Collection of Sacred Hymns for the Church of the Latter-day Saints* (Kirtland, Ohio, 1835).

22. For a detailed discussion of LDS hymnals, see Hicks, *Mormonism and Music,* 19–31, 128–39.

23. *Hymns of the Church of Jesus Christ of Latter-day Saints* (Salt Lake City: Church of Jesus Christ of Latter-day Saints, 1985); *Selected Hymns* (Salt Lake City: Church of Jesus Christ of Latter-day Saints, 1989).

24. *Hymns of the Church of Jesus Christ of Latter-day Saints,* 30.

25. "All Is Well," in Hugh McGraw, ed., *The Sacred Harp, 1991 Revision* (Bremen, Ga.: Sacred Harp Publishing, 1991), 122.

26. *Selected Hymns,* i.

27. *Church Music Handbook* (Salt Lake City: Office of Music Ministry, 1993).

28. Ibid.

29. Ibid.

30. Michael Moody, interview with author, Salt Lake City, March 21, 1993. All subsequent quotations are taken from this interview.

31. Hicks, *Mormonism and Music,* 39–40, 108–25.

32. Ibid., 202–3.

33. Ibid., 203.

34. Janice Kapp Perry and Joy Saunders Lundberg, *The Savior of the World: A Sacred Cantata* (New York: Carl Fischer, 1980), *I Walk by Faith* (Provo, Utah: Prime Recordings, 1985), and *For the Strength of Youth: LDS Standards in Song* (Provo, Utah: Prime Recordings, 1993).

CHAPTER 9

Troubadour for the Lord: Catholic Charismatics and Sacred Song

All Saints' Day 1992 in Boston: a long dark Saturday night of Halloween had given way to a brilliant Sunday morning. It was the kind of late fall day that New Englanders treasure. The sky was perfectly clear, the temperature a crisp 45 degrees. Such a day is precious for Yankees because it supplies one last sparkling respite before what Herman Melville so aptly called "a damp, drizzly November" that annually afflicts both soul and body in New England. On Boston Common squirrels and chipmunks scrambled to stock their nests against the approaching winter, while their human neighbors strolled by admiring the final flames of the foliage season. In the suburbs, chainsaws sounded the preparation of winter firewood as flocks of Canada geese flew south overhead.

More than a thousand New Englanders, however, rejected outdoor activities on this day to seek the voice within. Shortly after noon they began to arrive at the Cathedral of the Holy Cross in Boston's South End. Liturgical home of Boston's Roman Catholic archdiocese, the cathedral is a vast wooden Gothic revival structure typical of Catholic churches built in major American cities during the late nineteenth century. Its towering spires and rose windows could soar over New York, Philadelphia, Baltimore, Pittsburgh, Cleveland, Detroit, Chicago, or any other industrial city in the Northeast or Midwest. The features of Holy Cross, painstakingly fashioned to recall Limerick, Florence, and Chartres, stand as a monument to the Irish, Italian, and French Canadian immigrants who built it a century ago and whose grandchildren and great grandchildren still make up the core of Boston's Catholic community.

By 1:30, every possible parking space was taken within ten blocks of the cathedral. School and tour buses virtually surrounded Holy Cross. Boston police cordoned off the cathedral entrances, admitting only specially marked limousines to discharge their VIP passengers onto the front steps. Streams of worshipers converged at the cathedral doors from every direction. All had come to hear John Michael Talbot, Troubadour for the Lord, the most popular Catholic sacred-music artist in America. Tables in the cathedral's narthex entry hall were loaded with Talbot's books, cassette tapes, and compact disc recordings. They also offered brochures, newspapers, and clippings about Talbot and the community he founded, the Brothers and Sisters of Charity, as well as Mercy Corps, the international Catholic hunger relief agency to which the proceeds of the concert had been committed. Robed members of the Brothers and Sisters of Charity attended these tables: women arrayed in white or black, men in Franciscan brown. All wore little handmade signs around their necks cut out of paper in a distinctive heart shape. Written in crayon or magic-marker on each sign was the motto: "God is the musician and we are his instruments."

The crowd poured through the great wooden doorways, queuing up six-deep at the tables or proceeding directly into the cathedral to find seats in the fast-filling building. The assembly was very mixed: young people, elderly, and middle-aged; families, couples, and church groups; nuns and priests, nurses and teachers. Roughly two-thirds of the crowd was female; nearly half of it was under twenty-five years of age. At the head of the aisles, Brothers and Sisters of Charity greeted the people and pressed a simple photocopied program into their hands headed, "God Bless You, John Michael Talbot!" As concert time approached, the sun poured through the cathedral's seven bays of stained-glass windows. A brilliant beam of sunlight pierced the rose window in the west facade and shone directly upon a solitary chair set before the central altar. Everything was ready for the Troubadour for the Lord to sing for all the saints.

Instruments of God

About ten minutes after the announced concert time, the host of a local FM radio program stepped to the microphone to introduce Talbot. "We at the station are delighted to be cosponsoring this great event for Mercy Corps!" he said. "Let's show John just how much we love him and appreciate him! Brothers and sisters . . . John Michael Talbot!" As the ovation rose and the houselights dimmed, a solitary bearded figure emerged from stage right, his dark hair closely cropped in monastic style, his clothes in the Franciscan habit—hooded brown woolen robe, rope cincture, and sandals. He carried a guitar with loving familiarity as he crossed to his chair and sat, barely acknowledging the applause. He carefully arranged his robe, crossed his legs, adjusted the microphones, and checked the guitar's tuning. Without comment John Michael Talbot began to sing "Peace Prayer," his 1980 setting of the Prayer of Saint Francis.

Talbot delivered the words in a clear tenor voice with bell-like tone and burnished vibrato, accompanied only by his guitar, which he played simply but with masterful control. It was technically a solo performance, but its essence lay in the subtle interplay of two perfectly matched voices, one human, the other instrumental. Talbot's text came from one of the most beloved prayers of the Christian tradition; his musical setting, a fervent ballad in popular style, has proven to be one of his most characteristic and popular songs.

Without pausing, Talbot launched into "May I Never Boast," his 1987 setting of Galatians 6:14 and 17, Saint Paul's classic admonition to Christian humility. It was another ballad, more conversational and introspective in tone, with a strophic A–A–B–A–B–A structure. There was again no rhythmic break or key change after "May I Never Boast," simply a breath and a third spiritual ballad, Talbot's rendition of St. Paul's famous "love chapter" from the First Letter to the Corinthians (example 24 on page 365).

> Love is patient, Love is kind.
> Love is humble, does not put on airs.
> Love is never rude,
> Not prone to anger, does not seek itself.
> Love is patient, Love is kind.
> It does not brood over injuries, does not rejoice in what is wrong.
> Love rejoices always with the truth.
> Love never fails.
> There is no limit to Love,
> To its power to prevail, to its trust, to its hope, its power to endure.
> There are in the end three things that last:
> There is faith, there is hope, there is charity.
> And the greatest of these is Love, so after Love seek eagerly.

The three songs, all formally and stylistically similar, set a tone of prayerful expectation that gathered his cathedral audience into a single-minded congregation. At last he paused and permitted the people to respond with sustained but tentative applause. Talbot quickly launched into "The Master Musician," the title song from his latest album and companion book.[1] A more sprightly composition with a simple verse and chorus structure, it told the story of how we and the Master Musician are joined in a common purpose symbolized as a symphony that "rises, / Like incense from cathedral choirs of grace, / And a symphony sounding, / Like poetry from the pages yellowed in time."

As applause for Talbot's new song died away, the brown-robed singer began a homiletic commentary that would extend through the rest of the concert. "Truly God is with us," he began. "He desires us to bring his music into the world, a world filled with discord, hatred, darkness, and noise. He brings his music into this world by you and I becoming his instruments." Building upon the song's message, he amplified the metaphor of the Master Musician into a parable of divine grace and a discourse on Christian virtue. In order to become fit instruments for the Master Musician, he said, we must allow our natural selves to be cut down like the trees of the forest and learn the lesson of humility. "From that wood," Talbot said, "God can fashion an instrument upon which he can play his music."

Talbot then presented a spiritual and moral commentary on this imagery drawn from his companion book *The Master Musician*. He explained to the audience that after the tree is cut down, the wood must be aged so that it won't warp after it is shaped and joined. "Sometimes it's hard for us to wait for that aging process to happen in our lives," Talbot remarked. "We want everything now. [But] you have to have patience to follow the work of Jesus." Next the wood must be bent into shape. This is done by applying moisture to it after it has been dried. "Sometimes we don't know what God will do with us," Talbot said. "He dries us and then he gets us wet. [Laughter] He wets us so that he can bend us. But if he tries too quickly, the wood will crack. That water is a symbol of the action of the Holy Spirit that comes to us only in prayer."

When the pieces of the Master Musician's instrument have been prepared, Talbot said, he glues and clamps them into a complete whole. The glue is love, "the great fruit of the Holy Spirit, without which the instrument, no matter how mathematically perfect, will never hold together." The clamp is discipline, "which comes to us from the outside in, from the church and from the community." Then the instrument must be sanded by "everyday mundane activities of life that we do over and over and over. Yet those are the activities through which God smooths us flat. I don't know about you," Talbot joked, "but I have some real rough edges. I need to be sanded." Finally, the instrument becomes beautiful and strong through multiple coatings of "the lacquer of God [manifested through] our relationships," he said, "husbands and wives, parents and children, relationships at work and in the church. It happens at every level, everywhere that God's people are walking in faith."

In little more than a half-hour, John Michael Talbot had parsed a spiritual grammar for becoming an instrument of God. It was time for another song, "The Lord Is My Shepherd," his popular ballad setting of Psalm 23 in the unusual form of A–B–A–B2–B. Talbot introduced the song through a personal testimony. "I wrote this song when my father was converted to Christ and asked to be confirmed as a Catholic Christian. I sang it a year later at his funeral."

After "The Lord Is My Shepherd" Talbot again moved to another song without pausing for the congregation to respond. This time he choose one of his best-known songs, his 1980 setting of Mary's Magnificat in the Gospel of Luke, with a melodically complex verse and a powerful praise song refrain: "And Holy, Holy, Holy Is His Name." As Talbot began the second refrain, he asked the congregation to join in. They did so with the ease of singers long familiar with the words and tune. Three times they repeated the refrain, each time with more harmony and more intensity, eyes closed, bodies swayed, arms stretched upward in the classic charismatic prayer posture. When the song finally ended, Talbot received his largest ovation of the day.

Talbot proclaimed that like Mary we are called to do the will of God, but our calling is even more radical than hers. Not only can we bear Jesus into the world as she did, but it is also our mission to make ourselves like him. "He must be the absolute beginning and end, the very center of our life," Talbot declared, "or we cannot call ourselves Christians." "As I sing these [next two] songs," he prayed, "let the words permeate like the dew and sink into your soul. Let's be Christians, let's be like Christ." The first song was "Consider the Lilies," his immensely popular chorus based on Matthew 6:19, 33:

> So seek ye first the kingdom of God,
> And the cause of his righteousness;
> For wherever your treasure is,
> There will you find your heart.

As the last chords of "Consider the Lilies" still echoed through the cathedral, Talbot began a plaintive A–A–B–B2–A1 setting of Matthew 11:29–30, "All Who Are Weary," appealing to the congregation for deeper commitment to the all-sufficiency of Christ.

> All who are weary, come unto Me.
> All who find life a burden,
> I will refresh you; your soul will find rest.
> For My yoke is easy and My burden is light.

At this critical juncture in the concert Talbot issued a call to Christian service, returning to the imagery of his "Master Musician" theme, then giving way to moral and political exhortation: "If we are to bring harmony into the world, we must first change the discord of the disproportionate distribution of the world's wealth, where the United States, 5 percent of the world's population, uses 60 percent of the world's resources. We can try to rationalize it, socialize it, economize it, politicize it, even theologize it. That's really empty talk. That's sin, which means to miss the mark. We are missing the mark."

Talbot warmed to this peroration in language filled with evangelical Protestant rhetoric, but with an affective tone that remained affirming, not condemnatory, despite its prophetic message. "Perhaps the greatest abuse both of the sin of materialism and the sin of promiscuity is the sin of individualism gone wild," he proclaimed. "Have we allowed the Lord to order our lives in gospel obedience both as individuals and within the context of the church and the community of the church? We are first the church's people, and God would have us change."

Despite the exhortation, this was still a concert, and Talbot shifted back from the prophetic mode to the performance, returning once more to his metaphor of Christians as instruments of God. "Ultimately the music we learn from Jesus," he said, "is the music of the Beatitudes. I want to sing the Beatitudes to you as if you were musicians for God. Let us offer ourselves to be musicians, to be disciples of Jesus, to learn his music, to learn his order, his truth, and his greatest message, the love of God, in eight simple sentences, the heart of the Gospel message."

After performing his setting of the great text from Matthew 5:1–12, Talbot made an appeal for Mercy Corps International, the Catholic relief agency that he serves as honorary chairman. Why Mercy Corps?

> Because most of the world is hungry and sick. The majority of the world is poor. We're the minority of the world using the majority of the world's goods, but the majority of the world's population gets very little. That results in sickness both physical and psychological. What results is frustration, and sickness, and anger, and war. What results is death. So we feel if we're going to live counterculturally here in the United States, as we feel we should, we also want to have extensions of that, a practical way of helping the people throughout the world. We feel this is all part of the way that we are to make music for Jesus.

Talbot's final appeal for Mercy Corps was again steeped in the rhetoric of evangelical Protestants, the most prodigious religious fundraisers in American history.

> Today I want you to search your hearts to see how you can help Mercy Corps. I'm going to ask you to ask God what you're supposed to give, and believe that whether it is a still small voice or the loud shout of the Holy Spirit, he will tell you what to give. I'm going to ask you to pray, and when he tells you what to give, I can give you no better advice than what Mary gave to the women at the wedding at Cana: do whatever he tells you. If you will assent, you and I can become instruments not any more of war and discord and pestilence, but instruments of God's peace.

Here, finally, was closure. Talbot's sustained effort over almost two hours to form this congregation into instruments of God's peace had found its mission in the ministry of Mercy Corps. Faith was incarnated into action, the gospel action of selfless giving. Talbot's songs had been taken for the most part directly from scripture. His preaching had been Catholic in doctrine and Evangelical Protestant in rhetoric. His spirituality had been introspectively charismatic. It did not come as a surprise therefore that while the offering was being taken, he led the congregation in a slightly modified version of the famed 1926 gospel chorus by North Carolina Presbyterian Daniel Iverson, "Spirit of the Living God."

The congregation knew the song well. It has become a familiar part of Catholic charismatic renewal hymnody. After the chorus was sung, Talbot paused briefly to exhort yet once more: "Truly we are the people formed by the Spirit of God. We can intercede for one another and we can carry each other's burdens. But ultimately nobody can make the music of God for you. St. Paul said though Christ bears all our burdens, yet everyone must carry their own burdens. So we sing for the Spirit of God to fall fresh on each of us so that we can grow." He repeated the chorus, joined by a fuller and more harmony-filled voice singing back to him from the cathedral. It remained only to raise the spirit of the congregation before it went out to be the instrument of the Master Musician. In a concert remarkably free from emotional display, here was the opportunity to release the spiritual energy that had been building from the beginning. The time had come to sound the note of triumph, and everyone in the house knew that the right song for this moment was Talbot's trademark version of "Our God Reigns." The Troubadour for the Lord did not miss his cue, launching fervently into the 1974 praise song by Leonard E. Smith Jr. (example 25 on page 368).

> How lovely on the mountains are the feet of Him,
> Who brings good news.
> Announcing peace, proclaiming news of happiness.
> Our God reigns, Our God reigns!
>
> *Chorus:*
> Our God reigns! Our God reigns! Our God reigns! Our God reigns!
>
> He had no stately form, He had no majesty
> That we should be drawn to Him.
> He was despised and we took no account of Him.
> Yet now he reigns with the most High!
>
> It was our sin and guilt that bruised and wounded Him.
> It was our sin that brought Him down.
> When we like sheep had gone astray, our Shepherd came,
> And on His shoulders bore our shame!
>
> Meek as a lamb that's led out to the slaughterhouse,
> Dumb as a sheep before its shearer.
> His life ran down upon the ground like pouring rain
> That we might be born again!
>
> Out of the tomb, He came with grace and majesty.
> He is alive, He is alive.
> God loves us so see here His hands, His feet, His side.
> Yes, we know He is alive!

Everyone sang along. With each chorus, more hands reached skyward in the gesture of charismatic prayer, and more voices raised the song for all the saints and all of God's church.

Proffit, Profit, Prophet

John Michael Talbot's significance for American Catholic sacred song begins with his remarkable performing, recording, and publishing career. He has made forty-two Christian music recordings since 1976, amassing sales of more than four million units. Over the past twenty years, he has played an average of more than sixty dates per year in cities across the nation. Each year he leads sold-out pilgrimage tours to the Holy Land and has recently begun mendicant Prayer Walks, ministering door-to-door in poor Ozark towns. He has written fifteen books and compiled eight song collections.

His recordings have won high critical acclaim: *Light Eternal* won the 1982 Dove Award for Best Worship Music Album of the Year from the Gospel Music Association; nine of his other recordings have received Dove Award nominations. *Pulse!* magazine called *The Painter* the best Christian recording of the 1980s, while *Billboard* named Talbot Number One Male Christian Artist in 1988 and *The Birth of Jesus: A Celebration of Christmas* the best Christmas recording of 1990. Among Talbot's other notable recordings are *Come to the Quiet* (1980), his best-selling recording to date, consisting mostly of Psalm settings, and *Come Worship the Lord I and II* (1990), praise songs performed with the Brothers and Sisters of Charity. Most recently, Talbot has completed a signature album *Troubadour for the Lord* (1996); *Table of Plenty* (1997), a theme album on the Eucharist; *Pathways*, a six-volume series of instrumental recordings designed to lead the listener to specific spiritual states including quiet, solitude, and wisdom; and three albums in his classic spiritual ballad style, *Cave of the Heart* (1999), *Simple Heart* (2000), and *Wisdom* (2001). Talbot's books include *Changes: A Spiritual Journal* (1984), a spiritual autobiography; *The Fire of God* (1984), an exploration of spiritual healing; *Simplicity* (with Dan O'Neill) (1989), a collection of social teachings; three volumes of *Reflections on the Gospels* (1986–91); *The Master Musician* (1992); and, most recently, *The Lessons of St. Francis* (1997), *The Music of Creation* (1999), and *The Joy of Music* (2001).[2]

This is an impressive body of work by any standard, enough to make Talbot unquestionably the most popular American Catholic sacred-music artist in the last quarter century. There are some serious rivals, especially in the arena of liturgical music, where the Mass settings of John Foley, Richard Gelineau, and Richard Proulx have been used so frequently in eastern and midwestern parishes as to be almost canonical. But Talbot's unique combination of performance, recording, writing, and institutional leadership makes him preeminent in contemporary American Catholic music.

Talbot's story began in 1963 with ten-year-old "Johnny Mike" picking at a guitar alongside his older brother Terry in their Indianapolis home. Terry and John shared vocal and instrumental talent as well as the Talbot family's Methodist religious tradition. Playing in a series of bands around town, the brothers eventually caught on as principal members of a folk-rock band they called

Mason Proffit. The Talbots made their first Mason Proffit recording for Warner Records in 1967; John Michael was fourteen years old. Their debut album quickly moved up the charts, pushing aside such rock legends as the Beatles, the Beach Boys, Jefferson Airplane, the Rolling Stones, and the Byrds. Along with their Warner stablemates the Doobie Brothers, Mason Proffit established the acoustical folk-rock style as a major element in the burgeoning popular music culture of the late 1960s.

Commercial success brought predictable benefits and costs. For six years Mason Proffit flourished as a headline act on the country rock circuit. Young Talbot experienced both the highs—mostly booze and women—and the lows—tour burnout—of national celebrity while still a teenager. Talbot married and had a daughter, but the tour grind proved ever more burdensome. John and Terry witnessed first-hand the collapse of the flower child generation and the debacle of Vietnam. By 1974 the party was over. Terry experienced a Christian conversion and broke up Mason Proffit. John and his wife broke up too, beginning a protracted separation that lasted three years before they finally divorced. John, alone, famous, wealthy, and seeking he knew not what, experienced ontological freefall.[3]

He landed in the roiling waters of American charismatic piety. Never straying very far from his Methodist roots despite the band's popular success, Talbot as early as 1971 began to experience visionary episodes calling him to a Christian vocation. "The first vision," he reported in *Changes*, "was a vivid picture of an agrarian community of prayer painted for me by Jesus. Selfless love and unity characterized every aspect of this community of Jesus' followers, both in their dealing with one another and with nature. In this vision all of creation was reconciled to the way of Jesus; his followers not only spoke of his way, they also lived it." A second vision called him to "an apostolate of poverty among the churches of Jesus. I saw myself clothed in a brown, coarse garment resembling a habit and walking on foot from church to church to share the simple love of Jesus. In this vision Jesus called me to a ministry that did not depend on anything other than two legs and a voice to bring his message to the world."[4]

These visionary imperatives led Talbot first through a series of encounters with American evangelicalism. By the time twenty-one-year-old John Michael Talbot left Mason Proffit in 1974, the Jesus movement, the renewal of Pentecostalism, and the resurgence of Protestant fundamentalism were well under way, marking the Bicentennial Revival in American Protestantism. On his spiritual odyssey Talbot encountered all of these potent forces of "born again" religion. Out of their mutually reinforcing influence, Talbot's voice waxed prophetic, his vision countercultural, and his commitment to Christian ministry through music sure. He embarked on his mission with eschatological zeal "as a response from a call from the Lord. He told me to speak to issues, to urge the lazy and the self-righteous to repent and reform, to prepare a yet spotted and ugly Bride for the coming of her Groom by admonishing her to good works, forgiveness, and a love that would make her beautiful to behold."[5]

In 1976 he released *John Michael Talbot,* his first solo Christian music album. The recording presented Talbot as a seeker for Christ's kingdom, inviting listeners to join in his pilgrimage through the difficult spiritual terrain of the mid-1970s. This narrative and thematic approach, a spiritual "concept album," was an important innovation in Christian music and became a trademark of Talbot's recorded work. *JMT* proved to be an immediate and enduring success for Talbot and his new recording company, Billy Ray Hearns's Sparrow Records. By the end of 1976, Talbot had completed his transit from profitable secular country rocker to Christian prophet singing for the Lord.

Talbot joined forces with first-generation Christian contemporary music artists like Larry Norman, Barry McGuire, Nancy Honeytrees, and Keith Green to give the Bicentennial Revival a distinctive musical voice. "Most of that first generation had been successful in secular music," he recalled, "like my brother and myself. And we left it. We said 'This is not it. We are Christians, we don't agree with this, we want to do something else, something more.' It was not well thought out, we just did it."[6] They did it so well, however, that their success in the explosive Christian music market of the mid-1970s brought a new paradox of commercial stardom as religious artists. Talbot rejected the new star system, especially what he calls "the second generation of Christian contemporary artists," with its wealth, worldliness, and "big mansions in Nashville."

Talbot was keenly disappointed at this exchange of religious vision for commercial success. "At that turning point in Christian contemporary music," he recalled, "the language I heard from the industry was 'We don't want to lead the culture, we only want to reflect it. We know that will pay.'" For Talbot, Christian contemporary music had come to resemble the very kind of commercialism he had hoped to leave behind with Mason Proffit. "[The Christian contemporary music business] wasn't much different [from Warner Brothers]," Talbot recalled. "They were fairly ethical people: if they were cheats, they'd tell you so. The only difference is that it's a little more devious because it's got Jesus' name all over it." Reacting sharply to this rising commercialism, Talbot sought a more substantial approach to Christian music, one more congruent with his own sense of mission.

At a 1977 music seminar held at the First Church of the Nazarene in Denver, Talbot encountered fellow Christian sacred-music artist Barry McGuire in a conversation that permanently changed his sense of his music ministry. McGuire told Talbot, "*You* sing to God and *God* will take care of the people, because God can do that better than you can." From that moment, Talbot said, "my ministry changed forever. God said to me, 'I don't want you to play fancy riffs, I don't want people watching you play. I want people to watch me be God.' So I intentionally took a minimalist approach to playing and singing where less is more, so that people get their eyes off me and onto God. I tried that and it revolutionized my whole concept." That new minimalism first appeared on his 1977 release *The New Earth,* a collection of solo tunes more eschatological in their message, yet with a softer, more personal musical style. This shift in Talbot's public aesthetic prefigured a deeper and more important spiritual transformation about to alter his entire career.

Talbot's spiritual quest led him eventually to the Alverna Retreat Center, a Franciscan facility back home in Indianapolis. At Alverna Talbot confronted the finality of his divorce, the impending death of his father, the cost of supporting his family, the changing form of his music ministry, and the Franciscan imperatives of poverty and loving service to a broken world. From March 1978 to February 1980 he lived as a contemplative hermit at Alverna except for his concert trips. Under the guidance of Walter Molter, OFM, his spiritual director, Talbot converted to Catholicism and submitted his music ministry to its traditions and authority. On September 8, 1978, Talbot took the vows of a Third Order Franciscan, promising to be chaste, poor, and obedient in pursuing his vocation in the world.[7] Accordingly, he began to compose songs informed by Franciscan spirituality and to perform them in the simple brown-robed habit of the great thirteenth-century Italian saint. Even the specific course of his music ministry was revealed. Talbot wrote in June 1978 that "[the Lord] told me the degree of acceptance and popularity he would give me. He gave me the songs to sing, the albums to record, and the concerts in which to appear."[8]

Talbot's pilgrimage seemed to have found its end in the Franciscan movement, but he had in fact encountered something much larger: the Catholic Church progressing in full stride toward liturgical and spiritual renewal. John Michael Talbot—Indiana Methodist, rock star, Christian contemporary artist, and Franciscan convert—met the post–Vatican II Catholic Church in America head-on. There was much for him to learn.

Catholic Liturgical and Charismatic Renewal

The reasons for Talbot's extraordinary success extend far beyond his musical talents. His music reflects and expresses some of the most powerful forces that shaped late twentieth-century American Catholicism. Indeed his greatest significance may ultimately lie not in his musical artistry but in his ability to articulate and represent those forces. Two of them opened the way for Talbot's career: the Liturgical Renewal and the Charismatic Renewal. The first transformed the task and style of Catholic sacred music, admitting new artists like Talbot. The second provided a youthful, spirit-filled constituency that enthusiastically received his music and his vision. Without these two movements, it is doubtful that Talbot ever would have become Catholic or that the church would have accepted him and his music ministry.

The Liturgical Renewal was a century-long movement vindicated and finally authorized by the Second Vatican Council (1961–64).[9] The very first legislative act of Vatican II was the promulgation of *Sacrosanctum Concilium*, the Constitution on the Sacred Liturgy, on December 4, 1963. Like subsequent Vatican II legislation, this decree revolutionized church practice even as it affirmed the deep structure of Catholic tradition. *Sacrosanctum* is most famous for abandoning Latin as the exclusive language for the Mass and authorizing its celebration in vernacular languages as approved by local bishops. This epochal and controversial change, however, was itself the result of an even more fundamental revision of church thinking about liturgy and the sacred arts. Muting the Council of Trent's sixteenth-century emphasis on the valid performance of the liturgy, Vatican II shifted to a more qualitative standard for true worship based in the experience of the people.

Proclaiming that "something more is required than the mere observation of the laws governing valid and licit celebration" of the liturgy and that "all the faithful should be led to . . . full, conscious, and active participation in liturgical celebrations," *Sacrosanctum Concilium* acknowledged that "the liturgy is made up of immutable elements divinely instituted, *and of elements subject to change* [emphasis added]." Liturgical expression, the Council said in effect, should be open to ongoing experimentation and development. Its validity should judged by how effectively the people understand it and how authentically they participate in it. Hence, the language and ritual forms of liturgy should be those of the people.[10]

Sacrosanctum also presented a new theology of sacred music and a new set of guidelines for its production. Liturgical music should be familiar enough to encourage "active participation" and to build a "sense of community," the Council said. Far more than simply an ancillary medium for carrying sacred words, music itself can express a unique kind of holiness. It has the capacity to "unveil a dimension of meaning and feeling, a communication of ideas and intuitions that words alone cannot yield." As such, music holds a standing "greater even than that of any other art," and "as sacred song united to the words, it forms a necessary or integral part of the solemn liturgy."[11]

To reveal this dimension, sacred music must adhere to the three traditional Catholic criteria of sanctity, good form, and universality, but *Sacrosanctum* revoked the privileged status of Gregorian chant and Renaissance polyphony as the exclusive stylistic standards for liturgical music mandated by Trent. Any musical form or tradition was now to be regarded as capable of performing the functions of sacred music, so long as it conformed to the three criteria. Even the primacy of the human voice and the organ in liturgical music, absolute by Tridentine standards, was modified in *Sacrosanctum*. Other instruments could be used "on condition that the instruments are suitable, or can be made suitable, for sacred use, according with the dignity of the temple, and truly contribute to the edification of the faithful."[12]

Vatican II applied to liturgical music the principle of enculturation, the merging of universal Catholic teachings and forms with local, national, and ethnic traditions. "In certain parts of the world," *Sacrosanctum* taught, "especially in mission lands, there are peoples who have their own musical traditions, and these play a great part in their religious and social life. For this reason due importance is to be attached to their music, and a suitable place is to be given to it, not only in forming their attitude toward religion, but also in adapting worship to their native genius."[13]

At one stroke, the Council had opened Catholic sacred music to the forces of change and cultural diversity. The American church was quick to explore these implications. The U.S. Bishops Commission on the Liturgy warmly welcomed the new use of instruments. "The music of today," it wrote in 1972, "regularly presumes that song is accompanied. This places instruments in a different light. The song achieves much of its vitality from the rhythm and harmony of its accompaniment. Instrumental accompaniment is a great support to an assembly in learning new music and in giving full voice to its prayer and praise in worship."[14]

The United States offered a dramatic example of cultural and musical diversity, which the American bishops cited in a 1972 call for aggressively enculturated sacred music: "Liturgical music today must be as diverse and multi-cultural as the members of the assembly. Pastors and musicians must encourage not only the use of traditional music of other languages, but also the composition of new liturgical music appropriate to various cultures. Likewise the great musical gifts of the Hispanic, Black, and other ethnic communities in the church should enrich the whole church in the United States in a dialogue of cultures."[15]

The call for new sacred song coincided with the rise of folk and rock musical styles in America during the late 1960s and 1970s. The earliest response came from American Catholic composers who leapt into the breach with popular unison settings of the new English Mass grounded in the folksong revival style of Pete Seeger and Joan Baez. The introduction of "folk mass" music with guitar accompaniment sparked new liturgical interest among church youth, especially in the Northeast and Midwest. One of the earliest and most popular folk mass pieces was Peter Scholtes's 1966 setting of the Sanctus (example 26 on page 370). Just as these new norms and styles of the liturgical renewal were taking hold, John Michael Talbot was leaving Mason Proffit and taking up his vocation as a Christian sacred-music artist. There was now theological room in principle, where there had been none at all before Vatican II, for music of Talbot's popular American style to be integrated into Catholic worship and praise.

It was the Charismatic Renewal, however, that brought Talbot into Catholicism and provided him with a significant Catholic audience. Vatican II spoke often of the importance of reanimating the church through the action of the Holy Spirit. Indeed, one of its crucial debates concerned whether the charisms of the Spirit described in the New Testament, including the gifts of tongues, vision, and prophecy, had ended with the apostolic church. Leon Joseph Cardinal Suenens of Brussels led a successful effort to convince the council that scriptural charismata persisted into the present day. He also helped persuade the council to appeal for spiritual renewal as part of its *aggiornamento*, its adjournment agenda of 1964. The Charismatic Renewal began in America less than three years later. It exploded with enormous worldwide influence throughout the next two decades. Suenens, himself a charismatic, remained a stalwart sponsor and advocate of the movement.

The Renewal began among students at Duquesne University in Pittsburgh during a February 1967 retreat. "At a time of social and religious crises throughout their own country and the world at large," Suenens wrote in his 1975 book *A New Pentecost?* "some of these young people, realizing the impossibility of finding a human solution, met for a weekend of prayer and fasting to ask the grace of the Holy Spirit." At the retreat "an amazing spiritual transformation took place in them," Suenens reported. "They spoke of a new awareness of the love of God such as they had not experienced before; of a desire to pray and glorify God; of an insatiable thirst for Scripture. Moreover they felt power within them to bear witness to the risen Jesus. They talked of a 'baptism in the Holy Spirit' and of charisms given to them similar to those of which we read in the early Church."[16]

From Duquesne the Charismatic Renewal spread quickly to other American campuses, notably Notre Dame, Michigan, Loyola of New Orleans, and UCLA. "Soon prayer groups began to spring up," Suenens observed, "not only on university campuses but also in parishes, monasteries, and convents, first in the United States and then in the five continents." One illustration must suffice to suggest the immense scale of Catholic charismatic growth over just a few years. In 1967 the first national conference of American Catholic charismatics drew about one hundred people; by 1973 the International Catholic Charismatic Conference at Notre Dame was attended by 22,000 participants from thirty-five countries, including six hundred priests and ten bishops. A year later, 30,000 gathered. From the mid-1970s through the early 1990s the movement continued to expand at a remarkable rate everywhere in the Catholic world.

The Charismatic Renewal had important consequences for Christian sacred song. As millions embraced the presence of the Holy Spirit in their lives, they sought musical expression of their experience in worship. *Sacrosanctum* had brought simple folk settings of the Mass into wide circulation by the late 1960s. A few years later the Charismatic Renewal sought sacred songs in this same musical style to express their experience. On the Protestant side of the revival, Pentecostals and Evangelicals built on a well-established tradition of gospel hymns and gospel songs to construct new musical articulations for the movement of the Spirit. Around 1970 these musical and religious forces combined to create the praise song, the characteristic song form of the Charismatic Renewal.

Most closely akin to evangelical Protestant gospel songs and revival choruses, with historic roots in camp-meeting songs and gospel hymns, the praise song featured repeated refrains with melodies and simple harmonic progressions derived from folk, gospel, and pop styles. Textually, the praise song emphasized emotional first-person lyrics of intense Christological piety. The praise song also employed a new mode of transmission. Instead of relying on printed song collections, Catholic and Protestant charismatics used the then–avante garde overhead projector, which could fill an entire wall with text and melody to be sung by large worshipping assemblies.

Critics assailed praise songs as musically derivative and theologically self-centered, but these alleged flaws did not hamper their ever-increasing appeal. By the mid-1970s the praise song had become the most popular form of American Catholic sacred song, later embodied definitively in *Glory and Praise,* a hugely popular collection of post–Vatican II worship music first published in 1987. *Glory and Praise* created hymnological history by becoming the first American Catholic hymnal ever to enjoy wide circulation in the church, found in parish pews and retreat centers across the land. Typical of the collection was John Foley's 1978 eucharistic hymn, "One Bread, One Body." Foley was the leader of a group of young singer-composers universally known as "the Saint Louis Jesuits" whose songs and recordings fixed the form of the Charismatic movement praise song. "One Bread, One Body" was a classic of the new genre, fusing together the earlier folk mass harmonies with the popular ballad style of the 1970s (example 27 on page 372).[17]

From the very beginning, the Charismatic Renewal movement was marked by a synthesis of personal spirituality, community, and social action. Suenens listed four kinds of community that the movement had produced by 1975 on an increasing scale of commitment: weekly eucharistic meetings; households of social action where charismatics lived together and supported one another in their individual ministries; houses of prayer for charismatic contemplative communities; and covenant communities, which experimented in the community of goods and discipline by consensus.[18] During his time at Alverna, John Michael Talbot met with and performed for every kind of Charismatic Renewal community. The depth of their spirituality and commitment greatly influenced him.

After taking his Third Order vows, Talbot turned to the question of how to pursue his own vision of community. On September 11, 1978, Talbot wrote in his journal that "I feel closer to discovering the Catholic structure from which to bring forth my ministry. I feel it should be a combination of charismatic renewal and Third Order in a new move toward community that I will now call simply 'Charity.'"[19] Soon Talbot's vision of a multidimensional charismatic community of contemplation and action began to attract followers to Alverna. He received permission to remodel an old tool shed into a prayer chapel for his followers that he called "Little Portion" in honor of the Portiuncula at Assisi, the stable where St. Francis organized his first community in 1208. He also designed a modified Franciscan habit for his nascent community.

Meanwhile Talbot concluded work on his next album, *The Lord's Supper,* a collection of settings for eucharistic texts that signaled his embrace of Catholicism. By the spring of 1979 it was a certified hit. The content of the album and its popularity among Catholic audiences enabled Talbot to shift the focus of his music ministry. "God has told me to play only for credible sponsors who are

interested in unity and a return to early church catholicity," he wrote in his journal on April 25, 1979.

> With the success of *The Lord's Supper* album, many such Catholic sponsors are
> calling to ask me to come to their area and minister. I believe I will shortly be
> able to play almost exclusively for interdenominational renewal activities com-
> ing forth from the structure of the Catholic Church. The Charismatic Renewal
> and the Franciscan Order co-sponsoring the "Charity" program with other
> Catholic-minded fellowships seems to be a very real alternative to my past sit-
> uation. With all of this, I must simply recognize that Jesus doesn't ask you to
> do something unless he plans on helping you to do it.[20]

Eureka Springs

On an early summer evening nearly fifteen years after Talbot's Third Order
Franciscan vows, I was rolling through a beautiful Ozark Mountain landscape
in northern Arkansas. It looked a lot like Vermont or East Tennessee, emptier
than either, where distant fields, farms, and forests recalled the illustrations in
a child's storybook. I approached Eureka Springs, where I had arranged to visit
the Little Portion Hermitage of the Brothers and Sisters of Charity (BSC) and
to interview its general minister and superior, John Michael Talbot. Old Eureka
Springs turned out to be a resort town of postbellum yellow stone and brick
buildings built around the Carrol County Courthouse and the Old Basin Spring
Bath House. The town developed during the late nineteenth-century heyday of
hydrotherapy, when hot natural spring water baths were recommended to cure
ailments ranging from arthritis to dyspepsia. Today the storefront shops sell
quilts, souvenirs, clothes, ice cream, and curios to friendly crowds of young families and senior citizens.

But old Eureka Springs was not my destination. To find Little Portion Retreat
Center, I traveled a few miles further east to where new Eureka Springs bespoke
a very different cultural agenda: neon, country music, and the Christian tourist trade. The highway was lined with motels, theaters, fast food, moped rent-
als, and candy stores. I passed the Suwannee River Boys Country Review, the
Pine Mountain Jamboree, and the Anita Bryant Theater, where the veteran singer
was performing live. At the Ozark Mountain Hoedown Music Theater, a large
auditorium with a red barn false front, a large crowd had gathered to hear the
King's River Boys perform. The Original Cast Hoedown Gang were all there,
too. Past the Fun Spot water rides and go-karts, large billboards announced the
Great Passion Play and the Christ of the Ozarks Statue. Further down the highway, signs advised the traveler that Miracle Mansion was available for weddings,
as was the Crown of Thorns Chapel. As I drove the highway out of town, I saw
the Little Portion Community Store on the left in an old stone building.

Talbot's Little Portion Hermitage at Berryville bears an ambiguous symbolic relationship to nearby Eureka Springs. While Talbot and his followers seek to embody a post–Vatican II vision of Christian poverty, service, and community in a rural Arkansas setting, they are also enmeshed in a network of religious commerce that they themselves have promoted and from which they benefit. In this sense the Great Passion Play, Miracle Mansion, Crown of Thorns Chapel, and Little Portion are all linked together in the Christian entertainment industry that enriches Eureka Springs as much as it does Nashville. This commerce nurtures Talbot's community economically and threatens it spiritually. The challenge to Talbot and his people at Little Portion is the same one that Saint Paul articulated, namely, how to be Christians in the world but not of it. To his credit, Talbot has taken on that apostolic challenge directly, and appropriately so, because his ministry cannot prosper entirely in the world nor can it survive outside of it.

The Christ of the Ozarks and the Great Passion Play exemplify this tension. According to the official literature of the place, one day during the early 1960s Gerald Smith, discoverer and developer of Magnetic Mountain, remarked to his wife, Edna, "here should stand a giant monument as a memorial to Christ, to be known as 'The Christ of the Ozarks Statue.'" Smith commissioned sculptor Emmet Sullivan to create the statue, which was dedicated in 1966. This impressive statue, an angular image of the resurrected Jesus robed and hooded with his arms outstretched, stands seven stories high and weighs more than one million pounds.

The instant popularity of the Christ of the Ozarks Statue gave rise to the Great Passion Play, initiated on the grounds in 1968. The Smiths constructed a 1,300-seat amphitheater near the statue, containing a permanent set depicting their idea of the Jerusalem of Jesus' time. On this set they portrayed the story of Christ's Passion, "presented by a cast of more than 200 actors, live animals, authentic Biblical costuming, multi-level staging, [and] the latest in lighting and sound technology." By 1994 the Great Passion Play grounds had expanded to include a Sacred Arts Center, a Bible Museum, a Woodcarving Gallery, the Smith Memorial Chapel, the Church in the Grove, a memorial fragment of the Berlin Wall, two gift shops, a snack shop, a yogurt shop, and a "reconstruction" of "the Tabernacle in the Wilderness" described in Exodus 25:40, since expanded into a "New Holy Land Tour," a living biblical exhibition with thirty-seven more "reconstructed" sites.[21]

The Great Passion Play prospered during the Bicentennial Revival of the late 1970s and 1980s; by 1993, its twenty-fifth anniversary season, more than five million people had attended the production, touted as "America's foremost outdoor drama." From the beginning, the Passion Play offered songs and musical accompaniment as part of its presentation. During the early 1980s the play became closely associated with Talbot's own musical activity. In 1984 Phil Perkins, Talbot's producer, composed a new music program for the play, which was produced by Terry Talbot, John's brother, and distributed by Sparrow

Records, his label. Whether this association derived from Christian fellowship, artistic interest, profit, or simple neighborliness, it aptly illustrates the kind of religious and commercial forces swirling around Talbot's domain.

The intersection I wanted was marked out among the tourist clutter by a large sign of an Indian chieftain in full battle headdress advertising Onyx Cave. Just before the cave parking lot, I took the right-hand fork and drove several miles down a gravel road through woods and fields to a small hand-lettered sign marking a sharp left up a steep hill to Little Portion Retreat and Study Center. I pulled into the parking lot of a simple wooden structure that resembled a rural motel. The Retreat Center was comprised of three buildings, Alpha (office and a few visitors' rooms), Omega (kitchen, meeting hall, and chapel), and Walden (main retreat residence), linked by a porch with outdoor sofas and rocking chairs. The complex was built at the summit of a ridge looking out over fifty miles of Ozark foothills stretching north into Missouri. Nearby, an openwork belltower centered a sprinkling of small cottages housing the Retreat Center staff.

After settling into my room at Alpha, I explored the rest of the facility and met several people who earlier in the day had joined more than thirty others as the first "domestics" ever professed in the Brothers and Sisters of Charity. They had pledged to abide by the society's rule and its vows of poverty, chastity, and obedience while pursuing their daily lives and careers in the world. They spoke excitedly about a simple service of profession at the Little Portion chapel in which each of them recited promises of poverty, chastity, and obedience. After the service, the community celebrated this milestone in its history with several hours of spontaneous worship, praise, and charismatic gifts.

Walking back to my room under a star-studded Ozark sky, I reflected on the ironies of this peaceful place. Talbot bought the land in the fall of 1972, when he was nineteen years old and starring with Mason Proffit. He had purchased it in response to his 1971 vision of a rural community revealed to him by Jesus. In those days old Eureka Springs was pretty much the only significant town in the northern Ozarks. The beauty, peace, and religious fervor of the region had then drawn Talbot to buy 1,500 acres. His tract of land is still peaceful, still pristine. But only a few miles away up on the ridge, new Eureka Springs symbolizes much of what Talbot once enjoyed but now resists: mindless wasteful development, popular but insubstantial country music, and commercial promotion of the Christian message.

Little Portion

Little Portion Hermitage is located four miles down the ridge from the Retreat Center over dirt and gravel roads. The complex was laid out on a hillside with a more restricted view of the northern Ozark foothills. To the right, a row of twelve ultramodern wooden dwellings descended, built partially into the hill. Solar panels studded the roof of each structure and they were glazed with glare-resistant glass. Bicycles and toys strewn about the yard of each dwelling evidenced the presence of young families. At the end of the roadway a chapel rose, also built of wood and glass, surrounded by a traditional southern porch and surmounted by a cross. To its left stood a large refectory and all-purpose office building; beyond, two dozen smaller cabins lined a meandering stream. Gardens and barns spread farther down the hill past the cabins.

It was a blazing July day, and exhausting heat greeted me as I walked down the gravel driveway past the family dwellings. Talbot was sitting on the small porch of the refectory, chatting with some brothers and sisters. He was robed and shod in the same brown habit and sandals he wore at the Holy Cross Cathedral concert. He was taller than he appeared on stage yet slimmer, older looking than some of his publicity photos suggested yet still bearing the youthful look of early middle age. He welcomed me cordially and ushered me inside for our interview. The refectory contained a kitchen and a dining room that seated perhaps fifty people. The rest of the building was devoted to a suite of offices for Talbot and his chief staff members. We settled in the library to talk about Talbot's career, his Christian music, and his community.

We began with "The Master Musician" project, the book and compact-disc recording rehearsed at the Holy Cross concert. What was the inspiration for this project? "I [began] asking how did Jesus teach?" he answered. "He mainly used parables. They are very simple, they teach fundamentals, and they are mystical all at once. And that's my heart, because of my monastic bent and orientation. I said, 'Well, Lord, I'd like to do that too. I know how to garden and cut wood, but how do I do this?' He said, 'Well, what do you know?' I said 'I know music.' He said, 'Use that which you know.' I just sat down and a week later I had written this book." A book written in a week? "I work fast for trade books," Talbot remarked, "I didn't know what would come out. It was almost a one-write situation. We took it to Sparrow Publications, thinking of it first as a story, but it came off too contrived. I put it out as it was. And the music came the next week."

I asked him how the music "came to him." "Generally what happens is I pray," Talbot answered, "a melody will begin, and almost immediately, the particular text will float right in as an inspiration or as an adaptation. I rarely take a text and begin with it."

"You have the integration of text and tune immediately?" I asked.

"Yes," he said, "and then it just starts. I write pretty fast. I used to take time, but now I'm faster. For *Meditations in the Spirit* (1993), at one point I was writing two songs a day." The question of composition led quickly to Talbot's understanding of himself as an artist, a subject that revealed some of his strongest opinions about religious music culture in America. "I don't consider myself a Christian contemporary artist," he said, "not a liturgical artist. Some of what I write can spill over into that, but I consider myself a sacred music artist. I would like [my music] to be considered an icon in sound. In the spirit of the icon you pray, fast, and seek; then the music comes out."

For Talbot, the principal actions of sacred-music performer and audience should be worship, praise, and prayer, not aesthetic enjoyment or entertainment. This orientation led him in our interview to criticize Christian contemporary music not only for its commercialism but more fundamentally for its less-than-sacred intentionality. According to Talbot it makes the fundamental mistake of succumbing to the very worldliness against which it seeks to witness.

> Christian contemporary music sees people of this culture, which is a pagan culture, and says, they're way out there but they're starting to turn, so we're going to go way out where they are and walk them back. Now the problem I have with this is that it sometimes goes out and stays there. It does not pull the people, as individuals or as a cultural body, back into the wealth of the church. So what ends up happening is that instead of being Christians in America and forming society through the arts in a way that gets them to God, it simply degenerates by reaching out to the world and becoming worldly.

Talbot distinguished sharply between "entertainment-oriented ministry" and "ministry-oriented entertainment." Both are valid, but he argued that there is not nearly enough of the latter. The consequences of this situation are, in his view, dire. "There's nothing wrong with entertainment-oriented ministry," he said. "It's a fine thing, but when it becomes the focus, the center, and the determining factor and direction, then it becomes dangerous." Talbot objects not only to Christian contemporary music's excessively worldly style but also to the kind of religion it purports to advance. "I believe that American Christianity is a heresy and I believe that the industry of the Christian Broadcasters Association has become a Whore of Babylon. I've said this openly and that's why many of the industry people don't want to hang around with me. And I don't say this with any malice or judgment. It's up to God to judge hearts and souls."

Asked about his own music ministry, Talbot did not deny a certain necessary element of entertainment. "I hope my music is entertaining," he said, "because [otherwise] you won't listen to it. It's got to hold your interest. Even if it's quiet and prayerful and contemplative, there's got to be something about it on the psychological level and the artistic level that makes it interesting. I hope it's entertaining, but that's not my focus." When pressed to characterize his own music, Talbot was surprisingly vague. He located his own creativity by what it is not rather than by what it is. "My music is just my music," he responded, "it seems to be unique. I'm grateful for that. It doesn't fit into New Age, into World Music, into liturgical, into classical sacred music, into Christian contemporary music, or into traditional gospel music."

By contrast, Talbot was clear and emphatic about the intentionality behind his performance agenda. "I pray and I let the Lord take care of the people," he remarked. "I want them to get a catholic sense of the faith. And I don't mean the word in the denominational sense: the word means universal and complete.

I want them to get a full sense of the faith. So I go to the Old Testament, I do some things on Mary, which, surprisingly, non-Catholics like. [I] focus on Jesus, focus on the church, on the idea of sacrament, on the idea of some ecclesiology [the theology of the people of God]. And I try in an intuitive sense to walk people through it."

There is a strongly evangelistic cast to this agenda. Talbot is not simply singing to the converted. He carries a message of Franciscan spirituality melded with Vatican II activism and liturgical reform, along with not a little evangelical Protestant revivalism. He delivers this message to audiences primarily Catholic in identity but significantly Protestant as well, most of them charismatic, all of whom, he believes, need to hear his new articulation of God's word. Despite this evangelistic emphasis, however, Talbot understands his concert ministry to encompass more than just teaching and preaching. In prayer, in singing elements of the Mass, and in celebrating the presence of Christ, he seeks to make his concerts generate a spiritual synergy. "I hope that my concerts are liturgical, they are catechetical, they are sacramental. That's what I try to have happen."

What makes John Michael Talbot unique in American sacred music, however, is more than his successful blend of popular music style with Catholic and evangelical charismatic spirituality. He is the only sacred-music artist to have founded an officially sanctioned Catholic religious community, the Brothers and Sisters of Charity. This institutional innovation suggests the power of his vision and of his music, but it also raises important questions about the relationship between his music ministry and his role as a religious superior. Talbot himself has thought long and hard about these matters. Since the late 1970s he has been engaged in reconciling the demands and rewards of concert performance with his own quest for contemplative community and Christian moral action in the world. He has long since come to a settled position on these complex issues, embodied in the mission of Little Portion.

The BSC is a "public association of the faithful" given canonical status by the Vatican as an experimental form of ecumenical religious community. There are only ten such authorized "public associations" worldwide. BSC is the only one in the United States. Its ecumenical vision is rooted ultimately in the Franciscan tradition so formative for Talbot himself: "We say that we try to integrate the realities of all religions from a uniquely Christian base," he explained, "of all Christian faiths from a uniquely Catholic base, and of all Christian religious and monastic traditions from a uniquely Franciscan base. But we are not a Franciscan community. Franciscanism is our mother, we are its child."

As a Catholic religious community, the BSC looks most like an institutionalized combination of Cardinal Suenens's four social forms of the Charismatic Renewal. The community's rule, written by Talbot, is notable for its embrace of four different varieties of religious living: celibates, singles, and covenanted families—all living in monastic community at the Hermitage—and domestics living under vows in the world. Celibates follow traditional norms of Franciscan monasticism, poverty, chastity, and obedience. Singles, both male and female, observe the same standards but are free to marry if their vocations lead them in that direction. Covenanted families are the most innovative feature of Talbot's community. Inspired by his experiences in the Charismatic Renewal as well as the Catholic lay apostolic societies of the seventeenth century, Talbot insisted that whole families be included in his community and observe its precepts. The domestics—some single, some married—follow the BSC's norms in their professional lives and personal vocations while living outside the monastic community. All prospective members of the community must master Talbot's books *Changes, The Fire of God,* and *Simplicity,* which articulate his spiritual and social appropriation of the Charismatic Renewal, as part of their novitiate. Today there are about forty professed BSC monastics at Little Portion and five hundred domestics worldwide.[22]

My first question about the BSC concerned money. Talbot's recordings have grossed millions of dollars and he earns thousands for each appearance. The infusion of such large sums poses a problem of dependency for any religious community. That problem afflicted both Talbot's Alverna community and Little Portion after the BSC was founded in 1984. "Good people would come here," he recalled, "and those people became dependent on me. I became the sugar daddy. A love-hate psychological relationship developed and it became a very grown-in-on-itself, sick place."

In 1987 Talbot reformed the community, establishing a new set of regulations designed to limit his personal control of funding and to promote the traditional monastic norm of self-sufficiency. "I've taken a personal vow of poverty," Talbot told me. "I give everything I make to the community or to its civil corporation." Talbot's recording and concert income was restricted to certain specified uses. "The monies generated are used as what we call a benevolent benefactor," he explained. "It can be used for buying land, for building buildings, or sending out new ministries. It's dedicated. But the food, the utilities, and the daily stuff of running a community cannot be overly dependent on me."

Providing operating expenses is the community's collective economic task, not Talbot's. Some family members work out in the world, while others, along with the celibates and singles, concentrate on producing goods for sale at the community store and on developing Little Portion's farm, which now produces more than two-thirds of all food used by the Hermitage. The community's rules mandate a sliding scale of economic commitment. "The families in this community only have to give a third of what they may generate to the community," Talbot noted. "Singles have to give two-thirds, and the celibates give everything. So it's not a strict communism, it's a graduated social structure, and as people become more committed they usually want to give more. So we may end up that all of the permanently professed own all things in common."

Talbot and the BSC have applied the "evangelical counsels" of traditional Christian monasticism—poverty, chastity, and obedience—to create a prophetic community living over against contemporary American cultural values. "We're trying to live out poverty in the face of American consumerism," he proclaimed. "We're trying to live out chastity according to the single celibate or marital states of life in the face of what we believe to be rampant sexual promiscuity. We're trying to live out gospel values of dependency on God and interdependency on each other in obedience to God in the context of the church and the communities of the church, in contrast to rampant individualism."

Vatican authorities were at first skeptical that such an ecumenical, intergenerational community of contemplation and action could work in America. "They believe that our individualism is really at the bottom line," Talbot reported to me. "After all our worship services and all of our hymn sings and all our televangelist preachers, and all of our altar calls, and all of our sacraments, [they think] the bottom line of the Americans is, 'now I'm going to do what I want to do.' Therefore they ask the legitimate question: does Catholicism work in America? I believe it has to work here. If it doesn't work here, I don't believe Christianity can work here, and I'd hate to believe that." To the contrary, Talbot is convinced that the BSC is "a prototype of the church in the future" to redeem the corruption of American religious and cultural life. "I agree with Chuck Colson that we are in a moral and spiritual dark ages," he said, "and I believe that there need to be many communities such as this in the United States."

What is the relationship between Talbot's community and his music? Both monastics and domestics reported a wide range of responses to Talbot's performances and recordings varying from rapt enthusiasm to polite indifference. Talbot's 1987 reform removed most adherents drawn solely by his music and personality, but just three years later he recorded a two-volume album of praise songs, *Come Worship the Lord,* with the community in Little Portion Chapel. These authentic recordings of worship among the BSC rank with Talbot's most successful works and spawned a best-selling songbook. The title song is Talbot's 1980 setting of Psalm 95, a classic example of his synthesis of praise song style with biblically based text that became an anthem of the Charismatic Revival (example 28 on page 374).

The music and the community do, therefore, seem to be linked, and Talbot insisted that they are coordinated elements of his ministry because their common source lies in the charism of the Holy Spirit. "The music is part of the community," he said, "but the community charism is different in its present development. Ultimately I believe the music and the community's charism is the same. They are at different stages of development, but the community is ultimately similar to the music and the music to the community." When I asked him to specify the commonality between his music and his community, Talbot told of his community moving through a "fiery and zealous" beginning, then softening and flowering as its roots go deeper, and finally reforming in order to regain "the edge" for its true mission. The ongoing purification of the community, he believes, will eventually harmonize with his music in a common public expression of the Spirit.

Talbot's account of a fiery beginning, deeper rooting, then softening and flowering before reforming to regain "the edge" might just as appropriately describe his own twenty-five-year career as a sacred-music artist. After Mason Proffit he passed through the flaming spiritual power of the charismatic movement of the late 1970s, a historic moment of spiritual renewal that powerfully changed America's Catholic and Protestant Christians. He sent down roots at Alverna, embracing the Franciscan vision of mendicant poverty and service to the poor and placing his music at its good service. His vision has flowered at Little Portion, where he promulgates a new yet very American pattern of ecumenical, intergenerational community of married and celibate brothers and sisters committed to a life of prayer and social action. In the past few years he has reformed that community and brought it into conformity with the traditional monastic standards of the Roman Catholic Church while preserving its American experimentalism. With the profession of hundreds of new domestics and monastics worldwide, he now believes that both he and the BSC have regained "the edge" they need to reclaim America and the world. Meanwhile the music, the books, and the recordings pour forth as this Troubadour for the Lord continues on his pilgrim's way.

Notes

1. John Michael Talbot, *The Master Musician* (Grand Rapids, Mich.: Zondervan Publishing House, 1992), and Troubadour for the Lord Records TDD4620.

2. Copyright to Talbot's recordings and writings has since 1993 been consolidated under the colophon of Troubadour for the Lord, Eureka Springs, Ark. Additional information about them may be found at <http://www.john-michael-talbot.org> and <http://www.johnmichaeltalbot.com>.

3. John Michael Talbot, *Changes: A Spiritual Journal* (New York: Crossroads, 1984), 6.

4. Ibid.

5. Ibid., 14.

6. John Michael Talbot, interview with author, Little Portion Hermitage, Eureka Springs, Ark., July 9, 1994. All subsequent quotations are taken from this interview unless otherwise indicated in the text.

7. Kajetan Esser, *Origins of the Franciscan Order* (Chicago: Franciscan Herald Press, 1970), 203–17.

8. Talbot, *Changes*, 14.

9. See James Herbert Srawley, *The Liturgical Movement: Its Origin and Growth* (New York: Alcuin Club, 1957); Horton Davies, *Worship and Theology in England: The Ecumenical Century, 1900–1965* (Princeton, N.J.: Princeton University Press, 1965); and Herman Schmitt, ed., *Liturgy in Transition*, Concilium: Religion in the Seventies 62 (New York: Herder and Herder, 1971).

10. Miriam Therese Winter, *Why Sing?: Toward a Theology of Catholic Church Music* (Washington, D.C.: Pastoral Press, 1984), 50–52.

11. Ibid., 159; *Sacrosanctum Concilium*, Constitution on the Sacred Liturgy, December 4, 1963, trans. National Catholic Welfare Conference News Service, *AAS* 56 (1964): 112.

12. *Sacrosanctum Concilium*, 120.

13. Ibid., 119.

14. Bishops Committee on Liturgy, *Liturgical Music Today* (Washington, D.C.: U.S. Catholic Conference, 1972), 57.

15. Ibid., 55.

16. Leon Joseph Cardinal Suenens, *A New Pentecost?* (New York: Seabury Press, 1975), 77.

17. *Glory and Praise* (Phoenix, Ariz.: North American Liturgy Resources/GIA Publications, 1987).

18. Suenens, *A New Pentecost?* 79.

19. Talbot, *Changes*, 73.

20. Ibid., 116.

21. This account of the Great Passion Play/Christ of the Ozarks is based on promotional materials provided at Eureka Springs and current information on the play's Web site at <http://www.greatpassionplay.org>.

22. See Frances Ryan and John E. Rybolt, eds., *Vincent de Paul and Louise de Marillac: Rules, Conferences, and Writings* (New York: Paulist Press, 1995).

CHAPTER 10

The Conservatory Tradition:
Interviews with Daniel Pinkham
and Neely Bruce

Most of the sacred song we have explored to this point has been either traditional or popular. It was created by traditional sacred singers whose identity is long lost to memory or, more recently, by musicians whose training took place in popular venues: the singing school, the blues house, the rock concert. This salience of popular and traditional forms itself speaks volumes about the democratic roots of American sacred song, but there is another vitally important sector to be considered. It may best be called sacred art music, and its central institution is the conservatory, which sustains the elite composers and players who perform and create it.

Sacred art music employs two major public performance venues, the concert hall and the elite church-music program. Its primary repertory ranges from the Renaissance and baroque works of Palestrina, Bach, and Handel through the masses of Mozart and Haydn to the huge sacred works of the nineteenth century, including Beethoven's *Missa Solemnis,* Mendelssohn's *Elijah,* and the Requiem settings of Berlioz, Brahms, and Verdi. This is music of great difficulty requiring the finest players and conductors to perform. Urban and suburban Protestant congregations regularly undertake smaller works of this kind, but the larger compositions are almost exclusively the realm of symphony orchestras who perform them as part of the standard repertory. This concert-hall dominance is even more absolute for sacred works by recent and contemporary composers from Leonard Bernstein to Krzysztof Penderecki, György Ligeti, and Henryk Górecki.

Sacred art music is the public domain of sacred song where the conservatory's musical professionalism encounters urban religious culture. This encounter produces unique tensions for composers, performers, and their audiences. Conservatory programs in composition, for example, have a universal standard of excellence whether taught at the Juilliard School in New York, the Curtis Institute in Philadelphia, the New England Conservatory in Boston, or in major music programs attached to colleges and universities. Any well-trained composer ought to be able to write a choral or solo setting for a sacred text. But how does a composer approach the religious dimension of that task, if at all? Do they use religious tradition, or personal spirituality, or both? On the church side of the encounter, highly trained organists and choir directors guide the music of America's elite urban congregations, but by what criteria do they evaluate and select their musical materials? Are their choices a matter of musical proficiency and taste, religious identity and spiritual commitment, or both? And on the concert-hall side, is there any religious dimension at all to a public performance of a work like *Missa Solemnis* for either performers or audience? If so, what is it? What, if any, is the difference as public expression of religion between a performance in a church setting or in a concert hall?

To address these questions about sacred art music I interviewed Daniel Pinkham and Neely Bruce, two respected composers who have also long served as church music directors. While both possess conservatory training, they present sharp contrasts on most of the substantive questions. Many of those differences stem, no doubt, from their distance in age and cultural background. Pinkham is a senior composer and artist with deep roots in Boston and New England; Bruce is a generation younger, born and raised in Alabama and trained in the Midwest. Yet as the interviews make clear, their differing viewpoints are ultimately defined by their own practice of sacred-song composition and church music-making. These are the dimensions of sacred art music of greatest interest to our inquiry, and Pinkham and Bruce ably present two ends of the contemporary spectrum. Since the two interviews cover common questions with such different and free-flowing frames of reference, I have thought it best to present them verbatim rather than to attempt some sort of synthetic presentation.

Conservatory, Concert Hall, and Choir Loft: An Interview with Daniel Pinkham

Daniel Pinkham is the dean of American composers of sacred choral works. Trained by Aaron Copland, Walter Piston, and Archibald Davison at Harvard during the 1940s, Pinkham (b. 1923) is part of the postwar generation of composers who for a half-century have contributed liturgical music, psalm-settings, and hymn-settings written primarily for liberal Protestant churches and academic institutions.[1] Pinkham's career has been a paradigm for conservatory-trained composer-conductors in the church. For forty years he has occupied the forefront of the American composing scene, contributing a steady stream of distinguished choral and solo vocal works, most of which employ sacred or liturgical texts.

Pinkham's *Wedding Cantata* (1956), *Easter Cantata* (1957), and *Christmas Cantata* (1957) established his reputation as a composer and church musician. Appointments soon followed as director of music at Boston's prestigious King's Chapel in 1958 and as professor of composition at the New England Conservatory of Music in 1959. In the mid-1960s Pinkham experimented with other large liturgical texts and forms: *Requiem* (1963), *Stabat Mater* (1964), and *St. Mark Passion* (1965). Since this early burst of sacred compositions, Pinkham has continued to produce major religious works for chorus and orchestra, notably *Ascension Cantata* (1970), *Passion of Judas* (1973), *Hezekiah* (1979), *Conversion of Saul* (1981), and *Lauds* (1984).

Solo vocal compositions on biblical themes have accompanied these larger works, from *Song of Jephtha's Daughter* (1963) to *Manger Scenes* (1980). Even Pinkham's major instrumental works have borne religious titles, especially the chamber works: *Toccatas for the Vault of Heaven* (1972), *Blessings* (1977), *Epiphanies* (1978), *Miracles* (1978), *Proverbs* (1980), *Vigils* (1982), and *Psalms* (1983). Of this *oeuvre* the *New Grove Dictionary of American Music* comments: "his music has remained sturdy in architecture and energetically polyphonic, and his harmony has become more chromatic." In October 1981 *Boston Globe* music critic Richard Dyer called Pinkham "a national resource." The most recent edition of the *New Grove Dictionary of Music and Musicians* aptly summarizes Pinkham's contribution to sacred music: "his attraction to biblical stories and liturgy led to a large body of works for organ, short choral pieces, songs, and extended sacred compositions for choir and instruments." By any measure he is one of America's best-known and most frequently performed composers of sacred art music.[2]

Most of Pinkham's religious works have been premiered at King's Chapel, where he performed, planned service music, organized concert series, and conducted the renowned choir of that prestigious downtown congregation for forty-two years. Pinkham proved to be a perfect match for King's, a unique Unitarian Universalist parish. King's was the second-oldest Church of England parish founded in Boston before it turned Unitarian in 1783 under its Revolutionary-era minister James Freeman. One of America's first great Unitarian leaders, Freeman produced an original liturgy for his congregation by amending the Anglican Book of Common Prayer to reflect his low-church views and his theology of God as one person existing in three distinguishable modalities. As a founding mother of American Unitarianism, King's Chapel still uses Freeman's liturgy in worship at its galleried English baroque church, built in 1763 by Peter Harrison, Boston's chief colonial architect.[3]

A pioneer in church music as well as in theology, King's installed one of America's first pipe organs in 1713 and has presented centuries of sacred-music premieres in Boston. In 1958 Pinkham, a nonbeliever of Episcopal background, took over a well-mounted if artistically staid music program at King's and immediately brought it into the world of American avant-garde choral composition and performance. The arrival of Carl Scovel as senior minister eight years later cemented Pinkham's presence at King's. Scovel's keen interest in the entire range of church music combined with Pinkham's dedication to a diverse repertoire to produce one of the nation's finest and most innovative church music programs. Daniel Pinkham retired as director of music at King's Chapel in May 2000.

One afternoon during the week of his fiftieth Harvard reunion, Pinkham talked with me at his modest Cambridge house. Our conversation ranged across matters of sacred choral composition, conservatory training, performance in the church and the concert hall, and life at King's Chapel. Pinkham studded his conversation with many original stories, aphorisms, and remarks. Though Pinkham only hoped to give "something of a minority report that may be useful," the interview stands as both documentation of and commentary on his generation's experience of sacred song among America's liberal urban Protestants.

Sacred Texts

SM: Sacred music, and sacred song in particular, seems on the whole to be text-based. When you are writing a sacred composition, frequently it is based on a text—a psalm or part of the liturgy. How do you understand the saliency or relative importance of that text? Do you get really engaged in the text? Is it from there that the inspiration comes? Or is it rather a musical expression that you find a text for?

DP: That reflects very well on your understanding about music, because as you know, with every piece it's different. When I go about setting, say, a psalm text, if it's something I've decided to do or it's something someone has asked, I almost always go to a variety of translations. I was also a Latin scholar, so I'm very comfortable with that. Actually I have two different Latin translations of the psalter, the *Liber Usualis* of course and there's also a much more recent twentieth-century one in Latin.[4] And then, I'm not hesitant about making a composite, or sometimes a new translation if I find that I want to make a text's comprehensibility clearer. Or sometimes I will find a word or a sound which will work better with the singing voice. It's a combination of things, but the text always comes first when I'm writing a piece.

The text is always the central part. The most difficult thing still for me is to find a text, whether it is a sacred or a secular piece. Once I have a text, then the piece is done. It's a little bit like Nadia Boulanger [1887–1979] saying to Maurice Ravel [1875–1937], "how's your new piece?" He says, "Oh, well it's all done except for the notes!" Now people laugh at that, but the composer understands exactly what it means. The piece happened to be *Bolero,* by the way. Because there was an abstract principle of repetition with different orchestration. So the text is always the most difficult thing.

Sometimes I find myself writing texts. I've been sort of *force majeur* for a collection of pieces, a biblical book of beasts in which little animals would appear musically. This is for little kids. I'm doing [another piece] with the ACDA—the American Choral Directors Association. I've just taken the title "Waters." And well, in this piece there's something about Genesis—"before there was light there was water"—and then it continues with Noah and the Ark, and then there are a number of other instances of biblical water [in it]. I don't know if that is a sacred piece or not. It's certainly inspired by biblical things.

SM: You're giving various responses to texts. On the one hand, water is a theme or concept that informs, but on the other, it sometimes sounds as if there are particular words or images that you associate with particular sounds. Let's say we're talking about what we agree is a religious text, a scriptural passage or a hymn. There are various ways in which you seem to respond. And I assume that response is everything from autobiographical influence to personal spirituality to musical sensibility. In a sense the text brings something to you and it is different every time.

DP: But you see, it has to work two ways. I have to think of my clients. And so, choosing something like water, actually the title is "Alleluia for the waters."

SM: That's good.

DP: Yes, it is good. You know, a good title will get the church crowd! But for this particular group, the commission said it was a trust set up for a minister of music who had died, so actually it had to be religious or religiously oriented. But then again, when I was assembling these things I said, "Well, there isn't anyone who doesn't understand some aspect of water." So that it begins with a common denominator. I suppose it's just the cheap commercialism of my livelihood. No—I do mean that in some sense! [The piece was published as *Creation of the World* in 1994.]

Now to turn the other side of the coin. I am enormously interested in what we call basically liturgical texts, formulaic texts. I've written a Roman Catholic mass, a couple of Anglican masses, I have a year-old piece called *Missa Domestica*. It's the Kyrie, Sanctus, Benedictus, and Agnus Dei for voice, flute, and guitar. But then again, it's just taking the text that everyone knows. I've written a sabbath morning text in Hebrew, never did anything in Greek, though. Lots of liturgical pieces.

SM: Let's turn this textual question another way. You've done many of these liturgical pieces, but they're [based on universally known texts] like the mass. Then contextual elements come: patrons, possible audience, where you are in your own musical development, and so on. But what happens when you set a text several times? Especially something like the Kyrie. It's the simplest of texts, just three words. Now each one of those has enormous resonance, but the question is this: how does it feel when you return to a text that you've already set? Do you reflect on that at all, or do you just get ready and go to work?

DP: No, really each time I do a piece, it's always a new effort. If I come back to a text and reset it, it's always completely different. You know it's interesting,

[Canadian composer] Ned Rorem [b. 1923] did an extraordinary cycle of songs, *Poems of Love and the Rain* [1962–63], because he took a number of poems and set them each twice. And each time completely different. And it was really fascinating. The same thing with [French composer] Georges Auric [1899–1993], in Cocteau's *The Blood of the Poet,* which won all kinds of prizes for music. Auric was furious when, after everything was completed, Cocteau elected to take the very sad music and put it with happy scenes, and vice-versa. This so-called counterpoint of emotions can be very effective. When you hear a funeral going on and you hear some of the people being very carefully controlled and you hear a jazz band in the distance, it works. Now admittedly it's a cheap theatrical trick, but it works!

Tradition, Environment, and Experimentation

SM: There is something involved here about your voice as well. For all its variety, there is a voice, a compositional tradition in which you stand, that you continue to develop. Can you speak about how you understand what that musical voice is, especially when it's allied with a religious text or commission? The text sits there, you can mine it many different ways. I can understand that as a literary, intellectual, or conceptual act, but how does that translate into a musical style?

DP: When people ask, "How do things come to you?" I say, "Look, what I do is basically what an architect does." Because the first thing you want to know is how large is the plot. What are the code restrictions, how high can you build, how much bearing weight do you have to put on the pillars, what's the client going to use this for? Now those are the things which the layman is a little appalled to hear, because they don't think in those terms. They think of the Holy Ghost speaking to people. It doesn't work that way. Basically I set up parameters, I find out what has to be done. Then if I start a piece, and I have the text and all the rest set out, not to get spooky about this, but there is a certain amount of automatic writing that happens. It is there.

And, of course, it's based on all those ingredients—tradition, environment, and experimentation—those three things and certain knowledge. I always try to set for myself a new musical problem with every piece. There are also sometimes extramusical ones, maybe a funny little ostinato or maybe a crab canon that no one's going to hear except me. And if you have enough technique, then you can do those things for your own pleasure without ever thinking someone's going to spot it.

I think the best pieces have some kind of abstract logic to them: [Bach's] *The Well-Tempered Klavier,* his *Mass in B Minor,* all those things. There's always some place where you can't explain them entirely. And I'm not very religious in terms of saying these things, but there are times when you can step back from a piece and say, "I don't understand how I was able to write it." It doesn't happen always, but there are certain pieces I have written that I'm still touched by. It doesn't happen on a regular basis, and actually those are almost all texted pieces.

SM: A word that might work here is "ineffable." It's not overloaded theologically, but its reference is to something beyond logical calculus that goes on here, the synergy of all that simply happens. And you don't know how it came to be, but it did.

I like those three elements—tradition, environment, and experimentation—very much as a way of talking about the creative process.

DP: Henri Focillion was a great professor at Yale in architectural history. And I never met him, but I used to know a lot of architects and architectural historians who had a reverence for this man who was a thinker primarily. He said he thought the balance of those three were inherent in the works of great architects.

SM: Musically you almost need a challenge or problem or puzzle, and that would count as the experimental element.

DP: Parenthetically, those challenges and experimentations can, however, involve working with medieval techniques.

SM: Composing then is a true experiment, and there's no net. Either it works or it doesn't. And we talked a bit about the environment when we spoke about the specifications of a work. But I'm also interested in your sense of where you stand in the tradition, because you are celebrated as a composer in continuity with America's greatest compositional tradition, which comes out of [Harvard and Boston]. But on the other hand, your own sense of placement [may be different]. Can you talk about your own sense of musical tradition or traditions?

DP: I think that's an external view that's come to people who like to write books and make pigeonholes. I was interested when some years ago Wilfrid Mellers, who in *Music in a New Found Land,* spoke about my relationship to Charles T. Griffes [1884–1920].[5] You see it's interesting because his knowledge of my music at the time was exclusively from records, because he was writing in England. One piece that I think he heard was unlike anything else I ever wrote, *Concertante for Celeste and Harpsicord* [1963]. Just the two instruments, which has a lot of tinkling sounds that are like those in Griffes, but that's something I never thought of. I was very pleased to be associated with Griffes, but you see I don't really think of that as a direction. In the same way that [Claude] Debussy [1862–1918] in some ways was a dead end, nobody ever imitated that or forwarded that successfully. Lots of people followed [Maurice] Ravel, curiously enough, all the Hollywood people.

Of course I think that it's typecasting. People know largely my choral music. I suppose I'm as much performed as any living choral composer now. I didn't try to make it that way! I write a lot of instrumental music that people don't know anything about. And there are certain influences there: Walter Piston [1894–1976] and [German composer Paul] Hindemith [1895–1963]. I studied with Piston, but his influence on my vocal music is zero, yet on my instrumental music quite a bit. I'm much more rhythmic. I have much more shifting meter than Piston does. I have perhaps some of his rhythmic drive, but I'm more asymmetrical. Maybe some of this comes from reading Gerard Manley Hopkins!

SM: That would actually serve quite nicely.

DP: But I think it's very difficult to say that I have forwarded certain contributions or traditions, because I don't think about it, I just do it.

SM: That's really what I was curious about. Because there are all these labels and characterizations, textbook kinds of things, written about you. I wanted to test them out on you, but of course that is not how traditions work.

DP: Yes, but you know about twenty or thirty years ago there was enormous premium put on so-called originality. And the inventor became more important than the composer. You remember [Arnold] Schoenberg [1874–1951] speaking about [American composer] John Cage [1912–92]: "as an inventor, very impressive; as a composer, not much." But on the other hand there's no one in my generation who's not been touched by John Cage, from his thinking about music. Some of [his] controlled randomness in orchestral pieces I worked with a bit.

SM: That helps me, because it's the compositional tradition in the larger sense at work here, the whole musical tradition that you are free to sample and use any way you wish.

Degree of Difficulty

SM: Now I want to talk about some of your sacred choral works, because they are most important for my purposes. Some of your work is eminently singable, and some of it is taxing for moderately well-trained choruses, and some of it is really virtuoso choral writing. Is that difference a function of the ensemble commissioning the work?

DP: To a large extent. A woman by the name of Barbara Wallace who was with us for thirty-five years at King's Chapel, she retired just two years ago, used to sing with [the Boston] Handel and Haydn [Society] a lot, and recorded with them. Barbara was always that one soprano voice that was so beautiful especially when she was a younger talent, and where the voice turned over it was lustrous at certain points. Well, Barbara, who was my soprano of choice for years and years, said to me that every new piece of mine was so difficult for her at first, and she's a good musician, but that by the second rehearsal it's as if she'd been singing it all her life. There were certain pieces that, because I knew it was an amateur chorus, or because I knew there would not be much rehearsal time, I learned there were things I must not dare do. There were certain pieces that were written for specific groups for which there were no reasonable problems they could not confront. Maurice Casey, who for many years was director of choral activities at Ohio State University, who by the way has commissioned me for more pieces than anybody else, one day called me up and said, "Want to make some money? Would you write a piece which could go on the same program as [Beethoven's] Ninth Symphony?" I paused and said, "Well would it be on before or after?" You know it makes a difference! Well, that was the *Ascension Cantata* for chorus and wind orchestra. That's one of the most difficult pieces I've done. I was also supposed to conduct it, and had been given four hours' rehearsal, but everything was all done. Now that was really a more difficult piece than I would write today.

SM: Of course he had wonderful forces, but they were also able to own it somehow that quickly.

DP: Yes, he had wonderful forces, and I don't think I've ever heard a performance as good as that first one. I think perhaps I would say that as I've grown in a different direction, that I would probably be able to write a piece with that kind of brilliance and excitement, but with less technical problems for performers now. Mostly because I think I've put that aside as one of my priorities in writing pieces. [When performers are able to prepare my pieces quickly,] I always say to myself, "Well, I've done it right."

SM: So it does turn out that performability is a mark of "doing it right" for you.

DP: I think so.

SM: It's not like you want to put out a minefield for performers to navigate.

DP: Lukas Foss [b. 1922] has said in print, "It's only those excessively difficult pieces that are going to survive into the twenty-first century," an opinion with which I disagree. I have to ask myself if that is a question of development or of *zeitgeist*. As I said, as of twenty years ago, if you were understood or enjoyed, or people called your music pretty, that was damnation. I've never felt that way. For instance in 1946, my first year at Tanglewood, Ned Rorem and I became fast friends because we were interested in writing vocal music, and at that time if you were writing vocal music, people didn't take you seriously. You didn't get grants, it was the Princeton-Columbia axis—[Milton] Babbitt [b. 1916] and all those people—who did. And we've not changed. Ned and I haven't changed one bit. It's just that we're more fashionable now.

SM: I'm thinking about performability and accessibility now not only of the performers but also of the hearers. I know you can only be impressionistic, but I have several things in mind. One, in addressing the problem of religion and music, there is this question of what is really going on here? Why is it that music ultimately—whether in preaching, choral, organ, or hymnody—seems to be the emotional center, the heart? Do you have any thought about that now as a listener as well as a composer?

DP: Let me parry your question. There was a Unitarian church in Oklahoma, John Wolf was the preacher, Old Saints Church, I think. They commissioned me to write a piece, and I came back, and [King's Chapel minister] Carl Scovel and I were talking about that church, because it was one of the humanistic parishes, not at all Christocentric or theocentric. They were very bright people and [Wolf] spoke wonderfully, but there was no liturgy, no structure, no nothin'. And Carl said very simply: "Well, that's why the music program is so important," because basically there is no worship [without music].

Of Conservatories and Commissions

SM: Now let's go to the conservatory.

DP: I think the title gives you the thought of "conservative" or at least the idea of workman-like, the *atelier*.

SM: I assume it's as you say, it's about the workmanlike techniques, the professional-caliber skills needed to do music.

DP: Trade school.

SM: And yet liberal Protestant American sacred music has depended upon products of these schools for much of its worship music for at least the last century. The schools themselves are secular and pluralist. So the question is whether there is any place in the conservatory world for the creation of sacred music, or does that happen only after the training?

DP: Now I can't speak for places like the Yale Institute of Sacred Music, you see. Of course I really don't think there should be any dichotomy between sacred and secular: it's either quality or it isn't quality. I can only speak for New England Conservatory and there ain't nothin' there. None of the composition teachers is interested in that, and they're not terribly interested in vocal music at all, certainly not the sacred stuff. The experience that the students get [of sacred music] comes all through the choral activities department, because [those works] are looked on as elements of repertoire and literature.

SM: And studied that way.

DP: Yes, and taught that way. Now you know how atheistic I am, and I think people are sometimes surprised, but I was one of the people instrumental in having our commencement services [at New England Conservatory] detached from having a preacher come in and speak. I had a colleague, Judith Sutton, who was Jewish, and she was very unhappy about having a preacher come in. And I said, "Well, look, I'm the only person on the faculty who works in organized religion, so it falls to me." I brought this up in faculty council and they were appalled. They were very nervous, and they said, "Would you meet with the trustees?" And I said, "Of course." So I went and met with two or three [trustees] and I said, "I think that if at our commencement services we do a Beethoven string quartet or a Bach cantata, fine, but this is a secular school and that is part of our repertoire. But," I said, "I find it offensive that you bring [a sermon into our commencement] simply as a cosmetic, something that has nothing to do with it." Then they said, "But that makes sense!"

SM: I think it's important to say that therefore the source, the compositional training, for people who are writing this kind of church music is strictly secular, as opposed to, say, gospel singers who write their own stuff. I make no judgments, but I do think it's a different relationship between the artist and the congregation. And I think that's important to point out.

DP: [Long-time New England conservatory dean] Gunther Schuller [b. 1925] once told us that in certain African societies, there is no such thing as art, no concept of it. The music they make is all part of the expression of their religion. Of course, in the Roman Catholic Church in the Renaissance, [art] became the highest contribution one could make. The artistic setting involved great artists in the production of repertoire. I think in some ways we have that same dichotomy today, because the learned versus the improvised is, well, it's a class distinction. That's dangerous, but you have to say it.

SM: In that context, I want to ask you whether there is any problem for you about the range of outreach that this kind of sacred music has built into it. Obviously most black churches aren't going to perform it. But there is also a larger question of who you are writing for. Is there not in fact a presumably literate, and at least a middle-, if not upper-class audience for your music in American religious culture, and it's the one that turns out to be at the top? Isn't it of that character? Any thoughts about that?

DP: Again these are market forces. The publishers—well, the serious publishers—know that choral music is the most marketable. [William] Thorpe just called up, and said, "I'm going off to do some things with the Gregg Smith Singers." They wanted a brand-new piece that he's just published. We try to push our things, you see. For instance, there's my commission for ACDA, and Schirmer says, "Oh sure, we'll get it out in six months." Bill Thorpe has his piece—his official premier is next February—and it's out already!

SM: You were mentioning market and class elements: I would think that they work for you as an artist, and that likely people call you up and ask you for work. Has anyone unlikely asked you for a sacred piece?

DP: [A Jewish congregation] in Cleveland had a commissioning program for more than twenty-five years, in which on alternate years they commissioned a Jew and a non-Jew to write sacred music. It was very interesting because it worked two ways. It gave me time to figure out what they're all about, and also I think it invigorated their tradition by bringing in someone new to avoid inbreeding. In fact I scandalized them by saying, "This piece is twelve tone," which it was, although it really was very tonal. I said, "Twelve tones, one for each of the tribes."

"What Does Your Piece Mean?"

SM: Now I want to ask a different sort of question. You are a nonbeliever and yet also an artist who has written a great deal of—how can I put this—successful sacred music. Do you have any thoughts about what does go on in a singer or in a worshiper, and is it at all different from the concert experience? Does it make a difference whether the same work of yours is performed in a worship service or in a concert hall as part of a regular program, any difference phenomenologically, one might say?

DP: No. Not a bit. I think again you have to look and see what the situation is, because a lot of churches have a niche [in their service] that becomes a concert, so that doesn't make any difference.

SM: In that case they are parallel. But if there is any difference, it would be a matter of intentionality of presentation, but not of the music experience?

DP: I don't think so. People have said to me, "How long have you been a sacred composer?" I said, "I've *never* been a sacred composer! I'm a composer who writes a whole range of things."

SM: That's very interesting to me: from the composer's perspective [the piece] is workmanship, it is craft, it is form, it is all of those things, and that's what it is. Then it goes out and has its own life. And, as you say, our children get away from us. If an upper-class Southern Baptist church in Dallas performs one of your works as special music, they're going to do one thing with it, in their hearts and souls and lives; and if it's done at King's Chapel, it's going to be a different expression, and that's as it should be.

DP: Walter Piston said to us, "When someone says to you, 'What does your piece mean?' the best thing to say is, 'What does it mean to you?' First of all, they will be flattered that the composer will be interested, but then you will find out what their experience is, because what you're trying to do probably has nothing to do with it."

Let me give you a story about this: There is a fundamentalist college by the name of Houghton College ...

SM: In upstate New York. Oh yes, I know it.

DP: I went up there. I had been warned, but I had not realized how really repressive this was. I was to go up for a week's residency, and then there was supposed to be a so-called chapel service, which was in essence a midweek concert. They called me and said, "The program looks a little short. We could use another ten-minute piece."

Well, I thought we already had a full plate because I did not know their capabilities, which turned out to be very good. But at that time I was doing a lot of mixed-media pieces and I had a piece for electronic tape and slide projector. I had made both the tape and the slides. The tape I recorded directly and the slide projections I made by taking two slide binders, putting some acrylic paint on them, and smudging them together. Then I'd run them through the projector, and if they looked pretty or interesting, I'd include them. I arranged it so that they began first to look decorative and pretty decent, all nonrepresentational, and the music began to be frilly or whatnot, and then finally [became] sort of an inexorable sounding, like the heart. And then the slides became darker, more somber, and then lots of flashes of light. That was basically it. So I said I would do this. "What is the title?" they wanted to know. Well, I said "Aspects of the Apocalypse." Good title. So fine, we came and did the piece.

Afterwards, of course, it came to that mandatory Temperance punch that you have to go through. Of course they said "what does your piece mean?" And I said "What does it mean to you?" Oh, well then they said [all kinds of things]. Because, you see, for them the Devil is very much alive, and they began to cite demonology in it and so on. "Well, sit down," I said, "let me tell you a story. Once upon a time, a patient went to see a doctor, a psychiatrist." For them, Freud and the Devil of course go together, so they all knew what the Rorschach ink-blot test was. So I said, "The doctor gives out the cards and asks, 'What do you see?' And the patient says, 'Well, there are two people in bed.' Next card: 'There are two people in bed, but they're doing something different.' The third card: 'Three people in bed.' And the doctor says, 'You're a very sick man! You have a very unhealthy preoccupation with sex!' And the patient says, 'Don't look at me like that, Doctor, they're your dirty pictures!'"

SM: Did they get it?

DP: They got it. But there again, you see, beauty is in the eyes of the beholder.

SM: So the piece probably went down with them because they were seeing or imagining scenes from the Book of Revelation [in the slides].

DP: Yes, that's right.

SM: But meanwhile, you were selecting these images and sounds for entirely different aesthetic reasons.

DP: It was simply a theater piece, but [with] that kind of experience you have to be a little careful about explaining things too much, in the same way that I always put a barrier in front of people who want to talk about my religious experiences. For instance [at Houghton] they considered my lifestyle appalling, and yet I considered their denial of lots of things equally immoral. But I don't judge, they do.

SM: But as a composer of sacred works, among other things, it seems to be very important for you to shield or not be overt about your own religious beliefs or proclivities whether you have them or not. As you have laid things out, that really isn't anybody's business. What counts is the work itself.

DP: Yes. Precisely.

King's Chapel

SM: I want to finish with this question: do you have any remarks or reflections about your time at King's Chapel? How long has that been going on?

DP: Thirty-six years.

SM: I assume that you are very comfortable with that people, and they with you.

DP: Oh, they are very forgiving! You know that old adage: it's easier to ask for forgiveness rather than permission! There are certain situations you fall into where there's a lack of leadership. And if you go in there with the idea of [being a] new broom and set up something which is active and vibrant, even though it may be not what they're used to, a lot of people will respond positively.

SM: To the effort, at first, if nothing else.

DP: That's right. Exactly. And we've had remarkably smooth sailing at King's Chapel. A lot of times you can have people who will be terribly conservative and not want to go along. Years ago I did a piece in one of the concerts, not for service, and it was for tape and chorus. I'd done some tape pieces, but this was a fairly grating piece. And one of the ladies in the music committee, Lucy Putnam, she's now deceased, said very politely, without any suggestion of censorship, "Do you think King's Chapel is the place to be doing this kind of work?" It was very nice. I said, "Lucy, you know, it's very interesting because your ancestors raised the same question back in 1713 when we took in the organ. Now you're going to be able to say, 'We were the first kids on the block who were doing this.'" And I said, "I don't think this represents a threat and I don't even know how long the fashion's going to last. But this is something new and vital, and I would be remiss if I didn't let you see what was going on."

SM: And she bought it?

DP: Absolutely.

SM: Well, that was the right thing to say. The best way to handle objections from tradition is to let everyone know what the tradition actually is.

DP: Let me mention this before I forget it: You know the Episcopal Church about fifteen years ago put out a brand-new prayerbook?[6]

SM: Yes. Very controversial.

DP: I was in Richmond, Virginia, about ten years ago, and my counterpart there said there was an old woman, a big financial pillar of the church, who was very conservative. She took the new prayerbook and brandished it at him, as though he had been responsible for it, and said, "If Jesus Christ could see this book, he'd turn over in his grave!"

SM: So that I understand correctly: you have been innovating for the people of King's Chapel, consistently doing so, keeping them abreast of the best work as it comes out. But I don't know much about what your program looks like. I assume you don't necessarily have a formula, but what does a musical month at King's look like? Are you doing Bach or Scarlatti, or are you primarily modern?

DP: We're very eclectic. We do a lot of my pieces, we do all sorts of things. Here's a new slant. We've had—ever since I've been there—sixty services a year with full choir. Now like a lot of churches, we've had to cut back. I've just finished planning music for the summer [of 1994]. In the seventeenth century Heinrich Schütz [1585–1672] wrote the *Kleine Geistliche Concerte* [1636–39], he said, in response to the Thirty Years' War, in which his chapel choir was dismissed because they didn't have enough funds or enough people. And so he wrote these little pieces. This summer, we're doing only basically quartets. And so we're going through five or six Sundays doing only the *Kleine Geistliche Concerte*. Well, it's terrific repertoire. It will be not boring, we do it in German with the [English] translations [in the program]. But for me, it's fun to utilize the available resources—we have very good professionals there—in working with something or other that we can take pleasure in. I have to say that, after the singers, the congregation comes first! See?

SM: You have to keep the choir well fed and well cared for, and moving and feeling like they're growing. That translates into performance.

DP: Yes, it does. A lot of people say, "Oh, you shouldn't use the word 'performance' in church music." I say, "Well, what else is it?" The minister gives a performance, otherwise the people won't come back to church!

SM: And Carl [Scovel] is candid enough to admit it. Most pastors aren't.

DP: Carl is one of those people who never would think of suggesting that people in choir sit and listen to his sermon. A lot of people, you know, say to choir, "You've got to be there." But no, when the visiting preachers are there, choir people go out the back door. Fine, I never say anything about it. But inevitably when Carl's preaching they're there. They're listening.

SM: That speaks well of them and that's nice for him to know. And it's healthy in a larger sense. It means that the choir is owning its participation in the community, if I can put it this way, more than just as performers.

DP: Several of the choir people have joined the church. But I don't use that as a requisite: either they sing good or they sing bad.

SM: Yes, but that participation helps, it doesn't hurt. On the other hand, it is clear what everybody's role is. And so you have developed them into a very well-known ensemble in Boston where there's significant competition. Your program is very broad, it's all over the place: all shapes, styles, centuries, and that keeps the singers on their toes. It must be a wonderful music experience for them.

DP: It's fun because we have to call for different vocal colors. We're not like groups that only do Renaissance and chanson. We have to do a lot of different kinds of vocal colors, which is fun when you've got a lot of experienced people.

SM: You really do keep it moving. But I assume there are also hardy perennials in your repertoire?

DP: Oh, yes. Every Easter, for example, we do Randall Thompson's *Alleluia* (1940).

SM: The Unitarian tradition seems especially right for you, given your sense of things, because they are not going to push you on beliefs and doctrines and dogmas.

DP: But Unitarian churches, they are fundamentalists in reverse!

SM: There may be some truth to that, but the mixture of Unitarian liberalism and the Anglican heritage, with all of its musical and liturgical richness, makes King's Chapel truly a unique place. And as you say, you just fell into the job and the place. Certain conditions are necessary for the sort of church music career you've had, and I think that mixture has a lot to do with why it's been so successful for you and for them.

The Crisis in American Church Music: An Interview with Neely Bruce

Neely Bruce is one of America's most prolific and original younger composers. A contemporary of John Harbison and F. John Adams, Bruce (b. 1944) has composed more than five hundred works for every conceivable kind of ensemble in a host of genres. A particularly marked feature of his compositions is the integration of American musics, including hymns and fuging tunes in the Sacred Harp style, with his own contemporary musical sensibility. *The New Grove Dictionary of American Music* comments that "from 1976 [Bruce] has made a conscious effort to incorporate his understanding of the American music tradition into his own work, making use of elements of ragtime, bluegrass, and sentimental ballad style, as well as tunes in four-bar phrases based on 18th and 19th century models." Many of Bruce's pieces are settings of sacred texts for church or concert-hall performance, and his work generally is characterized by a prevailing tone of moral and spiritual reflection. Among his major works of a religious cast are seven settings of the Mass; *Psalms for the Nativity* (1971); *The Plague: A Commentary on the Fourth Horseman* (1982), a rock opera; *Hamm Harmony* (1992), "thirty-six compositions in shaped note style"; and *Shaker Shapes* (1992–98). The 2001 edition of *The New Grove Dictionary of Music and Musicians* observes that Bruce has "focused on assimilating the entire American musical tradition, including hymn tunes, marches, and ragtime" into his work and "with *Americana, or a New Tale of the Genji* [1978–83] he began a cycle of three operas each encompassing a century of America's musical heritage."[7]

Born in Memphis, Tennessee in 1944, Bruce attended the renowned Indian Spring School in Birmingham where he first acquired his taste for musical and spiritual exploration. Taking his cue from *The Autobiography of Benjamin Franklin*, Bruce attended worship services at a different Birmingham congregation each week for an entire school year.[8] The fruits of his search included a serious encounter with Judaism, the rejection of traditional southern Evangelical Protestantism, and a life-long commitment to Catholicism. After completing his undergraduate training at the University of Alabama, Bruce took the Ph.D. in composition and theory at the University of Illinois at Urbana-Champaign, where he taught for several years. In 1974 he joined the faculty of Wesleyan University in Middletown, Connecticut, where he now serves as professor of music and American studies. Over the past twenty years, Bruce has also held appointments as organist/music director at six different churches including Catholic, Episcopal, Lutheran, and United Church of Christ parishes. At the time of our interview he served as director of music at Asylum Street Baptist Church in Hartford. He is a founder of the New England Sacred Harp Singing Convention (1976) and founder/director of the American Music/Theater Group (1977), a choral and instrumental ensemble of international reputation for its live performances and recordings of Bruce's compositions.

I first met Neely Bruce in the summer of 1976 at the annual Sacred Harp singing held at Holly Springs Primitive Baptist Church in northwest Georgia. Since
then we have collaborated on a number of projects and workshops devoted to
early American sacred music in general and Sacred Harp singing in particular.
His knowledge and experience of American music ranges far beyond that realm,
however, to include virtually all of the traditions and movements treated in this
book. When I received the commission for this study, he was the first person I
thought to interview. We spent the evening of September 7, 1994, at Neely's 1743
farmhouse outside Middletown talking about his life in music and religion and
his understanding of sacred song in America. Though this transcript is but a frag-
mentary record of more than four hours of conversation, I believe it stands on
its own as a dialogue in which perennial questions about sacred song are opened
anew in the context of contemporary American Christianity and culture.

The Crisis in American Church Music

SM: You've used the term "crisis" to describe the circumstances under which
you have worked in the church. Do you want to say anything more about that?

NB: The crisis is on so many levels. One of the levels is what is being written
for churches both congregational singing and choirs? Another level is what is
the percentage of the church's budget going into music? What's the church's
budget in the first place? There are financial problems besetting practically all
of the major denominations.

Another part of the crisis mentality is that people don't know what they want
on a spiritual level. There's a sense of longing for something and they don't know
what it is. I think this is only inevitable in a culture which has been for at least
one hundred years systematically destroying community wherever you turn.

SM: Let's back up a minute and discuss the kind of music that is being written and for whom it is being written. It sounds like there's a critique there.

NB: The Catholic Church after Vatican II is a very clear example. It [had] just
happened with a great deal of optimism, then the '60s occurred. What should
the church do? There was a need for lots and lots of new church music. What
should have happened is that they should have identified the best composers
living and paid them to write music. And if they were not available to do it or
felt they couldn't or shouldn't, then ask for recommendations. The important
conception there is quality.

SM: Let's find another [Giovanni da] Palestrina [1543–1594], let's find another
[William] Byrd [1543–1623].

NB: Exactly. And if it doesn't work out with the first one, then go on to the next
one. And maybe Aaron Copland [1900–1990] might not be the right person, so
we'll find someone else. But no effort whatsoever was made to do anything along
these lines. Rather, what happened was that a vacuum was created, and nature
abhors a vacuum, so people were quite eager to come in and fill it with folk mass

music. It's an unspeakably sad lost opportunity. Now the reason this happened, I think, is basically people didn't want to spend the money on it.

SM: It's value and priority.

NB: Yes, people did not place a high priority on it in the parish. The church has paid a very big price for this, although they now have things. Oregon Catholic Press in fact has got some fairly distinguished things.[9] They have some good composers writing for them, but no great composers. But it's a great improvement. It has liturgical integrity, and it's quite singable music: there are some quite attractive and perfectly useful things. What you don't find coming out of this situation is the sort of thing that came out all over the place in England in the Renaissance and the early seventeenth century, where everyone was writing good church music, or at least competent church music. The reason they were doing so was that they all got paid to do so.

SM: But isn't it also the case that there was an international style that they could key on, and what Vatican II did was to relativize and nationalize and popularize the whole understanding of what church music is? Had there been something like a canonical musical style in the United States in 1965 that everybody already knew, they might have fallen to, but instead they went every which way. Isn't that a real factor?

NB: It's a very serious factor. Now one of the aspects of twentieth-century art that has to be dealt with by composers and patrons alike is stylistic diversity. This is one of the things that is a contributing factor to the alienation, because if you write music in a style that is unfamiliar to your audience, you may fascinate some people, and you may do a really good job of it and people admire it, but you always will create a situation in which people are having to relearn whatever the style is that they're listening to. Most people have a very limited ability to do that, and less patience. So eventually you create a situation in which the best stuff basically is written by professionals for other professionals, which is, of course, not building community. This is a very large problem and most people aren't dealing with it.

SM: We're busy celebrating diversity instead of coming together, especially religiously.

NB: Exactly. Now the solution to this is to recognize the problem. Certainly this generation of composers my age and younger has gotten tired of not having an audience. We want an audience. Some of the best work being done now does have an audience, and some of them are real successes. But neither Philip Glass's [b. 1937] nor John Harbison's [b. 1938] music is going to make it in the context of Christian religious music because that isn't what [their music is] about.

SM: Which brings us to the next point: What should the music be about?

NB: The first thing is you have to have the intention of writing music for worship. Intention is everything in this, because you have to recognize the problem, which is alienation and the lack of common language. Then you have to say we're going to solve this problem, we have to intend to solve it. We see the gap, now we're going to build a bridge over it. This intention is simply not there on the part of most composers, they do not think that way.

But there's a whole lot that can be done. We do not live in a society that is musically illiterate. We live in a culture where practically everyone is passionately involved in music. It's mostly that they are not involved in what we can call art music. And the problem with church music is that church attendance is sporadic and congregations, like the composers, are not thinking about what would be really good church music. Again, nature abhors a vacuum and there have been various ways of dealing with this. There's a sort of pseudo–Anglican English church anthem that has been proliferating everywhere, just generic early twentieth-century Anglican cathedral music with a few extra dissonances here and there and a few bows to popular tradition. I don't think it's sincere. I'm sorry, but it doesn't convince me in the least.

On the other hand you have this bad folk music which is being produced in vast quantities and not just by the Catholics. That act has spread to other parts. Actually the little things done by the Chorister Guild are among the most encouraging. Simple tuneful stuff that children relate to, with simple texts, and catchy tunes. It sounds corny, but a lot of that stuff is perfectly acceptable in my book. There's a lot more integrity there than in so many of these high-church anthems.

Musical Style and Worship Music

SM: What do you think accounts for that integrity? This question gets us over to a series of issues that have to do with sound, style, and text. Given your concept of identifying the problem and pursuing a solution, are you saying that at one level this is a matter of sheer musical craftsmanship? Or is it more as matter of pursuing matters of musical style for the late-twentieth and twenty-first centuries?

NB: Musical style involves a number of things. First, if you look in the history of music there is a kind of recurring pattern of increasing complexity and then at a certain point to proceed as an art form you simply cannot get any more complicated. So what you have to do is simplify, and what undercuts the whole thing is the dance. Now what is dancing? It's movement; it's basic bodily function. You move your hands, your feet, your whole body. There's a beat to it, you can move, you can enjoy yourself, and it's social. People almost never dance by themselves; it is a communal activity to one degree or other.

What's got to happen with worship music is that the corporeal element has got to be reintroduced. Now the whole notion of sacred dance has had a certain vogue in certain circles, but the unfortunate thing with it is that it is sort of watered-down modern dance.

SM: And it's performance art.

NB: And it's performance art, which is not at all what is needed. That's why

Pentecostals are right on. They move the body in worship and it will define a certain kind of music. But along with that comes a predictable rhythmic structure, a certain repetitive quality to the music that doesn't have to be ritualistic. So that corporeal element has to be there in church music. Now if you look around this culture, there's dance rhythms everywhere. We've got more dancing than we know what to do with. So why not get some of that into church music? You can do this with things like the gospel-music tradition. There's a strong rhythmic element, it's great, it's something you can build on, and it doesn't have to sound old-fashioned, even if you're doing old music. You can do all kinds of new things in that style.

Another thing that has to happen in terms of chorister skills is the basic simplicity of the material: Do-re-mi, fa-so-la, that's it. I am convinced one of the reasons why the whole shape-note [revival] is enjoying such a resurgence around the United States, and particularly around us here in New England, is because it is a simplification. Even though many of the pieces are big and complicated in terms of musical structure, on the level of the actual material it is a simplification. The idea of having four notes instead of seven—it's simplify, simplify, simplify!

SM: It's simplification without reducing the expressive range.

NB: In fact, quite the opposite happens. And what is simple? The breath comes in, the breath goes out. The body moves to the left, it moves to the right. Your heart beats. It contracts; it expands. These things are fundamental, they're inescapable, and music is like that, too.

The next thing is, if you think about people's aural experience, if you listen to American pop music, which is inescapable in this culture, they are listening to a very sophisticated level of musical achievement. Though the materials out of which it is built are simple, it is very sophisticated on a conceptual level and on various levels of detail. This is true certainly of American pop music taken as a whole. If you look at the music of the 1930s you have George Gershwin, Irving Berlin, Richard Rodgers, Jerome Kern, but this goes on. There's a different thing with early rock-and-roll and with the '60s and beyond, but people have actually heard a lot of sophisticated things. They have heard Jerome Kern songs with a lot of very subtle modulations, they've heard the Beatles who had all kinds of harmonic color or tape collage effects that are very sophisticated, or something like "Hey Jude" that had sophisticated structure and so on.

These are not esoteric things. People understand them. And occasionally popular artists come and they exploit these things, but to hell with that, why not have a church musician or a serious composer come along and exploit them! What you've got, you see, if you're a serious composer, you've got a technique for making structure out of materials that can be used perhaps in a less structured or more informal way in popular art. Somebody should have come along to feed on these things in the popular culture.

Another thing that should be noticed is that people go to the movies all the time, and at the movies they hear all kinds of dissonant harmony, anguished effects, strange instrumental sounds, and sound effects and noises, and all these things are associated with the dramatic content. Nothing I'm saying is original, but people have to apply it to the case in point. And the case in point is: don't throw people curve balls that land outside their experience. Look at what people's experience actually is, think about it, and realize that people hear all kinds of things.

The problem is not that people can't hear or perceive these things, but that somehow they don't put it all together, and when they begin to put it together they begin to feel a little bit offended. We need to figure out a nonthreatening way in which all these things can happen. And I think the solution to that, again, is the intention of the composer. If the intention is to worship, and it's a sincere intention, and you bring your late-twentieth-century life into your worship experience and your making of art, then all of these things are going to combine in a way that may even surprise you and become very original, but also will have lots of resonance with the people who hear it.

Text and Tradition

SM: What, then, is the role of liturgical tradition on the whole and of sacred texts in particular? Can a text that is not recognized as traditionally sacred become spiritually and worshipfully effective because of musical styles, or do you really have to use a text that people are going to recognize as sacred and worshipful, like the Bible? You've tried the whole range of these things in your own work, so what are your thoughts about text and tradition?

NB: For the moment let's leave aside the question of what's appropriate for the congregation to sing and just talk about what's appropriate for choirs to sing: what the choir or a soloist sings and what is listened to in the worship service. Now my own personal attitude about music to be listened to in a worship service—and there is quite a lot, because there are many places in the service for it—is that composers should express the text in the music, and it should be a direct emotional expression of the text in the manner of an art song.

And it is my considered opinion that one of the biggest things that's wrong in service music today is that texts are treated objectively. You hear music that clearly does not in any way connect with the inner life of the composer. There are composers who simply take words and put them to music in a sort of generalized way. Now the unfortunate thing is that they're doing this with the word of God. From my point of view this is simply not right, this should simply not happen.

There are many reasons for a composer to choose a text, but the most important thing is to make that text your own. It has to somehow become a part of you, and when that text is being sung, you are aware that it meant something to the person who wrote it. This is true of all great vocal music. We were talking about the *Missa Solemnis* and the extraordinary ability of Beethoven in the

Kyrie to take a text that has been set hundreds of times and somehow you hear Beethoven speaking. Not that Beethoven is the voice of God, but he is the voice of Beethoven!

I've gotten to the point where I cannot imagine setting the Ordinary of the Mass to music, because it's been done so many times. I've actually done it, but I don't know what I would think to do now. There are composers who feel compelled to write a Latin mass, but they have no connection to Catholicism and maybe even a minimal connection with Christianity, but somehow they glamorize this text.

SM: In part simply because of its Latinity?

NB: Yes, and of course it is a great text, there's no question about that, but there's a tremendous responsibility there. Now let's look at scripture. Scripture is full of passages that are quite singable and have not been set to music and are quite fresh.

SM: This is not the Psalms, it's more anthemic texts?

NB: Well, there are some things in the Psalms too. There are ten that get sung all the time and then there's the other 140! But outside of the Psalms there's amazing material for anthems, things that could be very expressive and very personalized.

I had this very serious problem confront me in my collection called *Hamm Harmony*. I did not write those pieces for church use, but I wrote them among other things as a devotion. And I thought, what am I going to use for texts? I had the great fortune to have been given a copy of an old Baptist hymnal by my sister, which I went through many times and picked out many texts. It is loaded, but nonetheless I had to find texts that I liked. Of course some of the poetry is just no good or even despicable or quaint or stupid, but then there are flashes of extraordinary imagery in that book that are not just your standard Watts hymns. There are some original things that just flash out at you, and the selections from Watts are not necessarily those that would have made it into a hymnal during the 1950s or 1960s.

SM: There are still a lot of rough edges in such hymnals that reflect popular use in the lives of real people.

NB: Yes, and of course I am drawn to that kind of thing anyway in many aspects of my art. I think those rough edges and texts being used in everyday life by everyday people is very important.

So that's one kind of source. The most disappointing search, however, is to try to find new material. People are not writing texts that really have a devotional or liturgical directness that can be set to music, which I think is a lack of faith or something.

SM: Do you know about Brian Wren and the so-called English hymn revival? There's a bit going on there, and then there are the feminists who are not only remodeling the traditional texts but writing new ones for a more inclusive vision of the church. There are glimmers out there.

NB: Now I do know some of that and I have sought it out, but what I've read of it was very disappointing as poetry, which is another problem. Here my opinion is that the crisis is on the level of the poetry. We have to find a way to get new singable texts. Now there's some fundamental flaws with the whole *Glory and Praise* approach of the Catholic charismatic movement. The big problem with that repertory is that to sing it well is difficult. It is not easy music; it requires long phrases and it's all in irregular rhythms. It would actually sound best done by professional singers, which is the exact opposite of what was intended.[10]

This is what you have to have for good poetry for singing by the congregation: you have to have short lines, simple vocabulary, a vivid but not simpleminded vocabulary that's capable of vivid imagery, that is fun to sing. Actually in the eighteenth century they understood this perfectly well and they had lots of people who did it well.

SM: You're talking about Isaac Watts's "improvement of psalmody."

NB: Exactly. But that is an idea that is easily transposed because in popular music it happens all the time. The vocabulary of the Beatles is not Faulkner by any means. It is a straightforward vocabulary that anyone can understand. But when you say, "We all live in a yellow submarine," you'll never forget that as long as you live because it has an immediate visual quality to it. There's nothing complicated about it, but it's fresh. Now unfortunately people get too convoluted, they try to say too much in this kind of poetry. You can't really say that much. You can say a few things and you can say them in a vivid way and capture everybody's imagination, and that's the quality that people should go for. Actually it's very Zen-like. The whole essence of so much Zen imagery is its simplicity and its immediacy and directness, and as a result it is very incisive.

SM: Watts called this "bathos." On the one hand he apologized for it to his poet colleagues, saying that he could write more artful poetry, but it would not have the same impact and it wouldn't move people. He had to self-consciously sink the metaphors to the level of maximum comprehension. But as we know, Watts was still a good enough poet so that what you are talking about worked in his poems. There's a balance point between creative genius and intelligibility, broad based intelligibility.

NB: Yes, exactly. Now people have just got to set out deliberately and try to make these things happen. There will be a certain awkwardness when they start out. Some of the new hymns I've seen and we've actually sung on occasion are perfectly good; they are certainly moving in the right direction. I'm not saying this is a hopeless situation by any means, but there's too much that's trying to do too much. Again it gets down to the quality of the people who are doing it. Who are the literary figures who are moving into this area?

It's just not what the young aspiring writer wants to do, which is too bad, because if the young aspiring writer were to do it and do it well, it could change the whole culture. Not only is the pen mightier than the sword, but if you sing it, it is mightier than if you read it. People don't understand that, but it's really true. Which is why those people still sing "All Hail the Power of Jesus' Name," and they are going to be doing that for a long time.[11]

The best hope in my opinion for American poetry is rap music, which is of very uneven quality, but it has energy and directness. The best of it is really quite good, and it solves a number of the musical problems we have talked about because it has the dance thing, but it is really quite avant-garde on every other level. It is electronically produced, it has all kinds of random elements and noise elements, it's like futurism come to life in the inner city and it works very well.

The Sacred Music Artist

SM: But this text issue raises the crisis question again in terms of who is promoting what, who is training whom, and why what is produced is so bad. Some people say it's a lack of nerve, or of will, or of confidence, but it may be worse than that, it may be a lack of genuinely informed religious identity. If poets and composers don't know who they are, how can they express their spirituality effectively?

NB: This brings us a little outside of religion, but let's talk a bit about the artist. The greatest task for the artist, I am convinced, is to know who you are. Because it is only by knowing who you are that you could ever say or do anything meaningful to anybody else. Once you realize the search for self-knowledge is really what it's all about, then it's endless, because we can never complete the task. But we have to make the attempt or we perish otherwise. The prerequisite for all of this is self-knowledge.

So you think, "Well, who am I?" and one of the questions that immediately comes from this is, "Who are my parents?" because they are you in [a] very real sense. Then you realize that you are connected to their parents and their brothers and sisters, then that we are all related in ways that are not necessarily only flesh and blood. I am not alone, no man is an island. And then you think, "Well, this self-knowledge thing is not just about learning about me, it's learning about everyone else and learning about the universe, because I contain the universe." Now most people don't want to know this, they don't want to have anything to do with this conception. Because the last thing they want is the responsibility, and the adventure, of "I am the Universe." Wow!

Then you start to ask how does God figure in all this, and how am I related to God and to all things in the universe? It just is an endless process. Then you start to figure out things. I like this and I don't like that, I'm a part of this and not of that, and you have to start making mature judgments about who you are and what you're going to do and what you're a part of and what you're not a part of. That leads to what you stand for. And all of these things are part of becoming a mature person.

When you really start putting all these things together and you're an artist, things start happening. Because all of a sudden whammo! an image comes, or a sound comes, or a shape comes. And where does it come from? It comes from inside of you, and it comes out of your realization. You sit alone in the middle of the night and ponder or sit in front of a blank piece of paper and say, "What is this all about, what should go down here and how can I control this?" Things start flowing through you, and ideas come and develop. Then you have a craft, too, and you start playing with them and working with these things.

Now I am convinced that a very large percentage of people who are working in the arts do not ever think about this stuff, because what comes out could not be the product of any real connection with themselves or with anybody else. It's either intellectualization or it's a cliché or it's nothing.

SM: How about it's market? I know that if I do this, people will buy it, and I can obviate the whole question of what it means and from whence it comes if I can sell it. Isn't that a common thing in the arts?

NB: Yes, it is. It's a very interesting thing. Before commodification the crafts-man—some little icon maker in some Byzantine village—comes up with some exquisite little thing. He's not doing it because someone can buy it. Yes, he's going to sell it because he needs something to eat, but something else is going on there that is really not possible now. That level of ordinary, everyday artisan is denied today. The furniture maker, the seamstress, this kind of person just is not going to make it these days because the rules of the game have changed, and that's really too bad. This is one place where artists should stand firm and say, "I'm not going to do this." I mean I'd love to have a larger audience, but there's a limit because you have to be true to yourself, and that means you have to have a self to be true to!

The hardest thing to learn to do as an artist in the twenty-first century, I'm convinced, is to be direct. Which is a cultural disease on another level. How many artists can you listen to and say that's sad, that's happy, that's ecstatic, that's depressed? I read Emily Dickinson. The woman can say so directly the most phenomenally obscure things. It's not that she can't have complicated thoughts, because the thought and expression is very complicated. But it's a knife, it goes right through you. It's got an incisive quality that I find all over the place in scripture. To me that's the real proof that it's the word of God. Because it goes through you, you can't resist it. All you have to do is read it and it goes boom! And of course it does it on so many levels so many times.[12]

You hear a Mozart aria, say, the Countess's two arias in *Don Giovanni*. They are beautiful tunes and so forth, but when you try to do the same thing, you realize it's exactly the right thing that this woman would sing. It's exactly the right feel-ings and right characterization. There's no ifs, ands, or buts about it. The artist who talked about this very clearly was William Blake, who was always aiming at absolute economy and directness of expression even in his convoluted manner.[13]

SM: It's a synthesis of form. This is a very interesting parallel. Blake was about word as language and word as object, like his illustrated books. There's a direct parallel there to word as song and word as text.

NB: Yes, of course, and those books take on all kinds of meanings that you don't see if you are looking only at the modern printed page. In the twentieth century there has been such an extraordinary expansion of technique for saying very complicated things, and of course we have very great artists who have done a wonderful job of this—Joyce, Faulkner, and so on. So the temptation now at the end of the century is to take that as the basis for art, forgetting of course where those guys came from, which was from a very different place.

It's a lot of fun to learn the technique. It's very powerful and it can help you from falling into cliché. But one of the greatest things about my job at St. Barnabas Episcopal Church was writing tunes that had to be sung and learned in one rehearsal, expressions of the text for the day. I had to hand them to the soloist sometimes on the morning it was going to be sung, who would learn it on the spot and go sing it. Simple, straightforward, tonal as could be.

SM: The term that keeps coming to me is "fitness," from Jonathan Edwards, not a bad source for thinking about these matters. The primary category for spirituality in Edwards is beauty, but he has a very Calvinist sense of that beauty which he sometimes calls "fitness."[14]

There's a sense in your conversation that when the artist has come to a mature knowledge of her- or himself, and then is presented with a text and a context from a commission or a congregation, there is a fitness of expression that gathers both the meaning invested in the text itself and the meaning that must be brought by the artist as one who is engaging in that text. When the two meanings meet, when the two absolutely fit together, you've got, potentially, greatness. You have right expression. I don't know what the right term would be.

NB: I think "right expression" is it. Whether it is great or not depends on the talents and the material and all kinds of other things, but you at least have a rightness and a sincerity that goes a long way. The problem with getting the fit gets back to realizing the problem. You have to realize that most things do not fit. A lot of people don't know how to read on any level but on the surface.

Recording and Performance

SM: Now let me ask you about some other things. What about recording and the impact of it on sacred music? On the one hand there's a half-billion-dollar-a-year gospel-music recording business, in which a lot of superficial stuff is being pumped out to the culture, and on the other hand you have used prerecorded materials and all kinds of media, and you want to record and promote your music. Does that have any bearing at all on the agenda of sacred song and sacred music composition? Instead of writing for live folks, you concentrate on writing a work to be recorded and therefore sold and disseminated.

NB: Let's talk first about recording and then about performance. Recording is an incredible can of worms. First, this brings up a movement in the beloved Southern Baptist Convention and other denominations to have canned accompaniments for choirs and for soloists. Now my brother is rather heavily involved in this and he's quite devoted to it. But I hear this and I can't tell you how much it turns me off. This is not the use of recording that has to do with sacred music. Another thing that I don't like is the use of recordings as prelude music, which is increasing in certain places.

SM: Especially in big Evangelical congregations that can't quite mount the music program to create live prelude music.

NB: They just pop in a tape instead. This is very disturbing. There are too many places in the culture where there's a canned equivalent. The theater orchestras went out when the movie soundtracks came in. They don't have half-time bands at football games as much as they used to. The church is one place where the people should insist on having live music, because it should be the offering of the congregation to God. And it is not an offering to God to pop in a cassette tape. I'm sorry, it isn't. I hope this is being done out of ignorance rather than out of malice, but it is better to have humble music made by your congregation or someone employed by your congregation. Humble is fine, but canned just doesn't cut it.

SM: Is there any up side at all?

NB: Perhaps the right way to think of recordings is as private devotion. I think one of the reasons to listen to music as a devotion is the whole notion of sacred music as something you can enjoy in your home, which is a very important idea from the Renaissance on, and from Protestant tradition. Why not reinvigorate that with some really good commercial recordings of sacred music?

One of the things I thought was the most promising about recording, but it seems not to be happening, is the whole Christian rock movement, which is an extremely interesting movement. Some of the rock groups are quite good, and they have the chops and the energy of many other rock bands that have a totally secular line of attack. They don't enter the mainstream, but they have a real place. And it would be fine with me if they became more popular. That would be an interesting alternative to what we have now. This music is much more popular in terms of how much it sells and how many have actually heard it than is generally realized. And there are many teenagers who like it, which is a very good sign.

SM: It is accomplishing the agenda you laid out earlier—it's taking the rhythms and the dance and so on.

NB: Yes, but it is concert music, it is not music for the worship service. I have heard interviews with people who do this music, who made it very clear that they were Christians, but this was not church music. They did not particularly care about church, they didn't go to church, and they would not think of [their music] as something that would enrich the worship service. So you think why not? Why not have something like this happen? But again you can't just do this by having some amateurs get up and try it. You have to have good musicians. Rock music is hard to play, the standard is extremely high, and everybody knows when it's bad.

SM: What about concert performance of sacred works? If we're talking about large works of serious sacred music, the place we're most likely to hear them is not in church but in the concert hall. People go to hear Seiji Ozawa and the Boston Symphony Orchestra perform something like Benjamin Britten's *War Requiem* and some of them say, "Gee, that's a good concert," while others come out profoundly moved by this statement about war and faith and suffering. Do you have a comment about concert performance vis-à-vis sacred song?

NB: What happens in the concert hall? We have to distinguish between art works that have religious subject matter and works that are designed for worship. There are many lamentable developments here on both sides. One is that there are many wonderful liturgical works from the past now heard almost exclusively in the concert-hall context. I guess it's better that they be heard in the concert hall than not at all, but it is an unavoidable distortion of the art. We are so familiar with this that we do not realize what a distortion it is. The Lutheran Cantatas, the Bach cantatas, are never done in churches anymore, but they are just not concert pieces. They are very intensely devotional and liturgical works which occupy a very special place, and they are to be considered as the musical equivalent of the sermon in the Lutheran service. If you take them out of that context and put them in a concert, which is of necessity a completely secular environment, people just don't know what they are hearing. You can't know unless you have prior knowledge of it and can interpolate it in the concert.

SM: They're not sharing the religious intentionality behind the work or the context for which it was designed. What they are doing is hearing those works, now with the early music ensembles playing it closer to historic performance practice.

NB: Well, that's what they say.

SM: All right, but let's grant it in theory. Even so, those performances occur in a context that not only isn't religious or spiritual, it's intentionally not that way! You don't run the Boston Symphony Orchestra or the Metropolitan Opera or the New York Philharmonic like a church.

NB: Why should you? Concert hall is for concerts and church is for church.

SM: What's the point, then, of putting on such a performance?

NB: None, in my humble opinion.

SM: I'm glad you said that, because it's the inference to be drawn from what you've said so far.

NB: But as I said earlier, it's better, I guess, that they are done at all, because the churches aren't going to perform those works. But why not? Why not have at least a few really good places as showcases for the great church musical works of the past? I'm not against having a few museums around. It's better to have sacred-music concerts in a church because at least you have an appropriate architectural environment and the mind is allowed to think on spiritual things. It's much better to do that.

SM: Now let's talk about works written for the concert hall on religious subject matter.

NB: The great contribution of the nineteenth century was to demonstrate conclusively that music could be the vehicle for great ideas. Those ideas can take many forms, and it is possible to write music on sacred subjects which is concert music, as you can make paintings and any number of things that are not liturgical and are sort of general humanistic statements but have Christian subject matter. A spectacular example is Beethoven's *Missa Solemnis,* which is a concert piece hands down. Beethoven might say you could do it in church, but it's never been done in church. The Verdi *Requiem* is even more that way. [Giuseppi] Verdi [1813–1901] never even pretended that his work was for the church. All his sacred music is nonliturgical, which is completely consistent with his vehemently anticlerical character. And he was not interested, I'm sure, in any of the things we have talked about.

But there is a real place for works of this sort. There is [Leos] Janacek [1854–1928] and his *Glagolitic Mass* that mixed sacred and secular elements. It's a tremendous piece. And there are many others, [for example] the notorious *Mass* of Leonard Bernstein, which is not as successful. Many people like it, but it's theologically confused and musically not Bernstein at his best. But then he has other things, the *Chichester Psalms* and the *Kaddish* symphony [Symphony No. 3], and both of those pieces are again concert works.

SM: Conceived that way?

NB: Yes, and there's a place for that sort of thing.

SM: What is that place?

NB: The place is the big concert hall. It's like the Boston Symphony Orchestra doing Britten's *War Requiem,* that's the place for it.

Concert Hall and Congregation

SM: Let's say you are commissioned to create a sacred work for the concert hall, you come up with a traditional text, and you do the composition. Are you writing for the concert-going audience or do you just disregard them and simply create in response to those words and the various forces working on you? Does the concert-hall destination make any difference? I'm trying to home in on what does take place there and what distinguishes it from the church context.

NB: What is the concert-hall-ness of it?

SM: Yes, because we agree on the distinction between church, concert-hall, and popular religious concerts, but what exactly is that distinction?

NB: Well, the whole idea of going to a concert is to create two basic things. One is that you are allowed to focus with uninterrupted attention on the music. What you are saying by the act of having a public concert is that this activity is worthy of your undivided attention and is important as music. This is relatively modern. Until the last few hundred years no one would think of giving music their undivided attention, and music would be part of liturgy, or part of ceremony, or part of social occasions. So by having public concerts we make the statement that this musical experience is worthy of your attention and will sustain your interest, and it's good enough.

Now the other thing that can happen in the concert hall is that you can assemble forces that are not practical anywhere else because of the concert hall's design. You can have large orchestras, large choruses, exotic instruments, fancy soloists. The economics of it allow for all sorts of importations that would not be in the budget in another context or would be totally irrelevant in most liturgical situations. You would not want a fancy opera star coming into a church service. So that allows for something really special to happen. Not only is the music something that you can give your undivided attention to, but we can provide a situation where you can hear that music done by people who are not going to get together otherwise, with forces that you're not going to hear otherwise. These are very, very good things to do.

SM: So concerts are occasional events, as they would have said in the eighteenth century: the event is unique to the occasion.

NB: Yes, that's right. Then you have to ask what is the subject matter of all this, because we now have a structure, and what are we going to do here? When you ask, is religion, the spiritual life, appropriate subject matter for this occasion, the immediate obvious answer is yes. Why not? The whole range of the human experience can be celebrated in this situation, and in fact composers use the widest possible variety of texts. As Beethoven and Verdi have done, you can take a liturgical text and put it in the concert situation and you come up with a concert work that has precisely these characteristics that I have been talking about. It demands your undivided attention and it requires forces that you are not going to have otherwise.

SM: Is the concert hall a place where religious matters can be presented as well as any others? Is that how you imagine your own pieces, as opposed to something you write for the liturgical context specifically?

NB: Yes, because in the liturgical context there are a number of other things that come into play. But the main thing is the communal aspect. In the concert hall, you have basically a passive performer-listener situation in which the listener is passive. Of course we want the listener to be active and engaged, but that is quite different from what a congregation is supposed to be doing, which is to be engaged in the act of worship along with every other member of the community. No, this, it seems to me, so obviously demands another sort of music. If you're aware of the difference of function, then you will write a different kind of music. I think that's pretty much what I have done. I see a big difference between my concert-hall pieces with religious content and the hundreds of things I have written for worship services.

SM: How would you characterize that difference?

NB: One thing is that none of those pieces would be done by congregations.

They are too complex, or too something, whatever it would be. Sometimes the piece is relatively simple but there's a little kink in it. A lot of art music is like that. It appears to be simple but there's a little kink in it, like [Gustav] Mahler [1860–1911] for example. It's really not appropriate for a congregation. You lose the subtlety if you do it with a large group of people like in church. Now what else? I think that there is a kind of rhythmic straightforwardness to the things I've done specifically for church choir and congregation. And that's just a practical matter on one hand but on the other it is more than practical. It has to do with the notion of doing it all together and making it accessible as well as practical.

One of the most profound differences between being in a congregation and being in a concert setting is the kinesthetic difference. Everybody knows this difference, but it's so profound. Congregations sit and stand up, or they kneel, or they get up in the aisle, or they pass the collection plate. They actually move. You move in ways that mean something. You're required to move, it's not an artificial thing at all.

SM: And in worship it's a communal movement that has a worship intentionality behind it. They are not normal or everyday movements.

NB: No, they aren't, but they are not stylized movements either. They are movements required by a particular situation of worship. When you move your body, you are automatically more involved in something than if you're not. That's just the way life is. So the congregational experience is a different experience on that level, which is a very profound level that permeates everything.

There's also the pure choice of instrument. Most concert halls don't have organs, most churches do. And the organ is a great instrument for all sorts of reasons. And we didn't talk about this, by the way, but there should be a concerted effort to get other instruments into the worship service whenever possible. There are lots of teenagers around who play saxophone or the flute or whatever. Get them involved and then you have a nice little ensemble you can use. Publishers, you know, won't publish music that has obligato instrument parts. They will do it a little more now.

SM: There are these technical differences of scale, instrumentation, complexity, rhythmic continuity, and so on, but it sounds to me that what it really comes down to is that the congregation is collectively engaging and participating in the music making and interacting with the music makers for a larger purpose, which is worship. Whereas the concert hall is the active-passive, performer-to-audience context in which the intention of the performers is to perform a work that may or may not be about religion. What you've really said is that for you there is a rather clear and distinct difference such that you can bring either of those two different intentionalities to a given work.

NB: Exactly. And they are not the only two possibilities. I could mention one that most people won't think of, and that is music that has no audience at all. Sacred Harp singing, for example. Any audience for it is a complete coincidence. Then there's the whole repertory of keyboard music for practice that's never intended to be presented in public. I mean, Bach wrote the *Klavieruebung* [*Cla-*

vier Exercises], and there's a lot to be said for that, because we tend to forget that there are many different contexts for music making. It doesn't even have to be public. It can be private, or communal. And there are many combinations of these that are also possible.[15]

SM: I can't resist asking about just one other term, the sacred. Just as the efficacious presence of the sacred actually is now available elsewhere than in churches, would you call concert-hall works with religious subject matter sacred music? Or is sacred music inherently, irreducibly a matter of both the behavioral and the intentional elements and actions of worship?

NB: Well, I believe everything is sacred!

Notes

1. Michael Steinberg, "Daniel Pinkham," in *The New Grove Dictionary of American Music,* ed. H. Wiley Hitchcock and Stanley Sadie (New York: Grove's Dictionaries of Music, 1986), 3:570–71 (hereafter *NGDAM*).

2. Sabine Feisst, "Daniel Pinkham," in *The New Grove Dictionary of Music and Musicians,* 2d ed., ed. Stanley Sadie (New York: Grove's Dictionaries, 2001), 19:756 (hereafter *NGDMM*).

3. Conrad Wright, *The Beginnings of Unitarianism in America* (Boston: Beacon Press, 1955), 210–12.

4. Benedictines of Solesmes, eds., *The Liber Usualis: With Introduction and Rubrics in English* (Tournai, Belgium: Society of St. John the Evangelist, Desclee, 1934).

5. Wilfred Mellers, *Music in a New Found Land: Themes and Developments in the History of American Music* (New York: Knopf, 1965); Barry Kernfeld, "Charles T. Griffes," *NGDAM,* 2:286–88.

6. Episcopal Church, *The Book of Common Prayer* (New York: Church Hymnal Corp., 1979).

7. William Duckworth, "(Frank) Neely Bruce," *NGDAM,* 1:314–15; Keith Moore, "Neely Bruce," *NGDMM,* 4:453.

8. *The Autobiography of Benjamin Franklin,* ed. Leonard W. Labaree (New Haven: Yale University Press, 1964).

9. Oregon Catholic Press (OCP) is the largest publisher of Catholic hymnals, music, and worship materials in America. Its collections are used by more than half of the nation's Catholic parishes. In addition, OCP's 10,000 music copyrights of original scores and choral arrangements are in universal use throughout the church.

10. *Glory and Praise* (Phoenix, Ariz.: North American Liturgy Resources/GIA Publications, 1987).

11. Edward Perronet, "All Hail! The Power of Jesus's Name," in *A Dictionary of Hymnology,* ed. John Julian (London: John Murray, 1892), 41–42.

12. See Beth Maclay Doriani, *Emily Dickinson: Daughter of Prophecy* (Amherst: University of Massachusetts Press, 1996); Roger Lundin, *Emily Dickinson and the Art of Belief* (Grand Rapids, Mich.: Eerdmans, 1998).

13. See David Erdman and John E. Grant, eds., *Blake's Visionary Forms Dramatic* (Princeton, N.J.: Princeton University Press, 1970); Leopold Damrosch, *Symbol and Truth in Blake's Myth* (Princeton, N.J.: Princeton University Press, 1980); Nelson Hilton, *Literal Imagination: Blake's Vision of Words* (Berkeley: University of California Press, 1983); and Nelson Hilton and Thomas Vogler, eds., *Unnam'd Forms: Blake and Textuality* (Berkeley: University of California Press, 1986).

14. On Edwards and "fitness" see Conrad Cherry, *The Theology of Jonathan Edwards: A Reappraisal* (Garden City, N.Y.: Anchor Books, 1966), 97–106; and Norman Fiering, *Jonathan Edwards's Moral Thought and Its British Context* (Chapel Hill: University of North Carolina Press, 1981), 89–90.

15. See Jaroslav Pelikan, *Bach Among the Theologians* (Philadelphia: Fortress, 1986), and Laurence Dreyfus, *Bach and the Patterns of Improvisation* (Cambridge, Mass.: Harvard University Press, 1996).

CHAPTER 11

Gospel Music:
Sacred Song and the Marketplace

Gospel music is unquestionably the most popular form of American sacred song today. It permeates the worship of both black and white Evangelical Protestant and Pentecostal denominations. Gospel is also the quintessential form of commercialized sacred song in contemporary America. While gospel musicians have been performing, recording, and broadcasting since the 1920s, contemporary gospel performers like Al Green, Andrae Crouch, BeBe and CeCe Winans, Amy Grant, Sandi Patti, Kirk Franklin, Stephen Curtis Chapman, and Michael W. Smith now command massive recording sales and concert fees and rank among America's most popular recording stars.

Billboard, the American music trade newspaper, devotes as much space to gospel as it does country music, including Top 25 charts for singles and albums. SoundScan, Inc., the industry compiler of direct-sales data, reported 49.965 million gospel albums and singles sold in 2001, divided roughly evenly between mainstream retailers and Christian Booksellers Association retailers. These figures cap a seven-year surge that has positioned Christian/Gospel as the music industry's fifth-largest selling genre, double the size of Latin and larger than classical, jazz, and New Age combined. These recording sales represent more than $600 million in revenues and do not include live concert gate, music publishing, production revenues, or nearly six million gospel music videos. At the beginning of the twenty-first century the gospel music business is a multibillion-dollar-a-year industry that exercises powerful cultural as well as commercial influence.

Gospel music constitutes a test case for a controversial set of issues raised by the interface of sacred song as public religious expression and the aggressive production and marketing that accounts for much of its popularity and economic importance. This dilemma opens profound questions about the cultural meaning of sacred song in contemporary America. To what extent can any traditional sacred-song form sustain the process of commercialization without losing its integrity? Alternatively put, is there a point at which sacred song capitulates its religious character for the sake of ever-greater sales and distribution? Exactly how sacred can media-generated and mass-produced gospel music be? How can, and why should, any sacred-song tradition seek to maintain itself against commercial pressures to market it successfully? Or is commercialization itself a distinctively American process that should govern the shape of our democratic popular culture, even our religious culture? Gospel music affords the classic example of how sacred song shapes, and is shaped by, these conflicting religious, cultural, and economic interests in contemporary America.

The dominant force in American gospel music today is the Gospel Music Association, located in a six-story contemporary office building along Nashville's Music Mile. The 6,400-member GMA is a membership network that brings together the elements involved in creating, producing, and marketing gospel music: artists, agents, distributors, festival organizations, licensers, managers, ministries, music publishers, producers, professional organizations, promoters, public relations, publications, radio and television broadcasters, record companies, recording studios, retailers, and video-production companies.[1] The association's everyday function is to facilitate relations and information flow among these many constituencies, but it is best known to millions of television viewers as sponsor of the annual Dove Awards for outstanding achievement in the field of gospel music, a program that presents the defining public image of the industry.

The Twenty-fifth Annual Dove Awards

The Family Network national cable channel televised the Twenty-fifth Annual Dove Awards on the evening of April 12, 1995, live from the Grand Ole Opry in Nashville, Tennessee.[2] In the show's opening shot, cameras panned around the Opryhouse auditorium filled with the elite of gospel music's performers and producers. This hall was not the Ryman Auditorium in downtown Nashville, best-known home of the Grand Ole Opry broadcast and legendary shrine of country music. It was, rather, a state-of-the-art performance hall designed and built in the 1980s for live and televised performance at the vast new Opryland complex twenty miles east of Nashville.

A very tight stage band played the show onto the air with the introduction to Michael W. Smith's current hit song "Love One Another." Smith, a handsome young man with long dark hair and a one-day beard dressed in jeans, gray T-shirt, and dark jacket, sang the song without introduction. It was a full-bore 1980s-style pop ballad production complete with dance moves rather uncertainly executed by the soloist and four male backup singers. Smith's song exhorted his hearers to feel the love proclaimed by Jesus. The refrain went: "Work it in and work it out, / 'Cause you know without a doubt, / You can change your world with God."

An enthusiastic ovation greeted Smith's performance, and over it the announcer intoned: "Ladies and gentlemen, your host for the Twenty-fifth Annual Dove Awards, Amy Grant!" Onto the stage strode Grant, the most popular American gospel artist of the 1980s, glamorous in long black tresses and a strapless black gown. "Tonight we are here to celebrate the best in gospel and contemporary Christian music," she said. "Nashville is home to me. We all grew up with our own gospel music, but now we recognize that it has no boundaries," she continued, setting the theme for the evening. "Tonight we will hear many different kinds of gospel music. You may not recognize it all, but listen to it with your heart."

Male Vocalist of the Year was the first award, a category made up of young men, all of them white except Larnelle Harris, all of them long-haired and casually costumed like Michael W. Smith in the opening number. Michael English won the award and offered thanks to the "special people" in his life and to God "for the opportunity to be part of [gospel music] for as long as I have." After these remarks English left the stage clutching his trophy, a crystal glass sculpture of the Holy Spirit rendered as a dove. Next Amy Grant introduced the 1993 Male Vocal Group of the Year, 4HIM, a group of two white and two black singers, to sing their current hit. Over the introduction to this intense pop ballad, 4HIM's lead singer asked the audience: "Who here believes that the only way to freedom is through the blood of Jesus?" then moved immediately into the song's first verse: "Everybody wants to be free, / Freedom can only be found in the blood of Jesus, / Freedom can only be known in the love of God."

4HIM's song concluded the first segment of the program. A barrage of commercials followed from Parable Member Stores, Spencer's Children's Clothes, Family Bookstores, Contemporary Christian Music Magazine, and Target Stores, all of them using gospel stars to sell their products. Later sponsors would also include the Visual Bible's production of the Gospel According to Matthew starring Richard Kiley, Arrival Music's video of the twenty-fifth anniversary broadcast, Hastings Locations, Integrity Music, and Nordic Track exercise machines.

The great black gospel singer Shirley Caesar, celebrating her silver anniversary season, opened the second segment with her version of "The Son Is Going to Shine Again," which she delivered in the classic spiritual-and-sermon style of the Black Church. "He will heal your body, / he will lift you up, / he will return your child" she sang. Amy Grant's comment: "The younger generation has nothing on that lady!" The award for Song of the Year followed, presented to Michael W. Smith, the singer who opened the show, for "In Christ Alone." Smith thanked his wife "for putting up with me."

By now it was clear that both the show onstage and the audience, dressed in tuxedos for men and black and navy-blue gowns for women, would be indistinguishable from any other major awards television presentation in the 1990s.

Indeed the Twenty-fifth Annual Dove Awards had been produced to convey exactly that mainstream image to viewers. Yet some of the award categories did confirm Amy Grant's opening remark about the diversity of contemporary gospel music. The Best Metal Gospel Group Award went to Bride Psychology for "Super Jesus," and Petra won Best Rock Gospel Group for "Wake Up Call." DC Talk, a racially mixed male group that combines rap, rock, soul, and traditional gospel, opened the third segment with its Best Rock Gospel Group single, a frenetic up-tempo version of the Byrds' classic "Jesus Is Just Alright," featuring a rap version of the verses. Twila Paris won Female Vocalist of the Year for the third time, thanking the GMA for the opportunity "to redeem myself," Christian Radio and Retail and Starsong Records for their help, and her husband: "I love you!"

The next segment began with eighteen-time Dove Award winner Steven Curtis Chapman performing his latest hit, "Heaven in the Real World." Video images of American desperation and despair preceded Chapman's voiceover asking "Where is the hope in a world demoralized by decay? Where is the hope? Not in who governs us but in the power of God working in the hearts of people." The tune then kicked in with Chapman's big white country/pop voice singing:

> He is the hope,
> He is the peace,
> That will make this life complete,
> Every boy and girl
> Looking for heaven in the real world.

Thunderous applause greeted the handsome blond singer's performance, then two Dove Awards for best gospel video were announced: Sandi Patti, Best Short Form Video for "Hand on My Shoulder," and Chapman, Best Song Video for "Heaven in the Real World." Chapman also picked up Songwriter of the Year honors. For his part, Chapman gave thanks "to all who have planted the seeds in me, my pastor, my parents, my family, my wife. As Chesterton said, 'a poet reminds us that we are not dead yet, that we are alive by the grace of God.'"

Amy Grant appeared in a navy-blue gown to open the fifth segment by introducing "a true giant of gospel music," veteran singer, songwriter, and perennial Dove Award winner Bill Gaither, accompanied by a quartet of traditional gospel luminaries. "It's important to remind our children who we are," Gaither said. "On this twenty-fifth anniversary of the Dove Awards, let's take a look at those who paved the way. Here's a classic from 1923, 'When all will be together, praising Him forever.'" The song brought down the house, evoking the largest ovation of the entire evening.

The next segment opened with a taped greeting from former President George H. W. Bush. "Gospel music has meant a great deal to me," he said. "It touches the soul and our hearts, brings out the best in people. I salute you all."

He added "a quick word about Amy Grant: She came to Camp David and sang in our chapel. She touched our soul and hearts. She is a friend, a wonderful Christian, and it's my privilege to introduce Amy Grant." The camera did not show Grant immediately. Instead it explored the faces of two dozen children who broke into the Sunday school classic "Jesus Loves the Little Children." Amy, now dressed in a splendid white gown, crossed to center stage and addressed the audience: "Every life, every beating heart has a searching soul inside seeking the truth. I refuse to believe that we're only here to live and die. Why would I then feel the hand of eternity? I want to live!" Then she sang these words in a deep alto, delivered with country timbre and ornament:

> For the children of the world, Every single boy and girl,
> Have in them a special seed, And we must have faith for these.
> Red and yellow, black and white, They are precious in his sight,
> Like a fallen seed, They have a special need.
> They have a destiny, And give them a light to see,
> For the children of the world.

Amy and her husband, gospel singer Gary Chapman, presented the Best New Artist Award to Point of Grace, a white women's quartet. After another interminable sequence of advertisements, Amy Grant returned to assert "the rhythm and blues roots of gospel" and to introduce Brian Duncan and Anointed as "the best of blue-eyed soul" to sing yet another black-influenced gospel ballad. 4HIM received the Group of the Year award for their album "Get Back to the Basics of Life." They thanked their record company, "our families who supported us on the road," Christian Radio and Retail, and, somewhat incongruously, the William Morris Agency, fabled New York advertising mavens. During the next commercial break, the Super Bowl–like competition of gospel-music retailers reached its zenith, led by the relentless campaign of Family Bookstores.

Black gospel greats BeBe and CeCe Winans presented the final award for Artist of the Year. The nominees were already familiar enough to the viewing audience: 4HIM, Steven Curtis Chapman, DC Talk, Michael English, and Michael W. Smith. English won and sang his current hit "In Christ Alone:"

> In Christ alone I place my trust,
> And trust the power of the cross.
> My source of life, my source of love,
> Is Christ alone.

Amy Grant wrapped up the broadcast with a few lines and a final song. "There are many different varieties of music all under the banner of gospel music," she said. "It's not just a style, it is a life transforming experience. We all share one thing:"

We believe in God, and we all need Jesus,
'Cause life is hard, and it might not get easier.
But don't be afraid to know who you are,
Don't be afraid to show it.
If you believe in God, if you say you need Jesus,
He'll be where you are, and He never will leave you.
Sing with me now, these words of the truth,
So all in this world will know it.
We believe in God, and we all need Jesus.

The Twenty-fifth Annual Dove Awards show was produced with state-of-the-art technical expertise and presented in a style indistinguishable from major awards shows like the Academy Awards, the Emmys, and the Grammys. The two-hour program also demonstrated that while historic gospel forms are still popular, a burgeoning contemporary diversity has begun to transform the genre. Above all, the broadcast asserted the same basic religious message of salvation through Jesus Christ again and again in the song lyrics and the brief personal testimonies of award winners. In this confluence of commercial production values, diverse musical styles, and religious content lies the challenge of gospel music for understanding sacred song in America.

What Is Gospel Music?

I grew up playing piano for Sunday-night song services at Baptist churches in metropolitan Philadelphia and New York. I also spent four summers in the mid-1960s singing radio broadcasts and Saturday evening concerts at Sandy Cove Bible Conference on the Chesapeake Bay near North East, Maryland, a fundamentalist resort founded by Orthodox Presbyterian evangelist George A. Palmer. I thought I knew what gospel music was. In my experience it meant above all the gospel-hymn tradition begun by Ira D. Sankey, Philip P. Bliss, William B. Bradbury, and Robert Lowry in the 1860s and 1870s and extended into the early twentieth century by successors like Homer Rodeheaver and Gypsy Smith. It meant songs like "What a Friend We Have in Jesus," or "The Old Rugged Cross," or "Power in the Blood," sung at revivals, missionary rallies, prayer meetings, and Sunday school. Along the way I had also come to know something of the Black Church tradition of gospel music embodied in songs like Charles A. Tindley's "Stand By Me" and Thomas A. Dorsey's "Take My Hand, Precious Lord" and of the bluegrass gospel heritage exemplified by Albert E. Brumley's song "I'll Fly Away" and Bill Monroe's recordings.

Given my background, I expected to hear a definition of gospel music based on those historic forms and styles from Don Butler, then director of the Gospel Music Association, when I conducted my first interview for this book with him in 1991 at the association's headquarters in Nashville. I was shocked when in response to my question, "What is gospel music?" he answered, "It's any music that tells the story." "Any music at all?" I asked. "Yes," Butler replied, "if it delivers the message, it's gospel music."[3]

Butler's definition sounded simple enough, but like most simple definitions it raised more problems than it solved. One was the nonmusical criterion whereby he had identified gospel music. Butler's definition was entirely text-driven: what makes music "gospel," he asserted, was not music at all, but rather the lyrical presence of the Christian message in some form. Such a standard was in the first place anachronistic because it made all of Christian hymnody since Ambrose of Milan a part of "gospel music," a term coined in the 1920s. A far more serious difficulty in Butler's formulation was its lack of any specification for what "the Christian message" is and is not. Would Butler accept the ancient hymns of Ambrose, or medieval ones by Hildegard of Bingen, or even the canticles of Francis of Assisi as "the Christian story?" I doubted it very much.

The Twenty-fifth Annual Dove Awards documented a rather different description of gospel music's "Christian message." Despite the musical diversity of the program, all of the song lyrics expressed the distinctive rhetoric of American Evangelical Protestantism, with its characteristic emphasis on the necessity of spiritual rebirth and a regenerate life of intense piety, moral purity, and public witness. Not all historic forms of "the Christian message" have contained these elements. In fact very few did until the eighteenth century, when German Pietists, English Methodists, and American Calvinists fused them together into the Evangelical movement that has dominated popular American Protestantism ever since.

Gospel music closely follows American Evangelicalism's classic pattern of textual and theological conservatism. Evangelicals have experimented with musical style far more than with lyrical content. The themes of sin and conversion, Christ's atoning sacrifice, and triumphant regenerate life have been constant elements of Evangelical sacred song for more than two centuries. While they differ in important ways, Sacred Harp singers and the Black Church offer up the same essential beliefs as do Amy Grant and Andrae Crouch. Grant implied as much in her claim that gospel music "is a life-transforming experience. We all share one thing: we believe in God and we all need Jesus."

Gospel music, then, is about "the Christian message," but it sings a very specific American Evangelical version of that message. Evangelical theology alone, however, does not differentiate sufficiently what makes gospel unique as sacred song. The historic marks of gospel music also lie in its musical forms and styles. The term itself has always been more generic than specific and its origin is unclear. The label "gospel music" seems to have first appeared during the 1920s in reference to the singing of black gospel quartets, but from 1870 to 1920, the closely related forms of gospel hymn, gospel song, gospel blues, and gospel bluegrass developed important aspects of Evangelical sacred song that would eventually combine in postwar gospel music.[4]

"Gospel hymn" was Ira Sankey's term for his much-imitated compositions of the 1870s that combined sentimental Evangelical lyrics with Victorian glee, barbershop, and parlor-room music styles. After 1900 the ecstatic beat-driven music of the black Pentecostal movement or "sanctified church" came to be called "gospel songs." While white gospel performers continued to incorporate popular styles into their gospel hymns, the decisive development in gospel music after World War I was the emergence of "gospel blues" in the Black Church, principally through the efforts of Chicago's Thomas A. Dorsey. Between the world wars white southern performers like Albert Brumley and Bill Monroe pioneered "gospel bluegrass," a style that combined lyrics of traditional doctrine and nostalgic southern cultural values with an up-tempo version of folk melodies, harmonies, and singing styles backed by a combo of guitar, mandolin, banjo, and bass.[5]

Until the 1970s "gospel music" meant this clearly delineated set of Evangelical sacred-song styles rooted in gospel hymns and developed in different but generically identifiable ways by the black and white branches of the movement. Into the 1980s Billy Graham shared his revival ministry with gospel-hymn soloist George Beverly Shea in much the same the same way Dwight Moody had with Ira Sankey a century earlier. Gospel music, moreover, was generally restricted to Evangelical communities and religious broadcasting. The Edwin Hawkins Singers' 1969 hit, "O Happy Day," a traditional lyric sung in a standard black gospel soloist and choir setting, was the rare crossover exception.

If the Twenty-fifth Annual Dove Awards are to be believed, much has changed in gospel music since then. But my interviews with a number of gospel artists suggest that there is at least as much continuity as change in gospel today and that the interaction of commercialism and sacred song is neither as simple nor as ominous as it might seem. To address the gospel phenomenon it seemed crucially important that I speak with gospel singers from both today's younger generation of artists and from their parents' generation whose experience reaches back to the roots of American gospel. I was fortunate to have available for interview two famous family acts of the bluegrass gospel genre whom I saw perform outdoors to a small, relaxed, and appreciative audience at the Peaceful Valley Bluegrass Festival on the banks of the Delaware River in Shinhopple, Sullivan County, New York, on August 17, 1996.

One of them, the legendary Lewis Family, "the first family of bluegrass gospel," has preserved the traditional white southern gospel style in a career that has spanned more than a half-century. The other group, the Isaacs, began as an unusual husband-and-wife act in the 1960s but they reached the mass gospel market only in the 1990s, thanks largely to the contemporary performing, composing, arranging, and producing of their three children and their spouses. Between them, the Lewis Family and the Isaacs ably represent the spiritual, musical, cultural, and market development of gospel music since 1945. For this project I interviewed Polly Lewis, veteran leader of the Lewis Family both onstage and off, and Ben Isaacs, twenty-four-year-old composer, arranger, and producer for the Isaacs who has already cowritten a number one gospel hit song and won a Dove Award. Other performers from other stylistic niches might have been chosen, but no other combination of performers exceeds the representative experience of the Lewises and the Isaacs in gospel music.

Two Generations of Gospel

The Lewis Family story began with Polly's parents, James Roy Lewis and Pauline Holloway, both born in Washington, Georgia, in 1910. The two grew up in a highly charged religious environment. "My momma's folks were Congregational Holiness," Polly reported, "and Pop's folks were Baptists, kind of straight like, you know, Southern Baptists."[6] The Lewis Family's spiritual origins blended together the two most powerful religious forces of the postbellum rural South, the Holiness and Pentecostal movement and fundamentalism. Those religious movements coalesced musically around the gospel hymn, and both the Lewises and the Holloways also embraced it.

Pop Lewis's father taught a gospel-hymn singing school, rejecting as did most Southern Baptists the older early American repertory of *The Sacred Harp* for the Victorian musical style of Ira D. Sankey. Though they lived just a mile apart on U.S. Route 378, Polly's parents "got acquainted going to the [gospel hymn] singing schools. They married when they were fifteen years old." Mom and Pop Lewis transmitted to their own burgeoning family the gospel hymns they sang at singing school. "From a small child," Polly remembered, "we would get the gospel books and just sing out of them."

By the late 1930s Pop Lewis and the eight children had begun to perform at singing conventions where hundreds would gather for several days to sing new gospel-hymn collections led by singing-school masters like Pop's father. "When we first started singing," Polly said, "we went to all of these singing conventions where people would sing by note, and we were kind of the featured part of it. Different song leaders would take a brand-new book and go through singing those songs and they would have us as a kind of extra treat for them."

As the Family matured musically, it embraced the songs of bluegrass gospel composer Albert E. Brumley, the hard-driving string-band style of bluegrass pioneer Bill Monroe, and the light-hearted stage presentation of Nashville's famed Grand Ole Opry. Crucial to this development was "Little Roy" Lewis, the youngest child, who in his early teens emerged as both a banjo virtuoso and an effective stage clown. The Lewis Family recorded several 78s immediately after World War II, but they gained their first major notoriety in 1954 from a thirty-minute, Sunday morning live television broadcast on an Augusta, Georgia, television station that continued weekly for thirty-eight years.

At the outset their program "followed four hours of Black Gospel," Polly recalled. That experience led the Family to incorporate what Polly calls "spirituals"—songs composed by Black Gospel pioneers like Charles Tindley and Thomas A. Dorsey—into their performances and recordings, a practice they still maintain today. "I always did like the spirituals," Polly remarked. "In every recording we try to put some spirituals to get a good variety of songs." Polly ascribed the relaxed, improvised style of the Lewis Family on stage to their early television experience. "On TV you have to do a lot of ad-libbing and fun to make the program enjoyable," she remarked, "and that's where I think we get our pet pattern." In concert the Lewises' "pet pattern" entails Polly delivering skillful introductions and spiritual testimony, while Little Roy plays virtuoso licks and capers about in fright wigs and physical comedy bits. Theirs is an old-fashioned concert style animated by a sense of improvisation learned at singing conventions and early television broadcasts.

Television shaped the Lewis Family in fundamental ways, none more important than the creation of a new market for their gospel music. Although they broadcasted from a small-market Augusta station, the Lewises attained media peerage with the two weekend broadcast giants of the emerging country music business, the Grand Ole Opry and the Louisiana Hayride. Broadcast appearances at the Opry in Nashville cemented the artistic and professional ties between the Lewises and mainstream bluegrass. "Bluegrass music features a lot of gospel anyway," Polly noted quite rightly. More than half of Bill Monroe's recordings, for example, were gospel songs. "And that's the reason we fit in good with them. We've never been put down for singing our gospel songs in any place. The bluegrass people love gospel songs."

The Lewises became a fixture on the bluegrass circuit and their record sales skyrocketed. Best-selling singles and albums followed during the 1960s and 1970s, along with Dove Awards and an immensely loyal following that continues to grow into the twenty-first century. The Lewis Family was a finalist yet again for two 2000 Dove Awards, Best Bluegrass Gospel Song and Album, for their 1999 release *So Fine.* They are one of the most enduring and successful of all gospel groups and yet through it all the Lewises preserve their classic sound and down-home personality, Little Roy continues to be the most outrageous stage presence in gospel music, and Mom and Pop Lewis keep celebrating wedding anniversaries, their seventy-second on the day of the Shinhopple concert.

Among Evangelicals the common religious justification for gospel music performers is that they are evangelists who proclaim the Word of God through song rather than through preaching.[7] I expected the Lewis Family to share this fervent sense of evangelism, but Polly demurred. When asked explicitly whether the family understood its career as a ministry, she gave a revealing answer: "There's a lot of groups that are really ministering to the people," she said, "but not our group. We more or less try to keep the people happy." She was clear that a Lewis Family concert is not an evangelistic effort per se. It is rather what Evangelicals call "witness" or "testimony," a public expression of their own spiritual experience given to what they presume is a Christian audience already "happy in the Lord." The overarching goal of the Lewis Family is not ministry or evangelism but rather consistency in testimony, musical style, and performance quality. "We try to be the same everywhere we go," Polly said. "I think we are consistent through the years; we've always maintained a good following. People can see that we don't fall out of the picture. We're always there!"

The Lewis Family's career recalls the great Evangelical itinerant tradition of traveling preachers and singing-school masters. Indeed it is not too much to claim that in the era of televangelism and mass-marketed recordings, groups like the Lewises, who still play small venues like Shinhopple, are the last remaining bearers of that tradition. I asked Polly why the Family carries on their difficult life of constant travel and almost daily musical performance. Her answer spoke of simple pleasures that might well have been shared by a nineteenth-century itinerant preacher. "Every year we have reached out a little farther and it just became our way of life because we enjoyed it," she said. "When we first started singing, we'd just gone about following our dream, and singing whatever we wanted to sing, and as it turned out, we've been at it for a long time." They simply love to entertain, and in the process to give witness to their Christian faith in song.

The Lewises do not write their own gospel songs. Performers first and last, they depend on songwriters to provide repertory for performance and recording. Most Lewis Family songs are early bluegrass gospel standards with their nostalgic language of Christian family, rural home, and hope of "gloryland." Especially important are those of their friend, the late Albert E. Brumley, whose 1932 song "I'll Fly Away" is the quintessential bluegrass gospel song and a Lewis anthem (example 29 on page 376). This repertory is also driven by the generational character of the Family's market. "We record some new songs," Polly noted, "but we don't like to do all new songs because one reason why you might buy a tape is because that's the old harmony style and you like that."

The demands of a successful gospel-music career, however, require new songs as well as old, and the source for most of those compositions has been Randall Hilton, who has written fifty-four songs for the Lewis Family, including "Slippers with Wings," "Hallelujah Turnpike," "What a Savior, What a Friend," and "I Stand Alone at God's Door." Hilton supplied not only promising melodies and lyrics, but also harmonizations designed specifically for the Lewis Family's performance style. "I love his songs," Polly said, "and when he sends them, you can always more or less say that it's going to be a good song."

The fame of the Lewis Family and other gospel groups attracted talented songwriters from the rural South into a new commercial milieu that eventually became the gospel-music business based in Nashville. With that talent nexus came agents, publishers, and broadcasters who made gospel music into a competitive recording industry. Early on the Lewis Family realized their need for a professional manager and settled on Herman Harper, a partner in the already well-established Don Light Talent Agency in Nashville. Harper eventually struck out on his own and the Lewises followed. They were together for twenty-four years until Harper died in 1993; the Lewises then signed with his son Clay, one of three brothers who took over the agency.

The kind of long-lasting industry relationships the Lewises enjoy is a much-desired feature of their work, but the Family has not made the selection of such colleagues a matter of religious preference. To the contrary, religion seems to have nothing to do with it, though traditional virtues of friendliness, honesty, and trustworthiness play a vital part. Polly said that successful work with writers and agents depends on "a feel" for the family's trademark sound and "a sense" of their goals in sacred song making. The same criteria apply in principle to producers and recording labels but the Lewis Family, like most gospel groups, has followed the best recording contracts from label to label. Nonetheless Polly's assessment of Daywind, the Family's current label, is still grounded in a feeling of mutuality. "We've been with a lot of labels," she said, "but the people we're with now are very friendly and nice to the Lewis Family and if you get that, you have a good feeling."

The Lewis Family is a gospel-music icon, honored by all gospel performers but most popular among the older generation. They might be expected to have some resistance to the new forms of gospel like rock, heavy metal, or hip-hop. In our interview Polly voiced some doubts about the contemporary direction of gospel music. "Some of it I don't care for," she said, "and if I did, maybe we'd be singing a different kind of song!" In Polly's view, much of nontraditional contemporary gospel is "too commercial" and lacks "sincerity." Her objections addressed both lyrics and musical style. "I think that for some of this music, if you very carefully listen to the words, you wouldn't know it's a religious song."

This issue of lyrical appropriateness is a very sensitive one in the age of gospel rock and gospel video. It engulfed even so acclaimed a gospel pop star as Amy Grant, some of whose songs and videos in the mid-1990s were broadcast on secular video networks and widely regarded by Evangelicals as crossing the line into romantic pop. Since then, Grant's recordings have hewn to a gospel-pop style clearly more in line with her audience and the broader Evangelical tradition of which it is a part. Her appearance as host of the Twenty-fifth Annual Dove Awards was a pointed statement of her full rehabilitation by the Gospel Music Association. Not coincidentally, during the show much was made of her then-recent marriage to gospel singer Gary Chapman.

Polly Lewis also objected to contemporary gospel on musical grounds. "Sometimes I have [on] a [gospel] radio station in my car," she said, and the song playing is "a rock song, a real heavy metal almost, and if I listen a little closer I can hear that it is gospel, you know, but some of it is just way, way out." Polly, like most of her generation, thought that certain musical styles were intrinsically more appropriate to the gospel message than others, and that in any case the music should be subordinate to the lyrics. "When I listen to a gospel song I like to listen to the message, to hear the Word," she said. "And if the music is loud and if the singing is where you can't hear the words, then you've lost that message." Polly's standard eliminated rock and heavy metal not just because of their beat-driven music but because of the sheer volume and distortion of their electronic instruments and voice amplification.

Was Polly's judgment a matter of theological principle or of generational musical taste? My interview with Ben Isaacs on his twenty-fourth birthday suggested that contemporary gospel performers still adhere to traditional theology, but they have a rather different attitude toward musical style. Ben is the youngest member of the Isaacs, a family bluegrass gospel act founded in the 1960s as a duo by his father, Joe, a Pentecostal from Kentucky, and his mother, Luly, a German Jewish Holocaust survivor who converted to Christianity after World War II.

Joe's musical background included Pentecostal gospel hymns and the bluegrass style of Bill Monroe and the Stanley Brothers.[8] By the late 1950s he had emerged as a bluegrass gospel composer and singer with a Decca recording contract. Luly pursued a solo folksong career and recorded folk-rock for Columbia Records in the early 1960s. They married and blended their performance practices into a unique and successful gospel style that Ben humorously called "kosher hillbilly." But the Isaacs took off commercially as their children joined the group in the late 1980s. By the mid-1990s the new generation of Isaacs were writing and arranging songs, producing recordings, and taking center stage as performers. Significantly, the Isaacs' first number one gospel hit single was "From the Depths of My Heart," written in 1993 by Ben and his sister Elizabeth. Since then sister Sonia has composed another hit, "Thank You," and married Tony Rice, an established gospel singer and producer. Ben has also emerged as a producer, nominated as a 2000 Dove Award finalist for both *Crabb Grass* with the Crabb Family and the Isaacs' *Increase My Faith* and winner in 2001 for the Isaacs' *Bridges*.

I asked Ben Isaacs the same questions about ministry, repertory, and the gospel-music business that I had asked Polly Lewis.[9] His answers revealed a different sense of purpose and practice. The Isaacs were introduced as "a gospel music ministry" at Peaceful Valley, and Ben clearly agreed with that designation. "Number one in my life is the Lord and our ministry," he said, "and then number two is the family and the playing of our music." Ben's concept of ministry was one of Christian witness, but rather than the "happiness" testimony of Polly Lewis, he emphasized the humble proclamation of the gospel in music and in lifestyle. "Whether we play a bluegrass festival or in a church or in an auditorium," he said, "we try to basically spread the light and to be the best a person can be because that's what God asks of me anyway. A person should not have to say he's a Christian for people to see it. We're not perfect, we're all going to make mistakes, but salvation and forgiveness come with Christianity."

Despite their commercial popularity the Isaacs, unlike the Lewises, perform mostly at churches. "We belong to the Church of God [a Pentecostal denomination]," Ben recounted, "and we play 70 percent Baptist churches, 15 percent Church of God, 5 percent Holiness, 1 percent Lutheran, and no Catholics. It seems like we've done everything possible." I asked him whether he was more comfortable in the church setting or the concert venue. "I'm more apt to feel more free in the spirit in the church than at a bluegrass festival," he answered. "If we live like we're supposed to, then it will show through us. But being a Christian, I'm going to be more comfortable around other Christians." Yet he felt at ease pursuing Christian music ministry in either setting, especially "when I have a bass in my hand!"

For Ben, as for Evangelicals generally, emotional authenticity is the mark of true Christian spirituality. He gauged the effectiveness of the Isaacs' performances by the emotional intensity and honesty of their audience interaction.

> We play what we feel, and most of the crowds we play to, if they don't get up and jump up and run around and laugh, that's fine, as long as they enjoy it. Of course, a responsive crowd makes it that much funner to play to. But if I see someone sitting there crying, that does the same thing for me. It's the emotion— it's kind of like an energy. There have been times in a festival, like when we sang "From the Depths of My Heart" at the Arcadia Bluegrass Festival, and I mean people were just bawling everywhere, and they talked about it for a year. It's one of those things. If you heed to God, then he will work through you.

It is fair to say that the Isaacs are far more intentional and explicit than the Lewises about their work as ministry grounded in a thoroughgoing Evangelical faith and lifestyle. The Lewises occupy the Christian entertainment end of the gospel spectrum; the Isaacs stand more toward its music evangelism end. This contrast also applies to repertory. The Lewises do not compose, the Isaacs do, and according to Ben, the same qualities of emotional and spiritual unity that suffuse the family's faith and interpersonal dynamics also inform its composition and performance of music. "Everybody in our family is a unit," Ben explained. "We all have ideas and we all try to work them in, and that gives us our style. Like the medley is going to be Dad's feelings about the Lord, whereas if you go to 'From the Depths of My Heart,' that my sister and I wrote, that's just the way we felt it. Then you get into stuff like 'Thank You' that Sonia felt."

What is most notable musically about the Isaacs is precisely this stylistic diversity. Joe writes "probably more than anyone else in the family," Ben said, and employs up-tempo rhythms and classic bluegrass harmonies reminiscent of the Lewises. But the younger generation seems to favor intense spiritual ballads rendered in contemporary pop harmonies, the music of the Bicentennial Revival. There is a lyrical component to this contrast as well. Joe's songs celebrate heaven and the community of the saints, while the children are more introspectively focused on the drama of sin and salvation.

Perhaps these are just the inevitable differences that subsist between mature adult Christians who have lived long in the faith and look forward to "meeting the Lord" and younger adults for whom the overcoming of sin and a secure

spiritual relationship with Christ have always been paramount. But in the Isaacs'
case, these differences are expressed in dramatically alternate musical styles.
Consider Ben's own musical influences: "I was raised up listening to old bluegrass, then Ricky Scaggs—a wonderful friend, I know him well—then the music that's adapted to me in the way I like to hear it, like Eagles and Bad Company. But I think anything that's telling the gospel is gospel, as long as it's the
Bible." From bluegrass to country to rock to pop and beyond, this is a postwar
syllabus of popular secular music in the American South, all of which blend
together in Ben's own composing and arranging.

The Isaacs are as close to musically self-sufficient as a major musical act can
be, gospel or otherwise. This feature has given them more control over the non-
musical aspects of their career than is typical. Since they write most of their own
songs, they are not dependent on relationships with industry songwriters like the
Lewises have been with Randall Hilton. "We don't have favored songwriters," Ben
observed. "We look at music for the message first. We have songwriters who say,
'You record all of your own stuff?' and we say, 'Of course not,' and they say, 'We've
got some some stuff we want to give you.' Well, we all sit down together, we listen to it together, and that's how we choose. It's like a process of elimination."

The same sort of autonomy characterizes the Isaacs' relationship to agents.
Since they write, perform, and produce their own recordings, they can determine conditions of recording contracts and ask Clay Harper, who manages them
as well as the Lewises, to make the deal. The Isaacs also exercise a firm hand on
Harper for booking performances. "Our booking agency has been, as far as I'm
concerned, the best," Ben remarked. "We'll play just about anywhere. Not a bar,
but we'll play coliseums, we'll play stockyards, fairs, the Opry, churches of any
kind. They are real supportive of us. If we don't want to take a place, they don't
make us do it just because we're signed with them. We have main control. They
work for us. We pay them to work for us, and that's what they do."

I concluded our interview by asking Ben what fame has done for him and
to him. He gave the obvious answer to the first part of the question. "Notoriety makes your lifestyle better, of course," he said, "and we're getting to play
more choice places." What fame has done to him and the Isaacs, however, was
more difficult to depict. One the one hand, "you tend to expect more respect
due to you, owing to your achievement," he admitted. After a pause he joked:
"It's just killing us!" But Ben's final comment turned the issue of respect on
its head and expressed the increased responsibility for integrity in their ministry that success has brought to the Isaacs. "In all seriousness, it is something
we all look forward to as growth. It does affect how you think about things. It
comes from playing gospel music. People are more judgmental about it than
any other kind of music in the world. Christians most of the time are the ones
that are hardest on other Christians. That's why we have to be really careful
what we do and not be offensive. And if someone falls in Christianity, the
Christian's job is to pray for them."

The Lewises and the Isaacs offer a series of contrasting experiences of ministry, music, and management in their milieu of bluegrass gospel. Much the same set of issues—entertainment versus ministry, traditional versus contemporary repertory, the dilemmas of popularity—besets the rest of the gospel-music world whether black or white, solo or ensemble. These issues, however, should not obscure the overriding fact that gospel groups participate in a kind of sacred song making categorically different from most of the other forms examined in this book.

Public performance and commercialization have begun to influence every kind of sacred song in America, from powwow and klezmer to Mormon and New Age, but gospel music is different. Gospel music created the modern American sacred-song industry and has consistently expanded beyond its original denominational constituencies and musical style. When they have commercialized, nongospel sacred-music traditions in the United States have followed the production and marketing strategies of the gospel-music business rather than develop alternate approaches. Whether one considers gospel as the archetype for the commercialization of all sacred music in the twentieth century or simply the first and most successful experiment in sacred-song marketing, the significance of the gospel music business cannot be gainsaid. That status, however, raises unavoidably the question of sacred song as a culture industry in contemporary America.

Culture Industry or Religious Culture?

Sometime, somewhere, gospel music began to depart the local community of sacred song making and became public performance. The defining moment of that process most likely occurred in 1872, the year that Ira D. Sankey stepped on stage with his harmonium to sing gospel hymns for Dwight L. Moody's revival campaign in Britain and the first tour of the Fisk Jubilee Singers arrived in New York City to perform their Victorian choral arrangements of slave spirituals. During the last three decades of the nineteenth century the strand of American Protestant sacred song we now call gospel music crossed the line that divides music by the people from music for the people. That transit created a new cultural location for sacred song in America, a new commercial relationship between sacred song–makers and their audience, and eventually a multibillion-dollar business.

These circumstances apparently do not trouble today's performers and producers of gospel music, who enjoy the economic benefits of their industry's success while maintaining their own sense of Christian witness and ministry. From the perspective of sacred song's role in American religious culture, however, questions must be raised about the integrity of gospel music as the public expression of religion. I have argued that gospel expresses the faith of a broad interdenominational Evangelical constituency, so why should there be doubt about its religious integrity? The suspicions arise, ironically enough, from gospel's very popularity, which results at least in part from the superimposition of market-driven production values and techniques onto a traditional religious culture.

At least 50 million Americans are members of Evangelical or Pentecostal churches. Despite many ecclesiastical and doctrinal divisions, this constituency shares central beliefs and a distinctive spirituality. Gospel-music lyrics appeal directly to this doctrinal and spiritual core and rarely depart from their confines. Musically, however, gospel became more stylistically diverse as the twentieth century proceeded, and now includes pop, rock, contemporary, hip hop, and other recent styles. The issue is whether this combination of lyrical conservatism and musical diversity is intrinsic to Evangelical religious culture or whether it has been promoted by the gospel-music industry for extrinsic reasons of market share and profit. If the former view is correct, then gospel may rightly be considered the most important American form of public sacred-song expression; if the latter, then gospel is a prime illustration of a perhaps equally characteristically American process of cultural commodification that has taken even religious expression captive.

To sort out this thorny issue is a task as difficult as it is important. For if sacred song is indeed captive to commodification, then all of its functions in religious culture that have been observed in this book are also subject to the economic imperatives of the culture industry. By inference, religion itself may well be at risk. The issue then is not simply theoretical. It amounts to the question of whether the production of religious commodities can at some point compromise the very religiousness they are designed to convey.

A critique of gospel music as commodification can be derived from Max Weber's sociology of religion and music and Theodor Adorno's theory of the culture industry. Both of these German social scientists identified rationalization and industrialization as the most powerful forces in modern society and applied that perspective specifically to music and culture. Weber saw both music and religion in the West as increasingly subject to the rules and organizational imperatives of rational calculation. He argued that the origins of both music and religion were to be found in the human experience of ecstasy, of what he called "charisma." For Weber it was the unbridled expression of ecstatic experience that first employed the human body as a musical instrument and created prophetic visions of the sacred.[10]

According to Weber, after these charismatic origins of music and religion had been exhausted their subsequent history has been a process of increasing organization and routinization governed by the logic of rational order. In his major essay on music, *The Rational and Social Foundations of Music* (1921), he argued that rationalization first took the form of organized scales in classical India and Greece, which reduced the range of tonal expression and musical form. Weber placed much emphasis on the further tempering of the scale in early modern Europe, which culminated in Bach's *Well-Tempered Clavier* (1722/1744), linking it to the growing industrial production of musical instruments and the increasing bureaucratization of religious and political institutions during the period.[11]

After Weber, the sociological interpretation of music in Western Europe passed to Theodor Adorno and Max Horkheimer, founders of the Frankfurt School of social theory. Both scholars wrote extensively on music, and coined the term "culture industry" in their 1947 book *Dialectic of Enlightenment,* but it was Adorno's further development of the culture industry concept that makes his work most relevant to a critique of gospel music. For Adorno, the culture industry is not so much an explicit set of enterprises that make profit from music, art, and literature as it is a fundamental change in the very nature and purpose of cultural expression caused by nineteenth- and twentieth-century capitalism. "The expression 'industry' is not to be taken too literally," Adorno wrote in a late essay. "It refers to the standardization of the thing itself—such as that of the Western, familiar to every movie-goer—and to the rationalization of distribution technique, but not strictly to the production process."[12]

Adorno understood the arts in the preindustrial world as expressions of individual freedom, human suffering, and cultural resistance to the dominant powers of society. The culture industry changed these essential features of artistic expression by standardizing their traditional forms and creating a mass audience for them. "The culture industry fuses the old and familiar into a new quality," Adorno wrote, to create "products which are tailored for consumption by masses, and which are manufactured more or less according to plan. This is made possible by contemporary technical capabilities as well as by economic and administrative concentration. The cultural commodities of the industry are governed by their realization as value, and not by their own specific content and harmonious formation. The entire practice of the culture industry transfers the profit motive naked onto cultural forms."[13]

Under this regime musicians, artists, and writers, now competing in a star system for performance fees and distribution contracts, remain free to create but only if they employ the standardized forms dictated by the culture industry. Their art, meanwhile, has been stripped of its liberating and humanizing essence in order to be more effectively marketed to passive consumers. The industry integrates the masses "from above" and regards them as "not primary, but secondary," Adorno wrote, "they are an object of calculation; an appendage of the machinery." Consumers purchase works that still speak of freedom and truth but lack those very qualities because they have become pure commodities. True cultural expressions, Adorno said, always "raised a protest against the petrified relations under which [their creators] lived. In so far as culture becomes wholly assimilated to and integrated in those petrified relations, human beings are once more debased. Cultural entities of the culture industry are no longer *also* commodities, they are commodities through and through."[14]

These critiques of musical culture by Weber and Adorno may seem harsh and inappropriate when applied to gospel music, but their perspectives give one genuine pause. To be sure, sacred song in America has always entailed the production of commodities. The hymn and tune book business flourished here for a century and a half before the rise of gospel music. But gospel music entailed something more than just salubrious effects on music publishing. Ira Sankey and the Fisk Jubilee Singers were the first sacred-song stars. American Protestants for the first time identified specific performers whose sacred songs they wanted to purchase and perform because those performers had sung them.

Sankey's *Gospel Hymns,* published between 1871 and 1894, sold millions of copies and remains the most successful sacred-song collection in American history. It established an economic link between popular sacred-song artists and music publishers that has flourished to the present. This linkage crossed racial as well as denominational lines. Thomas A. Dorsey, the father of gospel blues, was able to pursue his sacred-music career because of income derived from copyrights on his compositions beginning in 1932. Facilitated by the technological push of radio to sell phonograph recordings and television to sell music videos, gospel music has developed into one of America's major cultural industries.[15]

Since the Bicentennial Revival the cultural industrial development of standardized forms and new markets for gospel music has become increasingly overt. The most dramatic manifestation of these production and distribution motives has been found, as Adorno predicted, in the music itself, especially gospel's intensive and self-conscious effort to capture the mainstream popular music market. At the 31st Annual Dove Awards in 2000, for example, there were no less than forty-four categories representing more than a dozen stylistic genres including rap/hip hop/dance, modern rock/alternative, hard music, rock, pop/contemporary, inspirational, southern gospel, bluegrass, country, urban, traditional, praise/worship, children's, and Spanish language. These categories represent what amounts to a gospel overlay on the American popular music market, closely mirroring *Billboard* magazine's market sector charts.

Most of gospel's greatest current stars—Stephen Curtis Chapman, Michael W. Smith, Amy Grant, Avalon, Point of Grace—are classified as pop/contemporary and use musical styles and production values that make the sound of their recordings virtually indistinguishable from secular albums in that genre. Even their lyrics have blurred over into romantic ballads that voice Christian imperatives in more indirect moral and metaphorical language than traditional gospel lyrics of Christian experience. Most recently gospel video has been developed to compete with secular music video, posting explosive market growth over the past seven years, in 2001 accounting for nearly six million units.

It is difficult to believe that such well-developed market and stylistic parallels between gospel and secular popular music are accidental. If these parallels have indeed been managed by recording companies, producers, agents, distributors, and broadcasters, then it is reasonable to conclude that gospel is part of Adorno's culture industry. What are the implications of such a conclusion?

Adorno did not deal with religion or sacred song in his culture industry model, but some disturbing and paradoxical inferences can be drawn.

The heart of Adorno's critique is his moral claim that commodified music has lost its capacity to inspire individual freedom and articulate human suffering in the face of "petrified" social structures. Evangelical Protestants also address these issues of freedom and suffering, but in a different way. For them human freedom is an illusion-filled and easily abused quality that is best exercised in submission to God. Suffering is, of course, a human reality for Evangelicals, but their triumphalist gospel sees Jesus as overcoming our sin and suffering on the cross, his salvation and spirit prevailing over the world's harms. Such beliefs are a perfect religious and moral complement to Adorno's commodified music and it should therefore not be surprising that gospel music has consistently set its lyrics to simplified popular music styles.

It would follow from this analysis that gospel music expresses a socially conservative religious movement, which it manifestly does. But gospel's commodified music and self-satisfied morality also suggest that Evangelicalism may itself be captive to the culture industry. Not all forms of Christianity embrace capitalism with the same zeal as Evangelicals do today. Indeed, early American Evangelicals themselves were socially radical, opposing slavery and commercial economics. The independent lines and experimental harmonies of their sacred song, that of William Billings and the singing school, also embodied the critical and moral candor that Adorno ascribed to noncommodified music. Nor may it not be altogether coincidental that when southern Evangelicals shifted to proslavery hierarchical politics during the Second Great Awakening, their sacred song became suffused with simpler and more sentimental camp-meeting songs and spiritual ballads.

The crucial musical turning point for southern Evangelicals, however, was their acceptance of the gospel hymn and rejection of *The Sacred Harp* tradition in the late nineteenth century. Rival singing conventions sorted Evangelicals into what became the gospel-music majority and the Sacred Harp minority. The effects of that sorting are still visible today: Jeff Sheppard's grandfather championed the Sacred Harp conventions while Pop Lewis's father led gospel-hymn conventions. At precisely that moment, in the 1880s and 1890s, southern Evangelicalism was being transformed by the rise of the Southern Baptist Convention, the memorialization of the Civil War as "the Lost Cause," and the theological justification of racialism and segregationist social policies. In Rufus B. Spain's memorable phrase, white Evangelicals in the postbellum and early twentieth-century South lived "at ease in Zion," legitimating and presiding over a rigid social, political, and economic regime. During those long decades, their sacred song remained as stylistically "petrified," Adorno would say, as the social world it expressed.

The Bicentennial Revival signaled the reentry of southern Evangelicalism into the American cultural mainstream. Riding an immense wave of Pentecostal and fundamentalist resurgence that began in 1974, Evangelicals organized political, cultural, and media institutions from Jerry Falwell's Moral Majority to Pat Robertson's Christian Broadcasting Network. At first, a new generation of gospel artists wrote songs for the revival in traditional southern regional music styles, especially country and bluegrass. Soon, however, they were not only singing at local churches and revivals but also performing at massive gospel concerts and recording in Nashville. There they found a mainstream musical style dramatically changed by rock and pop and a music culture industry bristling with technical, distribution, broadcast, and marketing innovations. Evangelical entrepreneurs swiftly learned the transformed music business and created their own gospel-music publishing and production companies: Word, Maranatha, Sparrow, Myrrh. These now-massive media corporations have come to dominate every aspect of the gospel music industry and the Gospel Music Association. Weber would conclude that gospel music has become "fully rationalized" economically. Adorno would add that gospel has become a culture industry with its "profit motive transferred naked" onto sacred song.

This unsettling interpretation of gospel music as a culture industry can be countered, however, by examining the historical relationships between Evangelicalism and American democratic culture. Beginning with Sidney Mead's 1963 book *The Lively Experiment,* historians have explored the open-ended quality of American religious culture. Two fundamental conditions have enabled religion to thrive in America as nowhere else in the West. The first of these is religious liberty, which created competition between religious groups freed from prior political constraints or privileges. The other condition has been the persistent interpenetration of religion and politics in American public life, classically described by Alexis de Tocqueville in his 1840 book *Democracy in America* and interpreted as civil religion in Robert Bellah's *The Broken Covenant.*[16]

The combination of these two conditions has placed Evangelical Protestant denominations at the crossroads of American public culture. They have responded with an aggressive strategy of self-promotion grounded in the creation of dramatic religious products designed to persuade Americans to join them. Sacred song has played a central role in that strategy since it was conceived in the Great Awakening of the mid-eighteenth century. Evangelical itinerants George Whitefield, James Davenport, and Gilbert Tennent led singing of Isaac Watts's hymns at the Awakening's outdoor revival meetings, for which they were sometimes arrested, creating sensational publicity for their movement and its message. Whitefield also created an intercolonial Evangelical network during the revival through which he transmitted Watts's psalms and hymns as well as his own influential collection of English Evangelical hymns. That same network provided the postrevolutionary constituencies for the singing school, whose early tune books represented the most intense outburst of Evangelical music publication until Sankey's gospel hymns.

The Second Great Awakening contributed several important new dimensions to Evangelical sacred song. New Evangelical sects, especially Shakers, Disciples of Christ, Adventists, and Latter-day Saints, established their identities in part through the publication of distinctive hymn collections. The Second Awakening's most famous evangelist, Charles Grandison Finney, endorsed Joshua Leavitt's 1881 hymn collection, *The Christian Lyre,* carrying forward Whitefield's practice of designating specific hymnody as most genuinely Christian and establishing such designations as a permanent feature of modern revivalism. This evidence challenges the culture industry hypothesis at the level of production and distribution, because even if the Second Great Awakening created a sacred-song industry, which cannot reasonably be denied, it was designed, owned, and operated by Evangelicals as part of their revival agenda, not by profit-driven capitalist commodification that did not yet exist in America.

Most important, Evangelical sacred song in the Second Awakening rejected the compositional tradition of the New England singing school and embraced new vernacular musics to create camp-meeting songs and spiritual ballads. This development provides the first historic musical test of the culture industry hypothesis. At issue is the question of whether Evangelical embrace of new musical styles in the 1820s and 1830s reflected commodification and standardization, as Adorno would have it, or a religious imperative to employ any and all cultural expressions in the struggle to reach the unconverted.

The key element in this interpretive dispute is the status of musical popularity. From Adorno's late Marxist perspective, popularity of a musical form indicated its degree of market potential and potential profit. From the Second Great Awakening's religious perspective, as Nathan Hatch's landmark 1989 study *The Democratization of American Christianity* has shown, a musical form's popularity presented a new medium for offering God's grace. To be sure, Evangelical singing-masters and music publishers stood to gain by recasting secular fiddle tunes and folksongs into new revival hymns, but that worldly profit was regarded as a collateral blessing incidental to the advancement of God's kingdom.[17]

If the appropriation of popular music forms in the Second Great Awakening was part of Evangelicalism's specifically American agenda of competition in a spiritual, not economic, marketplace, then the subsequent development of Evangelical sacred song from Sankey's gospel hymns and Dorsey's gospel songs to the Dove Awards may be understood as the logical and legitimate extension of that religious strategy. The promulgation of the gospel through song in principle knows no limits of musical style. Evangelism by definition is culturally and musically inclusive. As successive waves of revival have reached new cultural and ethnic constituencies, Evangelical music artists have supplied new sacred songs to express the gospel in musical styles easily appropriated by them. For the Second Great Awakening the new style was fiddle tunes and folksongs, for Sankey it was Victorian parlor songs and glees, for Dorsey it was urban blues, for the World War II generation it was country and bluegrass, and for the Bicentennial

Revival it has been a remarkable new range of styles that encompasses all of musical America.

If publishers, distributors, and artists reap profit from creating such musical inclusivity it is a blessing, one not nearly as important, however, as the salvation that souls have found in part through those new sacred songs. All gospel-music artists, including the Lewis Family and the Isaacs, consistently articulate this theology of sacred song, as do industry leaders like agent Clay Harper, Sparrow Records founder Billy Ray Hearns, and current Gospel Music Association president and Christian Music Trade Association executive director Frank Breeden. There is no evidentiary reason to doubt their sincerity, or their faith.

Is the gospel-music business today a culture industry in Adorno's sense or the most public expression of American Evangelical religious culture? There can be little discourse or rapprochement between the two views. The culture industry hypothesis presupposes that human meaning has long since been eviscerated from cultural forms, including religion and music, by a sovereign capitalist order. Hence, gospel music exists ultimately to serve profit motive, not religious faith. The religious culture perspective places gospel music in the history of American religion and culture, in which the Evangelical movement has consistently exploited popular cultural forms to maximize its religious outreach. So successful have Evangelicals been at this populist strategy that they invented the sacred-song business in the early nineteenth century and have appropriated greater musical diversity ever since without losing the religious purpose for which it was created.

The culture industry and popular religious culture perspectives both make critical interpretive sense of gospel music. The impasse between them cannot be reduced to postmodern relativism without denying the interpretive claims of one side or the other. This hermeneutical impasse should not be lamented, however, because it forces once again, and in ultimate terms, the issue of sacred song's place in religious culture that has informed our study from the outset. If sacred song is merely an expressive appendage of religion, then it shares the same fate as religion itself in modern society. According to secular interpreters like Weber and Adorno, that fate is cooptation by the superior forces of capitalist market rationalization. If, to the contrary, sacred song is a constituting element of religious culture, then, as Mead and Hatch have argued, it can become a protean medium that expresses the deepest meanings of America's religious communities. Which interpretation to accept is a matter of one's own understanding of the contemporary world. But if, as I have argued throughout this book, sacred song is a substantive, not derivative, element of religious culture, then gospel music expresses in the most public way possible both the greatest promise and the gravest peril facing American religions in the twenty-first century.

Notes

1. Gospel Music Association, *The Resource Guide: An Official Publication of the Gospel Music Association* (Nashville: Gospel Music Association, 1990).

2. "The Twenty-fifth Annual Dove Awards," Family Network, April 12, 1995.

3. Don Butler, interview with author, Nashville, June 2, 1991.

4. Paul Oliver, Max Harrison, and William Bolcom, *The New Grove Gospel, Blues, and Jazz* (New York: Norton, 1986), 199–204. See also James R. Goff, *Close Harmony: A History of Southern Gospel* (Chapel Hill: University of North Carolina Press, 2002).

5. See Richard D. Smith, *Can't You Hear Me Callin': The Life of Bill Monroe, The Father of Bluegrass* (New York: Simon and Schuster, 2000).

6. Polly Lewis, telephone interview with author, August 17, 1996. All subsequent quotations are taken from this interview.

7. Ray Allen, *Singing in the Spirit: Black Gospel Quartet Singing in New York City* (Philadelphia: University of Pennsylvania Press, 1992), 50–75.

8. See Robert Cantwell, *Bluegrass Breakdown: The Making of the Old Southern Sound* (Urbana: University of Illinois Press, 1984), and Neil V. Rosenberg, *Bluegrass: A History* (Urbana: University of Illinois Press, 1985).

9. Ben Isaacs, telephone interview with author, June 9, 1996. All subsequent quotations are taken from this interview.

10. Max Weber, *From Max Weber: Essays in Sociology*, ed. H. H. Gerth and C. Wright Mills (New York: Oxford University Press, 1958), 51–54, 245–52, 262–66.

11. Max Weber, *The Rational and Social Foundations of Music* (Carbondale: Southern Illinois University Press, 1958), 11–31, 89–127.

12. Theodor Adorno and Max Horkheimer, *Dialectic of Enlightenment* (New York: Continuum, 1982); Theodor Adorno, "Culture Industry Reconsidered," in Adorno, *The Culture Industry: Selected Essays on Mass Culture*, ed. and trans. J. M. Bernstein (London: Routledge, 1991), 87.

13. Adorno, "Culture Industry Reconsidered," 85.

14. Ibid., 86.

15. Ira D. Sankey, James McGranahan, and George C. Stebbins, eds., *Gospel Hymns Nos. 1 to 6 Complete: For Use in Gospel Meetings and Other Religious Services* (New York: Christian Herald, Bible House, Biglow and Main, 1894); Sandra S. Sizer [Frankiel], *Gospel Hymns and Social Religion: The Rhetoric of Nineteenth-Century Revivalism* (Philadelphia: Temple University Press, 1978), 5.

16. Sidney E. Mead, *The Lively Experiment: The Shaping of American Religion* (New York: Harper and Row, 1963).

17. Nathan O. Hatch, *The Democratization of American Christianity* (New Haven: Yale University Press, 1989), 146–61.

Conclusion: American Sacred Song and the Meaning of Religious Culture

The goal of this book has been to isolate sacred song as a specific element of religion and to explore its roles and functions in a representative group of American religious communities. I chose this interpretive strategy both as a corrective to the virtual neglect of sacred song in academic studies of religion and as a search for new perspectives for understanding religious culture. The results of the inquiry have surprised me with their diversity and challenged me with their complexity.

I will not try to synthesize all of the findings into a grand conceptual scheme. To do so would betray the living reality of sacred song and violate the integrity of the religious traditions that it serves. Nonetheless, I believe this study has shown a much wider range of functions and meanings for sacred song than has previously been demonstrated, and it has suggested significant implications for the theory of religious culture. In concluding, therefore, I will briefly summarize what I take to be the most important of those functions, meanings, and theoretical implications.

Sacred song in America performs an immense array of religious functions. Some of them, discussed most thoroughly in part 1, are well established in the critical theory of religion. Especially notable among these is the ritual function of liminality and communitas of which Victor and Edith Turner have written so persuasively.[1] Native American song seems a perfect illustration of liminality, with its power to bring singers and dancers into a profound collective consciousness of spiritual and tribal identity. Likewise Chicano pilgrimage songs transform disparate individuals into a company of seekers whose penitential quest for God embodies the essence of Mexican American Catholicism.

In religious studies, sacred song is usually assigned to the ritual dimension precisely because examples like these seem so clearly to follow accepted theoretical models of ritual behavior. The performance of sacred song plainly has the capacity to transform individuals and communities. This ability to convey believers from everyday consciousness into sacred experience is a defining characteristic of religion. Sacred song's ancient capacity to mediate such ritual transformation continues undiminished in Native America and the Hispanic Southwest.

This placement of sacred song as ritual phenomenon seems even more appropriate in the case of the Black Church if one grants that the explicit Evangelical Protestant mythic content of its music is an overlay for the implicit and more fundamental African American religious reality of spirit possession. Yet on closer consideration, African American sacred song does not seem to operate in a classically Turnerian fashion.

Spirit possession is certainly a ritual mode, but as scholars of Afro-Caribbean religion have repeatedly shown, it does not bring the community together into a shared communitas, as the Turners would have it. Rather, souls who are ridden by the gods in, say, *vodun,* lose personal identity altogether in trance, while the rest of the community retains different ritual identities as priest/priestess, assistant, or worshiper. Certainly there is a powerful collective ritual sensibility in Black Church song, but it is not simply the "anti-structure" so prominent in Native American dance and Chicano pilgrimage. The lens of sacred song seems to bring into focus important comparative differences of this sort within theoretically monolithic categories like ritual. Native American, Chicano, and African American sacred song all facilitate ritual transformation, but they are significantly different kinds of transformation mediated by quite different musical, textual, and ritual forms.

The Black Church example also points to a very different way of understanding what sacred song means through the tools of literary theory, here Henry Lewis Gates Jr.'s concept of "signifyin(g)" as an improvisational mode that characterizes African and African American cultural expression. If Gates is right, and Samuel Floyd's application of "signifyin(g)" to music seems to bear out his case, then African American sacred song acquires its religious meaning not primarily because of its mythic text or ritual performance but because it embodies in a specially heightened manner a people's most fundamental way of communicating.[2]

The truly original contribution of Gates's theory to the study of sacred song is that sacrality lies not in what is said, but in how it is said. The more "signified" an utterance is, the more meaningful it becomes. When, in the Black Church, the endless rhythmic and melodic reiterations of African shout are covered by an improvising solo voice that "signifies" the text with prophetic energy, it is the call-and-response quality of this "signification" that confers sacred meaning. Articulation of traditional musical and textual figures with such extraordinarily intense "signification" is the key to the meaning of the sung sermon and the gospel shout, the two most powerful forms of sacred song in the Black Church.

This interpretation of Black Church song points to another dimension of Native American and Chicano sacred song that has escaped Turnerian ritual analysis. Gates invites us to consider sacred song not as a ritual medium that alters consciousness but as an interactive, layered form of expression with its own inherent meaning. Paying attention to expressive form yielded for Gates the notion of polyvocal "signifyin(g)." If we return to Native American sacred song with this same focus on expressive form, another interactive synergy appears, namely the profound link between song and dance. Native American sacred song does not fully disclose its religious meaning apart from the dance that it creates. Likewise the religious meaning of Chicano alabados is incompletely understood if the physical movement of pilgrimage is not included as an essential part of its public expression.

It is not clear what implications would attend a shift from ritual analysis to the interpretation of interactive expressive form for Native American and Chicano sacred song. There is indeed much more to be done along this line even with Black Church song. What is most important now is to acknowledge that ritual analysis of all three traditions does not exhaust their religious meanings. In religious culture form and function always exist in tension. While sacred song undoubtedly carries primary ritual functions in religion, its synergistic complexity invites us to think beyond ritual function to religious meanings inherent in the form itself.

In this study Native American, Chicano, and African American sacred song has expressed the most deeply traditional modalities of religious culture. The Sacred Harp and Jewish music revivals, on the other hand, articulate religious meaning at the opposite location, on the margin of secular society. Both of these examples displace traditional sacrality by locating sacred song in nontraditional performance contexts. This relocation is an emphatically postmodern phenomenon. Traditional southern singers may already be a minority within the Sacred Harp community, while very few traditional klezmer players are still alive and even fewer traditional Sephardic singers live in the United States. These sacred-song revivals have been driven by secular urban, professional, and university people who have encountered in Sacred Harp, klezmer, and Sephardic music something transcendent to embrace without requiring formal religious identity or behavior.

That "something," I think, is intense personal engagement with a mythic past through sacred song, either as a singer or as a listener. The conditions of postmodernity have reduced the ability of religious institutions to sustain a traditional belief system and have alienated individuals from those same institutions and beliefs. The "secondary sacrality" of Sacred Harp singings and the "paraliturgical" musics of largely lost Ashkenazic and Sephardic communities invite postmoderns to engage with the beliefs and practices presented in the singing and playing, but do not obligate them to affirm the beliefs or perform the practices. Participants in these sacred-song revivals engage with religious traditions and traditionally religious musicians, but they can hold the primary sacrality of religious commitment at arm's length.

What is remarkable for our inquiry is that in these cases sacred song both establishes the link to the traditional past and supplies the buffer to keep it from becoming too intrusive or all consuming. To sing Sacred Harp, attend a Sephardic concert, or hire a klezmer band brings the participant into direct contact with authentic sacred song and religious music-making. Yet it is, after all, only song and music-making, and not attendance at a Primitive Baptist church or Hasidic synagogue. Here sacred song supplies both authenticity and openness, engagement and optionality. Why sacred song can perform this extraordinary functional paradox is not clear. That it does so, however, opens the way for a new understanding of sacred song's potential meaning in postmodern society.

Part 2 of this book documents additional meanings and functions of sacred song from more contemporary contexts and religious movements. It presents a set of unlikely pairings that illustrate the range and diversity of those functions. One such pair, Kay Gardner's New Age and *The New Century Hymnal* of the United Church of Christ, indicates the power of sacred song to influence the realm of religious beliefs. The contrasts between the two cases are obvious enough. What fascinates are the comparisons.

The point of sacred song's impact differs in the two cases. Gardner's music and teachings have been foundational for the rise of the New Age movement, while the inclusive language that informs *The New Century Hymnal* is the latest of many historic reforms in the history of the UCC and its constituent communions. Yet both the New Age and *The New Century Hymnal* have had significant intellectual impact on American religious communities and, not coincidentally, they are both rooted in late twentieth-century feminism. The New Age, and especially Gardner's Wiccan branch of it, is preponderantly female and took its intellectual origin from the radical feminism of the 1960s and 1970s. The UCC, historic heir of the Puritans, has become increasingly female in membership and leadership, as have most liberal Protestant denominations. Many UCC women ministers and lay leaders, like their New Age sisters, are products of the postwar feminist movement.

The most striking similarity between these two examples of sacred song's influence on beliefs, however, is that neither of them has been primarily concerned with sacred-song performance. *The New Century Hymnal* controversy is about inclusive editing of traditional hymn texts, not about the tunes assigned to them or how and when to sing them. Gardner's initial fame rested on the popularity of her meditation music, but her influence as a New Age *savant* derives from her cosmological teachings about music.

Gardner's New Age cosmologies and the UCC's inclusive-language movement have been successful feminist religious movements that shaped the thought of their religious constituencies. Their teachings are not fundamentally about women but rather about how women's realities must be incorporated into any religious culture. Initially, both movements encountered little institutional resistance. The decentralized pluralism of the New Age allowed Gardner's teachings to float freely, embraced whole or in part by the movement's eclectic constituencies. Inclusive language triumphed in the UCC as a 1970s liberal Protestant theological renewal movement, combining with civil rights, Vietnam War pacifism, and a social justice agenda to produce a new standard for religious speech. Significantly, however, it was in its reform of sacred song that inclusive language encountered its greatest resistance in the UCC. Both movements offered new language for and about sacred song, but when the inclusive language movement sought to reform a traditional canon of hymn texts it faltered, but has not failed.

Another unlikely pairing, the Mormon Tabernacle Choir and John Michael Talbot, may seem to make an inauspicious functional combination, but they both exemplify the powerful effects of sacred song on religious institutions. In the choir's case, the institutional function of sacred song has been to legitimate a once-radical and remote religious sect. In Talbot's case sacred song has made possible the creation of a new religious institution, the Brothers and Sisters of Charity. These examples document sacred song's impact at two different stages of institutional development, but the larger function they both illustrate is sacred song's ability to mold the fate of religious institutions in contemporary America. This is an altogether new phenomenon in Christian history and has rarely if ever been seen in world religions.

Two other crucial parallels between the choir and Talbot are the power of media exposure and the performance of popular music repertory used to generate financial and cultural support for experimental religious communities. The choir has aggressively presented a repertory of Christian sacred classics since the Chicago Columbian Exposition of 1893. Technology and taste blended together in the national popularity of the choir's Sunday evening broadcast during the golden age of radio and in its successful recording collaboration with the Philadelphia Orchestra, the ensemble filmed during the same postwar period by Walt Disney in *Fantasia*. There is no other example of sectarian legitimation through sacred song in American history remotely as successful as the choir's. It is not likely to be repeated. Yet it serves notice of sacred song's power to shape American attitudes toward entire religious communities.

Similarly, Talbot's live performances and successful recordings have laid the popular and financial foundations for his religious community. Talbot's recordings have always been beautifully engineered to capture the nuances of his singing and playing. He quickly changed over to cassette and compact-disc formats when those new audio technologies became available, and now he is producing videos. More directly relevant to sacred song's function is the simplicity of musical style and biblical lyricism in his songs. As a composer of spiritual ballads and praise songs, Talbot has kept it simple without sacrificing musical or textual substance. These qualities make his songs ideal for congregational singing, and thereby for consistent popularity and sales.

No one will confuse Talbot's *Come to the Quiet* with the Tabernacle Choir's recording of Handel's *Messiah,* but both performances play to a broad-based

American audience with a taste for familiar works and musical styles. And now the choir has embarked on a new concert anthem style that brings it into mainstream Evangelical church music. This combination of advanced media and recording technology with popular musical repertory has provided large financial and cultural capital for the Latter-day Saints and the Brothers and Sisters of Charity to legitimate and launch major religious institutions.

A final combination of examples, conservatory composers and gospel music, highlights yet another dimension of sacred song's function in religious culture, this time at the frontier of religion and commercialization. Daniel Pinkham and Neely Bruce offer different understandings of the task of the conservatory-trained sacred art music composer, but they both make their livings teaching, writing, and performing sacred music in elite institutional settings. Their differences take the measure of the discourse among sacred-music composers today on matters of textual interpretation, stylistic appropriateness, creative autonomy, and personal religious investment. Yet both of them inhabit an artistic world dependent on financial patronage and the influence it wields, implicitly or explicitly, on the works they and their colleagues compose and perform.

Gospel music presents a musical, cultural, and religious surface quite different from the world of conservatory and choir loft, but at base it too faces the challenge of maintaining religious and artistic authenticity in the face of ever-increasing influence from patrons, producers, and distributors. These commercial interests seek excellence of composition and performance in both the classical and the gospel music industries. By supplying commissions and contracts, however, their patronage imposes constraints on the very qualities of creativity it seeks to sponsor.

The conservatory seems to escape the worst of Adorno's culture industry afflictions, though the musical conservatism of concert audiences is the bane of contemporary composers.[3] Classically trained composers seem more stylistically free than their gospel counterparts, but then innovation is a prime value of the elite contemporary music industry while fidelity to traditional forms is a fundamental imperative of the gospel-music business. If conservatory-trained composers and gospel artists can continue to resist the market forces that increasingly determine their survival, then both styles of American sacred music can hope to embody the heroic qualities with which Adorno would have endowed them. If not, then both kinds of sacred song will prove American in another, lesser sense, prone to the manipulation and commodification that so deeply marks our culture in the twenty-first century.

One other problematic has informed this study from beginning to end: the problem of public versus private or communal expressions of religion. This issue has not achieved canonical theoretical status because it is of such recent origin. Made possible by twentieth-century America's cultural environment of mass media and instant telecommunications, the distinction between public and private expressions and meanings of religion presents new issues quite beyond the reach of standard theories of religion. While important work has been done on religious conflict and religious pluralism, the problem of publicity is a new and peculiarly, if not uniquely, American one.

The issue is not how to describe hostility between or coexistence among different religious communities in a single society. The question is rather how to interpret the meaning of a genre of religious expression, in this case sacred song, in a cultural regime that makes it available and attractive to believers and non-believers alike. American religious liberty has served, as James Madison predicted in his 1785 *Memorial and Remonstrance*, to encourage religious diversity and give religion a secure place in the nation's public culture. What has happened since World War II, however, is the creation of a media environment that has transformed religious diversity into market competition. Specific genres of religious expression, and especially sacred song, have thereby become public in a new sense. To a significant degree they have been detached from their traditional religious communities and relocated into a new public dimension of commercial cultural commodity.[4]

Though massive and growing, this market transformation of public religious expression is still quite incomplete. American sacred song today exists both in the new cultural commodity environment and in traditional religious contexts. This study has noted the impact of the new commercialization on every variety of sacred song that has been examined. That impact has ranged from the cottage-industry recordings of Native American and Sacred Harp groups through the burgeoning of klezmer and New Age as world-music genres to the vast commercial domain of gospel music. All of these examples have one common reality: American sacred-song performers today routinely produce and sell recordings in order to keep performing. To perform sacred song is to sell it. This marketing reality in turn opens sacred-song traditions to nonbelievers as well as believers. The question is whether the nonbelievers are purchasing and consuming music or religion.

I have resisted the temptation to issue a blanket condemnation or endorsement of sacred-song commercialization. It is frankly too soon to know how sacred song will fare as a commodity. What is more important for understanding public religious expression in America is the inclusion of commercialization as a primary process whereby religious expression becomes public. It will no longer suffice to interpret American religious culture as if the market did not profoundly influence its forms of public expression. Whether the new market economy sustains or distorts the religious meaning of sacred song, it unquestionably provides a new functional relationship between religious expression and the public that demands theoretical assessment.

Finally, this study has also prompted broader reflections on how religious culture might be understood through these meanings and functions of sacred song. Along the way, many theoretical categories have been invoked to explain how sacred song works in different religions: liminality, primary and secondary sacrality, kratophany, repristination, legitimation, and so on. But the inquiry has also suggested a larger commentary on the very concept of religious culture itself.

The study of religion has consistently employed theories of religion that are reductionistic or factorial. Both kinds reflect the dominance of social scientific method on the field. From Marx, Durkheim, and Freud came the legacy of theories that reduce religion to something else: capitalist ideology, societal representation, psychological neurosis. Other theorists, including Weber, Eliade, and Turner, have contributed models that interpret religion in terms of historical cause and effect, social structure and function, or the human capacity to create symbols and rationally order the world.[5]

Both varieties of theory have made vitally important contributions to understanding religious culture, but they conspicuously fail to address the problem of how different aspects of religion might relate to one another. I began this book by citing one theory that does promise to consider that problem, Clifford Geertz's concept of religion as a cultural system of beliefs, institutions, rituals, and moral and spiritual norms. While Geertz tried to introduce the notion of interaction between these elements in his definition, it was only a one-way dynamic beginning with beliefs and ending with behavior. In his field studies, however, Geertz has proved a much more flexible practitioner of his own theory, especially in his famed studies of Islam and of Balinese ritual. Yet even in this work, the theoretical formulation of religious culture tended toward the mechanical as it does almost everywhere else in the study of religion.[6]

If this study has demonstrated one truth, it is that sacred song does not act in religious cultures in a monolithic or mechanical manner. Sacred song is not a static factor of religiousness set in fixed relationships to a primal cause or to a series of reified elements of religious culture. To the contrary, sacred song interacts with and can alter all of Geertz's elements. Different varieties of sacred song, moreover, can have differential impact on the same factor. Sacred song's role in religion today extends even beyond explicit or formal religious cultures into the realms of secondary sacrality and the paraliturgical.

What all of this means, quite simply, is that when we place sacred song at the center of inquiry, it shows us more than a set of different functions within a fixed model of religious culture. It reveals the moving, protean, interactive reality that gives religious cultures their dynamism and vitality. In this sense sacred song comes close to disclosing what makes religion live as an expression of human meaning. This is precisely the dimension of religious culture that twentieth-century reductionistic and factorial theories have failed to address. The exploration of expressive forms of religious culture like sacred song therefore invites a larger critique of the very idea of religion as a factorial or functional entity.

While analytical categories and theoretical models are absolutely necessary to the critical study of religion, they must always be tested against the living cultural reality they claim to comprehend. This book has provided one sort of test, and current theories, at least in the arena of sacred song, have been found wanting. Factorial and functional theories provide a rationally ordered explanation of religious cultures without which critical discourse would be impossible. But the exploration of sacred song also reminds us that religious expression is not simply rational in nature. There is a voice in the expressive forms of religious culture that belies and persistently challenges theoretical efforts to silence it by functional and factorial rationalization. More important, that voice, in the form of sacred song, speaks through and beyond every element of religious culture. Sometimes its message is one of order, sometimes one of change, but its archetypal power always resists rational reduction and therefore invites us to think about religious culture as a dynamic whole animated by its expressive forms as well as by its factorial and functional elements. For in the end it is the living reality of human religiousness that moves the believer to sing and compels the scholar to understand.

Notes

1. Victor Turner, *The Ritual Process: Structure and Anti-Structure* (Chicago: Aldine Press, 1969), and *Dramas, Fields, and Metaphors: Symbolic Action in Human Society* (Ithaca, N.Y.: Cornell University Press, 1974); Victor Turner and Edith Turner, *Image and Pilgrimage in Christian Culture* (New York: Columbia University Press, 1978).

2. Henry Louis Gates Jr., *The Signifying Monkey: A Theory of African-American Literary Criticism* (New York: Oxford University Press, 1995); Samuel A. Floyd, *The Power of Black Music: Interpreting Its History from Africa to the United States* (New York: Oxford University Press, 1995).

3. Theodor Adorno, "Culture Industry Reconsidered," in Adorno, *The Culture Industry: Selected Essays on Mass Culture,* ed. and trans. J. M. Bernstein (London: Routledge, 1991), 85–87.

4. James Madison, "A Memorial and Remonstrance against Religious Assessments," in *The Papers of James Madison,* ed. Robert A. Rutland, William M. E. Rachal, Barbara D. Ripel, and Frederika J. Teute (Chicago: University of Chicago Press, 1973), 8:295–306.

5. Karl Marx, *Marx on Religion,* ed. John Raines (Philadelphia: Temple University Press, 2002); Emile Durkheim, *The Elementary Forms of the Religious Life,* trans. Joseph Ward Swain (New York: Macmillan, 1915); Sigmund Freud, *The Future of an Illusion,* trans. James Strachey (New York: Norton, 1961); Max Weber, *The Protestant Ethic and the Spirit of Capitalism,* trans. Talcott Parsons (London: G. Allen and Unwin, 1930), and *The Sociology of Religion,* trans. Ephraim Fischoff (Boston: Beacon Press, 1963); Mircea Eliade, *The Sacred and the Profane: The Nature of Religion,* trans. Willard R. Trask (New York: Harcourt, Brace, 1959); and Turner, *The Ritual Process.*

6. Clifford Geertz, "Thick Description: Toward an Interpretive Theory of Culture," in Geertz, *The Interpretation of Cultures* (New York: Basic Books, 1973), 3–32.

Appendix: Music Examples

No. 196. Song of the Grass Dance (a) (Catalogue N. 5960)

Sung by KILLS-AT-NIGHT

VOICE ♩= 116
DRUM ♩= 116
Drum-rhythm similar to No. 19

Śuŋ - ka- wit- ko   ǩoŋ   he- ye - lo   he- wa -

wo - ki- ya   he   wa - oŋ   *we*   he - e - ye - lo   *o   a*   *he*   *yo*

WORDS

Suŋ′ka-witko′ ǩoŋ	Crazy Dog himself
he′yelo	said
hewawo′kiya he	"I helped"
waöŋ′	living
he′yelo	he said (this)

Example 1. "Song of the Grass Dance (a)," Frances Densmore, *Teton Sioux Music and Culture*, 196.

332

Mañanitas A La Virgen De Guadalupe

MORNING SONG TO THE VIRGIN   Tradicional

ESTROFAS:

1. Oh Vir - gen,__ la más her - mo - sa del Va - lle__ del A - na-huac,__ tus hi-
2. Cuan-do mi - ro tu ca - ri - ta lle - na de__ tan - to can-dor,__ qui-sie-
3. Ma - dre de__ los Me - xi - ca - nos di - jis - te__ ve - ní-as a ser; __ pues ya
4. Re - ci - be,__ Ma-dre que - ri - da, nues-tra fe - li - ci - ta-ción__ hoy por
5. A - que-lla a - le - gre ma - ña - na en que a-pa - re - cis-te a Juan__ mien-tras
6. Mi - ra que__ soy Me - xi - ca - no y por e - so tu - yo soy; __ bus-ca en
7. Re - ci - be,__ Ma-dre que - ri - da, nues-tra fe - li - ci - ta-ción;__ mí - ra-
8. En - vi - dia__ no ten-go a na - die si - no al án - gel que a tus pies__ ha - ce
9. Sal - ve, Vir - gen sin man - ci - lla, de be - lle - za sin i - gual, de Gua-da-
10. Tú bri - llas - te, Vir-gen San - ta, co-mo es-tre - lla ma - ti - nal, __ a-nun-
11. Hoy a tus pi - es a - cu - di - mos, díg - na-te, __ Ma - dre, mi-rar __ a tus

1. jos muy de ma - ña - na te vie - nen a __ sa - lu - dar.
2. ra dar - te mil be - sos pa - ra mos - trar - te mi a - mor.
3. lo ves, Mo - re - ni - ta, sí te sa - be - mos que - rer.
4. ser el dí-a tan gran - de de tu tier - na a - pa - ri - ción.
5. Dios me dé la vi - da nun-ca se me ol - vi - da - rá.
6. va - no en el mun - do quien te qui - e - ra más que yo.
7. nos a - quí pos - tra - dos y da - nos tu __ ben - di - ción.
8. cua - tro - cien-tos a - ños que te sir - ve__ de es - ca - bel.
9. lu - pe es tu nom - bre y tu tro - no el__ Te - pe - yac.
10. cian - do la al-bo - ra - da que i-ba pron-to a__ co - men - zar.
11. hi - jos que llo - ran-do ve - ni - mos an - te tu al - tar.

ESTRIBILLO:

Des - pier - ta, Ma-dre, des - pier - ta; mi - ra que ya a-ma-ne-

Fin

ció, mi-ra es - te ra-mo de flo - res que pa - ra ti__ trai - go yo.

Example 2. "Mañanitas a La Virgen de Guadalupe," *Flor y Canto,* 209.

333

Alabado Sea El Santísimo

PRAISE TO THE HOLY SACRAMENT

Tradicional

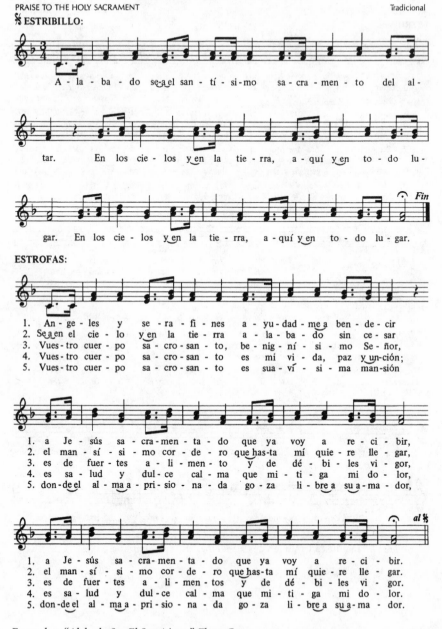

Example 3. "Alabado Sea El Santísimo," *Flor y Canto*, 291.

Grita, Profeta

CRY OUT, PROPHET

Emilio Vicente Matéu

ESTROFAS:

Example 4. Emilio Vicente Mateu, "Grita, Profeta," *Flor y Canto*, 351.

Example 4. Con't.

De Los Cuatro Vientos

FROM THE FOUR WINDS

Arsenio Córdova

Example 5. Arsenio Cordova, "De Los Cuatro Vientos," *Flor y Canto,* 358.

Bendito, Bendito

Tradicional

1. Ben - di - to, ben - di - to, ben - di - to se - a Dios, los
2. Je - sús de mi al - ma, te doy mi co - ra - zón; y en
3. A - do - ro en la hos - tia el cuer - po de Je - sús, su
4. A tus plan - tas lle - go con - fu - so de do - lor, de
5. Yo cre - o, Dios mí - o, que es - tás en el al - tar, o -
6. Oh cie - lo y tie - rra, de - cid a u - na voz, ben -

1. án - ge - les can - tan y a - la - ban a Dios, los
2. cam - bio te pi - do me des tu ben - di - ción, y en
3. san - gre pre - cio - sa que dio por mí en la cruz, su
4. to - das mis cul - pas im - plo - ro tu per - dón, de
5. cul - to en la Hos - tia te ven - go a a - do - rar, o -
6. di - to por siem - pre, ben - di - to se - a Dios, ben -

1. án - ge - les can - tan y a - la - ban a Dios.
2. cam - bio te pi - do me des tu ben - di - ción.
3. san - gre pre - cio - sa que dio por mí en la cruz.
4. to - das mis cul - pas im - plo - ro tu per - dón.
5. cul - to en la hos - tia te ven - go a a - do - rar.
6. di - to por siem - pre, ben - di - to se - a Dios.

Example 6. "Bendito, Bendito," *Flor y Canto*, 424.

Example 7. Charles Wesley and Thomas Waller, "Love Divine," *The Sacred Harp*, 30.

339

HOLY MANNA. 8s & 7s.
"Worship the Lord in the beauty of holiness." -- Ps. 29:2.

C Major George Atkin, 1819.

William Moore, 1825.

1. Breth-ren, we have met to wor-ship, And a - dore the Lord our God;
Will you pray with all your pow - er, While we try to preach the word?
All is vain un - less the Spir - it of the Ho - ly One comes down; Breth-ren, pray and

ho - ly man - na   Will be show-ered all   a - round.

2 Brethren, see poor sinners round you,
   Trembling on the brink of woe;
   Death is coming, hell is moving,
   Can you bear to let them go?
   See our fathers, see our mothers,
   And our children sinking down;
   Brethren, pray and holy manna
   Will be showered all around.

3 Sisters, will you join and help us?
   Moses' sisters aided him;
   Will you help the trembling mourners,
   Who are struggling hard with sin?
   Tell them all about the Saviour,
   Tell them that He will be found;
   Sisters, pray, and holy manna
   Will be showered all around.

4 Is there here a trembling jailer,
   Seeking grace, and filled with fears?
   Is there here a weeping Mary,
   Pouring forth a flood of tears?
   Brethren, join your cries to help them;
   Sisters, let your prayers abound;
   Pray, O pray that holy manna
   May be scattered all around.

5 Let us love our God supremely,
   Let us love each other, too;
   Let us love and pray for sinners,
   Till our God makes all things new.
   Then He'll call us home to heaven,
   At His table we'll sit down;
   Christ will gird Himself, and serve us
   With sweet manna all around.

Example 8. George Atkin and William Moore, "Holy Manna," *The Sacred Harp*, 59.

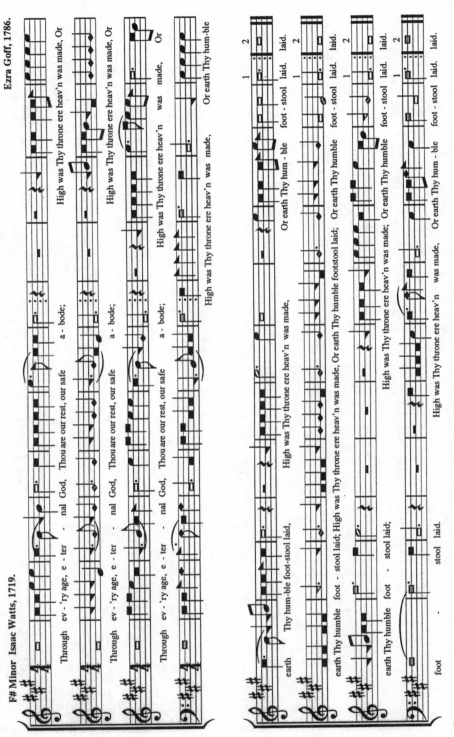

Example 9. Isaac Watts and Ezra Goff, "Stratfield," *The Sacred Harp*, 142.

PARTING HAND. L.M.

"But as touching brotherly love ye need not that I write unto you: for ye yourselves are taught of God to love one another." -- 1 Thes. 4:9.

G Major   John Blain, 1818.

Arr. - William Walker, 1835.

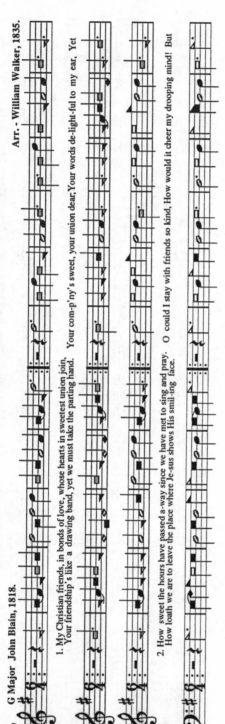

1. My Christian friends, in bonds of love, whose hearts in sweetest union join,
Your friendship's like a drawing band, yet we must take the parting hand.
Your com-p'ny's sweet, your union dear, Your words de-light-ful to my ear, Yet

2. How sweet the hours have passed a-way since we have met to sing and pray.
How loath we are to leave the place where Je-sus shows His smil-ing face.

when I see that we must part, You draw like cords around my heart.

du - ty makes me un-der-stand That we must take the part - ing hand.

3. And since it is God's holy will,
We must be parted for a while,
In sweet submission, all as one,
We'll say, our Father's will be done.

My youthful friends, in Christian ties,
Who seek for mansions in the skies,
Fight on, we'll gain that happy shore,
Where parting will be known no more.

4. How oft I've seen your flowing tears,
And heard you tell your hopes and fears!
Your hearts with love were seen to flame,
Which makes me hope we'll meet again.

Ye mourning souls, lift up your eyes
To glorious mansions in the skies;
O trust His grace -- in Canaan's land
We'll no more take the parting hand.

5. And now my friends, both old and young,
I hope in Christ you'll still go on;
And if on earth we meet no more,
O may we meet on Canaan's shore.

I hope you'll all remember me
If on earth no more I see;
An interest in your prayers I crave,
That we meet beyond the grave.

6. O glorious day! O blessed hope!
My soul leaps forward at the thought
When, on that happy, happy land,
We'll no more take the parting hand.

But with our blessed holy Lord
We'll shout and sing with one accord,
And there we'll all with Jesus dwell,
So, loving Christians, fare you well.

Example 10. John Blain and William Walker, "Parting Hand," *The Sacred Harp*, 62.

342

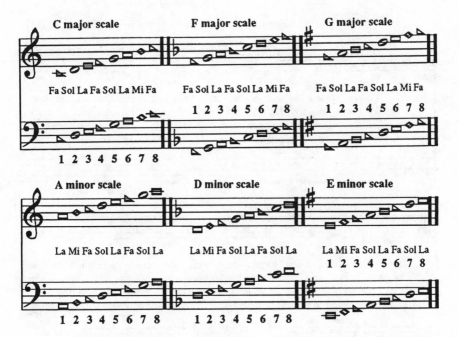

Example 11. The Shape Note Gamut, *The Sacred Harp*, ix.

343

"We'll Understand It Better By and By" (Charles Albert Tindley, orig. © 1905).

Example 12. Charles Albert Tindley, "We'll Understand It Better By and By."

Example 12. Con't.

Take My Hand, Precious Lord (original)

Example 13. Thomas A. Dorsey, "Take My Hand, Precious Lord (Original)," Michael W. Harris, *The Rise of Gospel Blues*, 127.

mm. 20-22 When my way grows—— drear, Pre-cious

mm. 23-25 Lord, lin-ger near,—— When my life—— is——

mm. 26-28 al - most—— gone,———————— Hear my

mm. 29-31 cry, hear my— call,—— Hold— my hand lest I

mm. 32-34 fall,— Take- my hand,— Pre-cious Lord,— lead me

mm. 35-36 home.————————————

Example 13. Con't.

What a Friend We Have in Jesus

Greater love has no one than this — John 15:13 NIV

1. What a friend we have in Je - sus, All our sins and griefs to bear!
2. Have we tri - als and temp - ta - tions? Is there trou - ble an - y - where?
3. Are we weak and heav - y lad - en, Cum-bered with a load of care?

What a priv - i - lege to car - ry Ev - 'ry-thing to God in prayer!
We should nev - er be dis-cour - aged, Take it to the Lord in prayer:
Pre - cious Sav - ior, still our ref - uge; Take it to the Lord in prayer:

Oh, what peace we of - ten for - feit, Oh, what need-less pain we bear,
Can we find a friend so faith - ful Who will all our sor-rows share?
Do thy friends de - spise, for - sake thee? Take it to the Lord in prayer;

All be - cause we do not car - ry Ev - 'ry-thing to God in prayer!
Je - sus knows our ev - 'ry weak - ness, Take it to the Lord in prayer.
In His arms He'll take and shield thee; Thou wilt find a so - lace there.

WORDS: Joseph Scriven, 1819-1886
MUSIC: Charles C. Converse, 1832-1918

CONVERSE
8.7.8.7.D.

Example 14. Joseph Scriven and Charles C. Converse, "What A Friend We Have in Jesus."

What A Friend We Have In Jesus

Words by
JOSEPH M. SCRIVEN
Arr. by Hubert Powell
Chorals arr. by Carol Cymbala

Example 15. Carol Cymbala and Hubert Powell, arr., "What A Friend We Have in Jesus," *The Brooklyn Tabernacle Choir: Live with Friends*, 96–98.

Example 15. Con't.

Example 15. Con't.

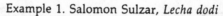

Example 1. Salomon Sulzar, *Lecha dodi*

Le - cha do - di li - krat ka - lah p' -

nei___ sha - bat___ ne - ka - be - lah le - lah.

♪ = very short note   • = long note   ↑ = pitch slightly higher than notated

• = medium note   ○ = very long note

Example 2. Lewandowski, *Lecha dodi*

Le - cha do - di li - krat ka - lah p' -

nei___ sha - bat ne - ka - be - lah le - lah.

Example 3. Second most-commonly submitted melody

Le - cha do - di li - krat ka - lah p' - nei sha - bat ne - ka - be - lah, le -

cha do - di li - krat ka - lah p' - nei sha - bat ne - ka - be - lah. Le -

cha do - di le - cha do-di li-krat ka - lah le - cha do-di li-krat ka -

lah, le - cha do-di li-krat ka - lah p' - nei sha-bat ne-ka - be - lah.

Example 16. Six Settings of *Lecha dodi*, Mark Slobin, *Chosen Voices*, 199–200.

Example 4. Hasidic-style *Lecha dodi*

Le - cha___ do - di_____ li - krat__ ka -
lah____ le - cha do - di li - krat___ ka - lah.

Example 5a. Seasonal variant: *Lecha dodi* for three Friday nights before Tisha b'Av

Le - cha do - di li - krat_ ka - lah p' - nei sha - bat ne - ka - be -
lah, le - cha do - di li - krat ka - lah p' - nei sha - bat ne - ka - be - lah.

Example 5b. Seasonal variant: *Lecha dodi* for the month of Elul

Le - cha do - di li - krat__ ka - lah p' -
nei____ sha - bat ne - ka - be - lah.

Example 16. Con't.

Example 17. "Vayhí miqéts burmuelos con miel," Isaac Levy, *Antologia de Liturgia Judeo-Espanola*, 17.

"Zuni Song"
(from "Changes")

traditional
arranged by R. Carlos Nakai

Example 18. R. Carlos Nakai, "Zuni Song," *The Art of the Native American Flute*, 59.

"Lunamuse" is a meditative work in circular form. The ostinato and the theme are constants; contrasting sections (B, C, and B¹) are to be improvised if possible. (Flute melody in section B is suggestion only.) All percussion is to be played with great subtlety. Note: Section C is the climax and should be played as such without breaking the flow of the entire work.

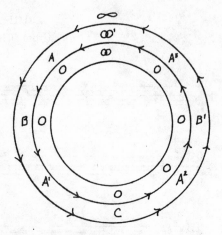

Example 19. Kay Gardner, "Design for Lunamuse," *Sounding the Inner Landscape,* 200–201.

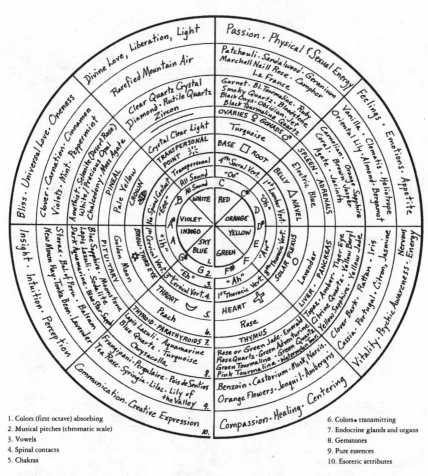

1. Colors (first octave) absorbing
2. Musical pitches (chromatic scale)
3. Vowels
4. Spinal contacts
5. Chakras

6. Colors• transmitting
7. Endocrine glands and organs
8. Gemstones
9. Pure essences
10. Esoteric attributes

Example 20. Kay Gardner, "Chart of Color, Sound, and Energy Correspondences," *Sounding the Inner Landscape*, 26–27.

Come, Come, Ye Saints

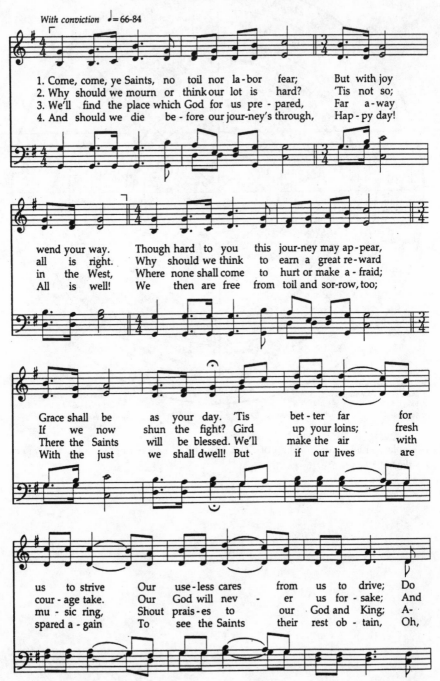

Example 21. William Clayton, "Come, Come, Ye Saints," *Hymns of the Church of Jesus Christ of Latter-day Saints*, 30.

this, and	joy your hearts will	swell— All	is well!	All is well!
soon we'll have this	tale to	tell — All	is well!	All is well!
bove the rest these	words we'll	tell — All	is well!	All is well!
how we'll make this	cho-rus	swell— All	is well!	All is well!

Text: William Clayton, 1814-1879
Music: English folk song

Doctrine and Covenants 61:36-39
Doctrine and Covenants 59:1-4

Example 21. Con't.

ALL IS WELL. P.M.

"Through the righteousness of God and our Savior Jesus Christ." -- 2 Peter 1:1.

A Major *Revival Melodies, 1842.*

Arr. - J. T. White, 1844

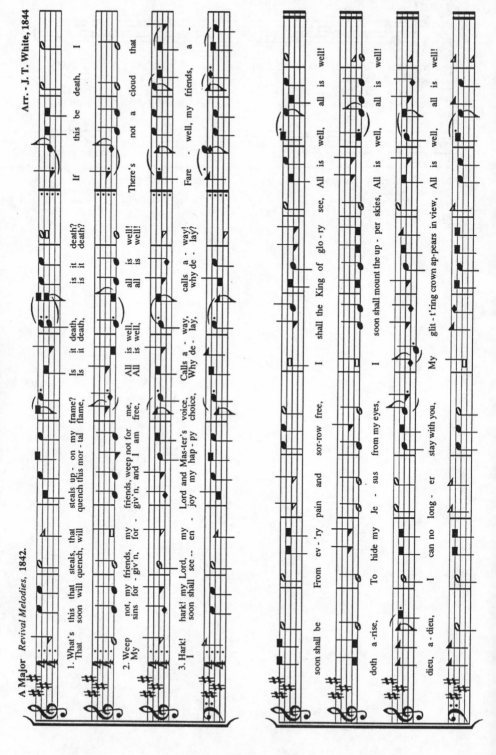

1. What's this that steals, that steals up - on my frame? Is it death, is it death? If this be death, I
   That soon will quench, will quench this mor - tal flame, Is it death, is it death?

2. Weep not, my friends, my friends for - giv'n, There's not a cloud that
   My sins for - giv'n, and I am free, All is well, all is well!

3. Hark! hark! my Lord, my Lord and Mas-ter's voice, Calls a - way, calls a - way, Fare - well, my friends, a -
   I soon shall see -- en - joy my hap-py choice, Why de - lay, why de - lay?

soon shall be From ev - 'ry pain and sor-row free,   I shall the King of glo - ry see, All is well, all is well!

doth a - rise, To hide my Je - sus from my eyes,   I soon shall mount the up - per skies, All is well, all is well!

dieu, a - dieu, I can no long - er stay with you, My glit - t'ring crown ap-pears in view, All is well, all is well!

360

Seven Values
I Walk by Faith
(Moroni 7:28)

Words and Music by:
Janice Kapp Perry

With Conviction ♩=70

I will pre-pare to make and keep sa-cred cov-e-nants, Seek prom-ised bless-ings of the priest-hood through o-be-di-ence, Live my life to claim the bless-ing sweet of ex - al - ta-tion, My

Example 23. Janice Knapp Perry, "I Walk by Faith."

Example 23. Con't.

Example 23. Con't.

Example 23. Con't.

I Corinthians 13

Words and Music by
John Michael Talbot

Example 24. John Michael Talbot, "1 Corinthians 13," *Come Worship the Lord*, 5.

Example 24. Con't.

Example 24. Con't.

Our God Reigns

Words and Music by
Leonard E. Smith, Jr.

Example 25. Leonard E. Smith Jr., "Our God Reigns."

Example 25. Con't.

Holy, Holy, Holy
(Hosanna)

Music by
Peter Scholtes

Example 26. Peter Scholtes, "Holy, Holy, Holy (Hosanna)."

Example 26. Con't.

One Bread, One Body

Based on 1 Corinthians 10:16,17; 12:4;
Galatians 3:28
The Didache 9

JOHN FOLEY, S.J.

REFRAIN

One bread, — one bod-y, _____ one Lord of all, one cup of bless - ing which we bless. ____ And we, __ though man-y, ____ through-out the earth, we are one bod - y in this one Lord.

Example 27. John Foley, S.J., "One Bread, One Body," *Glory and Praise*, 180.

VERSES

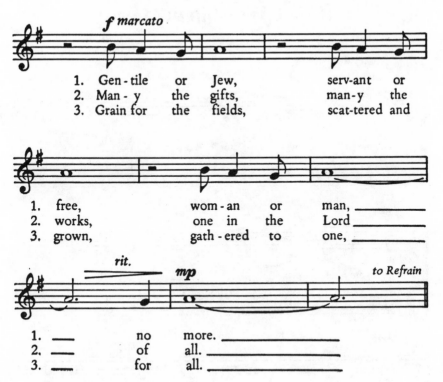

1. Gen-tile or Jew, serv-ant or free, wom-an or man, ___ ___ no more. ___
2. Man-y the gifts, man-y the works, one in the Lord ___ ___ of all. ___
3. Grain for the fields, scat-tered and grown, gath-ered to one, ___ ___ for all. ___

Example 27. Con't.

Psalm 95
(Come Worship the Lord)

Words and Music by
John Michael Talbot

Example 28. John Michael Talbot, "Psalm 95 (Come Worship the Lord)," *Come Worship the Lord*, 34.

Example 28. Con't.

I'll Fly Away

We would prefer to be away from the body and at home with the Lord. 2 Corinthians 5:8

TEXT: Albert E. Brumley
MUSIC: Albert E. Brumley

I'LL FLY AWAY
9.4.9.4. with Refrain

Example 29. Albert Brumley, "I'll Fly Away."

Index of Titles and First Lines

"Alabado de Dios," 48
"Alabado Sea El Santísimo," 48–49, 50, 291
Alleluia (Thompson), 278
"All Is Well," 233, 360
Amazing Grace, 85
Amazing Grace with Bill Moyers, 85
"America," 224
Americana (Bruce), 278
American Christmas Harp, An, 85
"America the Beautiful," 203
Ancestral Voices, 167
Ascension Cantata (Pinkham), 266
"Aurelia," 216
Autobiography of Benjamin Franklin, The, 279

Baptist Faith and Message, 193
Baptist Hymnal, 1991, The, 189–93, 208–10
"Battle Hymn of the Republic, The," 226
"Battle of San Pietro, The," 225
Bay Psalm Book, The, 74, 75, 78, 79
"Bendito, Bendito," 63–65, 338
Billboard Magazine, 296, 314
Blood of the Poet, The, 268
Bolero (Ravel), 267
Book of Doctrine and Covenants, The, 214, 231
Book of Mormon, The, 213–14; Moroni 7:28, 361–64
Boston Handel and Haydn Collection of Church Music, The, 81
Brazilian Mass (Berger), 217
Bridges, 308
Brief Introduction to the Skill of Music, 74
"Bright Morning Stars Are Shining," 165

Broken Covenant, The, 221, 316

Cánticos Espirituales, 63
Cánticos Mexicanos, 63
Cantos Sagrados Populares, 63
Changes (book), 247
Changes (recording), 167
Chant, 178
"Chart of Color, Sound, and Energy Correspondences," 357
Chichester Psalms (Bernstein), 292
Children's Songbook, 235
Christian Harmony, The, 81
Christian Lyre, The, 317
Christmas at Temple Square, 229
Christmas Cantata (Pinkham), 266
Christmas Sampler, 229
Church Music Handbook, 233–34
"Church's One Foundation, The," 216
Collection of Best Psalm Tunes, 78
Collection of Hymns and Spiritual Songs, 109
Collection of Sacred Hymns for the Church of the Latter-day Saints, 231
"Come, Come Ye Saints," 225, 232–33, 358–59
"Come, my Beloved, to meet the Bride," 134
"Come, O Fount of Every Blessing," 200–203
"Come, Thou Fount of Every Blessing," 199–203
Come to the Quiet, 325
Come Worship the Lord, 261
Commentary, 155
Concertante for Celeste and Harpsichord (Pinkham), 270
"Consider the Lilies," 243

Conversion of Saul (Pinkham), 266
Crabb Grass, 308
Creation of the World (Pinkham), 268
Cycles, 167

December: Piano Solos, 167
"De Los Cuatro Vientos," 56–57, 337
Democracy in America, 316
*Democratization of American Christianity,
    The,* 317
Deseret Sunday School Union Music Book, 235
Deseret Sunday School Union Song Book, 235
Destination Culture, 145
Dialectic of Enlightenment, 313
*Directory and Minutes of Sacred Harp Sing-
    ings,* 81
Don Giovanni (Mozart), 288
Drawing Down the Moon, 170
"Dr. Watts Hymns," 109, 111, 122, 127

Earlier American Music Series, 83
Easter Cantata (Pinkham), 266
Easy Instructor, The, 79
Eclectic Harmony, 85
Ein Heldenleben (Strauss), 180
Elijah (Mendelssohn), 218, 225, 264
Emerald Streams, 85

Fantasia, 325
Favorite Songs, 85
Fiddler on the Roof, 144
Fiddler on the Move, 145
Fifth Symphony (Beethoven), 272
Fire of God, The, 260
"I Corinthians 13," 365–66
Flor y canto, 54
Fools of Chelm, The, 137
"For the Children of the World," 300
For the Strength of Youth, 235
"From All That Dwell Below the Skies," 76
"From the Depths of My Heart," 308, 309

Genevan Psalter, 74
"Give It All to Jesus," 105
Glagolitic Mass (Janacek), 292
Glory and Praise, 253, 286
Godspell, 106
Gospel Hymns, 116, 314
Gospel Pearls, 116
"Grita, Profeta," 55–56, 335–36

Grounds and Rules of Musick, The, 75
"Gypsy Sweetheart," 224

"Hallelujah Chorus," 219, 224
"Hallelujah Turnpike," 306
Hall's New Collection, 71
Hamm Harmony (Bruce), 278, 285
"Hand on My Shoulder," 299
Healing Voice, 169
"Hear My Supplication," 225
"Heaven in the Real World," 299
"He Understands; He'll Say, 'Well Done,'" 116
Hezekiah (Pinkham), 266
His Fullness, 112
"His Grace Was Greater," 122
"Holy, Holy, Holy (Hosanna)," 191, 369–70
"Holy Manna," 70–71, 340
Horae Lyricae, 75
"How I Got Over," 118
How Shall We Sing the Lord's Song? 204–6
Hymnal (Evangelical and Reformed Church),
    194, 210
Hymnal of the United Church of Christ, 194
"Hymnos Sagrados dedicados a Nuestro Pa-
    dre Jesus de Nazareno," 63
*Hymns: The Church of Jesus Christ of Latter-
    day Saints,* 231
Hymns and Spiritual Songs, 75
*Hymns of the Church of Jesus Christ of Latter-
    day Saints,* 232

"I Am Crucified with Christ," 104
"If I Don't Get There," 116
"I'll Fly Away," 301, 306, 375
"I'm Glad to Be at Service," 103
"In Christ Alone," 298, 300
*Inclusive Language Guidelines for the Use and
    Study of the United Church of Christ,* 194–95
Increase My Faith, 308
Introduction to the Singing of Psalm Tunes, An,
    75
Invisible Religion, The, 86
"I Stand Alone at God's Door," 306
I Walk by Faith, 235
"I Walk by Faith," 361–64

"Jesus Christ Is Risen Today," 219
"Jesus Is Just All Right with Me," 299
"Jesus, Lover of My Soul," 80
"Jesus Loves the Little Children," 300

Jesus Only, 112

"Jesus Only," 112

Jesus Only, Nos. 1 and 2, 112

"Jesus Walked This Lonesome Valley," 219

Jewish Liturgy and Its Development, 131

John Michael Talbot, 248

Journeys, 167–68

"Joy to the World," 76

Kaddish (Symphony No. 3) (Bernstein), 292

Klavieruebung (Bach), 294–95

Kleine Geistliche Concerte (Schütz), 277

Latter-day Saint Hymns, 231

Latter-day Saints Psalmody, 231

Lauds (Pinkham), 266

Lecha dodi, 134, 352–53

Liber Usualis, 267

"Lift Thine Eyes," 225

Lively Experiment, The, 316

"Liverpool," 71

Live with Friends, 126

"Living Hoop, A," 20–21

"Llanfair," 219

"Lord Is My Shepherd, The," 242

Lord's Prayer, The, 226

Lord's Song in a Strange Land, The, 135

Lord's Supper, The, 254

"Love Divine," 69, 339

"Love Divine, All Loves Excelling," 80

"Love One Another," 297–98

Lunamuse, 164, 173, 356

"Maitland," 117

"Make a Joyful Noise unto the Lord, All Ye Lands," 106

"Mañanitas a La Virgen de Guadalupe," 44–46, 209

"Manchester Hymnal," 231

Mass (Bernstein), 292

Mass in B Minor (Bach), 269

Master Musician, The, 242

"Master Musician, The," 241, 257

"May I Never Boast," 241

Meditations in the Spirit, 257

Memorial and Remonstrance, A, 327

Messiah (Handel), 226, 325

Midwest Supplement to the Sacred Harp, 85

Minhag America, 130

Missa Domestica (Pinkham), 268

Missa Gaia/Earth Mass, 166

Missa Solemnis (Beethoven), 264, 284–85, 292

Missouri Harmony, The, 80

Mooncircles, 173

"Move On Up a Little Higher," 118

Music and Musicians in Early America, 83

Music and Trance, 123, 168–69

Music in a New-Found Land, 270

Music of Black Americans, The, 109

"Must Jesus Bear the Cross Alone?" 117

Nature Religion in America, 166

"Nauvoo Hymnal," 231

"Nettleton," 199

New Century Hymnal: A Sampler, The, 198

New Century Hymnal, The, 194–210, 328; controversy, 203–7, 323–24; debate in UCC General Synod XIX, 199–200; editorial process of, 195–98; inclusive language editing of, 199–203; and *Inclusive Language Guidelines,* 194–95; origins of, 194–95; reception of, 209–10; as reform hymnal, 208–9; research for, 195

New-England Psalm-Singer, The, 78, 79, 81

New Grove Dictionary of American Music, The, 118

New Harp of Columbia, The, 81

New Northampton Collection, The, 85

New Pentecost? A, 252

Night Chant, 167

Ninth Symphony (Beethoven), 272

Northern Harmony, 85

Norumbega Harmony, The, 85

"O, for the Wings of a Dove," 218

"O Divine Redeemer," 219

"Oh, Happy Day," 118, 303

"Old Rugged Cross, The," 301

"One Bread, One Body," 253, 371–72

OneSpirit, 181

"Onward, Christian Soldiers," 191

Open Any Door, 235

Oration on Church Music, An, 80

"O Sacred Head Now Wounded," 218

"Our God Reigns," 245, 367–68

Ouroboros (Gardner), 174, 179, 180

"Parting Hand," 73–74, 342

Passion of Judas (Pinkham), 266

"Peace Prayer," 240

"Perdona a Tu Pueblo," 50

Peter Schlemihl, 137

Pilgrim Hymnal, The, 194, 209

Plague, The (Bruce), 278

Plain and Easie Introduction to Practicall Musicke, A, 79

Plan, The, 235

Poems of Love and the Rain (Rorem), 268

"Power in the Blood," 301

Power of Black Music, The, 125

Prairie Home Companion, A, 84, 143

Prayer of St. Francis, 219, 240

Prelude in D Major (Bach), 225

Primitive Hymns, Spiritual Songs, and Sacred Poems, 87

"Psalm 95 (Come Worship the Lord)," 373–74

Psalms for the Nativity (Bruce), 279

Psalms of David Imitated in the Language of the New Testament, The, 75

Public Worship, Private Faith, 92

Rainbow Path, A, 171, 174

Rational and Social Foundations of Music, The, 312

Repository of Sacred Music, 80, 199

Requiem (Berlioz), 219, 264

Requiem (Pinkham), 266

Requiem (Verdi), 292

Revival Melodies, 233, 360

Rivers of Delight, 84

Royal Harmony Compleat, The, 78

Sacred Canopy, The, 86

Sacred Harp, The, 68, 80, 85, 199; and gospel hymns, 315; lyrical content of, 76, 79, 184; McGraw revision of, 96; and Mormon hymnody, 233; and narrative, 93; performance of, 94

Sacred Harp Bicentennial, 85

Sacred Harper's Companion, The, 85

Sacred Harp Singings, 82, 87, 90, 96

Sacred Hymns and Spiritual Songs, 231

Sacrosanctum Concilium, 249–51

Saint Mark Passion (Pinkham), 266

Saturday's Warrior, 235

Savior of the World, The, 235

"Schenectady," 72

Schlemiel the First (Netsky), 137–40

Scottish Psalter, 74

Selected Hymns, 232, 233

Shaker Shapes (Bruce), 279

Shaman's Cave, 181

"Shape Note Gamut, The," 343

Signifying Monkey, The, 125

Simplicity, 257

Sing with Me! 235

Slave Songs of the United States, 110

"Slippers with Wings," 306

Social Harp, The, 81

"Song of the Grass Dance (a)," 28, 332

Songs of Zion, 231

"Son Is Going to Shine Again, The," 298

Sounding the Inner Landscape, 171

Southern Harmony and Musical Companion, The, 80

Spectrum Suite, 166

Spiral Dance, The, 170–71

"Spirit of the Living God," 244

Stabat Mater (Pinkham), 266

"Stand by Me," 116, 301

Starborn Suite, 167

"Steal Away," 203

"Stratfield," 71, 341

Subcultural Sounds, 154–55

"Super Jesus," 299

"Take My Hand, Precious Lord," 116–17, 301, 346–47

"Thank You," 308

"There'll Be Peace in the Valley," 116

Thesaurus of Hebrew-Oriental Melodies, 135

"Through It All," 104

Toccata in F (Widor), 225

Tuning the Human Instrument, 167

Urania; or a Choice Collection of Psalm-Tunes, Anthems, and Hymns, 78

"Vayhí miqéts burmuelos con miel," 150–51, 354

Vedas, 7

"Villulia," 93

Viriditas (Gardner), 174

"Wake Up Call," 299

"Warrenton," 199

War Requiem (Britten), 291

"Waterfall Improvisation," 164

Wedding Cantata (Pinkham), 266

Well-Tempered Klavier, The (Bach), 269, 312

"We'll Understand It Better By and By," 116, 344–45

West Side Story (Bernstein), 182

"We Will Meet Him in the Sweet By and By," 116

"What a Friend We Have in Jesus," 126, 301, 348–51

"What a Savior, What a Friend," 306

"What Did the Lady of the Passover Eat?" 150

"When All Will Be Together," 299

"Where Are the Nine?" 106–8

Whole Booke of Psalmes, The, 74

World of Our Fathers, The, 155

"Yes, God Is Real," 118

Zlateh the Goat, 137

Zodiac Suite, 166

"Zuni Song," 167, 355

Index of Names and Subjects

Abena, Nurudina Pili, 181
Abeyta, Bernardo, 51, 52, 53, 61
Adler, Margo, 170
Adler, Samuel, 136
Adorno, Theodor, 313, 314–16, 317, 318, 326
Adventists, 317
African Methodist Episcopal Church, 100, 109, 111
African Methodist Episcopal Church Zion, 100, 111
Alabados, 62–65. *See also* Penitentes
Albanese, Catherine, 166
Aleichem, Sholem, 137
Alkabetz, Solomon, 134
Allen, George N., 117
Allen, Richard, 109
Alverna Retreat Center, 249, 253, 260
Ambrose of Milan, 302
American Choral Directors Association, 268
American Music Theater Group, 94
Anglican cathedral music, 282
Anointed, 300
Antigua style, 52
Anti-Mission Baptists, 88
Apostolic Church of God (Chicago), 101–8; architecture in, 102–3; music ministry of, 119–22; worship service, 103–8. *See also* Brazier, Bishop Arthur M.; Pentecostal Assemblies of the World; Wilson, Stuart
Aragón, José Rafael, 47
Aragón, Miguel, 47
Arcadia Bluegrass Festival, 309
Archibeque, Miguel, 61
Arianism, 205

Aristotle, 6
Arrieta, Pedro de, 41
Ashanti, 108
Atkin, George, 70, 340
Auden, W. H., 5
Augusta, Georgia, 304
Augustine of Hippo, 7
Auric, Georges, 269
Avalon, 314
Azevedo, Lex de, 235
Azusa Street Revival, 113

Baal Shem Tov, 141
Babbitt, Milton, 272
Bach, Johann Sebastian, 1, 77, 218, 312; and Mormon Tabernacle Choir, 224, 225, 269
Bad Company, 310
Bad Hand, Howard, 20, 22, 25–26, 27, 31–33
Baptist Hymnal, 1991, The: as consensus hymnal, 209–10; and fundamentalism, 192–93; and inclusive language, 191–92; origins of, 189–90; reception of, 192, 209; selection of hymns for, 190–92; as theological statement, 193
Baptists, 78; Anti-Mission, 88; in Chicago, 116–18, 119; in Georgia, 80; hymnals, 285; Primitive, 69, 88, 280; in the rural South, 81; and Watts, 78, 184
Baroque, German, 77
Barrand, Anthony G., 85
Barriero, Antonio, 60
Barron, Sam, 172
Bates, Katherine Lee, 203
Bausch, Michael G., 185

Bayley-Hazen Singers, 83

Beach Boys, 247

Beale, John, 92, 93, 94

Beatles, 247, 283, 286

Beethoven, Ludwig van, 4, 264, 272, 284, 292

Bellah, Robert N., 221–22, 316

Ben-Asher, Aharon, 133

Benedict XIV, 41

Ben Eliezer, Israel, 141

Bennett, Lerone, 100

Ben-Yosi, Yosi, 133

Berger, Jean, 217

Berger, Peter, 86

Berlin, Irving, 283

Berlioz, Hector, 216, 219

Bernstein, Leonard, 264

Bestor, Kurt, 236

Beza, Theodore, 74

Bible citations: Acts 2:1–4, 112; Acts 2:38, 114; 1 Corinthians 10:16–17 and 12:4, 371; 1 Corinthians 13, 365–66; 1 Corinthians 14:15, 121; Deuteronomy 6:4–9, 132; Didache 9, 371; Ephesians 5:19, 121; Galatians 2:20, 104; Galatians 3:28, 371; Galatians 6:14 and 17, 241; John 15:13, 348; Lamentations of Jeremiah, 77; Luke 1:46–55, 77, 243; Matthew 5:1–12, 244; Matthew 6:19 and 33, 243; Matthew 11:29–30, 243; Nehemiah 8:8, 133; Psalm 17, 76; Psalm 23, 242; Psalm 95, 261, 373; Psalm 117, 76; Romans 8:28–34, 103; 1 Samuel 7:12, 201; Song of Solomon, 77

Bicentennial Revival, 248, 255, 314, 315, 317

Billings, William, 78, 79, 95, 315

Birmingham, Alabama, 82, 84, 90, 279

Black Christ (El Christo Negro), 52

Black Church: and black gospel, 304–5; chanted sermon in, 114–15; and "Dr. Watts Hymns," 109, 111; and gospel hymns, 111–12; and gospel songs, 115–19; Jubilee style in, 111; sacred song in, 100–127; sanctified style in, 111–12, 303; and shout, 110–11; and slave spirituals, 109–10; tongue-songs in, 112–13. *See also* Signifyin(g)

Blackstone Singers, 21

Black Virgin, 52

Blain, John, 73, 342

Blake, Ran, 142

Blake, William, 288–89

Blanding, Montana, 25

Bliss, Philip P., 301

Bock, Jerry, 144

Boggs, Lilburn, 222

Bohlman, Philip, 46

Booth, Mark, 5

Boston, Massachusetts, 75, 83, 131, 147, 195, 239

Boulanger, Nadia, 267

Boulder, Colorado, 84

Bourgeois, Louis, 74

Bowman, David B., 205, 208

Boyer, Horace Clarence, 116

Bradbury, William B., 301

Bradford, Barlow, 229

Brady, Byron, 18

Brahms, Johannes, 3, 264

Brazier, Bishop Arthur M., 103; musical leadership of, 114, 119–22; sermon of, 106–8

Breeden, Frank, 318

Brewster, William Herbert, 118

Brico, Antonia, 173

Bride Psychology, 299

Britten, Benjamin, 291

Brooklyn, New York, 147–48

Brooklyn Tabernacle Choir, 118, 122, 126

Brothers and Sisters of Charity (BSC): finances of, 260, 326; Franciscan roots of, 259; as public association of the faithful, 259; rule of, 259–60; Talbot as superior of, 260; uniqueness of, 260–61; Vatican response to, 261–62

Brown, Tony, 24–25

Bruce, Neely: on church performance of sacred music, 293–95; on commodification, 288; on concert performance of sacred music, 291–93; on the crisis in church music, 280–82; principal works by, 279; on recording, 289–90; on religious texts, 284–87; and the Sacred Harp revival, 83, 84; on the sacred music artist, 287–89; on styles in sacred music, 282–84; training of, 279; on Vatican II, 280–82

Brumley, Albert E., 301, 303, 304, 305; music example for, 375

Brustein, Robert, 137, 139, 140

Buber, Martin, 145

Buchanan, James, 223

Budapest, Z., 170, 173, 179

Budd, Malcolm, 3

Burne, Edwin, 61

Burrows, Derek, 148

Bush, George H. W., 229, 299

Bush, George W., 229

Butler, Don, 301–2

Byrd, William, 280
Byrds, 247, 299

Caesar, Shirley, 298
Cage, John, 271
Calvin, John, 74
Calvinism, 75, 207. *See also* Great Awakening;
    Second Great Awakening
Cambridge, Massachusetts, 83, 137, 147
Camisso, Adelbert von, 137
Campbell, Don, 169, 178
Campbell, Lucie E., 116
Canyon Records, 167
Carden, Allen D., 80
Carnegie Hall, New York, 225
Carthage, Illinois, 214
Casas, Bartolomé de Las, 62
Casey, Maurice, 271
Catano, Quirio, 52
Catholic Church: and the Charismatic Re-
    newal, 249, 251–53, 314; and "folk mass,"
    251; *Glory and Praise* hymnal of, 253; and
    the Liturgical Renewal, 249–51; praise
    songs in, 253–54; and *Sacrosanctum Conci-
    lium,* 249–51; Second Vatican Council of,
    249–52
Celtic calendar, 179
Central Illinois Sacred Harp Convention, 84
Chant, 6, 177–78. *See also* Lyrics
Chapman, Gary, 307
Chapman, Steven Curtis, 299
Charismatic Renewal. *See* Catholic Church
Charleston, South Carolina, 130
Chaucer, Geoffrey, 57
Chaves family, 53
Chavez, Cesar, 42
Chiapas, Mexico, 42
Chicago, Illinois, 83, 101–2, 113, 116–19
Chicago Sacred Harp singers, 92
Chimayó, New Mexico, 46
Chorister Guild, 282
Christ, Carol, 170
Christensen, Richard L., 204–8
Christian, Meg, 170
Christian Broadcasters Association, 258
Christian Broadcasting Network, 316
Christian Church (Disciples of Christ), 185,
    186, 317
Christian contemporary music, 258, 308
Christian Methodist Episcopal Church, 100
Christian Music Trade Association, 318

Christian Radio and Retail, 299
Christian Science, 172
Christ of the Ozarks, 254–55
Christ Temple Cathedral Church of Christ,
    Holiness (Chicago), 119
Churches of Christ, 90
Churchill, Ward, 36
Church of Christ (Holiness), 113
Church of God, 308
Church of God in Christ, 100, 113, 118
Church of Jesus Christ of Latter-day Saints
    (Mormons), 213–15; and hymnody, 230–31,
    233–34, 236; and the Mormon Tabernacle
    Choir, 221–24, 225, 317, 327
Ciclo de los pastores, 52
Cincinnati, Ohio, 131, 136
Civil religion in America, 221–22, 225, 227–28,
    316
Clayton, William, 232–33, 358–59
Cleveland, James, 118
Clyde, Arthur G., 204, 208
Cocteau, Jean, 269
Coltrane, John, 100
Columbus, Ohio, 84
Commercialization: of gospel music, 312–16;
    of powwows, 22, 37–38, 327; of sacred song,
    9–10. *See also* Culture industry; Public cul-
    ture
Communitas. *See* Liminality and communitas
Condie, Richard P., 226
Cone, James, 110, 122
Congregational Holiness Church, 304
Congregationalists, 75, 78, 81, 184, 194; English,
    75
Converse, Charles, 126; music examples from,
    348–51
Cooke, Deryck, 2
Copland, Aaron, 265, 280
Córdova, Arsenio, 56; music example from,
    337
Cornwall, J. Spencer, 224
Cortés, Hernán, 40
Cox, Harvey, 185
Crabb Family, 308
Crawford, James, 195–99, 203, 208
Creel, Harrison, 69, 70, 72
Creeltown, Alabama, 69
Crist, Carol, 216
Crosby, Fanny J., 185
Crouch, Andrae, 119, 302
Crouch, Sandra, 119

Cultural tourism, 34–38; war declared against, 36
Culture industry, 312–16, 326
Cymbala, Carol, 126; music example from, 349–52

Dakota Nation (Santee Sioux), 36
Daly, Mary, 170, 185
Dance, 28–31; African American, 108–9, 110; as communitas, 30–31; Native American, 28–31; and sacred musical style, 282–83
Davenport, James, 316
Davie, Donald, 76
Davis, Mark, 70, 72, 74
Davis, M. C. H., 71
Davison, Archibald, 265
DC Talk, 299
Debussy, Claude, 270
DeLong, Richard, 95
Deloria, Vine, Jr., 26–27
Densmore, Frances, 27–28, 332
Denver March Powwow, 18–23
Denver Symphony, 173
Dianic music, 149, 150, 178
Díaz, Porfirio, 42
Dickinson, Emily, 288
Dipko, Thomas E., 199
Disciples of Christ. *See* Christian Church (Disciples of Christ)
Disney, Walt, 325
Dixie Hummingbirds, 118
Docetism, 206
Dodson, Anne, 164, 165
Don Light Talent Agency, 306
Doobie Brothers, 247
Doran, Carol, 185
Dorsey, Thomas A., 100, 116–19; and commodified music, 314, 317; and gospel music, 301, 303, 304; music example from, 346–47
Dove Awards, 297–301, 304–7, 314, 317
Drone, 177
Drum in powwow songs, 19, 20, 25, 125
Du Bois, W. E. B., 122
Duck, Ruth C., 185
Duncan, Brian, 300
Duquesne University, 252
Durham, William H., 113
Durkheim, Emile, 220, 328

Eagles, 310
Ebenezer Baptist Church (Chicago), 118

Edwards, Jonathan, 4, 77, 78, 289
Edwin Hawkins Singers, 118, 303
Elegba, 127
Eliade, Mircea, 114, 328
Elizondo, Virgil, 44
Ellington, Duke, 100
Elliott, Willis, 203, 205
Ellsworth, Maine, 163
Ely, Ginnie, 91
Emerson, Ralph Waldo, 4
English, Michael, 298, 300
English country parish style, 76–77
Episcopal Church, 166, 185, 289. *See also* Anglican cathedral music
Eriksen, Timothy, 85
Esquipulas, Guatemala, 52–53
Esu, 127
Eureka Springs, Arkansas, 254–56
Evangelical and Reformed Church, 186, 194
Evangelicalism, American, 77–78, 80, 207; and African Americans, 100–101, 109–14, 123–24; and contemporary Christian music, 290; and gospel music, 302, 312; and Sacred Harp singing, 88–90, 95–97. *See also* Great Awakening; Holiness movement; Pentecostalism; Second Great Awakening
Evans, Richard, 224
Extremadura, Spain, 40

Fackre, Gabriel, 205
Falwell, Jerry, 316
Faulkner, William, 286
Feminism, 173, 174, 185. *See also* Women's spirituality
Fergason, John, 204
Feuerbach, Ludwig, 206
Figueroa, Pedro Pardo de, 53
Finney, Charles Grandison, 317
Fisk Jubilee Singers, 111, 311, 314
Five Blind Boys, 118
Flagg, Josiah, 78
Flathead Lake, Montana, 25
Fletcher, Harvey, 224, 225
Floyd, Samuel A., 125–27
Focillion, Henri, 279
Foley, John, S.J., 246, 253; music example from, 371–72
Forbis, Wesley L., 190, 191, 192, 193
4HIM, 298, 300
Forty Families, 42
Fox, Matthew, 169

Franc, Guillaume, 74
Franciscans, Third Order (Tertiaries), 60; and Penitentes, 60–61; and Talbot, 240, 253, 259
Francis of Assisi, Saint, 166, 302
Franklin, Aretha, 9
Franklin, Kirk, 296
Fraternidad Piedosa de Nostro Señor Jesus Nazareno, 59
Frazier, E. Franklin, 110
Freeman, James, 266
Freud, Sigmund, 206, 328
Fromm, Herbert, 136
Frost, Robert, 181
Frye, Northrop, 6
Fulani, 108

Gabon, 108
Gaither, Bill, 299
Gante, Pedro de, 62
Gardner, Kay, 164, 171–81, 324; music examples from, 356, 357
Gardner-Gordon, Joy, 169
Gates, Henry Louis, Jr., 125–27, 322–23
Geertz, Clifford, 10, 11, 328
Gelineau, Richard, 246
Geophagy, 51, 53
German Pietists, 302
Gershwin, George, 283
Gilbert, W. S., 191
Glade, Earl J., 224
Glass, Philip, 137, 167, 281
Glencoe, Alabama, 87
Glorietta, New Mexico, 188
Goddess movement, 170–71
Godfrey, Illinois, 204
Goff, Ezra, 71; music example from, 341
Górecki, Henryk, 264
Gordon, David, 140
Gordon, Larry, 83–85
Gospel hymns, 185, 302–3, 314, 316
Gospel music: agents and producers of, 306–7, 310, 318; as American Evangelical sacred song, 302–3, 317; bluegrass, 303, 304, 308; as culture industry, 312–16; defined, 301–2; and democratization, 317; diversity of musical styles in, 296, 298, 301, 307, 309–10, 314; lyrics, 297–301, 307; as ministry, 305–6, 308–10; popularity of, 296–97; as rationalization, 312–13, 316; songwriters, 306, 310; and television, 305; as testimony, 306; video, 314. *See also* Dove Awards; Isaacs; Lewis Family

Gospel Music Association, 297, 307, 316
Gounod, Charles, 219, 224
Graham, Billy, 303
Graham, Martha, 167
Grammy Awards, 213, 226, 301
Grand Ole Opry, 297, 304
Grant, Amy, 298, 302, 307, 314
Grant, Bill, 217–18
Great Awakening, 77–78, 109, 184
Great Passion Play, 254, 255
Green, Al, 296
Green, Keith, 190, 248
Gregg Smith Singers, 83, 274
Gregorian chant, 177
Gregory, Poppy, 83
Grey, Joel, 139
Griffes, Charles T., 270
Guido of Arezzo, 79
Guthery, Henry, 70

Habermas, Jürgen, 8
Hafiz, 181
Halpern, Steven, 166–67, 169, 174, 178, 181
Handel, George Frideric, 224, 226, 229, 325
Hanukah, 150–51
Harbison, John, 281
Harmonic Convergence of 1988, 165, 181
Harmonics (overtones), 176
Harnick, Sheldon, 144
Harper, Clay, 307, 310, 318
Harper, Herman, 306
Harris, Larnelle, 298
Harris, Michael, 117
Harrison, Peter, 266
Hatch, Nathan O., 317, 318
Hauff, Judy, 96
Hawkins, Edwin, 118
Hawkins, Walter, 118
Haywood, G. T., 114
Hazzanim (cantors), 135–37, 147–48
Hearns, Billy Ray, 248, 318
Herbert, Victor, 224
Hewlett, Lester, 226
Hicks, Michael, 231
Hidalgo y Costilla, Miguel, 42
Hildegard of Bingen, 174, 302
Hill, Phyllis, 119
Hilton, Randall, 306
Hindemith, Paul, 270
Hitchcock, H. Wiley, 83
Hocutt, John C., 96

Holiness movement, 111–12, 124
Holloway, Pauline, 304
Holly Springs, Georgia, Primitive Baptist Church, 280
Holocaust (Shoah), 131, 155
Holy Cross Cathedral, Boston, 239–40
Honeytrees, Nancy, 248
Hope Publishing Company, 189
Hopkins, Thomas, 74
Hopkinson, Francis, 78
Horkheimer, Max, 313
Horse Pasture, George, 29, 30–31
Houghton College, 275–76
Howe, Irving, 155
Hughes, Rosa, 82
Hymnals, 184–210; recent mainline Protestant, 185–86
Hymns, 7; meter in, 76, 184–85

Ibo, 108
Idelsohn, A. Z., 132, 135, 153
Inclusive language, 185, 194–95, 199–203; in *New Century Hymnal*, 199–203
Indianapolis, Indiana, 246, 249
Indian Country Tourism 2000, 35–36
Institute for Early American Culture, 94
Institutional Democratic Party (PDI), 42
International Catholic Charismatic Conference, 252
Isaacs, Ben, 304
Isaacs (bluegrass gospel group), 304, 308
Islam, 130, 133
Israeli folksong, 142
Ithaca, New York, 84
Iturbide, Agustín de, 42
Iverson, Daniel, 244

Jackson, George Pullen, 83
Jackson, Mahalia, 117, 118
Jagoda, Flory, 148
James, William, 4
Janáček, Leoš, 292
Jarrett, Keith, 167
Jazz, 100
Jefferson Airplane, 247
Jessop, Craig, 229
John Paul II, 42
Johnson, Daniel L., 204, 205, 208
Johnson, Lyndon B., 226
Johnson, Ted, 96

Jones, Charles Price, 111–12
Jones, Sam, 185
Jourdain, Robert, 3–4
Juan Diego, Saint, 40–41
Judaism: American, 130–31; Ashkenazic, 131, 138, 139; Conservative, 131, 141–42; Hasidic, 131, 138; Orthodox, 131, 147–48; Reconstructionist, 131, 153, 154, 155; Reform, 130, 155; Sephardic, 130; and Six Days War of 1963, 155; and Yom Kippur War of 1973, 155

Kapelye, 143
Kaplan, Mordecai, 131, 153
Katchko, Adolph, 136
Keillor, Garrison, 84, 143
Kern, Jerome, 283
Kimball, Spencer, 226
King, E. J., 80
King's Chapel, Boston, 266, 276–78
Kirschenblatt-Gimblett, Barbara, 145
Kirtland, Ohio, 231
Kivy, Peter, 3
Klezmer Conservatory Band, 139, 143
Klezmer music, 137–46; and *Fiddler on the Roof*, 144; Hasidic origins of, 141; and Havurah movement, 144–45; as heritage music, 145–46; as paraliturgical music, 152–57, 323–24; performance of, 141–43; as repristination, 156–57; response to, 143–46; revival of, 142–46; as subcultural music, 154–56. *See also* Klezmer Conservatory Band; Netsky, Hankus; *Schlemiehl the First*
Klezmorim, 143
Knapp, William, 77
Knox, John, 74
Koussevitsky, Moshe, 136
Kratophany, 114–15
Kulbach, Lisle, 148
Kundalini yoga, 174
Kyle, Juanita, 83

Ladd, Boye, 23–24
Lake Junaluska Conference Center, 186
Lakota Nation (Teton Sioux), 35
Lamy, Jean Baptiste, 61
Lane, Julia, 164
Lang, Andrew, 205
Langer, Suzanne, 2
Latter-day Saints, Church of Jesus Christ of, 213–36; founding of, 213–15; and the Great Trek and "State of Deseret," 223; opposi-

tion to, 222–23; and polygamy controversy, 223–24

Latter-day Saints music: children's music, 234–35; church teaching about, 233–34; continuity and change in, 236; hymnody, 230–34; local church program of, 230, 233–34; theology of praise in, 214; youth music, 235–36

Lavendar Jane, 172
Leavitt, Joshua, 317
Levi-Bruhl, Lucien, 26
Levy, Yitzak, 148
Lewandowsky, 352
Lewis, James Roy, 304, 315
Lewis, Polly, 303–8
Lewis, Roy ("Little Roy"), 304, 305
Lewis Family, 303–8
Liberation theology, 42
Liberman, Lev, 155
Ligeti, György, 264
Liminality and communitas: in pilgrimage, 54–58; in powwow dancing, 30–31; in powwow song, 31–32; and sacred song, 321–22
Little, William, 79
Little Portion Hermitage, 254, 257
Little Portion Retreat and Study Center, 256
Little Vine, Alabama, Primitive Baptist Church, 69
Liturgical Renewal, 249
Lloyd, Benjamin, 87
Lomax, Alan, 83
Longhurst, John, 215, 219
Louisiana Hayride, 305
Lowens, Irving, 83
Lowry, Robert, 301
Loyola University of New Orleans, 252
Luckmann, Thomas, 85
Lund, Anthony, 224
Lundberg, Joy Saunders, 235
Lyon, James, 78
Lyrics: as chant, 6; as element of sacred song, 5–6; as "iterative" myth in sacred song, 5–6; as *melos*, 6; as *opsis*, 6; in powwow songs, 25–26; "vocable" forms of, 26

McAllester, David, 167
McAllister, Stanley, 224
McGraw, Hugh, 82, 83, 95, 96
McGuire, Barry, 248
McKay, David O., 225, 226
McMurray, Pat, 90

Maderno, Francesco, 42
Madison, James, 327
Madison, Wisconsin, 84
Magnificat, 243
Mahler, Gustav, 3
Maine WomenFolk, 164
Maloney, Nick, 142
Mampre, Susan, 85
Marot, Clement, 74
Martin, Roberta, 117
Martin, Sallie, 118
Marx, Karl, 206, 328
Mason, Charles H., 112
Mason, Lowell, 81
Mason Proffit, 246–47
Mateos, Fr. Miguel, 48, 49, 50, 59, 60
Matéu, Emilio Vicente, 55; music example from, 335–36
Mays, Benjamin, 110
Mead, Sidney E., 316, 318
Medicine Eagle, Brooke, 181
Medinas family, 53
Mellers, Wilfrid, 270
Melody, 3; in *alabados*, 63; Neely Bruce on, 283–84; in New Age music, 168–69, 173, 177; in powwow songs, 27–28; in Sacred Harp singing, 70, 73; as signifyin(g), 124–27; in synagogue song, 135; in Talbot's music, 240–43, 257
Melville, Herman, 239
Mendelssohn, Felix, 130, 218, 224, 225, 264
Mendelssohn, Moses, 130
Mercer, Ted, 96
Mercy Corps, 240, 244
Methodists, 80, 184, 302; in the rural South, 81
Mexico City, Mexico, 40, 41
Meyer, Leonard, 2
Middletown, Connecticut, 83
Mighty Clouds of Joy, 118
Millennialism, 181–82
Minneapolis, Minnesota, 84
Modal scales, Greek, 94, 172, 176
Molleno, Antonio, 47
Molter, Walter, O. F. M., 249
Monitor Radio, 90
Monroe, Bill, 303, 304, 305, 308
Montclair, New Jersey, 84
Montgomery, Marlene, 147, 150
Montpelier, Vermont, 83
Montreat Conference Center, 187
Moody, Carole, 85

Moody, Dwight L., 80, 111, 185, 311

Moody, Michael, 234, 236

Moore, Jennie, 113

Moore, R. Laurence, 221

Moore, William, 70; music example from, 340

Moral Majority, 316

Morley, Thomas, 79

Mormon pop, 236

Mormons. *See* Latter-day Saints

Mormon Tabernacle, 215–16; Aeolian-Skinner organ at, 215–16, 219

Mormon Tabernacle Choir: and American civil religion, 221–22, 225, 227, 228; as archetype, 220; at Chicago World's Columbian Exposition, 223; as church choir, 227; and commercialization, 224–29, 325–26; commitment of members of, 217–18; and legitimation, 220–30, 325; musical skills in, 217; as "national treasure," 213, 215; and phonograph recording, 224–27; and radio, 213, 224, 228; recent changes in, 229; and rehearsal, 215–20; selection of members for, 217–18; and television, 229

Morning Star Baptist Church (Chicago), 116

Morris, Kenneth, 118

Morton, Henrietta Mann, 23

Mozart, Wolfgang Amadeus, 224, 288

"Mozart effect," 3

Mujerista theology, 42

Music: deconstructionist definition of, 2–3; and emotion, 2; as experience, 2; physiological processing of, 3–4; psycholinguistic model of, 3; as symbol, 2

Myth: as element of sacred song, 4–6. *See also* Lyrics

Nakai, Carlos, 167, 181; music example from, 355

Nakota Nation (Yankton Sioux), 36

Nashville, Tennessee, 188, 297

National Baptist Convention, USA, 100, 116

National Baptist Convention of America, 100

National Public Radio, 84

National Sacred Harp Singing Convention, 82, 93

Native Americans, 17; religions of, 26–27; and sacred song, 17–18. *See also* Powwow; Powwow songs

Nauvoo, Illinois, 214, 222

Near, Holly, 170

Neo-Paganism, 170–72, 179

Netsky, Hankus, 139–46, 154

New Age, 164–82; defined, 165–66

New Age music: and *chakras,* 166, 174; composition of, 173–75, 178, 179, 180; and cosmology, 175–76; as Dianic, 178; as ecstatic expression, 169; and healing, 174, 176–78; and kundalini yoga, 174; and lyrics, 168, 179; and performance, 163–65, 175, 180; and religious beliefs, 169, 324–25; response to, 180; styles of, 166–68, 176–77; and Wiccan movement, 178–79; women's spirituality, 173, 174

Newbury, Massachusetts, 75

New England, 74–79, 83–85

New England Conservatory of Music, 139, 142, 273

New Jersey Mass Choir, 118

Newport, Rhode Island, 130

New York, New York, 130–31, 136, 166

Niebuhr, H. Richard, 221

Nix, W. M., 117

Nixon, Richard M., 226

Norman, Larry, 248

Norumbega Harmony, 84, 85, 90–93

Notre Dame University, 252

Nuckolls, Ivory, 102

Old Horn, Dale, 19, 20, 21

Old Joe Clark's, 83

Old Town School of Music, 83

Oliver, Paul, 118

Ometeotl, 41

Orchestra at Temple Square, 229

Oregon Catholic Press, 281

Orlando, Florida, 197

Ormandy, Eugene, 226

Osmond Family, 235

Ottley, Jerold, 217, 227

Otto, Rudolf, 26

Packer, Boyd K., 233

Palestrina, Giovanni da, 280

Palmer, George A., 301

Palmyra, New York, 214

Parham, Charles, 112–13

Paris, Twyla, 299

Parker, Nora, 81

Parr, Bob, 91, 92

Paskemin, Randall, 22

Patti, Sandi, 9, 190, 299

Paul, Saint, 241

Paul VI, 42

Paz, Octavio, 43

Peaceful Valley Bluegrass Festival, 303

Penitentes: as Franciscan Tertiaries, 60–61; in New Mexico, 60–62; origins of, 60; performing *alabados*, 59–60; practices of, 61; as preservers of *alabados* tradition, 62–64

Pennekeep, Walter, 19

Pentecostal Assemblies of the World, 101, 114

Pentecostalism, 112–14, 124

Penterecki, Krzysztof, 264

Perry, Janice Kapp, 235; music example from, 361–64

Petra, 299

Philadelphia, Pennsylvania, 116, 130–31, 136, 140–42

Philadelphia Orchestra, 225, 226, 229, 325

Phillips Theological Seminary, 204

Pilgrimage: as communitas, 54, 58, 321; and geography, 56–57; of *Guadalupanas*, 56; and intentions, 54; preparation for, 55; *promesa*, 54; and songs, 55–57; and vocations, 56

Pilgrim Baptist Church (Chicago), 116

Pinkham, Daniel: approach of, to religious texts, 267–68; on commissions, 273–74; on conservatories and sacred music, 273–74; and King's Chapel, 266, 276–78; on market forces, 274; on the meaning of his sacred music, 274–76; on musical composition, 269–70, 272–73; musical influences on, 270–71; on originality, 271; principal works by, 266; training of, 265

Pintchik, Pierre, 136, 147

Piston, Walter, 265, 270

Pittsburgh, Pennsylvania, 131

Pius X, 42

Playford, John, 74

Podhoretz, Norman, 155

Point of Grace, 314

Pop music style: and gospel music, 297–98, 312, 314–16; and Mormon music, 236

Portiuncula of Assisi, 253

Portland, Oregon, 84

Potok, Chaim, 155

Powell, Hubert, 126; music example from, 349–52

Powers, William, 26, 28

Powwow, 17–38; and blessing the dancing ground, 19–20; competition dancing in, 22; dancing in, 28–31; defined, 23, 24; drums in, 20; and the feather, 22; and geography, 24; and Grand Entry, 20–21; and the whistle, 21–22

Powwow movement, 24–25; and cultural tourism, 34–38

Powwow song: ceremonials, 17–18; drum and, 25; as liminality and communitas, 30–34; lyrics, 25–26; "making," 26–27; melodies, 27–28; and socials, 17; structure, 28. *See also* Lyrics; Powwow

Pratt, Orson, 231

Presbyterians, 78, 185

Primitive Baptists, 87, 88

Progressive National Baptist Convention, 100

Prosser, Gabriel, 123

Proulx, Richard, 246

Psalms, metrical, 74–75

Public culture: and commercialization of sacred song, 9; performance and ritual in, 8–9; "public sphere" defined by Habermas, 8; Sacred Harp singing as, 86; and sacred song, 8

Pueblo Indian Revolt, 60

Puritans, 74

Pythagoras of Samos, 176

Quadrivium, 147, 148

Rabinowitz, Solomon, 137

Raboteau, Albert, 110

Raga, 177

Ralliere, Juan de, 63

Randall, Bruce, 96

Ravel, Maurice, 165, 267, 270

Reconquista, 41

Religion: and culture, 10, 327–29; diversity of, 1–2, 327

Repristination, 156–57

Revere, Paul, 78

Reza, Mary Frances, 54, 58, 62, 63

Rhythm: in African American sacred song, 110, 113, 123–25; Bruce on, 282–83; in Chicano pilgrimage songs, 57–58; in New Age music, 176, 178; in powwow songs, 25–26

Rice, Tony, 308

Ridgecrest Conference Center, 186

Riesman, David, 145

Ripplinger, Don, 215–20, 227–29

Ritual, 7. *See also* Turner, Edith; Turner, Victor

Robbins, Kathleen, 71, 73

Roberts, Cliff, 23, 24

Robertson, Pat, 9, 316

Robinson, Robert, 199–203
Rocky Boy's Powwow, 22
Rodeheaver, Homer, 301
Rodgers, Richard, 283
Romney, George, 226
Roosevelt, Franklin D., 225
Rorem, Ned, 269, 272
Rosenberg, Jay, 148
Rosenblatt, Yosele, 136, 147
Ross, Randy, 35
Rouget, Gilbert, 123, 168–69
Rousseau, Jean-Jacques, 221
Rovner, Seidel, 136
Roxbury, Massachusetts, 75
Ruether, Rosemary Radford, 185
Rutter, John, 229

Sachs, Kurt, 2
Sacks, Oliver, 3
Sacred art music, 264–95; defined, 264–65
Sacred Harp singing: at Birmingham, 82; and gospel hymns, 81, 315; at Little Vine, 69–74; northern revival of, 82–85, 304; and northern singers, 90–93; regional and musical differences in, 93–95; regional rapprochement within, 95–97; in the rural South, 88–90; as secondary sacrality, 86–93, 323–24
Sacred song, 3–12; defined, 8
Sagra Familia (Holy Family) Church, 58–59
Saint Louis, Missouri, 84, 197
Saint Louis Jesuits, 253
Salpointe, Juan Battista, 61
Salt Lake City, Utah, 213, 215–16
Sanchez, Robert Fortune, 61
Sandy Cove Bible Conference, 301
San Francisco, California, 84, 170
Sankey, Ira D., 81, 111, 116, 185; and culture industry, 314, 317; and gospel music, 301, 303, 304, 311
Santería, 100
Santero style: *bultos,* 48; *reredos,* 48; *santos,* 48. *See also* El Santuario de Chimayó
Santo Niño de Atocha, 50, 53
Santuario de Chimayó: architecture of, 47; and Holy Child of Atocha, 50; interior decoration in, 47–48; and the *legenda* of Chimayó, 51; and Miraculous Cross of Our Lord of Esquipulas, 48, 50; Palm Sunday liturgy at, 48–50; pilgrimage to, 54–58; and *el posito,* 47, 50; Tewa and Tano background of, 51. *See also* Liminality and communitas

Saraswati, 180
Satie, Eric, 165
Schoenberg, Arnold, 271
Scholtes, Peter, 251; music example from, 369–70
Schuller, Gunther, 274
Schütz, Heinrich, 277
Scovel, Carl, 267, 272, 278
Scriven, Joseph, 126, 348–51
Second Great Awakening, 80–81, 184, 315, 316–17
Second Vatican Council, 249
Separate-Baptists, 186
Sephardic music: *coplas,* 149; as Dianic, 149, 150; as Jewish folksong, 153; Yitzak Levy's compilations of, 148; as *Midrash,* 149; as paraliturgical music, 152–57, 323–24; performance and interpretation of, 148–51; as repristination, 156–57; response to, 151–52; as subcultural music, 154–56
Seymour, William J., 113
Shakers, 317
Shape-notes, 79–80
Shea, George Beverly, 303
Shepherd, Thomas, 117
Sheppard, Jeff, 87, 89, 94–96, 315
Sheppard, Shelbie, 82, 87–89, 96, 97
Sherman, Ben, 35
Shiloah, Amnon, 133, 154
Shumway, Nehemiah, 71
Signifyin(g), 122, 125–27; illustrated, 126–27, 322–23
Simos, Miriam. *See* Starhawk
Singer, Isaac Bashevis, 137, 140
Singing school, American: and Billings, 78–79; English origins of, 76–77; and Great Awakening, 77–78; lyrical resources of, 75–76; and Mason, 81; New England origins of, 74–75; as noncommodified music, 315; postbellum decline of, 81; as reaction to psalter tradition, 74; and "regular singing," 75; and shape-notes, 79–80; southern tradition of, 80; and Watts, 75–76
Sirota, Gershon, 136
Sitka Tribe of Alaska, 35
Skaggs, Ricky, 310
Slobin, Mark, 135, 144–46, 154–55
Sloboda, John A., 3
Smith, Edna, 255
Smith, Emma, 231
Smith, Gerald, 255

Smith, Gypsy, 301

Smith, Hyrum, 214, 222–23

Smith, Joseph, 213–14, 222–23, 231, 234

Smith, Joseph F., 223

Smith, Joseph Fielding, 226

Smith, Leonard E., Jr., 245; music example from, 367–68

Smith, Michael W., 297, 298, 314

Smith, William, 79

Smithsonian Institution, 83, 85

Smoot, Reed, 223

Snow, Eliza, 235

Social Gospel, 185

Southern, Eileen, 109, 110, 118

Southern Baptist Convention: fundamentalist agenda of, 192–93, 315; growth of, 89–90, 186–93; historical relationship of, to United Church of Christ, 186; musical organization in, 187–89; during postbellum era, 315; and recorded worship music, 289; and the Ridgecrest Conference Center, 187–89; in the rural South, 81, 90; and Sacred Harp singing, 88; Sunday School Board (Life Way Ministries), 188–89; and worship, 89

Southern Methodists, 81, 90

Spain, Rufus B., 315

Spanish Inquisition, 149–50

Sparrow Records, 248, 316

Spencer, Jon Michael, 110, 115, 122, 123

Spirit possession, 123–25, 322

Staheli, Ron, 231

Stainer, John, 224

Stanley Brothers, 308

Staple Singers, 118

Starhawk (Miriam Simos), 170–71, 181

Starsong Records, 299

State University of New York at Stony Brook, 172, 175

Stephens, Evan, 223

Stephenson, Joseph, 77

Sternhold, Thomas, 74

Stokowski, Leopold, 225

Stone, Samuel S., 216

Storr, Anthony, 3

Strauss, Richard, 180

Structure and antistructure. *See* Liminality and communitas

Suenens, Leon Joseph Cardinal, 251–52

Sulzar, Salomon, 352

Summit, Jeffrey A., 135

Sun Dance, 36

Sunday, Billy, 185

Sutton, Judith, 273

Sweat lodge, 36

Synagogue song: *amida,* 132; and cantillation, 133; on holy days, 132; *lecha dodi,* 134, 352–53; *piyyutim,* 133–35; *Shema,* 132; *sheva,* 132

Taft, William Howard, 224

Talbot, John Michael: and Bicentennial Revival, 247–48; and Brothers and Sisters of Charity, 259–61; and the Charismatic Renewal, 253; and commercialization, 254–56, 325; as composer and writer, 257–58; as critic of contemporary Christian music, 248, 258–59; and Franciscans, 249, 253; and Little Portion Hermitage, 256–57; and Little Portion Retreat and Study Center, 256; and the Liturgical Renewal, 251; and Mason Proffitt, 246–47; and *The Master Musician,* 241–42, 257; and Mercy Corps, 240, 244; music examples from, 365–66, 373–74; as performer, 239–45, 258–59; relationship of music by, to religious institutions, 261–62, 325–26; as religious superior, 260; as sacred music artist, 257–59; social teachings of, 243. *See also* Brothers and Sisters of Charity

Talbot, Terry, 246, 247, 255

Tano Indians, 51

Tans'ur, William, 77, 78

Tate, Edith Creel, 71, 72

Taylor, John, 231

Te Kanawa, Kiri, 227

Temple Square Chorale, 229

Tennent, Gilbert, 78, 316

Tenochtitlan, 40, 41

Tepeyac, Mexico, 40, 42

Tewa Indians, 51

Thick description, 11

Third Order Franciscans (Tertiaries), 60, 253

Thompson, Randall, 278

Thoreau, Henry David, 181

Thorpe, William, 274

Thurman, Howard, 110, 122

Tindley, Charles Albert, 115, 301, 304; music example from, 344–45

Tiomkin, Dmitri, 225

Tocqueville, Alexis de, 316

Tonantzin, 41

Troeger, Thomas H., 185

Truex, Barb, 164

Tuckey, William, 78
Tufts, John, 75, 79
Tulsa, Oklahoma, 204
Turbak, Sue, 91, 92, 93
Turner, Edith, 54, 321
Turner, Nat, 123
Turner, Victor, 30, 54, 321, 328
Turner, William, 114–15

UCLA, 252
United Church of Christ: General Synod IX,
    194; General Synod XVII, 195; General Syn-
    od XIX, 197–99; historical relationship of,
    to Southern Baptists, 186; *Inclusive Lan-
    guage Guidelines*, 194
United Methodist Church, 186, 191
United States Council of Catholic Bishops, 251
University of Chicago, 101
University of Illinois, 279
University of Michigan, 252
Utah Symphony, 229

Valéry, Paul, 6
Van der Leeuw, Gerardus, 29
Vasquez, Pedro Ramirez, 42
Veitia, Diego de, 51
Verdi, Giuseppe, 264, 292
Vesey, Denmark, 123
Village Harmony, 84, 94
Virgen de Guadalupe, 40–46; apparition, 40;
    and Juan Diego, 40–41; interpreted by Paz,
    43–44; *legenda*, 40; in Liberation Theology,
    42; and "Mañanitas a La Virgen de Guada-
    lupe," 44–46; in Mexican politics, 42; mi-
    raculous healings attributed to, 41; and *la
    morenita*, 43–44; in *mujerista* theology, 42;
    name of, 40–41; in popular religion, 42, 43;
    Spanish, 40–41, 52
Vision quest, 36
Vodun, 100
Voice: as instrument of healing, 178
Voice of the Turtle, 147
Von Stade, Frederica, 227

Wachs, Judith, 147–52, 154, 157
Wacker, Grant, 114
Walker, William, 73, 80; music example from,
    342
Wallace, Barbara, 271
Waller, Thomas, 69, 70; music example from,
    339

Walter, Thomas, 75
Ward, Clara, 118
Washington, D.C., 84, 166
Washington, Georgia, 304
Watts, Isaac: and African American hymnody,
    109, 111; in Evangelical hymnody, 184, 316;
    lyrical style of, 76; and "system of praise,"
    75–76, 286
Weber, Andrew Lloyd, 106
Weber, Max, 220, 312, 318, 328
Weinstein, Arnold, 140
Welch, Jay, 226
Wellesley College, 83, 84
Welsh, Andrew, 6
Wesley, Charles: and Black Church hymnody,
    109, 111; and Evangelical hymnody, 184, 339;
    and *The Sacred Harp*, 70, 77, 80
Wesley, John, 77, 111, 193
Wesley, Samuel S., 216
Wesleyan University, 83, 84
West Africa: instruments common to, 109;
    musical traditions of, 109; religious culture
    of, 108–9
Western Wind Ensemble, 83
White, Benjamin Franklin, 80
White, J. T., 360
Whitefield, George, 77, 78, 316, 317
White Plume, Alex, 35
Whitman, Walt, 73
Wiccan movement, 170–71, 178
Widor, Charles-Marie, 225
Wilberg, Mark, 229
Willard, Karen, 85
Williams, Aaron, 77
Williams, Robert, 219
Wilson, Stuart, 102, 119–22
Winans: BeBe, 296, 300; CeCe, 296, 300
Winston, George, 167, 181
Winter, Paul, 166, 181
Wise, Isaac Meyer, 130
Women's spirituality, 170–72, 174, 178–79, 181
Woodruff, Wilford, 223
Woods, Gertrude, 71
Woodward, Ken, 203, 205
Word, Incorporated, 189, 316
Word of Mouth Chorus, 83
World's Columbian Exposition, 101, 223, 325
Wren, Brian, 185, 190
Wright, Glen, 85, 96, 285
Wright, Ted, 35
Wyeth, John, 80, 199

Yale Institute of Sacred Music, 273
Yiddish literature and theater, 137–39, 140
York, Terry, 187–92, 207
Yoruba, 108
Young, Brigham, 214, 215, 223, 231
Young, Carlton, 191

Zapata, Emiliano, 42
Zapatistas, 42
Zen Buddhism, 286
Zubiría y Escalante, José, 61
Zuckerkandl, Victor, 5
Zumárraga, Juan de, 40

Among his many publications, Stephen A. Marini has written
Radical Sects of Revolutionary New England. He is Elisabeth Luce
Moore Professor of Christian Studies at Wellesley College.

Public Expressions of Religion in America

Producing the Sacred: An Essay on Public Religion   *Robert Wuthnow*
Unsecular Media: Making News of Religion in America   *Mark Silk*
Uncivil Rites: American Fiction, Religion, and the Public Sphere   *Robert Detweiler*
Houses of God: Region, Religion, and Architecture in the United States
   Peter W. Williams
Private Needs, Public Selves: Talk about Religion in America   *John K. Roth*
Sacred Song in America: Religion, Music, and Public Culture   *Stephen A. Marini*

The University of Illinois Press
is a founding member of the
Association of American University Presses.

Composed in 10.5/12.5 Minion
with Minion display
by Jim Proefrock
at the University of Illinois Press
Manufactured by Maple-Vail
Book Manufacturing Group

University of Illinois Press
1325 South Oak Street
Champaign, IL 61820-6903
www.press.uillinois.edu